PENGUIN BO

A TOWN CALLED

R.K. Narayan was born in Madras in 1
Maharajah's College in Mysore. His first novel *Swami and Friends* (1935) was set in the enchanting fictional territory of Malgudi. Narayan's other novels are *The Bachelor of Arts* (1937), *The Dark Room* (1938), *The English Teacher* (1945), *Mr Sampath* (1949), *The Financial Expert* (1952), *Waiting for the Mahatma* (1955), the Sahitya Akademi award-winning *The Guide* (1958), *The Man-eater of Malgudi* (1962), *The Vendor of Sweets* (1967), *The Painter of Signs* (1976), *A Tiger for Malgudi* (1983), *Talkative Man* (1986) and *The World of Nagaraj* (1990).

Besides six collections of short stories (*A Horse and Two Goats*, *An Astrologer's Day and Other Stories*, *Lawley Road*, *Malgudi Days*, *Grandmother's Tale* and *Under the Banyan Tree*), Narayan published two travel books (*My Dateless Diary* and *The Emerald Route*), five collections of essays (*Next Sunday*, *Reluctant Guru*, *A Writer's Nightmare*, *A Story-teller's World* and *Salt and Sawdust*), translations of Indian epics and myths (*The Ramayana*, *The Mahabharata* and *Gods, Demons, and Others*, published together as *The Indian Epics Retold*) and a memoir, *My Days*. *A Town Called Malgudi*, *The World of Malgudi*, *The Magic of Malgudi* and *Memories of Malgudi*, collections of Narayan's fiction, and *Malgudi Landscapes*, a selection of his best writings, are available from Penguin Books. *Malgudi Schooldays*, a volume of Narayan's children's writing, is available in Puffin, while *The Writerly Life*, a volume of his selected non-fiction, is available in Viking.

In 1980 R.K. Narayan was awarded the A.C. Benson medal by the Royal Society of Literature and was made an Honorary Member of the American Academy and Institute of Arts and Letters. In 1989 he was made a member of the Rajya Sabha. In 2000 the Government of India conferred on him the Padma Vibhushan.

R.K. Narayan died in May 2001.

S. Krishnan taught English literature at Madras Christian College and at Annamalai University. He spent many years with the United States Information Agency in their educational and cultural programmes. He is now a weekly columnist for the *Hindu*, consulting editor with the *Indian Review of Books* and senior editor of *Shruti*, a music and dance magazine. Krishnan has edited several volumes of R.K. Narayan's writings for Penguin Books. He lives in Chennai.

By R.K. Narayan in Penguin Books India

The Emerald Route
The Indian Epics Retold
Indian Thought: A Miscellany
The Magic of Malgudi
Malgudi Landscapes
Malgudi Schooldays
Memories of Malgudi
My Dateless Diary
The Ramayana
Salt and Sawdust
A Story-teller's World
A Town Called Malgudi
The World of Malgudi
A Writer's Nightmare
The Writerly Life: Selected Non-fiction

A TOWN CALLED MALGUDI

Dear Rosie
Many Happy Returns

The Finest Fiction of

R.K. Narayan

of the Day. Hope this
year ahead is full of

Edited *with an introduction by*

S. Krishnan

love luck & happiness
for you.
love
Ananyaa, Ikram & Ashima
March 22, 03'.

PENGUIN BOOKS

Penguin Books India (P) Ltd., 11 Community Centre, Panchsheel Park, New Delhi 110 017, India
Penguin Books Ltd., 80 Strand, London WC2R 0RL, UK
Penguin Putnam Inc., 375 Hudson Street, New York, NY 10014, USA
Penguin Books Australia Ltd., 250 Camberwell Road, Camberwell, Victoria 3124, Australia
Penguin Books Canada Ltd., 10 Alcorn Avenue, Suite 300, Toronto, Ontario, M4V 3B2, Canada
Penguin Books (NZ) Ltd., Cnr Rosedale and Airborne Roads, Albany, Auckland, New Zealand

First published in Viking by Penguin Books India 1999
Published in Penguin Books 2002

Copyright © R.K. Narayan 1999
Introduction copyright © S. Krishnan 1999

The Man-eater of Malgudi was first published by William Heinemann Ltd. 1961
Talkative Man was first published by William Heinemann Ltd. 1986
The short stories were first published as part of
Malgudi Days (first published by William Heinemann Ltd. 1982),
Under the Banyan Tree (first published by William Heinemann Ltd. 1985) and
Salt and Sawdust (first published by Penguin Books India 1993)

All rights reserved

10 9 8 7 6 5 4 3 2 1

For sale in the Indian Subcontinent and Singapore only

Typeset in Sabon by SÜRYA, New Delhi
Printed at Chaman Offset Printers, New Delhi

This book is sold subject to the condition that it shall not, by way of trade or otherwise, be lent, resold, hired out, or otherwise circulated without the publisher's prior written consent in any form of binding or cover other than that in which it is published and without a similar condition including this condition being imposed on the subsequent purchaser and without limiting the rights under copyright reserved above, no part of this publication may be reproduced, stored in or introduced into a retrieval system, or transmitted in any form or by any means (electronic, mechanical, photocopying, recording or otherwise), without the prior written permission of both the copyright owner and the above-mentioned publisher of this book.

CONTENTS

INTRODUCTION

R.K. NARAYAN WILL be ninety-three this year. He makes light of his age. When asked about it by curious but well-meaning people, sometimes he responds like a joke-book: 'Well, if you live long enough, you can also be ninety.' In his foreword to the special edition of his autobiography, *My Days*, which Penguin India brought out in honour of his ninetieth birthday, he writes more frankly but typically enough: 'Perhaps it (turning ninety) could be (a personal achievement) if one were unaware of the insidious symptoms of senility—such as fumbling for a name or constantly treasure-hunting for a key or a document, which one's hand—acting independently—misplaces. The mileage covered in an evening walk is also reduced, not worth reckoning. Earlier I used to walk eight to ten miles a day; now it is along the garden path up to the gate. My doctor's only advice is "Don't have a fall!" which means watching one's step, avoiding steeps and slopes and children chasing each other, and above all hanging on to the four-pronged aluminium walker night and day. Apart from these I do not have much to do for self-preservation.' Actually when one meets Narayan one is likely to be struck by his healthy appearance. He has gone through some of the ills the flesh is heir to at his age, but his only serious problem is with his hearing.

R(asipuram) K(rishnaswami Iyer) Narayan Swami was born on 10 October 1906 in his grandmother's house in Purasawalkam, an old section of Madras city. Here he grew up with his grandmother—who had offered to take care of him as several other siblings occupied his mother's attention—and uncle in a rambling old house with a large compound, a peacock and a monkey (which duly disappeared) for company. His grandmother, affectionate though she was, firmly supervised his lessons—he went to a local school—and taught him Sanskrit slokas and told him tales from Hindu myths and epics. Though Narayan is not very religious in a conventional sense, the Hindu values he had imbibed in his early youth have always remained with him, and are unobstrusively reflected in his writing. During his early teens, he moved to Mysore, where his father had become headmaster of a prestigious high school in the old Mysore State. From being a lonely child, Narayan had the experience of living with brothers and sisters in a large joint family. As he grew older he went for daily rambles in Mysore city, which was full of natural and man-made beauty. He also read voraciously—as the headmaster's son, he had unlimited access to the school library. He also had first crack at the many British and American magazines to which the school subscribed and which were delivered to the headmaster's house. But despite having a martinet of a headmaster for a father, and despite the fact that English was his best subject, he had difficulty in obtaining a college degree, which he eventually did. In those days, and one supposes now also, it was not done to stay idle, and one had to get a job quickly. Narayan had two shots at teaching but gave up the attempts after a few days. It was not really essential for him to work as the large, affectionate joint family absorbed him and his casualness in its bosom, but he felt he should contribute in some fashion towards the expenses of the family, which was surviving precariously enough after his father's death. And he made a few rupees every month by acting as a reporter for a Madras journal. Earlier he had tried his hand at writing imitative heroic poetry which was much admired by his brothers and their friends, but he realized that his talent lay in the prose narrative. He started contributing sketches and short stories to Madras journals, notably the *Hindu*. He began working on his first novel, *Swami and Friends*, which he started on an auspicious day in the house of his grandmother in Bangalore where she had come to stay. He also fell in love, an unusual idea in those days of arranged marriages. When the families displayed reluctant interest, astrologers stood in the way, pointing out horoscopical discrepancies. But Narayan stood his ground and married Rajam, the girl of his choice. She bore him a girl-child who became the centre of his universe. That the marrige was star-crossed was obvious when Rajam died of typhoid within six years. He was desolate beyond words, and finally some spiritual experiences he had in Madras gave him a measure of serenity, and brought him back to normal. He has described his married life, his wife's death, and the recovery he made through spiritual experience in detail in *The English Teacher*, published in 1944, a watershed in his writing in which there is very little fiction.

In the meantime, while Rajam was still alive, after passing through the hands of many publishers, the manuscript of *Swami and Friends* reached Graham Greene, who arranged for it to be published by Hamish Hamilton. Narayan's next novel, *The Bachelor of Arts*, was published by Nelson in 1937, and *The Dark Room* was published by Macmillan in 1938. None of them sold particularly well, partly because the shadow of war was looming over England (most of the copies of his books were destroyed during the blitzkreig), and partly because Narayan was an unknown foreign author, but all the books were critical successes in varying degrees. Today he laughs: 'I had the unique experience of having a new publisher for each book. One book, one publisher—and then perhaps he said to himself, "Hands off this writer",' but it must have hurt then.

When he felt a little more at peace with himself, at the recommendation of friends, he started a journal named *Indian Thought* which ran for three issues, and duly folded, partly because of war-time restrictions on paper and so forth, but Narayan got a mixture of dread and delight while getting the issues ready. Finally he was ready to write *The English Teacher*, mentioned above, which many Narayan aficionados consider his best work. As he himself has said, the book is almost entirely autobiographical except for the name changes from real life. Considering the theme and the fact that the author was writing of his own experience, it is really astonishingly unsentimental. The first half is an idyll of married life, while the second deals with the writer's recovery from the depth of grief and gloom, in the sure knowledge that he is still in communication with his wife.

The other three of Narayan's first four novels are based

on his own experiences. *Swami and Friends* is the story of a small boy and his joys and sorrows, written with delightful ease and a sure insight into the psyche of a very small person. The hero of *The Bachelor of Arts*, Chandran, is really Swami grown up, and now a college student. The college life of those days is perfectly delineated, and the older ones among us will find the lecturers resembling the ones we had. The union debates, the antinomian student, the outings after hours which students on the verge of manhood are entitled to are all there. There is a good bit of Narayan in this book, especially in the episode of Chandran falling in love with a girl, whose horoscope unfortunately does not match his. Narayan's third novel, *The Dark Room*, is quite unusual for him, as a closely concealed anger runs through the book. It is the story of a Hindu woman, who is neglected by her husband because of his infatuation with another, and who decides unsuccessfully to run away from home. It is a sombre book, and later Narayan was to say: 'This must have been an early testament of the "women's lib" movement.' One suspects it may have been suggested by a happening in the family. It is of interest that every one of the protagonists of the first four novels runs away from their routine life at some point—Swami, because he is afraid to return home after an anarchical act at school, Chandran because of thwarted love and the heroine of *The Dark Room* because of an unfeeling husband and a loveless life. The English Teacher's plunge into the world of spiritualism may also be considered a running away of a sort.

Once he got back in the stride of writing again, rising from the slough of despondency as it were, novels, short stories and occasional sketches started flowing from Narayan's pen (incidentally, he almost always uses a fountain pen, writing usually slightly diagonally on the page). John Updike described Narayan as 'a writer immersed in his materials'. The next novel he published was *Mr Sampath*, inspired partly by his experience with his printer during the brief life of *Indian Thought*, and partly by his brief sortie into the film world—he wrote some scripts for the Gemini Studio in Madras. *Mr Sampath* was the harbinger of the great reputation he was to make as writer, not only in the English-speaking world, but also in other countries, in languages ranging from Hebrew to Japanese. As in the case of *Mr Sampath*, almost all of his fiction is based on a person or an incident with which he was familiar. The next novel, *The Financial Expert*, had its origin in a story he heard from his brother, about an employee in the latter's office, who had no business to be there as he had been dismissed, but continued to skulk around outside, acting as an adviser to illiterate villagers who needed money. Narayan may also have been influenced by the real-life story of a financier in Bangalore who banked money for many people, including well-known members of society, and then defalcated.

Waiting for the Mahatma, which followed, is Narayan's only fictional attempt to take notice of the freedom struggle that had gone on in the country. By the time he wrote the novel, the country had been free for ten years, and one assumes that he had an irresistible desire to bring Mahatma Gandhi into one of his stories. In the novel, the Mahatma plays an important role in the romance of Bharati, a dedicated young follower of his and Sriram, a feckless but

rich young man. Some readers were critical of the novel,
feeling that the Mahatma should not have been made a
fictional character, but the story is really about the
transformation of Sriram from a lackadaisical youth into a
stronger person, thanks both to his brief association with
the Mahatma, and his profound love for Bharati. Actually,
the minor characters—Sriram's grandmother, Kanni, the
shopkeeper, the chairman of the town council and others—
are interestingly drawn, but while not a failure, the book
does not command the same attention from his faithful
readers as others do.

The following year, 1956, was an important one in
Narayan's life. His daughter, Hema, married her cousin,
Chandru, and went away to Coimbatore to live with him.
'Having practised the role of a protective father all along,
I found myself unemployed . . . but I realized they were a
happy couple.' Also, he made his first trip abroad, to the
United States, at the invitation of the Rockefeller Foundation.
The idea for his best known novel, *The Guide*, had been
germinating in his mind for some time. He took a hotel
room in Berkeley, California, and finished writing it in
three months in the beginning of 1957. 'At this time I had
been thinking of a subject for a novel: a novel about
someone suffering enforced sainthood. A recent situation in
Mysore offered a setting for such a story. A severe drought
had dried up all the rivers and tanks . . . As a desperate
measure the municipal council organized a prayer for rains
. . . A group of brahmins stood knee-deep in water
(procured at great cost) on the dry bed of Kaveri, fasted,
prayed and chanted certain mantras continuously for eleven
days. On the twelfth day it rained, and brought relief to the

countryside.' With this idea as the core, Narayan weaves a brilliant story around Raju, the sinner turned saint, in *The Guide*. In his autobiography Narayan says casually, '*The Guide* attained a certain degree of popularity.' In reality it is not just his most popular novel, it is also the most brilliantly crafted. It has continually been in print in many different editions, has been translated into several languages, and been made into a play and a film, neither of which met with Narayan's approval. It won him the Sahitya Akademi award, the highest the Indian government gives for literature. In *The Guide*, Narayan tells the story of Raju, a railway guide, whom circumstances, after a period of good fortune when he acted as the agent of a dancer, put in prison for criminal misappropriation. When he comes out after doing his term, he settles down under a tree near a temple in a village. The simple villagers take him to be a holy man despite his telling them the story of his life in crime, and continue to pay daily tribute to him. When a drought occurs, they look to him to produce rain. One has to read the novel oneself to see how brilliantly Narayan achieves an ambiguous ending, which is quite satisfactory just the same. Told on two levels which closely mesh, this is probably Narayan's most polished work of fiction. This novel was followed by *The Man-eater of Malgudi*, which is included in this selection and discussed elsewhere.

Narayan's subsequent novels are all still set in Malgudi, but vary widely in themes which show an attempt to move along with the rest of the world. His next novel has quite a daring theme—for Narayan. Jagan in *The Vendor of Sweets* is a man of high philosophy and ideals, and a follower of Mahatma Gandhi's teachings. He is very proud of his son, Mali, who has gone to study abroad. One can imagine Jagan's mental travail when Mali returns, accompanied by a Korean wife. Soon enough Jagan realizes that they are not even married. This is a classic story of the generation gap, made the more palpable as father and son are quite sure of the correctness of their attitudes. Neither will give in, but Narayan resolves the whole tangle in his own amiable fashion, making each give in a little to the other.

If one thought *The Vendor of Sweets* was a rather unusual work in the Narayan canon, one can only call *The Painter of Signs* revolutionary. In this novel, Narayan meets sex head on—at least as far as his old-fashioned views and gentle humour would allow him. The hero, Raman, is a sign-painter who, in the course of his professional work, meets Daisy and falls in love with her. But Daisy is a government-employed family planning propagandist. She is not unattracted by him but she is a stern woman to whom her job means more than anything else. Narayan tells the story of these star-crossed lovers—there is no real resolution as Daisy is transferred to another town where the propaganda for birth control is not doing so well—with his usual humour but also a measure of poignancy.

The next novel, *A Tiger for Malgudi*, was inspired, as so often with Narayan, by an account he read about a Swamy having a tiger for a companion, which followed him with docility even in great crowds at famous festivals. This set Narayan thinking about whether there may not be an inexplicable communion between animals and human beings—at least between some of them. In his novel, a tiger breaks loose from a circus, walks into Malgudi where the people are of course terrified by it. The people's attempt to pen in the tiger gives wide scope for Narayan's special kind of drollery. In the end the tiger befriends a Swamy to whom it tells its story.

In *Talkative Man*, Narayan finds himself in contemporary times. This novella is included in this selection and is discussed elsewhere.

The World of Nagaraj, the most recent of Narayan's full-length novels, has a serious theme in that it deals with both the generation gap and family dissensions. Nagaraj is conservative and well-to-do. Respected by the denizens of Malgudi, childless, living with his mother and wife, his great ambition in life is to write a book on the sage Narada. This never really gets off the ground, but he derives a lot of gentle pleasure from talking about the book, tracking down sources of information, and generally doing research for a book which he cannot admit to himself, he will never finish. His placid life is suddenly disrupted when Tim, the rebellious son of his older brother, suddenly appears to stay with him. Nagaraj's brother is furious, his wife is embarrassed, and Nagaraj is in a quandary as he loves Tim, but also has the greatest respect for his older brother whom he dare not offend. On one level, the novel is about the present young generation the values of which mystify a conservative Hindu like Nagaraj, yet he cannot bring himself to abandon Tim, who, however difficult, has come to him for refuge. (The reader should remember that Nagaraj has been childless during his best years.) On another level, the attitudes moulded by hundreds of generations, the expectations of the joint family, and the deep traditional respect he has for his older brother leave Nagaraj in a welter of conflicting emotions.

The most recent book that Narayan has published is a novella, titled *The Grandmother's Tale* (1993). This is the story of his great-grandmother as he heard it from his grandmother. His great-grandmother was a spirited young woman, who, deserted by her young husband at an early age, went after him all by herself, picking up clues here and there, and finally found him in distant Poona. She also succeeded in bringing him back with her. Narayan says that 'this is mainly a story writer's version of a hearsay biography of a great-grandmother. She was seven when she got married, her husband being just ten years old.' One would not decry Narayan if one were to suggest that *The Grandmother's Tale* belongs with the recently popular genre of 'faction', that is fiction based on facts. Narayan himself gives sufficient indication in the narrative that it may be so. Whatever it is, it is an absolutely delightful period-piece with a heroine who is tough and tender at the same time. An interesting feature of the novella is that it is the only one of his works of fiction not to have Malgudi as its locale.

Narayan has also written retellings of the Indian classics, *Ramayana* and *Mahabharata*, as well as tales from Hindu myths and legends. These are told with a novelist's skill, and may well serve as introductions to the great books, especially for foreigners. The writing is easy and limpid and the narratives flow effortlessly. Being a perfectionist who left nothing to chance in his writing, he worked with scholars in the preparation of these works. He has also written a number of short stories, some of which are included in this selection and discussed elsewhere. He wrote two travelogues on Mysore, both commissioned by the government. His account of writing and publishing the earlier in 1939, when a Maharajah ruled the state and administration was in the hands of Indian officials ingrained in the British tradition, forms a hilarious chapter in his autobiography.

Which brings us to that autobiography, *My Days*. To use a word out of a women's journal, it is enchanting. Graham Greene said about it: 'Since the death of Evelyn Waugh, Narayan is the novelist I most admire in the English language. His autobiography is worthy of his novels.' First published in 1974, the book is emotion recollected in tranquillity, and coloured by the imagination of a great writer. Starting with his early years in Madras, his education and subsequent attempts to be a teacher in the Mysore school system, his early travails as an author, the editing of *Indian Thought* which as we saw had only a fleeting existence, the autobiography brings his life to the point where he is a contented man in his sixties, taking pleasure in watching his grandchildren. He has steadfastly refused to bring it up to date, partly because of the effort involved in finding long-forgotten dates, but more because: 'A composition which is wholly subjective begins and ends rather arbitrarily—brooking neither addition nor subtraction. Subtraction will mutilate; addition will stick out as an appendage. My friend Graham Greene once said: "Autobiography cannot be concluded. I must add that it cannot be extended either".' Incidentally, the friendship between Greene and Narayan lasted from the early thirties, when Greene found publishers for Narayan's first few books—in fact, *Swami and Friends* could be called a discovery of Greene's as he was the first person to be impressed by its merits—until Greene's death in 1991. The two constantly corresponded with one another, and met whenever Narayan was in London. The friendship was a valuable aspect of Narayan's literary thinking.

A town called Malgudi. Where is it? One won't find it on any map, though an intrepid American academic once drew a city map of Malgudi which was pretty much like the real Malgudi, if it had ever existed outside the imagination of its creator. It is easier to say what Malgudi is not. It must first be stated categorically that it is not Mysore city. An old Mysore-resident and long time friend of Narayan states pretty affirmatively: 'His locale is Mysore.' Nothing could be farther from the fact. Malgudi is no way resembles Mysore which has stately palaces and beautiful buildings, broad avenues flanked by huge flowering trees, and a picturesque hill within walking distance for the sturdy of limb. Nor does Malgudi resemble William Faulkner's sin and gloom ridden Yoknapataupha County, to which it has been sometimes compared because both writers created their own landmarks and people. The name Malgudi occurred to Narayan when he started writing *Swami and Friends*. He wrote: 'The train stopped at Malgudi.' And Malgudi became his town (actually the train stops for the first time only at the end of the book). If anything, Malgudi has a strong resemblance to small provincial towns of those days, complete with a Taluq Office, a municipal building, clock-tower, and a central statue with steps leading to it on which young and old sat of an evening, while hawkers peddled their wares. Malgudi is a dusty little town, with winding lanes, tenement houses with one water-tap for all the families. The people of Malgudi are by and large gentle and nervous, while some of them are always looking for easy wasy to become rich. Narayan's genius lies in giving airy nothings a local habitation and a name. Of course the denizens of Malgudi are all not airy nothings. There is the Scrooge of a landlord who will not live in any of the premises he owns as he wants to make rental money on every square inch, and bathes under the street tap. There is the pseudo-professor who has a sex-book to offer to the highest bidder, which Margayya, the financial expert, believes can be printed and sold under a euphemistic title. There are also the holy man who helps himself to flowers from other people's houses for his pooja, a variety of shop-keepers, and a dozen other minor characters to whom Narayan has given individual voices. One should not forget the drunkard, who, when in his cups, says, 'Mother is a sacred commodity, sir.' It all seems very real to the true Narayan admirer who also has some idea of real towns like Malgudi. As Graham Greene says, 'We have been as familiar (with Malgudi) as with our own birthplace. We know, like the streets of childhood, Market Road, the snuff stalls, the vendors of toothpaste, the Regal Haircutting Saloon, the river, the railway.' To settle the question once and for all, Narayan said, on the occasion of being presented with the membership of the American Academy and Institute of Arts and Letters by Ambassador Harry S. Barnes: 'I didn't consider too long when I invented this little town. It had just occurred to me when I started on my first novel, *Swami and Friends* in September 1930, that it would be safer to have a fictitious name for the background of the novel which would leave one to be free to meddle with its geography and details as I pleased, without incurring the wrath of any city-father of any actual town or city. I wanted to be able to put in whatever I liked and wherever I liked—a little street or school or a temple or a bungalow or even a slum, a railway line, at any spot, a minor despot in a little world. I began to like my role, and I began to be fascinated by its possibilities; its river, marketplace, and the far-off mountain roads and forests acquired a concrete quality, and have imprisoned me within their boundaries, with the result that I am unable to escape from Malgudi, even if I wished to . . .' Thank God for that. We are the beneficiaries. Malgudi, with its dusty streets and lanes, the river Sarayu which is dry half the time and provides a place to relax in for young and old, the Mempi hill and forest at a distance, all of which are the background for little boys desperately wanting hoops to wheel around, young men ogling girls drawing water from the Sarayu, the financial expert who gulls illiterate peasants and a score of others, is so much a part of our life that we would feel deprived if it were taken away from us suddenly.

Critics have tried to analyse Narayan's art but without much success. What E.B. White said about humour in general has a particular application to Narayan's work. Humour, White said, is like a frog; when dissected the thing dies in the process and the innards are of interest only to the specialist. A reviewer put it less clinically when he said that Narayan's stories are like drops of water trembling on a lotus leaf. All of which simply means that Narayan is a nonpareil.

In the autumn of his life, Narayan, having got over the trauma of his daughter's death in 1994, leads a serene existence. He reads the newspapers, studies his mail and throws away letters from strangers, rests a while after lunch, walks in a park some days, and always goes to his granddaughter's house in the evening to spend a couple of hours with his great-granddaughter, Madhavi, who calls him G.G. (great-grandfather). His quad cane with its four prongs accompanies him everywhere. He says it is more reliable than a brother.

July 1999   **S. Krishnan**

NOVEL

The Man-eater of Malgudi

FOR THE THEME of this novel, or rather, the idea of it, Narayan went to Hindu mythology. He takes the story of Basmasura, a Rakshasa (demon is the closest approximation), who obtains a boon from the god Siva that anybody he touches will be burnt to a cinder immediately. The Rakshasa uses this power widely and indiscriminately until gods and humans turn to the god Vishnu for succour. Vishnu takes the form of a beautiful woman, and when Basmasura desires her, he/she agrees to yield to him if he can repeat, gesture perfect, a dance that he/she will perform. The arrogant and infatuated demon agrees, and after several movements, Vishnu touches his own head. Basmasura follows suit, and is promptly burnt to ashes by his own touch. In *The Man-eater of Malgudi*, the gentle and placid life of Nataraj and his close friends, a poet and journalist, is suddenly disturbed when Vasu, a powerful and unpleasant taxidermist, moves into Nataraj's domain with his stuffed animals, despite Nataraj's feeble protests. Things go from bad to worse when Vasu lives an uproarious life, carousing and bringing his fancy women into the private areas of Nataraj's printing press. Vasu also wants to kill a temple elephant that Nataraj has befriended. This is too much, and while Nataraj fumes impotently, Vasu is found dead one morning. Was it a murder? If so, were Nataraj and any of

his friends involved? The reader will have to find out the
solution for himself, and the relevance to the myth. Despite
the intrusion of Vasu, perhaps the only totally evil person
in Narayan's fiction, this is a delightful story of Malgudi.
Market Road, Albert Mission School and Kabir Street are
mentioned in the very first page of the book, which teems
with the special people which Malgudi alone can produce.
This is Narayan's most carefully crafted story in which he
combines humour and pathos with mystery.

CHAPTER ONE

I COULD HAVE profitably rented out the little room in
front of my press on Market Road, with a view of the
fountain; it was coveted by every would-be shopkeeper in
our town. I was considered a fool for not getting my
money's worth out of it, since all the space I need for my
press and its personnel was at the back, beyond the blue
curtain. But I could not explain myself to sordid and
calculating people. I hung up a framed picture of Goddess
Laxmi poised on her lotus, holding aloft the bounties of
earth in her four hands, and through her grace I did not do
too badly. My son, little Babu, went to Albert Mission
School, and he felt quite adequately supplied with toys,
books, sweets, and any other odds and ends he fancied. My
wife, every Deepavali, gave herself a new silk sari, glittering
with lace, not to mention the ones she bought for no
particular reason at other times. She kept the pantry well-
stocked and our kitchen fire aglow, continuing the traditions
of our ancient home in Kabir Street.

I had furnished my parlour with a high-backed chair
made of teak-wood in the style of Queen Anne, or so the

auctioneer claimed who had sold it to my grandfather, a roll-top desk supported on bowlegs with ivy-vines carved on them, and four other seats of varying heights and shapes, resurrected from our family lumber-room.

Anyone who found his feet aching as he passed down Market Road was welcome to rest in my parlour on any seat that happened to be vacant. While they rested there, people got ideas for bill forms, visiting cards, or wedding invitations which they asked me to print, but many others came whose visits did not mean a paisa to me. Among my constant companions was a poet who was writing the life of God Krishna in monosyllabic verse. His ambition was to compose a grand epic, and he came almost every day to recite to me his latest lines. My admiration for him was unbounded. I was thrilled to hear such clear lines as 'Girls with girls did dance in trance', and I felt equally excited when I had to infer the meaning of certain lines; that happened when he totally failed to find a monosyllable and achieved his end by ruthlessly carving up a polysyllable. On such occasions even the most familiar term took on the mysterious quality of a private code. Invariably, in deference to his literary attainments, I let him occupy the Queen Anne chair, while I sat perched on the edge of my roll-top desk. In the next best seat, a deep basket-chair in cane, you would find Sen, the journalist, who came to read the newspapers on my table, and who held forth on the mistakes Nehru was making. These two men and a few others remained sitting there till six in the evening when the press was silenced. I had no need to be present or attend to them in any way. They were also good enough to vacate their chairs without being told and disappear when anyone came to discuss business with me.

Between my parlour and the press hung a blue curtain. No one tried to peer through it. When I shouted for the foreman, compositor, office-boy, binder or accountant, people imagined a lot of men working on the other side; if I had been challenged I should have gone in and played the ventriloquist. But my neighbour, the Star Press, had all the staff one could dream of, and if any customer of mine insisted on seeing machinery, I led him not through my curtain, but next door to the Star, where I displayed its original Heidelberg with pride as my own acquisition (although in my view the owner had made a mistake in buying it, as the groans of its double cylinder could be heard beyond the railway yard when formes were being printed). The owner of the Star was a nice man and a good friend, but he hardly got any customers. How could he when all the time they were crowding my parlour, although all I could offer them was an assortment of chairs and a word of welcome? But as few had ever stepped beyond the blue curtain, everyone imagined me equipped for big tasks, which I certainly attempted with the help of my well-wisher (I dare not call him staff) Sastri, the old man who set up type, printed the formes four pages at a time on the treadle, sewed the sheets, and carried them for ruling or binding to Kandan four streets off. I lent him a hand in all departments whenever he demanded my help and my visitors left me alone. On the whole I was a busy man, and such business as I could not take up I passed on next door to be done on the original Heidelberg. I was so free with the next-door establishment that no one knew whether I owned it or whether the Star owned me.

I lived in Kabir Street, which ran behind Market Road. My day started before four in the morning. The streets would be quite dark when I set out to the river for my ablutions, except for the municipal lamps which flickered (if they had not run out of oil) here and there in our street. I went down Kabir Street, cut through a flagged alley at the end of it, trespassed into the compound of the Taluk office through a gap in its bramble fencing, and there I was on the edge of the river. All along the way I had my well-defined encounters. The milkman, starting on his rounds, driving ahead of him a puny white cow, greeted me respectfully and asked, 'What is the time, master?'—a question I allowed to die without a reply as I carried no watch. I simpered and let him pass suppressing the question, 'Tell me the secret of your magic: how you manage to extract a milk-like product out of that miserable cow-like creature to supply thirty families as you do every morning? What exactly are you, conjuror or milk-vendor?' The old asthmatic at the end of our street sat up on the *pyol* of his house and gurgled through his choking throat, 'Didn't get a wink of sleep all night, and already it's morning and you are out! That's life, I suppose!' The watchman at the Taluk office called from beneath his rug, 'Is that you?'—the only question which deserved a reply. 'Yes, it's me,' I always said and passed on.

I had my own spot at the riverside, immediately behind the Taluk office. I shunned the long flight of steps farther down; they were always crowded, and if I went there I was racked with the feeling that I was dipping into other people's baths, but this point upstream seemed to me exclusive. A palmyra tree loomed over the bank of the river, festooned with mud pots into which toddy dripped through a gash in the bark of the tree. When it fermented, it stank to the skies, and was gathered in barrels and sold to the patrons who congregated at the eighteen taverns scattered in the four corners of the city, where any evening one could see revellers fighting or rolling in the gutters. So much for the potency of the fluid dripping into the pot. I never looked up at the palmyra without a shudder. 'With his monopoly of taverns,' I thought, 'Sankunni builds his mansions in the New Extension and rides about in his four American cars driven by uniformed chauffeurs.'

All the same I was unable to get away from the palmyra. At the foot of the tree was a slab of stone on which I washed my *dhoti* and towel, and the dark hour resounded with the tremendous beating of wet cloth on granite. I stood waist-deep in water, and at the touch of cold water around my body I felt elated. The trees on the bank stood like shadows in the dusk. When the east glowed I sat for a moment on the sand reciting a prayer to the Sun to illumine my mind. The signal for me to break off from contemplation was the jingle of ox-bells as country carts forded Nallappa's grove, bringing loads of vegetables, corn and fuel from the nearby villages to the market. I rose and retraced my steps, rolling up my washing into a tight pack.

I had more encounters on my way back. My cousin from the fourth street gave me a cold look and passed. She hated me for staying in our ancestral home, my father having received it as his share after the division of property among his brothers. She never forgave us, although it had all happened in my father's time. Most of the citizens of this area were now moving sleepily towards the river, and everyone had a word for me. The lawyer, known as the adjournment lawyer for his ability to prolong a case beyond the wildest dream of a litigant, came by, a sparse hungry-looking man who shaved his chin once a fortnight. When I saw him in the distance I cried to myself, 'I am undone. Mr Adjournment will get me now.' The moment he saw me he cried, 'Where is your bed? Unless you have slept by the river how can you be *returning* from the river at this unearthly hour?'

There was one whom I did not really mind meeting, the septuagenarian living in a dilapidated outhouse in Adam's Lane, who owned a dozen houses in our locality, lived on rent, and sent off money-orders to distant corners of the Indian subcontinent, where his progeny was spread out. He always stopped to give me news of his relations. He looked like a new-born infant when he bared his gums in a smile. 'You are late today,' I always said, and waited for his explanation, 'I sat up late writing letters. You know how it is with one's children scattered far and wide.' I did not mind tarrying to listen to the old man, although my fingers felt cramped with encircling the wad of wet clothes I was carrying home to dry. The old man referred to four sons and their doings and five daughters, and countless grandchildren. He was always busy, on one side attending to the repairs of his dozen houses, about which one or the other of his tenants was always pursuing him; on the other, writing innumerable letters on postcards, guiding, blessing, admonishing, or spoiling with a remittance of cash one or the other of his wards.

I was content to live in our house as it had been left by my father. I was a youth, studying in Albert Mission, when the legal division of ancestral property occurred between my father and his brothers. I well remember the day when his four brothers marched out with their wives and children, trundling away their share of heirlooms, knickknacks and household articles. Everything that could be divided into five was cut up into equal parts and given one to each. Such things as could not be split up were given to those who clamoured the loudest. A rattan easy chair on which my grandfather used to lie in the courtyard, watching the sky, was claimed by my second uncle whose wife had started all the furore over the property. She also claimed a pair of rosewood benches which shone with a natural polish, and a timber wooden chair that used to be known as the bug-proof chair. My father's third brother, as compensation for letting these items go, claimed a wooden almirah as his own and a 'leg' harmonium operated by a pedal. The harmonium was also claimed by another uncle whose daughter was supposed to possess musical talent. It had gathered dust in a corner for decades without anyone's noticing it. No one had even asked how it had come to find a place in our home, although a little family research would have yielded the information. Our grandfather had lent a hundred rupees to a local dramatic troupe and attached their harmonium as their only movable property after a court decree, lugged it home, and kept it in a corner of our hall. He died before he could sell and realize its value, and his successors took the presence of the harmonium in the corner of the hall for granted until this moment of partition.

All the four brothers of my father with their wives and children, numbering fifteen, had lived under the same roof for many years. It was my father's old mother who had kept them together, acting as a cohesive element among

11

members of the family. Between my grandmother, who laid down the policy, and a person called Grand-Auntie, who actually executed it, the family administration ran smoothly. When my grandmother died the unity of the family was also gone. The trouble started with my father's second brother's wife, who complained loudly one day, standing in the passage of the house, that her children had been ill-treated and that she was hated by everyone; her cause was upheld by her husband. Soon various other differences appeared among the brothers and their wives, although all the children continued to play in the open courtyard, unmindful of the attitude of the elders to each other.

Before the year was out, on a festival day, they had their biggest open quarrel, provoked by a minor incident in which an eight-year-old boy knocked down another and snatched a biscuit from his mouth. A severe family crisis developed, as the mother of the injured child slapped the offender on his bare seat. My father and his brothers were sitting around, eating their midday meal. My father muttered mildly, 'If Mother were alive she would have handled everyone and prevented such scenes.'

Two of his brothers, incensed at the incident, got up without touching their food. My father commented, without looking at anyone in particular, 'You need not abandon your food. This is a sacred day. Such things should not be allowed to happen.' My mother, who was bending over him, serving ghee, whispered, 'Why don't you mind your business? They are not babies to be taught how to conduct themselves on a festive day.'

My father accepted her advice without a word and resolved at that moment to break up the joint family in the interests of peace. The next few days saw our family lawyers, assisted by the adjournment expert, walking in and out with papers to be signed, and within a few weeks the house had become empty. It had been a crowded house since the day it was built by my father's grandfather, numerous children, womenfolk, cousins, relations and guests milling in and out all the year round, and now it became suddenly bare and empty. The household now consisted of my parents, Grand-Auntie, me and my two sisters. My brother was away in Madras in a college hostel. As he grew older my father began to spend all his time sitting on the *pyol*, on a mat, reading Ramayana or just watching the street. Even at night he never went beyond the *pyol*. He placed a small pillow under his head and stretched himself there. He hardly ever visited the other parts of this immense house. Occasionally he wandered off to the backyard to pluck the withered leaves off a citrus tree, which had been his favourite plant. It had been growing there for years, and no one knew whether it was an orange or lime tree; it kept people guessing, never displaying on its branches anything more than a few white flowers now and then. This plant was my father's only concern. He hardly ever looked up at the six tall coconut trees that waved in the sky. They were my mother's responsibility and Grand-Auntie's, who regularly had their tops cleared of beetles and withered shoots, sent up a climber once a month, and filled the granary with large, ripe coconuts. There were also pumpkins growing in the backyard, and large creepers covered the entire thatched roof of a cow-shed, which used to house four of Malgudi's best-bred cows, years before.

After my father's death my mother lived with me until

Babu was a year old, and then she decided to go and live with my brother at Madras, taking away with her her life-companion Grand-Auntie. Thus I, with my wife and little Babu, became the sole occupant of the house in Kabir Street.

CHAPTER TWO

SASTRI HAD TO go a little earlier than usual since he had to perform a puja at home. I hesitated to let him go. The three colour labels (I prided myself on the excellence of my colour-printing) for K.J.'s aerated drinks had to be got ready. It was a very serious piece of work for me. My personal view was that the coloured ink I used on the label was far safer to drink than the dye that K.J. put into his water-filled bottles. We had already printed the basic colour on the labels and the second was to be imposed today. This was a crucial stage of the work and I wanted Sastri to stay and finish the job. He said, 'Perhaps I can stay up late tonight and finish it. Not now. Meanwhile will you . . .' He allotted me work until he should be back at two o'clock.

I had been engrossed in a talk with the usual company. On the agenda today was Nehru's third Five-Year Plan; my friend Sen saw nothing but ruin in it for the country. 'Three hundred crores—are we counting heads or money?' His audience consisted of myself and the poet, and a client who had come to ask for quotations for a business card. The discussion was warming up, as the client was a Congressman

who had gone to prison fourteen times since the day
Mahatma Gandhi arrived in India from South Africa. He
ignored for the time being the business that had brought
him and plunged into the debate, settling himself inexorably
in a corner. 'What's wrong with people is they have got into
the habit of blaming everything on the Government. You
think democracy means that if there is no sugar in the
shops, Government is responsible. What if there is no
sugar? You won't die if you do not have sugar for your
morning coffee some days.' Sen disputed every word of the
patriot's speech.

I listened to the debate until I noticed Sastri's silhouette
beyond the curtain. Sastri, when there was any emergency,
treated me as a handy-boy, and I had no alternative but to
accept the role. Now my duty would be to fix the block on
the machine and put the second impression on all the labels
and spread them out to dry, then he would come and give
the third impression and put the labels out to dry again.

He explained some of the finer points to me, 'The
blocks are rather worn. You'll have to let in more ink.'

'Yes, Mr Sastri.'

He looked at me through his small silver-rimmed glasses
and said firmly, 'Unless the labels are second-printed and
dry by three o'clock today, it's going to be impossible to
deliver them tomorrow. You know what kind of a man K.J.
is . . .'

What about my lunch? Sastri did not care whether I had
time for food or not—he was a tyrant when it came to
printing labels, but there was no way of protesting. He
would brush everything aside. As if reading my mind he
explained, 'I'd not trouble you but for the fact that this

satyanarayana puja must be performed today in my house; my children and wife will be waiting for me at the door . . .' As it was he would have to trot all the way to Vinayak Street if his family were not to starve too long.

Wife, children. Absurd. Such encumbrances were not necessary for Sastri, I felt. They were for lesser men like me. His place was at the type-board and the treadle. He produced an incongruous, unconvincing picture as a family man. But I dared not express myself aloud. The relation of employer and employee was reversed at my press whenever there was an emergency.

I accepted the situation without any fuss. According to custom my friends would not step beyond the curtain, so I was safe to go ahead with the second impression. Sastri had fixed everything. I had only to press the pedal and push the paper on to the pad. On a pale orange ground I had now to impose a sort of violet. I grew hypnotized by the sound of the wheel and the dozen kinks that were set in motion by the pressure I put on the pedals. Whenever I paused I could hear Sen's voice, 'If Nehru is practical, let him disown the Congress . . . Why should you undertake projects which you can't afford? Anyway, in ten years what are we going to do with all the steel?' There was a sudden lull. I wondered if they had been suddenly struck dumb. I heard the shuffling of feet. I felt suddenly relieved that the third Five-Year Plan was done with.

Now an unusual thing happened. The curtain stirred, an edge of it lifted, and the monosyllabic poet's head peeped through. An extraordinary situation must have arisen to make him do that. His eyes bulged. 'Someone to see you,' he whispered.

'Who? What does he want?'

'I don't know.' The whispered conversation was becoming a strain. I shook my head, winked and grimaced to indicate to the poet that I was not available. The poet, ever a dense fellow, did not understand but blinked on unintelligently. His head suddenly vanished, and a moment later a new head appeared in its place—a tanned face, large powerful eyes under thick eyebrows a large forehead and a shock of unkempt hair, like a black halo.

My first impulse was to cry out, 'Whoever you may be, why don't you brush your hair?' The new visitor had evidently pulled aside the poet before showing himself to me. Before I could open my mouth, he asked, 'You Nataraj?' I nodded. He came forward, practically tearing aside the curtain, an act which violated the sacred traditions of my press. I said, 'Why don't you kindly take a seat in the next room? I'll be with you in a moment.' He paid no attention, but stepped forward, extending his hand. I hastily wiped my fingers on a rag, muttering, 'Sorry, discoloured, been working . . .' He gave me a hard grip. My entire hand disappeared into his fist—he was a huge man, about six feet tall. He looked quite slim, but his bull-neck and hammer-fist revealed his true stature. 'Shan't we move to the other room?' I asked again.

'Not necessary. It's all the same to me,' he said. 'You are doing something? Why don't you go on? It won't bother me.' He eyed my coloured labels. 'What are they?'

I didn't want any eyes to watch my special colour effects, and see how I achieved them. I moved to the curtain and parted it courteously for him. He followed me. I showed him to the Queen Anne chair, and sat down at my usual place, on the edge of my desk. I had now regained the feeling of being master of the situation. I adopted my best smile and asked, 'Well, what can I do for you, Mr . . .?'

'Vasu,' he said, and added, 'I knew you didn't catch my name. You were saying something at the same time as I mentioned my name.'

I felt abashed, and covered it, I suppose, with another of those silly smiles. Then I checked myself, suddenly feeling angry with him for making me so uneasy. I asked myself, 'Nataraj, are you afraid of this muscular fellow?' and said authoritatively, 'Yes?' as much as to indicate, 'You have wasted my time sufficiently; now say quickly whatever you may want to say.'

He took from his inner pocket a wad of paper, searched for a handwritten sheet and held it out to me. 'Five hundred sheets of note-paper, the finest quality, and five hundred visiting cards.'

I spread out the sheet without a word and read, 'H. Vasu, MA, Taxidermist'. I grew interested. My irritation left me. This was the first time I had set eyes on a taxidermist. I said, assuming a friendly tone, 'Five hundred! Are you sure you need five hundred visiting cards? Could you not print them one hundred at a time? They'd be fresh then.'

'Why do you try to advise me?' he asked pugnaciously. 'I know how many I need. I'm not printing my visiting cards in order to preserve them in a glass case.'

'All right. I can print ten thousand if you want.'

He softened at my show of aggressiveness. 'Fine, fine, that's the right spirit.'

'If you'd like to have it done on the original Heidelberg . . .' I began.

19

'I don't care what you do it on. I don't even know what you are talking about.'

I understood the situation now; every other sentence was likely to prove provocative. I began to feel intrigued by the man. I didn't want to lose him. Even if I wanted to, I had no means of getting rid of him. He had sought me out and I'd have to have him until he decided to leave. I might just as well be friendly. 'Surely, whatever you like. It's my duty to ask, that's all. Some people prefer it.'

'What is it anyway?' he asked.

I explained the greatness of Heidelberg and where it was. He thought it over, and suddenly said, 'Nataraj, I trust you to do your best for me. I have come to you as a friend.' I was surprised and flattered. He explained, 'I'm new to this place, but I heard about you within an hour of coming.' He mentioned an obscure source of information. 'Well, I never give a second thought to these things,' he said. 'When I like a man, I like him, that's all.'

I wanted to ask about taxidermy, so I asked, looking at his card, 'Taxidermist? Must be an interesting job. Where is your er . . . office or . . .'

'I hope to make a start right here. I was in Junagadh— you know the place—and there I grew interested in the art. I came across a master there, one Suleiman. When he stuffed a lion (you know, Junagadh is a place where we have lions) he could make it look more terrifying than it would be in the jungle. His stuffings go all over the world. He was a master, and he taught me the art. After all we are civilized human beings, educated and cultured, and it is up to us to prove our superiority to nature. Science conquers nature in a new way each day; why not in creation also?

That's my philosophy, sir. I challenge any man to contradict me.' He sighed at the thought of Suleiman, his master. 'He was a saint. He taught me his art sincerely.'

'Where did you get your MA?'

'At Madras, of course. You want to know about me?' he asked.

I wonder what he would have done if I had said, 'No, I prefer to go home and eat my food.' He would probably have held me down. He said, 'I was educated in the Presidency College. I took my Master's degree in History, Economics and Literature.' That was in the year 1931. Then he had joined the civil disobedience movement against British rule, broken the laws, marched, demonstrated and ended up in jail. He went repeatedly to prison and once when he was released found himself in the streets of Nagpur. There he met a *phaelwan* at a show. 'That man could bear a half-ton stone slab on his cheek and have it split by hammer strokes; he could snap steel chains and he could hit a block of hard granite with his fist and pulverize it. I was young then, his strength appealed to me. I was prepared to become his disciple at any cost. I introduced myself to the *phaelwan*.' He remained thoughtful for a while and continued, 'I learnt everything from this master. The training was unsparing. He woke me up at three o'clock every morning and put me through exercises. And he provided me with the right diet. I had to eat a hundred almonds every morning and wash them down with half a *seer* of milk; two hours later six eggs with honey; at lunch chicken and rice; at night vegetables and fruit. Not everyone can hope to have this diet, but I was lucky in finding a man who enjoyed stuffing me like that. In six months I could

understudy for him. On my first day, when I banged my fist
on a century-old door of a house in Lucknow, the three-
inch panel of seasoned teak splintered. My master patted
me on the back with tears of joy in his eyes, 'You are
growing on the right lines, my boy.' In a few months I
could also snap chains, twist iron bars, and pulverize
granite. We travelled all over the country, and gave our
shows at every market fair in the villages and in the town
halls in the cities, and he made a lot of money. Gradually
he grew flabby and lazy, and let me do everything. They
announced his name on the notices, but actually I did all
the twisting and smashing of stone, iron, and what not.
When I spoke to him about it he called me an ungrateful
dog and other names, and tried to push me out. I resisted
. . . and . . .' Vasu laughed at the recollection of this
incident. 'I knew his weak spot. I hit him there with the
edge of my palm with a chopping movement . . . and he fell
down and squirmed on the floor. I knew he could perform
no more. I left him there and walked out, and gave up the
strong man's life once and for all.'

'You didn't stop to help him?' I asked.

'I helped him by leaving him there, instead of holding
him upside down and rattling the teeth out of his head.'

'Oh, no,' I cried, horrified.

'Why not? I was a different man now, not the boy who
went to him for charity. I was stronger than he.'

'After all he taught you to be strong—he was your
guru,' I said, enjoying the thrill of provoking him.

'Damn it all!' he cried. 'He made money out of me,
don't you see?

'But he also gave you six eggs a day and—how much

milk and almonds was it?'

He threw up his arms in vexation. 'Oh, you will never understand these things, Nataraj. You know nothing, you have not seen the world. You know only what happens in this miserable little place.'

'If you think this place miserable, why do you choose to come here?' I was nearest the inner door. I could dash away if he attempted to grab me. Familiarity was making me rash and headstrong. I enjoyed taunting him.

'You think I have come here out of admiration for this miserable city? Know this, I'm here because of Mempi Forest and the jungles in those hills. I'm a taxidermist. I have to be where wild animals live.'

'And die,' I added.

He appreciated my joke and laughed. 'You are a wise guy,' he said admiringly.

'You haven't told me yet why or how you became a taxidermist,' I reminded him.

'H'm!' he said. 'Don't get too curious. Let us do business first. When are you giving me the visiting cards? Tomorrow?' He might pulverize granite, smash his guru with a slicing stroke, but where printing work was concerned I was not going to be pushed. I got up and turned the sheets of a tear-off calendar on the wall. 'You can come tomorrow and ask me. I can discuss this matter only tomorrow. My staff are out today.'

At this moment my little son Babu came running in crying 'Appa!' and halted his steps abruptly on seeing a stranger. He bit his nails, grinned, and tried to turn and run. I shot out my hand and held him. 'What is it?' I asked. He was friendly with the usual crowd at my press, but the

23

stranger's presence somehow embarrassed him. I could guess why he had come; it was either to ask for a favour— permission to go out with his friends, or cash for peppermints—or to bring a message from his mother.

'Mother says, aren't you coming home for food? She is hungry.'

'So am I,' I said, 'and if I were Mother I wouldn't wait for Father. Understand me? Here is a gentleman with whom I am engaged on some important business. Do you know what he can do?' My tone interested Babu and he looked up expectantly.

Vasu made a weary gesture, frowned and said, 'Oh, stop that, Mr Nataraj. Don't start it all again. I don't want to be introduced to anyone. Now, go away, boy,' he said authoritatively.

'He is my son . . .' I began.

'I see that,' Vasu said indifferently, and Babu wriggled himself free and ran off.

Vasu did not come next day, but appeared again fifteen days later. He arrived in a jeep.

'You have been away a long time,' I said. 'You thought you were rid of me?' he asked, and, thumping his chest, 'I never forget.'

'And I never remember,' I said. Somehow this man's presence roused in me a sort of pugnacity.

He stepped in, saw the Queen Anne chair occupied by the poet, and remarked, half-jokingly, 'That's my chair, I suppose.' The poet scrambled to his feet and moved to another seat. 'H'm, that's better,' Vasu said, sitting down.

24

He smiled patronizingly at the poet and said, 'I haven't been told who you are.'

'I'm—I'm . . . a teacher in the school.'

'What do you teach?' he asked relentlessly.

'Well, history, geography, science, English—anything the boys must know.'

'H'm, an all-rounder,' Vasu said. I could see the poet squirming. He was a mild, inoffensive man who was unused to such rough contacts. But Vasu seemed to enjoy bothering him. I rushed in to his rescue. I wanted to add to his stature by saying, 'He is a poet. He is nominally a teacher, but actually . . .'

'I never read poetry; no time,' said Vasu promptly, and dismissed the man from his thoughts. He turned to me and asked, 'Where are my cards?'

I had a seasoned answer for such a question. 'Where have you been this whole fortnight?'

'Away, busy.'

'So was I,' I said.

'You promised to give me the cards . . .'

'When?' I asked.

'Next day,' he said. I told him that there had been no such promise. He raised his voice, and I raised mine. He asked finally, 'Are we here on business or to fight? If it's a fight, tell me. I like a fight. Can't you see, man, why I am asking for my cards?'

'Don't *you* see that we have our own business practice?' I always adopted 'we' whenever I had to speak for the press.

'What do you mean?' he asked aggressively.

'We never choose the type and stationery for a customer.

It must always be the customer's responsibility.'

'You never told me that,' he cried.

'You remember I asked you to come next day. That was my purpose. I never say anything without a purpose.'

'Why couldn't you have mentioned it the same day?'

'You have a right to ask,' I said, feeling it was time to concede him something. The poet looked scared by these exchanges. He was trying to get out, but I motioned him to stay. Why should the poor man be frightened away?

'You have not answered my question,' said Vasu. 'Why couldn't you have shown me samples of type on the first day?'

I said curtly, 'Because my staff were out.'

'Oh!' he said, opening his eyes wide. 'I didn't know you had a staff.'

I ignored his remark and shouted, 'Sastri! Please bring those ivory card samples and also the ten-point copper-plate.' I told Vasu grandly, 'Now you can indicate your preferences, and we shall try to give you the utmost satisfaction.'

Sastri, with his silver-rimmed glasses on his nose, entered, bearing a couple of blank cards and a specimen type-book. He paused for a second, studying the visitor, placed them on the table, turned and disappeared through the curtain.

'How many are employed in your press?' Vasu asked.

The man's curiosity was limitless and recognized no proprieties. I felt enraged. Was he a labour commissioner or something of the kind? I replied, 'As many as I need. But, as you know, present-day labour conditions are not encouraging. However, Mr Sastri is very dependable; he has been with me for years . . .' I handed him the cards and

26

said, 'You will have to choose. These are the best available.'
I handed him the type-book. 'Tell me what type you like.'

That paralysed him. He turned the cards between his
fingers, he turned the leaves of the type-book, and cried,
'I'm damned if I know what I want. They all look alike to
me. What is the difference anyway?'

This was a triumph for me. 'Vasu, printing is an
intricate business. That's why we won't take responsibility
in these matters.'

'Oh, please do something and print me my cards,' he
cried, exasperated.

'All right,' I said, 'I'll do it for you, if you trust me.'

'I trust you as a friend, otherwise I would not have
come to you.'

'Actually,' I said, 'I welcome friends rather than
customers. I'm not a fellow who cares for money. If anyone
comes to me for pure business, I send them over to my
neighbour and they are welcome to get their work done
cheaper and on a better machine—original Heidelberg.'

'Oh, stop that original Heidel,' he cried impatiently. 'I
want to hear no more of it. Give me my cards. My business
arrangements are waiting on that, and remember also five
hundred letterheads.'

CHAPTER THREE

AN ATTIC ABOVE my press was full of discarded papers, stacks of old newspapers, files of dead correspondence and accounts, and, bulkiest of all, a thousand copies of a school magazine which I used to print and display as my masterpiece and which I froze in the attic when the school could not pay the printing charges.

I called up a waste-paper buyer, who was crying for custom in the streets, and sent him up the rickety staircase to make a survey and tell me his offer. He was an old Moslem who carried a sack on his back and cried, 'Old paper, empty bottles,' tramping the streets all afternoon. 'Be careful,' I told him as I sent him up the stairs to estimate. 'There may be snakes and scorpions up there. No human being has set foot in the attic for years.' Later, when I heard his steps come down, I prepared myself for the haggling to follow by stiffening my countenance and assuming a grave voice. He parted the curtain, entered my parlour and stood respectfully pressing his back close to the wall and awaiting my question.

'Well, have you examined the lot?'

'Yes, sir. Most of the paper is too old and is completely brown.'

'Surely you didn't expect me to buy the latest editions for your benefit, or did you think I would buy white paper by the ream and sell it to you by weight?' I spoke with heavy cynicism, and he was softened enough to say, 'I didn't say so . . .' Then he made his offer. I ignored it completely as not being worth a man's notice.

At this point, if he had really found my attitude unacceptable, he should have gone away, but he stayed, and that was a good sign. I was looking through the proofs of a cinema programme and I suddenly left him in order to attend to some item of work inside the press. I came out nearly an hour later, and he was still there. He had set his gunny sack down and was sitting on the door-step. 'Still here!' I cried, feigning astonishment. 'By all means rest here if you like, but don't expect me to waste any more time talking to you. I don't have to sell that paper at all. I can keep it as I have kept it for years.'

He fidgeted uneasily and said, 'The paper is brown and cracks. Please have consideration for me, sir. I have to make one or two rupees every day in order to bring up my family of . . .' He went into the details of his domestic budget: how he had to find the money for his children's school-books, food, and medicine, by collecting junk from every house and selling it to the dealers for a small margin of profit, often borrowing a loan at the start of a day. After hearing him out, I relented enough to mention a figure, at which he picked up his sack and pretended to go. Then I mitigated my demand, he raised his offer, and this market fluctuation went on till three o'clock. Sastri came at three with a frown

on his face, understood in a moment what was going on
and muttered, 'Sometimes it's better to throw old paper
into a boiler to save firewood than sell it to these fellows.
They always try to cheat,' thus lending support to my own
view.

Presently Vasu arrived in his jeep, and unpacked his
valise, mumbling, 'Let me note something before I forget it.'
He sat in the Queen Anne chair, took out a sheet of paper
and wrote. Both of us, the parties to the waste-paper
transaction, watched him silently. A lorry was passing
down the road, raising a blanket of cloud; a couple of
jutkas were rattling along on their wooden wheels; two
vagrants had stretched themselves on the parapet of the
fountain, enjoying a siesta; a little boy was watching his
lamb graze on the lawn which the municipality was struggling
to cultivate by the margin of the fountain; a crow sat on top
of the fountain, hopefully looking for a drop of water. It
was an ideal hour for a transaction in junk.

Vasu stopped writing and asked, 'What's going on?'

I turned to the waste-paper man and said, 'You know
who he is? I'll have him to explain to if I give the paper
away too cheap.'

Vasu raised his eyes from the paper, glared at the
Moslem and asked, 'What are you supposed to be doing?
Have a care!' The trader grew nervous and said, 'My final
offer, sir. It's getting late; if I get nothing here I must at
least find another place for my business today.'

'All right, go,' I said. 'I'm not stopping you.'

'Twenty-five rupees, sir.'

'If this gentleman approves,' I said. Vasu seemed pleased
at being involved. He tapped the table and hemmed and

hawed. The ragman appealed to him, 'I'm a poor man. Don't squeeze me. If I invest it . . .'

Vasu suddenly got up, saying, 'Let's have a look at your loot anyway,' and, led by the Moslem, passed beyond the curtain and clambered upstairs. I was surprised to see Vasu enter the spirit of the game so completely.

Presently the Moslem came down with a pile of paper and took it to the front step. He came up to me, holding twenty-five rupees in currency, his face beaming, 'The master has agreed.' He made three more trips upstairs and barricaded my entrance with waste paper. He beckoned to a *jutka* passing down the street and loaded all the bundles into it. I asked, 'Where is that man?'

'He is up there.'

'What's he doing there?'

'I don't know,' said the old man. 'He was trying to open the windows.'

Presently Vasu called me from the attic, 'Nataraj, come up.'

'Why?' I cried. I was busy with the cinema programme. He repeated his command, and I went up. I had not gone upstairs for years. The wooden stairs creaked and groaned, unused to the passage of feet. There was a small landing and a green door, and you stepped in. Vasu was standing in the middle of the room like a giant. He had opened a little wooden window with a view of the fountain, over the market road; beyond it was a small door which led to a very narrow terrace that looked southwards on to the neighbouring roof-tiles. The floor was littered with pieces of waste paper; age-old dust covered everything.

Vasu was fanning around his ears with a cover of the

school magazine. 'That fellow has done you a service in carrying away all that waste paper, but he has dehoused a thousand mosquitoes—one thing I can't stand.' He vigorously fanned them off as they tried to buzz about his ears. 'Night or day, I run when a mosquito is mentioned.'

'Let us go down,' I said, flourishing my arms to keep them away from my head.

'Wait a minute,' he said. 'What do you propose to do with this place?'

I ruminated for a moment; I had no plans for it, but before I could say so he said, 'I'll clean it up and stay here for a while. I want some place where I can throw my things and stay. The important thing will be to get a mosquito-net for sleeping in, a bed and one or two chairs. The roof comes down too low,' he added. He swung his arms up and down and said, 'Still a couple of feet above my arms, not too bad.'

I gave him no reply. I had never thought of the attic as habitable.

He asked, 'Why are you silent?'

'Nothing, nothing,' I said. 'I shall have to . . .'

'What?' he asked mercilessly. 'Don't tell me you want to consult your seniors or partners, the usual dodge. I will stay here till a bungalow is vacated for me in the New Extension. I wouldn't dream of settling here. So don't be afraid. After all you would only put junk into it again.'

I said nothing and went down to my office. He followed me, drove away in his jeep and returned an hour later with four workmen carrying brooms and buckets. He led them past the curtain, up the stairs. I heard him shouting and bullying them and the mops and brooms at work. He discovered the water-closet below the staircase and made them carry up buckets of water and scrub the floor. Next day he brought in a builder's man and spent the whole day washing the walls of the attic with lime. He passed in and out, and hardly found time for a word with me. I watched him come and go. Two days later he brought a bedstead and a few pieces of furniture. Since I found it a nuisance to have Vasu and his minions pass up and down by the press I opened a side gate in the compound, which admitted his jeep into a little yard from Kabir Lane and gave him direct access to the wooden stairs. It took me another week to realize that without a word from me Vasu had established himself in the attic. 'After all,' I thought to myself, 'it's a junk-room, likely to get filled again with rubbish. Why not let him stay there until he finds a house?'

He disappeared for long periods and would then suddenly drop in. I had no idea where he went. Sometimes he just came and lounged in my parlour. My other visitors always tried to run away at the sight of him, for they found it difficult to cope with his bullying talk. The poet left if he saw him coming. Sen, the journalist, who was always loudly analysing Nehru's policies, could not stand him even for a minute. He had been unwittingly caught the very first day, while he was expatiating on the Five-Year Plan. Vasu, who had come in to collect some stationery, listened for a moment to the journalist's talk and, turning to me, asked, 'Who's he? You have not told me his name.'

'A good friend,' I said.

Vasu shook his head patronizingly and said, 'If he is so much wiser than Nehru, why doesn't he try to become the Prime Minister of India?'

The journalist drew himself up haughtily and cried, 'Who is this man? Why does he interfere with me when I am talking to someone? Is there no freedom of speech?'

Vasu said, 'If you feel superior to Nehru, why don't you go to Delhi and take charge of the cabinet?' and laughed contemptuously. Words followed, Sen got up in anger, Vasu advanced threateningly. I came between them with a show of courage, dreading lest one of them should hit me. I cried, 'All are friends here. I won't allow a fight. Not here, not here.'

'Then where?' asked Vasu.

'Nowhere,' I replied.

'I don't want to be insulted, that's all,' the bully said.

'I am not going to be frightened by anyone's muscle or size. Do you threaten to hit me?' Sen cried. He pushed me out of the way and stepped up to Vasu. I was in a panic.

'No, sir,' said Vasu, recoiling. 'Not unless I'm hit first.' He raised his fist and flourished it. 'I could settle many problems with this, but I don't. If I hit you with it, it will be the end of you. But that doesn't mean I may not kick.'

Vasu sat in my parlour and expounded his philosophy of human conduct. 'Nataraj!' he would say. 'Life is too short to have a word with everyone in this land of three hundred odd million. One has to ignore most people.' I knew it was just a fancy speech, because his nature would not let him leave anyone in peace. He'd wilt if he could not find some poor man to bully. If he found someone known to him, he taunted him. If he met a stranger or a new face, he bluntly demanded, 'Who is he? You have not told me his name!'

No maharaja finding a ragged commoner wandering in the halls of his durbar would have adopted a more authoritative tone in asking, 'Who is this?'

Vasu's habit of using my front room as an extension of his attic was proving irksome, as I had my own visitors, not to speak of the permanent pair—the poet and the journalist. For a few days Sen and the poet left the moment they heard the jeep arrive, but gradually their views underwent a change. When Vasu came in, Sen would stick to his seat with an air of defiance as if saying, 'I'm not going to let that beefy fellow . . .' The poet would transfer himself without fuss from the high-backed Queen Anne chair to a poorer seat. He had developed the art of surviving Vasu's presence; he maintained a profound silence, but if he were forced to speak he would confine himself to monosyllables (at which in any case he was an adept), and I was glad to note that Vasu had too much on his mind to have the time for more than a couple of nasty, personal remarks, which the poet pretended not to hear. Sen suppressed the expression of his political opinions in Vasu's presence (which was a good thing again), but it did not save him, as Vasu, the moment he remembered his presence, said, 'What are the views of our wise friend on this?' To which Sen gave a fitting reply, such as 'If people are dense enough not to know what is happening, I'm not prepared to . . .', which would act as a starting point for a battle of words. But the battle never came, as on the first day, to near-blows—it always fizzled out.

I left everyone alone. If they wrangled and lost their heads and voices, it was their business and not mine. Even if heads had been broken, I don't think I'd have interfered.

I had resigned myself to anything. If I had cared for a peaceful existence, I should have rejected Vasu on the first day. Now it was like having a middle-aged man-eater in your office and home, with the same uncertainties, possibilities, and potentialities.

This man-eater softened, snivelled and purred, and tried to be agreeable only in the presence of an official. He brought in a khaki-clad, cadaverous man one day, a forestry officer, seated him and introduced me, 'This is my best friend on earth, Mr Nataraj; he and I are more like brothers than printer and customer or landlord and tenant.'

'Actually, I am not a landlord and don't want to be one,' I said, remembering how much more at peace I used to be when my attic was tenanted by junk. Woe to the day I had conceived the idea of cleaning it up.

Vasu said, 'Even among brothers, business should be business.'

'True, true,' said the forester.

Now Vasu turned to the art of flattery. I would never have guessed his potentialities in this direction. He said, 'I have brought Mr . . . because I want you to know him. He is a very busy man, but came with me today.'

'Do you live in the forest?'

Before the forester could speak, Vasu answered, 'He is Mempi Forest. He is everything there. He knows and has numbered every beast, and he has no fear. If he were a coward he would never have joined this department.'

The forester felt it was time for him to put in a word about himself, 'I have put in thirty years in the department. They gave me a third extension of my service only two weeks ago.'

'See how he looks? Can you guess his age?' (I wanted to say that I could do so unerringly.) 'He is like a teak tree—thousands of those trees in Mempi Range are in his charge, isn't it so, sir?'

'Yes, yes, that's a big responsibility,' he said.

'And you know, he looks wiry, but he must be like a teak log in strength. I am a strong man, as you know, but I'd hesitate to challenge him. Ha! Ha! Ha!' Vasu stopped laughing and said, 'Seriously, he is one of the best forestry officers in India. How many times has he been attacked by a rogue elephant?'

'Eighteen times,' said the man statistically.

'And you just gave it a four-nought-five charge at point blank range?'

'Yes, what else could one do?' asked the hero.

'How many tigers has he tracked on foot?'

'An average of at least one every half-year,' he said.

'And in thirty years you may guess how much he must have done and seen,' Vasu said. He asked the hero, 'What did you do with all those skins?'

'Oh, presented them here and there,' said the man. 'I don't fancy keeping trophies.'

'Ah, you shouldn't say that. You must let me stuff at least one animal for you, and you will know the difference,' said Vasu. 'Nataraj,' he added suddenly, 'the main reason why I have brought him to you is he wants a small book printed.' My heart sank. It was terrible enough to have Vasu for a customer, and now to have to work for someone he was championing! The three-colour labels were still undelivered. 'Nataraj, you will have to clear your desk and do this.'

37

I held out my hand mechanically. The forester took out of his bag a roll of manuscript, saying, 'I have made a habit of collecting Golden Thoughts, and I have arranged them alphabetically. I wish to bring them out in book form and distribute them to schoolchildren, free of cost. That is how I want to serve our country.'

I turned over the manuscript. Virtues were listed alphabetically. 'My Tamil types are not good,' I said. 'My neighbour has the best Tamil types available and his original Heidelberg . . .'

'Oh,' Vasu groaned, 'that original again!'

I looked at him compassionately. 'As a man of education, Vasu,' I began, 'you should not shut your mind to new ideas.'

'But why on earth should I know anything about the original what's-its-name?' he cried with mild irritation; it was evident that he was struggling to be on his best behaviour before the man in khaki.

'It's because,' I replied with the patience of a saint explaining moral duty to an erring soul, 'it's the machine on which fast printing has to be done. For instance work like our friend's here—Golden Thoughts—the right place for it would be the original Heidelberg, a lovely machine. What do you say, sir?' I said, turning to the man. I had spent a lifetime with would-be authors and knew their vanities from A to Z.

The forester said, 'Yes, I want the best service possible—the book must look nice. I want to send a specially bound copy to our Chief Conservator at Delhi through our chief at Madras.'

'So you want two special copies?' I asked.

'Yes, yes,' he agreed readily.

I looked through the pages of the manuscript. He had culled epigrammatic sentiments and moralizings from every source—*Bhagavad-Gita, Upanishads,* Shakespeare, Mahatma Gandhi, the Bible, Emerson, Lord Avebury and Confucius— and had translated them into Tamil. It was meant to elevate young minds no doubt, but I'd have resented being told every hour of the day what I should do, say, or think. It would be boring to be steadfastly good night and day. All the same the book contained most of the sentiments Vasu had missed in life and it would do him no harm to pick up a few for his own use. I told him, 'I'm sure you will enjoy going over the manuscript, in case our friend does not find the time to give it a final look-over.'

'Oh, yes, yes, of course,' Vasu said faintly.

I was confident now that I could dodge, at least for the time being, the responsibility of printing the golden book, but I couldn't judge for how long. If I took it on, with Vasu living overhead, he would storm the press night and day when the man in khaki was out of sight. There was going to be no money in it; I was positive about that. The whole transaction, it was patent, was going to be a sort of exchange between the two: Vasu wanted to win the other's favour through my help. I had already printed stationery for Vasu, and he had shown no signs of paying for the work.

I told the man, handing back the manuscript, 'Please go through it again and make all the final revisions and additions. Then if you are satisfied with the final form, we'll do something with it. I do not want you to incur any unnecessary expense later—corrections are rather expensive,

39

you know. All the time you can give for revision in manuscript will be worthwhile.' Once again my experience of would-be authors saved me: authors liked to think that they took infinite pains to attain infinite perfection.

I could see Vasu's bewilderment: he could not make out whether it was a good thing or a bad thing that had happened: the manuscript had changed hands too swiftly. He looked at my face and then at the other's. I was a seasoned printer. I knew the importance of shuffling off a manuscript without loss of time. Once the manuscript got lodged with you, you lost your freedom, and authority passed to the writer. Vasu began to argue, 'How can you get him to come again? Do you know the distance he has to come—from Peak House, where he is camping.' Very encouraging! Sixty miles away. It would not be often that he would find the time, or the conveyance, to come downhill.

'He won't have to come here! You can fetch the manuscript,' I said, and Vasu agreed with alacrity. 'Yes, yes, that's a good idea. I'll always be round you, you know,' he said with servility.

A week later, a brown envelope from the Forest Department arrived for Vasu. His face lit up at the sight of it. 'Must be my game licence. It was embarrassing to go into the jungle without it. Now you will see what I shall do . . . The swine!' he cried when he had read the contents. 'They think I want to go sightseeing in the forests and permit me to shoot duck and deer—as if I cared!' He remained in thought for a while. 'Now they shall know what I can do.' He carelessly thrust the paper into his pocket.

CHAPTER FOUR

A MONTH LATER Vasu stopped his jeep in front of my office and sounded the horn; he sat at the wheel, with the engine running. I looked up from a proof of a wedding invitation I was correcting. The adjournment lawyer was sitting in front of me—his daughter was to be married in two weeks and he was printing a thousand invitation cards. This was one piece of work I was obliged to deliver in time, and I didn't want to be interrupted. I shouted back to Vasu, 'Anything urgent?'

'Yeah,' he said. He seemed to have picked up his American style from crime books and films.

'I am busy,' I said.

'Come on,' he said aggressively. I placed a weight on the proof and went out. 'Jump in,' he said when I approached him.

'I really can't,' I said. 'That man is waiting for me.'

'Him! Don't be silly, jump in.'

'Where are you going?'

'I'll bring you back in ten minutes,' he said. 'Can't you spare ten minutes for my sake?'

I said, 'No, I can't spare ten minutes.'

'All right, five minutes then.' I climbed into the jeep and he drove off. We crossed Nallappa's Grove and drove for ten miles on the trunk road; he drove recklessly. I asked him where he was going.

'I thought you might enjoy a visit to Mempi.'

'What . . . what's the meaning of this?' I asked angrily.

'So you don't like being with me! All right. Shall I stop? You may get down and go back.'

I knew it would be futile to exhibit temper. It'd only amuse him. I concealed my chagrin and said, 'I certainly should enjoy walking back ten miles, but I wish I had had the time to pick up my shirt buttons before leaving.' I had mislaid my buttons at home. My shirt was open at the chest.

He cast a look at me. 'No one will mind in the jungle,' he said and rocked with laughter. Now that I was at his mercy, I thought I might as well abandon myself to the situation. I only wished I had not left the adjournment lawyer sitting in my chair. How long was he going to be there and what was to happen to the marriage of his daughter without invitation cards? I said, assuming the most casual tone possible, 'It was a matter of an urgent marriage invitation.'

'How urgent is the marriage?' he asked.

'It's coming off in fifteen days, and they must have time to post the invitation cards. A printer has his responsibilities.'

'If the man is willing and the woman is willing—there is a marriage. What has a printer to do with it? It's none of a printer's business. Why should you worry?'

I gave up all attempts to explain; he was not prepared

to pay any attention to my words. He was the lord of the universe, he had no use for other people's words. 'Why should you worry?' he asked again and again. It was so unreasonable and unseasonable that I didn't think fit to find an answer. I noticed that the speedometer needle was showing a steady sixty. 'Mind the road,' I said, as I saw villagers walking in a file, stepping aside as the jeep grazed them. Lorries and buses swerved away, the drivers muttering imprecations. Vasu enjoyed their discomfiture and laughed uproariously. Then he became suddenly serious and said, 'More people will have to die on the roads, if our nation is to develop any road sense at all!' A peasant woman was sitting on the roadside with a girl whose hair she was searching for lice. He saw them and set his course to run into them, swerving away at the last moment after seeing them tumble over each other in fright.

'Oh, poor creatures,' I said. 'I hope they aren't hurt.'

'Oh, no, they won't be hurt. These women are hardy and enjoy a bit of fun. Didn't you see how they were laughing?'

I felt it best to leave his words without comment. Even that seemed to annoy him. After we had gone a couple of miles, he said, 'Why are you silent? What are you thinking about? Still worrying about that invitation?'

'Yes,' I said to be on the safe side.

'Only fools marry, and they deserve all the trouble they get. I really do not know why people marry at all. If you like a woman, have her by all means. You don't have to own a coffee estate because you like a cup of coffee now and then,' and he smiled, more and more pleased with his own wit.

I had never known him so wild. He had seemed to practise few restraints when he visited me at my press, but now, in his jeep on the highway, his behaviour was breath-taking. I wondered for a moment whether he might be drunk. I asked testily, 'What do you think of prohibition, which they are talking about nowadays?'

'Why?' he asked. As I was wondering what to say, he said, 'Drink is like marriage. If people like it, it's their business and nobody else's. I tried to drink whisky once, but gave it up. It tastes bad.' He sat brooding at the wheel for a moment and said, 'I wonder why anyone should want to drink.'

My last hope that the man might be drunk was gone. A man who could conduct himself in this way dead sober! I shuddered at the thought. When we arrived at Mempi village I was glad to jump out. Riding in the jeep with one leg dangling out had made me sore in all my joints and my head reeled slightly with the speed of his driving.

Mempi village, at the foot of the hills, consisted of a single winding street, which half a mile away disappeared into the ranges of Mempi. A few cottages built of bamboo and coconut thatch lined the wayside; a tea-shop with bananas dangling in bunches from the ceiling was a rallying point for all buses and lorries plying on this road; a touring cinema stood in the open ground flanking the road, plastered over with the picture of a wide-eyed heroine watching the landscape. The jungle studded the sides of the hill. A small shrine stood at the confluence of the mountain road with the highway, and the goddess presiding was offered coconut and camphor flames by every driver on the mountain road.

Vasu pulled up his jeep and asked the man at the tea-shop, 'What's the news?'

The man said, 'Good news. There was a prowler last night, so they say. We saw pug-marks on the sand and sheep were bleating as if they had gone mad. Not where I live, but I heard Ranga talk of it today.'

'Did he see anything?' asked Vasu; and added eagerly, 'What did he see?'

The tea-shop had a customer waiting, and the owner mechanically handed him a bun and drew strong red tea from a sizzling urn and poured it into a glass tumbler. I had been starving. I cast longing looks at the brown buns arranged on a shelf, although normally I would not have dared to eat anything out of a shop like this, where flies swarmed over the sugar and nothing was ever washed or covered; road dust flew up whenever a car passed and settled down on the bread, the buns, the fruit, sugar, and milk. The shop had a constant crowd of visitors. Buses and lorries halting on their way up to the coffee estates, bullock carts in caravans, pedestrians—everyone stopped here for refreshment.

When I put my fingers in my pocket, I did not find a single coin, but only the stub of a pencil with which I'd been correcting the proof of the wedding invitation. I called pathetically like a child at a fair tugging at the sleeve of his elder, 'Vasu!' He was busy discussing the pug-marks and the circle round him was growing: a coconut-seller, the village idiot, the village wag, a tailor, and a man carrying a bundle of tobacco on his head. Each was adding his own to the symposium on the tiger's visit.

Vasu did not hear me call him. I had to cry out, 'Vasu, lend me some cash; I want to try the tea here.'

He paused. 'Tea! Why?'

I felt silly with my shirt open at the chest and the *dhoti* around my waist. 'I'm hungry. I had no time for breakfast this morning.'

He looked at me for a minute and resumed his discussion about the pug-marks. I felt slighted. Hunger had given an edge to my temper. I felt indignant that I should have been dragged out so unceremoniously and treated in this way. I called out, 'Have you or have you not any loose coin on you? I'll return it to you as soon as I am back home.'

'So you think we are going back home, eh?' he said irresponsibly. I was struck with a sudden fear that this man was perhaps abducting me and was going to demand a ransom for releasing me from some tiger cave. What would my wife and little son do if they were suddenly asked to produce fifty thousand rupees for my release? She might have to sell the house and all her jewellery. I had not yet paid the final instalment on that gold necklace of hers that she fancied only because someone she knew had a similar one. Good girl, this had been her most stubborn demand in all the years of our wedded life and how could I deny her? Luckily I had printed the Cooperative Bank Annual Report and with those earnings paid off half the price of the necklace. But, but, that necklace cost in all only seven hundred rupees—how would she make up fifty thousand? We might have to sell off the treadle; it was rickety and might fetch just thirteen thousand, and then what should I do after my release, without my printing machinery? What was to happen to Sastri? He'd be unemployed, or would he go over to operate the Heidelberg? If my wife appealed to him would he have the sense to go to the police and lead

them to the tiger cave guarded by this frightful man with
the dark halo over his head? Suppose he mounted guard
over me and the tiger returned to the cave and found him,
would the beast have the guts to devour him first and leave
me alone, retching at the sight of any further food?

All this flashed through my mind. It made me swallow
my temper and smile ingratiatingly at Vasu, which had a
better effect than any challenge. He relented enough to say,
'You see, when I'm out on business I rarely think of food.'
('Because you'll not hesitate to make a meal of any fool
who has the ill-luck to go with you,' I remarked mentally.)
Suddenly he left me, got into his jeep and said, 'Come on,'
to someone in the group, and was off. I felt relieved at his
exit, but cried like a lost child, 'When . . . ? When . . . ?'
He waved to me saying, 'Stay here, I'll be back,' and his
jeep raced up the mountain road and disappeared round a
bend. I could hear the whining of its gears for a while.

I looked down at my chest, still unbuttoned. I felt
ridiculous, standing there. This was no doubt a very beautiful
place—the hills and the curving village road, and the
highway vanishing into the hills. The hills looked blue, no
doubt, and the ranges beyond were shimmering, but that
could hardly serve as an excuse for the liberties Vasu had
taken with me. I sat down on a wooden plank stretched
over two empty tins, which served for a bench, and addressed
myself to the tea-shop man, 'Is there a bus for Malgudi
from here?'

'Yes, at two o'clock coming from Top Slip.'

It would be a good idea to catch it and get back to
town, but how was I to pay for the ticket? I didn't have
even a button to my shirt. I cursed myself for entertaining

and encouraging Vasu, but I also felt relief that he had gone away without a word about the ransom. I explained my situation to the tea-shop man. He was very happy when he heard that I was a printer. 'Ah, I'm so happy, sir, to know you. Can you print some notices for me, sir?'

'With pleasure,' I said, and added, 'I'm here to serve the public. I can print anything you want. If you prefer to have your work done on a German machine, I can arrange that too. My neighbour has an original Heidelberg, and we are like brothers.' I became loquacious at the unexpected opening offered for a friendly approach.

The man explained, 'I have no time to leave this place and attend to any other business in the town, and so I have long been worrying how to get some printing work done.'

'Oh, you don't have to worry as long as I'm here. Your printing will be delivered to you at your door, that's how I serve my customers. I print for a wide clientele and deliver the goods by bus or train, whichever goes earlier.'

'Ah, that's precisely how I would like to be served,' he said. Then he launched on his autobiography. He was a self-made man. Leaving his home in Tirunelveli when he was twelve years of age, he had come to Mempi in search of work. He knew no one, and he drifted on to the tea plantations in the hills and worked as an estate-labourer, picking tea-leaves, loading trucks, and in general acting as a handy-man. In the August of 1947, when India became independent, the estate, which had been owned by an English company, changed hands, and he came downhill to look for a new job. He established a small shop, selling betel nuts, peppermints and tobacco, and expanded it into a tea-shop. Business prospered when a new dam construction was started somewhere in a valley ten miles out; engineers, ministers, journalists, builders and labourers moved up and down in jeeps, lorries and station-wagons, and the place buzzed with activity night and day. His tea-shop grew to its present stature. He built a house, and then another house, very near the shop in a back street. ('I can go home in five minutes for a nap or a snatch of food,' he boasted.) He began to take an interest in the shrine at the confluence of the mountain and the plains. 'Hundreds of vehicles go up to those summits and to this day we have never heard of an accident—although some of those roads are narrow and twisting, and if you are careless you'll dive over the ridge. But there has not been a single accident. You know why?' He pointed at the little turret of the shrine showing above the roadside trees. 'Because the Goddess protects us. I rebuilt the temple with my own funds. I have regular pujas performed there. You know we also have a temple elephant; it came years ago of its own accord from the hills, straying along with a herd of cattle returned from the hills after grazing. It was then about six months old, and was no bigger than a young buffalo. We adopted it for the temple. His name is Kumar and children and elders alike adore him and feed him with coconut and sugarcane and rice all day.'

After all this rambling talk he came to the point. He was about to celebrate the consecration of the temple on a grand scale, carrying the Goddess in a procession with pipes and music, led by the elephant. He wanted me to print a thousand notices so that a big crowd might turn up on the day.

I readily agreed to do it for him, and asked, 'When do you want it?'

He was flabbergasted. 'I don't know. We shall have to discuss it at a meeting of the temple committee.'

I was relieved to note that it was only a vague proposal so far and said, 'Write to me as soon as your plans are ready, and I will do my best for you. I will print anything you want. By the way, why don't you let me taste your tea and a couple of those buns? Who is your baker in the town? He has given them a wonderful tint!' He concocted a special brew of tea for me and handed me a couple of brown buns on a piece of old newspaper. I felt refreshed and could view my circumstances with less despair now. At the back of my mind was a worry as to whether the adjournment lawyer might still be sitting waiting for my return. Return home? Ah, there was no such prospect. I would have been wiser if I had written my will before venturing out with Vasu. 'I'll pay your bill next time I visit you,' I said, 'maybe with the printed notices. You see, I had to come away suddenly and didn't know I'd come so far.' And then I made another request, 'Do you know these bus people? What sort are they?'

'Every bus must stop here for tea,' he said boastfully.

'I knew it'd be so. Can you do me a favour? Could you ask one of the conductors to take me back to town and collect the fare at the other end? The bus has to pass in front of my press, and I could just dash in . . .'

'Why do you want to go away? Aren't you going to wait for Vasu?'

I felt desperate. Was this man in league with Vasu? Probably they had plans to carry me to the cave at night—all kidnappers operated at night. They were saving me up for their nocturnal activities. I said desperately, 'I must get back to the press today; the lawyer will be waiting for me. A wedding invitation. You know how important it is.'

'But Vasu may ask why I didn't keep you here. I know him, and he is sometimes strict, as you may know.'

'Oh,' I said casually, 'he is a good fellow, though his speech is blunt sometimes. We are very close, and he knows all about this marriage invitation. He'll understand and . . . he is a good friend of mine. The trouble is I came away without picking up my buttons or cash.' I laughed, trying to import into the whole situation a touch of humour. 'I wonder when Vasu will be back!'

'Oh, that nobody can say. When he hears about a tiger, he forgets everything else. Now he'll be right in the jungle following the pug-marks, and . . .'

'A fearless man,' I cried in order to please the tea-seller. 'What is your name?' I asked.

'Muthu,' he said. 'I have four children, and a daughter to marry . . .'

'Then you will understand better than anyone else how anxious that lawyer will be.'

'Which lawyer?' he asked.

'Our adjournment lawyer, whom I left sitting in my office.'

'I'm sure you will help me to find a good bridegroom for my daughter.' He lowered his voice to say, 'My wife is scheming to marry her off to her own brother's son, but I have other ideas. I want the girl to marry a boy who is educated.'

'She must marry someone who is at least a BA,' I said.

He was so pleased with this that he gave me a third bun and another glass of tea. 'This is my treat. You don't have

51

to pay for this cup,' he said.

Presently his customers began to arrive—mostly coolies carrying pick-axes, crow-bars and spades on their way to that mysterious project beyond the hills. Caravans of bullock carts carrying firewood and timber stopped by. Loudspeaker music blared forth from the tent-cinema, where they were testing their sound again and again—part of some horribly mutilated Elvis Presley tune, Indianized by the film producer. I sat there and no one noticed me: arms stretched right over my head for glasses of tea; sometimes brown tea trickled over the side of the glass tumbler and fell on my clothes. I did not mind, though at other times I'd have gone into a rage at any man who dared to spill tea over my clothes. Today I had resigned myself to anything—as long as I could hope for a bus-ride back to town on credit and good will. I glanced at the brown face of a very old timepiece kept on a wooden shelf inside the tea-shop. It was so brown that I could hardly make out the numerals on it.

Still an hour before the bus arrived and two hours since Vasu had gone. I only hoped that he would not return before the bus arrived. I prayed he would not: I reassured myself again by asking, over the babble of the tea-shop, if Muthu could tell when Vasu would be back, and he gave me the same reply as before. This was the only silver lining in the cloud that shrouded my horizon that day. Even so my heart palpitated with apprehension lest he should suddenly appear at the tea-shop and carry out his nefarious programme for the evening. He could pick me up between his thumb and first finger and put me down where he pleased. Considering his enormous strength, it was surprising that he did not do more damage to his surroundings. I sat in a trembling suspense as men came and went, buying tobacco, betel leaves, and cigarettes and tea and buns. I could hardly get a word with Muthu. I sat brooding over what I'd have to face from Sastri or my wife when I got back . . . Get back! The very phrase sounded remote and improbable! The town, the fountain, and my home in Kabir Street seemed a faraway dream, which I had deserted years ago . . .

The crowd at the tea-shop was gone. I sat on the bench and fell into a drowse. The hills and fields and the blindingly blue sky were lovely to watch, but I could not go on watching their beauty for ever. I was not a poet. If my monosyllabic friend had been here, perhaps he would have enjoyed sitting and staring; but I was a business man, a busy printer. I bowed my head and shut my eyes. I felt weak: I might eat all the buns in the world, but without a handful of rice and the sauce my wife made I could never feel convinced that I had taken any nourishment. The air far off trembled with the vibration of an engine. Muthu declared, 'The bus should be here in ten minutes.' Amazing man with ears so well attuned; I said so. I wanted to do and say anything I could to please this man, whom at normal times I'd have passed as just another man selling tea in unwashed tumblers.

The bus arrived, on its face a large imposing signboard announcing 'Mempi Bus Transport Corporation', although the bus itself was an old one picked off a war surplus dump, rigged up with canvas and painted yellow and red. It was impossible to guess how many were seated in the bus until it stopped at the tea-shop and the passengers wriggled and jumped out as if for an invasion. They swarmed around the tea-shop, outnumbering the flies. The conductor, a very thin man, in a peaked cap and khaki shirt over half-shorts, emerged with a cash-bag across his shoulder, and the driver jumped out of his seat. Men, women, and children clamoured for attention at the tea-shop. The driver and the conductor exchanged a few words, looked at the cash-bag, took out some coins for themselves. The conductor then addressed the gathering in a general manner, 'I am not stopping for more than five minutes; if anyone is left behind he will be left behind, that's all. I warn you all, don't blame me later,' and he looked around like a schoolmaster watching his erring pupils and passed into the tea-shop. He was given a seat of honour beside the owner. He called for a glass of tea and buns. He lit a cigarette. After he was well settled, I went to show myself to Muthu, who, I feared, might forget me in the midst of his booming business—a fear which was well-founded, for as soon as he saw me he said, 'Ah, I'd forgotten about our printing master.' Then he told the conductor, 'Brother, give him a seat to the town; he will pay at the other end.' The brother took time to grasp the meaning of the proposition. He looked at me with sour suspicion. 'Why should he not pay now?'

'Because he has left all his cash in town.'

'Then why did he come here? You know how many tell me that each day?' He moistened his upper lip with his tongue as smoke emerged from his nostrils. 'Another monster in league with Vasu,' I thought, and felt desperate. He demonstrated with his hands the act of wringing a neck. 'I'd like to do this to anyone who comes up with such a proposal. If our inspector checks mid-way, it'll end my career, and then I and my family will have to take a begging bowl and go from door to door.'

The man had a far-fetched imagination. Having always lived within the shelter of my press, I had probably grown up in complete ignorance of human nature, which seemed to be vicious, vile, vindictive and needlessly unfriendly everywhere. I went up to him with chest thrown out and said haughtily, 'I'll guarantee that you will not have to carry a begging bowl. Today I am stuck here, but generally I'm not a passenger in any bus, having a car—if not mine, my friend's which is as good as mine.'

'What car do you use?'

'Well . . .' I said, reflecting, 'a Morris, of course,' mentioning the first make that came into my head.

'Model?' he asked, pursuing the subject.

'Fifty one, I think . . .'

'Four-door?'

'Yes.'

'Oh, you are lucky; it's worth its weight in gold, that particular model. I know several people who are searching for one desperately. Do you think you would care to quote a price for it?'

I shook my head. 'Oh, dozens of persons ask me that every day, but I want to keep it till it falls to bits, you know. I don't want to sell.'

He had now developed a wholesome respect for me as a member of the automobile fraternity. He was prepared to overlook my unbuttoned shirt and dishevelled appearance and ticketless condition; I wished I had some more jargon to impress him further, but I had to manage as best I could with whatever rang in my memory as a result of the printing I had done for Ramu of Ramu's Service Station, who sometimes dropped in to talk of the state of the nation in the motoring world.

The bus-conductor said, 'Any time you want to dispose of your Morris, you must tell me.' He turned to Muthu and confided, 'Sooner or later I want to give up this endless ticket-punching and drive a baby taxi—I know a man who earns a net income of fifty rupees a day with just one baby vehicle. I have saved enough to buy a car now.'

Muthu nudged him in the midriff and muttered, 'Don't I know!' darkly, at which both of them simpered. I knew at once they meant that the conductor made money by pocketing a lot of the cash collected from passengers. I said, to add to the mood of the hour, 'One has to make money while one can. Otherwise, when one is old or down and out, who would give a paisa?'

When the conductor started nearly half an hour later, I walked along royally beside him and took my seat in the bus. I had taken leave of Muthu briefly but in touching terms; he assured me that he would write to me for any help he might need. I sat in the royal seat, that is, beside the driver. The conductor leaned over my shoulder from behind, to say, 'You will have to move and make space at the next stop. The Circle is expected.' The word 'Circle' in these circumstances indicated the inspector of police for this circle, whose seat at the front was always reserved. If another passenger occupied it, it was a matter of social courtesy to vacate it or at least move up closer to the driver and leave enough space at the end of the seat for the Circle. Once, long, long ago, a planter returning to his estate created a lot of unpleasantness by refusing to make way for the Circle, with the result that the Circle was obliged to travel in one of the ordinary seats inside the bus, with the rabble, and at the next stop he impounded the whole bus with the passengers for overcrowding.

The bus travelled for an hour. I felt happy that after all I'd slipped away from Vasu. I cast a look behind once or twice to see if his jeep was following us. Coming back from tracking the tiger, he might want to embark on the bigger expedition of tracking a printer who had escaped from a tea-shop.

The bus stopped under a tree on the road and the conductor issued a warning, 'We are not stopping for more than a minute. If anyone is impatient to get out, let him get out for ever. Don't blame me afterwards.' In spite of this threat a few of the passengers wriggled out and disappeared behind the bushes by the roadside. A constable in uniform was seen coming across a maize field, sweating in the sun and bearing under his arm a vast load of papers and files. He gesticulated from a distance to catch the eye of the driver. He arrived and placed the files on the scat next to me. I moved up to the inferior side of the seat close to the driver and cleared a space for the Circle. I couldn't, after all, be choosy as I was there on sufferance.

The constable said to the driver, 'The Circle is coming; you'll have to wait.'

'How long?' asked the conductor.

The constable clung to the rail, rested his feet on the step, pushed his turban back on his head, and spurned answering. Instead he said, 'Give me a *beedi*,' and held out his hand. The driver produced from his pocket matches and a *beedi*. The constable smoked: the acrid smell of *beedi* leaf and tobacco overpowered the smell of petrol. The constable's face shone with perspiration. He said, 'I feared I might lose the bus; the Circle would have chopped off my head.' A couple of children started crying, a woman sang a soft but tuneless lullaby, someone was yawning noisily, someone else was swearing, a couple of peasants were discussing a litigation, someone asked wearily, 'Are we going to go on at all?' and someone else made a joke about it. I looked back furtively for Vasu's jeep coming in pursuit. I grew tired of the policeman's face, and the road ahead, and everything. I was beginning to feel hungry, the buns having been assimilated into my system long ago. All the passengers subsided into apathetic, dull waiting.

Finally the Circle turned up, a swarthy man in a khaki uniform, appearing suddenly beside the bus on a bicycle. As soon as he jumped off, work started: the constable held the handlebars; the conductor heaved the bicycle up to the roof; the Circle climbed into his seat and said, 'Start.' The driver squeezed the bulb of the rubber horn, and its short raucous bark resounded along the highway, past the hill, and brought a dozen passengers at the run who had strayed away from the suffocating bus into the surrounding country. For a brief while there was the disorder of people trying to clamber back to their original seats. One heard grumblings and counter-grumblings—'I was sitting here,' 'No, this was my place,' until the conductor said, 'Keep quiet, everyone,' in deference to the presence of the Circle. The Circle, however, sat stiffly looking ahead; it was evident he did not want to embarrass the conductor by noticing the overcrowding.

I was overwhelmed by the proximity of this eminent person, who smelt of the sun, sweat and leather. I hoped he'd not take me for an ex-convict and order me out. He had a nice downward-directed short moustache. He wore dark glasses and his nose was hooked and sharp; his Adam's apple also jutted out. The driver drove with great caution; he who had been swerving away from collisions for over an hour (a pattern of driving which Vasu had already accustomed me to), now never exceeded twenty miles an hour, applied the brake when a piece of paper drifted across, and gently chided any villager who walked in the middle of the road. At this rate, he would not reach the town before midnight. His speed depended on where the Circle was getting out. I felt it imperative to know at once his destination. 'You are going to town, I suppose?' I said to him. Where was the harm in asking him that? There was no law against it.

He turned his sunglasses on me and said, 'I'll be getting off at Talapur.'

'Is that where you stay?' I asked.

'No. I'm going there for an investigation,' he said, and I shuddered at the thought of the poor man who was going to be investigated. He talked to me about crime in his area. 'We've a lot of cattle-lifting cases in these parts, but the trouble is identification when the property is traced; they mutilate the animals, and then what happens is the case is dismissed and all the trouble one takes to frame a charge-sheet is simply wasted. We have a few murders too, and a certain amount of prohibition offences around the dry-belt areas.' I found that he was a friendly sort of man, in spite of all his grim looks. 'This is a difficult circle,' he said finally. 'Offenders often disappear into the jungles of Mempi, and sometimes one has to camp for days on end in the forests.'

At the Talapur bus-stand, which was under a tree, with
a replica of Muthu's tea-stall, a constable was there to
receive the Circle and haul down his bicycle from the roof.
The Circle got on his cycle and pedalled away. Talapur was
a slightly larger town than Mempi and was regarded as an
important junction. It had more shops lining the street. The
conductor uttered the usual warning to the passengers and
vanished into the tea-shop. Most of the passengers followed
suit and some dispersed to various corners of the city. I sat
in the bus, nursing my hunger in silence, having no credit
here.

When the bus started again, it was obvious that the
Circle was no longer there to impede its freedom. It was
driven recklessly and brought to a dead stop every ten
minutes, to pick up a wayside passenger. The conductor
never said 'no' to anyone. As he explained to me, 'These
poor fellows will get stranded on the highway if we are not
considerate. After all they are also human creatures.' He
was a compassionate conductor, who filled his pockets with
the wayside fare, never issuing a ticket. 'At this rate he
could buy a Rolls Royce rather than a Morris Minor,' I
thought. The bus left the highway and darted across devious
side-tracks through corn-fields in search of passengers. It
would draw up at a most unexpected spot, and, sounding
the horn, the driver would cry, 'Come on, come on,
Malgudi, last bus for the town.' The bus penetrated into the
remotest hamlet to ferret out a possible visitor to the town,
and all the passengers had to go where the bus went and sit
there patiently watching the antics of the driver and
conductor, who seemed to have a fixed target of income for
the day and determined to reach it. That was how a three-

hour jeep ride in the morning was stretched out to eight on the return journey and it was eleven at night when the bus came to a halt in the public square beyond the market in Malgudi.

At eight o'clock next morning I sat correcting the proof of the adjournment lawyer's invitation. Sastri came in half an hour after I had opened the door of the press. He stood transfixed at the sight of me and said, 'We all waited till nine last night.'

'I've always told you that you should lock up the door at your usual time whether I am in or out,' I said grandly, and added, 'Sometimes I get so much else to do.'

'But that lawyer would not move. He kept saying you promised to be back in five minutes, in five minutes, and then there were the fruit-juice labels. He was very bitter and said . . .'

'Oh, stop that, Sastri,' I said impatiently. I did not like the aggrieved tone he was adopting. I'd had enough of nagging from my wife all night, after she had been forced to get up from sleep and feed me at midnight. 'If I disappeared abruptly it was my own business. Why should I be expected to give an explanation to everyone? If the fruit-juice man wants to print his labels elsewhere, let him clear out, that's all. I can't be dancing attendance on all and sundry. If he can find any other printer to bring out his magenta shade in the whole of south India . . .'

Sastri did not wait for me to finish my sentence but passed into the press, as it seemed to me, haughtily. I sat correcting the proof: the corrections were in the state I had

left them on the previous day. 'Mr . . . requests the pleasure
of your company . . .' Wrong fonts, and the bridegroom's
name was misspelt. 'Company' came out as 'cumbahy'. I
never cease to marvel at the extraordinary devils that dance
their way into a first proof. The sight of 'cumbahy' provoked
me to hysterical laughter. I was light-headed. I would not
have to beg at a tea-shop and starve or go about without
a button to my shirt. I had a feeling that I was in an
extraordinarily fortunate and secure position, enough to be
able to say 'fie' to Sastri or anyone. Life in Market Road
went on normally. It was good to watch again the *jutkas*
and cycles going round the fountain and the idlers of our
town sitting on its parapet and spitting into it. It produced
in me a great feeling of security and stability. But that lasted
only for a few minutes. The adjournment lawyer, looking
unshaven as ever, his shoulders draped in a spotted *khadi*
shawl, a *dhoti* above his knee, and an umbrella dangling
from his arm, stepped in, his face set in a frown.

'Do you think . . .' he began.

One look at him and I knew what he was going to say,
'Won't you come in and take a seat, first?'

'Why should I?' he asked. 'I'm not here to waste my
time.'

I was still motioning him to a chair, but he seemed
afraid that once he sat there I'd abandon him and disappear
again for the day.

He said, 'I'm printing my invitation elsewhere, so don't
trouble yourself.'

'Oh, no trouble whatever. This is a free country, you
are a free man. Our Constitution gives us fundamental
rights. How can I compel you or anyone to do what you

may not want to do?' I knew he was lying; if he had wasted his time till nine last evening and was back so soon, when had he found the time to seek a printer? Anyway it was not my business; this was a free country, fundamental rights, every citizen was free to print his daughter's marriage card where he pleased, but if he had his wits about him he'd watch out where he got the best results.

'Sastri!' I called aggressively. 'Bring this gentleman's original draft—lawyer so-and-so's daughter's wedding.' Sastri from his invisible world responded with his voice, but made no effort to bring the original. This gave everyone time to cool. The lawyer edged a step nearer the chair.

'Won't you take a seat, please? Mr Sastri should be with us in a minute.' He sat down, but remained in a state of hostile silence. I said, 'I suppose all your other arrangements are ready?'

He shook his head. 'How truly have our elders said . . .' He quoted a proverb to the effect that building a house and conducting a marriage were the two Herculean tasks that faced a man. I added a further sentiment that a man who marries off his daughter need perform no other meritorious acts in life as he is giving away his most precious treasure—which moved the lawyer so deeply that tears came to his eyes. He said, blowing his nose, 'Susila is the gentlest of my children. I hope she will have no trouble from her mother-in-law!' He sighed deeply at the thought and I said consolingly, 'Mother-in-law! "Down with them," says the modern girl, college-educated and modern-minded.'

'I've given her the best possible education,' he said morosely. 'What more could I do? I pay her music master fifteen rupees a month, her school fees amount to fifteen rupees, and I pay ten rupees for her school bus . . .'

'And you have to manage all this,' I thought, 'by securing endless adjournments.' But I said aloud, 'Yes, life today is most expensive.' After this agreeable *tête-à-tête*, I cried suddenly, 'Sastri, this gentleman is waiting to take away his invitation copy. After all we must give him time to print elsewhere.'

The lawyer behaved like one who has been stung. 'Oh no. Oh no,' he cried. 'Even if it means stopping the marriage, I will not go anywhere else for my printing.'

I said, 'I'm here to help humanity in my own humble way. I will never say no to anyone. Don't hesitate to command me for anything you may want me to do.' He took my offer promptly, and said, 'A thousand cards—or do you think we could do with less?'

Late that evening Vasu's jeep drew up before my press. It was past eight and the traffic in the street was thin. Vasu looked at me from his driving seat. His hair was covered with dust and stood up more like a halo than ever. He beckoned to me from his seat. I was overworking in order to finish the lawyer's invitations, and I had even undertaken to address and distribute them if he so ordered. He had acquired so much confidence in me that he did not feel the need to sit up with me, and had gone home. I shouted back to Vasu, 'Why don't you come in?' I was now on my own ground, and had no fear of anyone. He said, 'Hey, come on! I want you to see what I have here.' I went out, making up my mind not to step into the jeep, whatever might happen. I'd stand at a distance to see whatever it was that he was going to show me. There was dust and grime on his face, but also a triumphant smile exposing his teeth; his eyes had widened, showing the whites. I edged cautiously to the jeep. I only hoped that he would not thrust out his arm, grab me and drive off. He took a flashlight and threw the beam on to the back seat, where lay the enormous head of a tiger. 'How did you manage that?' I asked, there being no other way of talking to a man who had brought in the head of a tiger. A couple of curious passers-by slowed their pace. Vasu shouted to them, 'Get away and mind your own business.' He started his car to take it through the side gate and park it in the yard. I went back to my seat and continued my work. I could hear his steps go up the wooden stairs. When the breeze blew in from his direction, there was already a stench of flesh—it might have been my imagination.

The curtain parted; he came in and took a seat. He lit a cigarette and asked, 'Do you know what he measures? Ten and a half tip to tip; the head is almost eighteen inches wide! I got him finally in the block, you see; they will have a surprise when they next check the tiger population in their block.' He then described how he got information from various people, and had followed the foot-marks of the tiger from place to place. He had to wander nearly six miles within the jungle, and finally got it at a water-hole, at about two in the morning. He showed me the bleeding scratches on his feet from having to push his way through thickets; at any moment it might have sprung on him from some unsuspected quarter. 'I was prepared to knock him down with my hands and ram the butt of my rifle between his jaws if it came to that,' he said. It was evident that he was not going to wait for others to pay him compliments. He showered handfuls of them on himself.

'What about the permit? You didn't have one?'

'The tiger didn't mind the informality.' He laughed aloud at his own humour. 'That swine double-crossed me! Probably because you didn't print Golden Thoughts for him.' He never let slip an occasion to blame me or accuse me. I gave no reply, but I became curious to see his animal.

He took me to his room. This was my first visit there since he had occupied it. He had his bed draped over with a mosquito-net, a table in a corner, heaped with clothes and letters, and a trunk with its lid open with all his clothes thrown about. He had tied a string across the room and had more clothes hanging on it. On the little terrace he had put out some skins to dry; there was a tub in a corner in which the skin of the tiger was soaking. Skins of smaller animals lay scattered here and there, and jungle squirrels and feathered birds were heaped in corners. A lot of wooden planks and moulds and all kinds of oddments lay about. Ever since I had given him the attic, I had left him fairly alone, not wanting to seem an intrusive host, and all the while he had been surrounding himself with carcasses. The room smelt of decaying flesh and raw hide; he had evidently been very active with his gun, which now rested on his bed. ('I'm a man of business, and I cannot afford to waste my time. Each day that I spend without doing my work is a day completely wasted.') There was a resinous odour in the air which made me retch. I couldn't imagine any human being living in this atmosphere. Sastri now and then in the past weeks had complained of a rotting smell somewhere. We had searched our garbage cans and odd corners of the press to see if the paste we were using had gone bad. Once I had to speak severely to our binder; I called him names for possibly using some nasty slaughter-house material in binding. He was apologetic, although he had used no such material. Even after his promise to improve his material, the smell persisted. It was pervasive and insistent and Sastri found it impossible to stand at the type-board and compose. Then we thought a rat might be dead somewhere and turned up every nook and corner of the press, and finally we blamed the health department. 'Next time that fellow comes around for votes, I'll make him stand at the type-board and perform inhaling exercises,' I said bitterly. Sometimes my neighbour of the original Heidelberg came to ask if I noticed any smell around. I said emphatically that I did and asked his views on the municipal administration, little thinking that the fountainhead of all the stink was the attic over my own machine.

I sat down on an iron chair because the whole problem loomed enormously before me. If this man continued to stay here (I had really no idea how long he proposed to honour me with his presence), what was to happen to me and to my neighbourhood?

Vasu was stirring the broth in the tub with a long pole, at which the stench increased. I held my nostrils with my fingers and he ordered, 'Take your fingers away. Be a man.' When I hesitated, he came and wrenched my fingers apart. 'You are imagining things,' he said. 'What do you think that tub contains? Tiger blood? Ha! Ha! Pure alum solution.' He began to instruct me in the higher realms of carcass treatment. 'Actually the whole process of our work is much more hygienic and clean than paring the skin of vegetables in your kitchen.' I shuddered at the comparison. 'After all one takes a lot of care to bleed the animal, and only the skin is brought in. In order to make sure that there is no defect, I attend to everything myself. The paws and the head are particularly important.' He lifted the paw of the dead tiger and held it up. 'If there is the slightest flaw in the incision you will never be able to bring the ends together. That is what Suleiman taught me; he was an artist, as good as a sculptor or a surgeon, so delicate and precise! I killed the tiger last night. What do you think I was doing till tonight?'

'Hiding yourself and the carcass from the eyes of forest guards,' I thought.

'Bleeding, skinning, and cleaning it so that sentimentalists may not complain. To make still surer, we pack, or rather pickle, the skin in tins of salt immediately after flaying. So you will understand it is all done under the most hygienic conditions.' He swept his hand around, 'I do everything myself, not because I care for anyone's comments, but . . .'

'There are bits of flesh still there,' I said, pointing at the new tiger-skin.

'What if there are! Don't you have flesh under your own skin? Do you think you have velvet under yours?' This was his idea of humour and I had no way of matching it. I looked around. On his work bench in a corner stood a stuffed crow, a golden eagle, and a cat. I could recognize the cat as the one that used to prowl in my press hunting for mice. 'Why did you shoot that cat? That was mine!' I cried shuddering. I fancied I could still hear its soft 'mew' as it brushed its back against my legs at the treadle.

'I didn't know,' he said, 'I only wanted it for study;

after all, it's the same family as the tiger. I am trying to make a full mould of the tiger. There are some problems of anatomy peculiar to the *felis* family in this area and I needed a miniature for study and research. Without continuous application one cannot prosper in my line.'

'What did that crow do to you?' I asked.

'It's to serve as a warning to other crows to let Vasu's skins alone and not to peck at them when they are put out to dry.'

'And that golden eagle?'

'It was wheeling right over this roof four days ago; it's only five days old and do you notice any smell?' he asked victoriously. He had such a look of satisfaction and victory that I felt like pricking it a little.

'Yes, of course, there is a smell.'

'Oh, come on, don't be a fussy prude, don't imagine that you are endowed with more sensitive nostrils than others. Don't make yourself so superior to the rest of us. These are days of democracy, remember.' I was appalled at his notion of democracy as being a common acceptance of bad odours.

'What did that poor eagle do to you?' I asked. I could not bear to see the still, glazed look of the bird. 'See its stare!' I cried.

'Aha!' he said. He picked it up and brought it closer to me. 'So you think it's looking at you with its eyes!' Its dilated black pupils, set in a white circle, seemed to accuse us. He was convulsed with laughter and his voice split with mirth. 'So you are taken in! You poor fool! Those eyes were given it by me, not by God. That's why I call my work an art.' He opened a wooden chest and brought out a cardboard carton. 'See these.' He scooped out a handful of eyes—big round ones, small ones, red ones in black circles. The ferocious, striking, killing glare of a tiger, the surprise and superciliousness of an owl, the large, black-filled softness of a deer—every category of gaze was there. He said, 'All these are from Germany. We used to get them before the war. Now you cannot get them for love or money. Just lenses! Sometimes I paint an extra shade at the back for effect. The first thing one does after killing an animal is to take out its eyes, for that's the first part to rot, and then one gives it new eyes like an optician. I hope you appreciate now what an amount of labour goes into the making of these things. We have constantly to be rivalling Nature at her own game. Posture, look, the total personality, everything has to be created.' This man had set himself as a rival to Nature and was carrying on a relentless fight.

'You have no doubt excelled in giving it the right look, but, poor thing, it's dead. Don't you see that it is a *garuda*?'

'What if it is?'

'Don't you realize that it's sacred? That it's the messenger of God Vishnu?'

'I want to try and make Vishnu use his feet now and then.'

'You may be indifferent, but haven't you seen men stopping in the road to look up and salute this bird when it circles in the sky?' I wanted to sound deliberately archaic and poetic.

He ruminated for a second and added, 'I think there is a good business proposition here. I can supply them stuffed eagles at about fifty rupees each. Everyone can keep a sacred *garuda* in the puja and I'll guarantee that it won't fly off. Thus they can save their eyes from glare. I want to be of service to our religious folk in my own way.'

I shivered slightly at the thought and the way his mind worked. Nothing seemed to touch him. No creature was safe, if it had the misfortune to catch his eye. I had made a mistake in entertaining him. I ought to send him away at the earliest possible moment. His presence defiled my precincts. My mind seethed with ideas as to how to throw him out, but he noticed nothing. He settled himself down on the easy chair, stretched his legs, and was preparing for a nice long chat. 'This is a minor job. I really don't care for it. My real work you will see only when the tiger is made up. You see it now only as a beast with a head and a lot of loose skin soaking in alum, but I'll show you what I can do with it.'

CHAPTER FIVE

HE WAS A man of his word. He had said that he never wasted his time. I could see that he never wasted either his time or his bullets. Whenever I heard his jeep arrive, I would see some bloody object, small or big, brought in, if I cared to peep out. But nowadays, as far as possible, I tried to shut my eyes. I was having a surfeit. Not in my wildest dream had I ever thought that my press would one day be converted into a charnel house, but here it was happening, and I was watching helplessly. Sometimes it made me very angry. Why couldn't I ask him to get out? This was my own building, laboriously acquired through years of saving and scraping, and the place would not have come to me but for a good Moslem friend who migrated to Pakistan and gave me the first offer. If I opened the back door, I stepped into Kabir Street, and right across it to my own home. But all this had come about only to harbour the murderer of innocent creatures.

I had been brought up in a house where we were taught never to kill. When we swatted flies, we had to do it without the knowledge of our elders. I remember particularly one of my grand-uncles, who used the little room on the *pyol* and who gave me a coin every morning to buy sugar for the ants, and kept an eye on me to see that I delivered the sugar to the ants in various corners of our house. He used to declare, with approval from all the others, 'You must never scare away the crows and sparrows that come to share our food; they have as much right as we to the corn that grows in the fields.' And he watched with rapture squirrels, mice and birds busily depleting the granary in our house. Our domestic granary was not built in the style of these days with cement, but with a bamboo matting stiffened with mud and rolled into cylinders, into whose wide mouth they poured in the harvest, which arrived loaded in bullock carts. That was in the days before my uncles quarrelled and decided to separate.

I was appalled at the thought that I was harbouring this destroyer, but I hadn't the courage to go up to him and say, 'Take yourself and your museum out of here!' He might do anything—bellow at me, or laugh scornfully, or rattle my bones. I felt dwarfed and tongue-tied before him. Moreover it was difficult now to meet him; he was always going out and returning late at night; sometimes he was away for three days at a stretch. He returned home late because he did not want his booty to be observed. When he was at home he worked upstairs with the broth and moulds; one beard the hammering, sawing, and all the other sounds belonging to his business, and sometimes during the day he hauled down packing cases and drove off to the railway station. I noted it all from my seat in the press and said to myself, 'From this humble town of Malgudi stuffed carcasses radiate to the four corners of the earth.'

He worked single-handed on all branches of his work. I admired him for it, until I suddenly realized that I too laboured single-handed at my job, with the slight difference that Sastri was with me; but Vasu had, I suppose, all those ruffians of Mempi lending him a hand in his nefarious trade. I do not know why I should ever have compared myself with him, but there it was. I was getting into an abnormal frame of mind. There was no person in whom I could confide, for I had always played that role myself. My visitors were, as usual, the journalist and the poet, both of them worthless as consultants. All the same I made an attempt to ascertain their views.

The journalist was frankly dumbfounded when he realized that there was no aspect of this particular problem which he could blame directly on the Government. He merely snapped, 'Why do you tolerate such things? As a nation, we are what we are today because of our lack of positive grip over our affairs. We don't know where we are going or why. It is part of the policy of drift, which is our curse.' I paid no attention to what he was saying; it was all too vague and roundabout and irrelevant to the present case; the idea of Vasu provoked Sen into incoherent unpredictable statements. I left him alone. After all one should learn to bear one's burdens.

Still, two days later, the oppression on my mind was so great that I buttonholed the poet when he was struggling to start on the seventh canto of his opus and asked what he would do in my place. I feared that he might suggest reading poetry aloud as a possible step towards driving out the killer. He took time to comprehend my problem; even to myself, the more I attempted to speak of my problem, the more incomprehensible it seemed. I was left wondering if I were making too much of a very simple matter.

When he did understand, the poet asked, 'Why don't you try to raise the rent?'

I beat my brow, 'Oh, Kavi! Do I have to tell you that I am not a *rentier*? I let him in as a friend and not as a tenant. Do you want to heap on my head the reputation of being a man who takes rent for his attic space?'

The poet looked bewildered and said, 'Then you could surely tell him to go. Why not?'

It was impossible to explain. My wife also said the same thing. In my desperation I had turned to her, though I rarely discussed my problems with her. I had become abnormal. I was brooding too much on Vasu. His footsteps on the wooden stairs set my heart racing. I knew that it was involuntary anger which stirred my heart; the trouble was that it was both involuntary and suppressed! My wife said simply, sweetly, as she served my supper, 'Ask him to go, that's all. Babu is frightened of him, and refuses to go when I send him to you.'

All this worked on my mind. I waited for a chance to have a word with the man. It was like waiting for my father, in my childhood. I often had to spend days and days hoping to catch my father in a happy mood to ask him for a favour, such as cash for purchasing a bat or ball or permission to go out scouting. Most times he was preoccupied and busy, and I lost the taste for food until I was able to have a word with him. I would confide in my grand-uncle and he would help me by introducing the subject to my father at the appropriate moment, when he was chewing betel leaves after a contented dinner. When my father turned to question me, I would squirm and find myself tongue-tied, unable to go on with my proposition. I was in a similar predicament now, with the added handicap of not having my grand-uncle around. I recollected that on the day I saw his dead body stretched out on the bier my first thought was, 'Oh Lord, who is going to speak for me hereafter?'

At last I stuck a note on Vasu's attic door when he was away, 'May I have a word with you when you have the time?' and waited for results. One morning, three days later, he parted the curtain and peeped in while I was at the treadle, printing the monosyllable forms. I had now barricaded the passage beyond, from the attic stairs to my treadle, with steel mesh, so that Vasu always had to come by the front door whenever he wanted to see me. The first thing he said was, 'You take a pleasure in making me go round, is that it?' My heart sank at the sight of him. There was a frown on his terrible brow. 'Perhaps he missed a target or his gun backfired!' I thought to myself. It was more dangerous than asking for a concession from my father. He flourished the note and asked, 'Is this for me?' He seemed to possess a sixth sense. He looked grim and unfriendly. I wondered if someone had been talking to him. I looked up from my proof and just said, 'Nothing urgent. Perhaps we could meet later, if you are busy.'

'If *you* are busy it is a different matter, but don't concern yourself with my busyness. I am always busy.'

'Yes,' I added mentally, 'as long as the forests are full.'

He added, 'I cannot afford to lounge about, if you know what I mean. If I had the same luck as your other friends who congregate in your press, reading verse or criticizing the Government, I might . . .'

That settled it. He was in a challenging mood. I suppressed the qualms I had all along and said, 'Will you kindly take a seat? I will join you in a moment.' He was sitting in his chair when I came to him two minutes later, after taking enough time to put away the paper in hand. He said, 'You have made a fetish of asking people to sit in this room.' This was a surprise attack.

'I like to observe the ordinary courtesies,' I said.

'Do you mean to say that others don't?' he asked with his face puckering into the usual lines, and I knew he was getting back into his old mood of devilish banter. I felt relieved. I might have even gone to the length of inquiring about his dead or dying animals, but I checked myself, feeling an aversion to the subject. I said, 'Vasu, I don't want you to mistake me. Have you been able to secure a house?'

'Why?' he asked, suddenly freezing.

'I just thought I might ask you, that's all.'

'Not the sort of question a supposedly hospitable person should ask of his guest. It is an insult.'

I fought down my racing heart and my tongue which was ready to dart out like a snake's. I said very casually, 'I asked because I require the place for . . .'

'For?' he asked aggressively, cocking his ear, and waited for my answer.

'Someone is coming to stay with us, and he wants . . .'

'How many rooms in your own house are occupied?'

'Should one go into all that now?'

'Yes, the question is of interest to me,' he said, and added, 'Otherwise I would not mind if you had all your relatives in the world come and live with you.'

I suppressed the obvious repartees. Aggressive words only generate more aggressive words. Mahatma Gandhi had enjoined on us absolute non-violence in thought and speech, if for no better reason than to short-circuit violent speech and prevent it from propagating itself. I toned my repartee down to a cold business-like statement, 'My guest is a man who likes to stay by himself.'

'Then why should he seek solitude in this noisy press?'

I had no answer, and he said after some reflection, 'For years you did nothing more than house old decaying paper there; now I have made it slightly habitable you are getting ideas. Do you know how much it has cost me to make it livable in? The mosquitoes and other vermin would eat you up if you were slightly careless, the roof-tiles hit your head, there are cobwebs, smoke, and in summer it is a baking oven. No one but a fool like me would have agreed to live there!'

I remained silent. All I could say was obvious, such as, 'Is this the return I get for giving you shelter?' 'If you remember, you volunteered to stay,' and the most obvious one, 'After all you are living on my hospitality; get out if you do not like it.' 'You are not obliged to be here, you know,' etc. etc. I swallowed all such remarks. Instead I said sentimentally, 'I never expected you would be so upset.'

'Who says I am upset? You are fancying things. It takes a lot more to upset me. Well, anything else?' he asked, rising.

Not until his jeep moved did I realize that he had given me no answer to my question. He had treated it lightly, viciously, indifferently, but all to no purpose. He was gone; my problem remained unsolved, if anything made worse by my having irritated the man. Stag-heads, tiger-skins and petrified feathers were going to surround me for ever and ever. My house was becoming a Noah's Ark, about which I had read in our scripture classes at Albert Mission. There was going to be no help from anywhere. Nobody seemed to understand my predicament. Everyone ended up with the monotonous conclusion, 'After all, you invited him to stay with you!' I felt completely helpless. Sastri alone grasped the situation and now and then threw in a word of cheer such as, 'These things cannot go on for ever like this, can they?' Or sometimes he was brazen enough to say, 'What can he do after all, if you really want him to clear out?' as he stuck alphabet to alphabet on his composing stick. He felt it necessary to cheer me up as nowadays I was involving him in a lot of worrying transactions with our customers. The co-operative society report and ledgers were overdue because I could not muster enough sharpness of mind to check the figures. The cash bill of Anand Bhavan Hotel remained half done for the same reason, and it was he who had to battle with the customers and send them back with a convincing reply. Anyway it was a slight comfort in a world where there seemed to be no comfort whatever. I was lulled into a state of resignation. Vasu saw me less and less. I could hear his steps treading the staircase more emphatically than ever. I detected in that stamping of feet a challenge and a sense of ownership. I raged within myself every time I heard those footsteps and I knew I had lost him as a friend. From now on our relationship was going to be of the coldest. I would be grateful if he left me alone and did not think of bringing that terrific fist of his against my chin.

That he had not been idle came to light very soon. Five

days passed uneventfully, and then came a brown envelope brought by a court process-server. I received it mechanically, signing the delivery note. Opening it, I read, 'You are hereby asked to show cause why proceedings should not be instituted against you . . .' etc. It was from the House Rent Controller, the most dreaded personality in the town. The charges against me were: one, that I had given part of my press for rent without sanction to one Mr Vasu; and two, that I was trying to evict a tenant by unlawful means. It took me time to understand what it meant. Vasu had filed a complaint against me as a landlord. There were also other minor complaints, such as that I was not maintaining the house in a habitable condition, and was involving the said tenant in great loss, damage, and expense.

This involved me in a set of new activities. Up till now I had not known what it was to receive a court summons. I really did not know where to start and what to do next. Litigation was not in my nature. It was a thing I avoided. I had a shuddering fear of courts and lawyers, perhaps from the days when my uncles let them loose on my father and there was no other topic of discussion at home for months on end. I hid the summons away: they had given me three days' time to attend to it—a sort of reprieve. It gave me a feeling of being on parole. I did not confide even in Sastri. I realized that it would be futile to speak about it to anyone: no one was going to understand. Everyone would treat me as if I had done some unlawful act on the sly and was now caught, or trot out the old advice, 'After all it was *you* who agreed to take the man in. You have only yourself to blame.'

The situation seemed so dark that I surrendered myself

to a mood of complete resignation. I even began to look relaxed. I attended to my work, listened to jokes and responded to them normally at my press. I counted the days—seventy-two hours more, sixty, twenty-four . . . 'Tomorrow, I shall probably be led off straight from the court to the jail.' Everyone was going to have a surprise. Vasu would chase out Sastri and my customers and utilize my front room and all the rest of the space for arranging his 'art' pieces. People would get used to it in due course, cease to refer to the place as a press, and rather call it a museum. My wife and child would fend for themselves and visit me in prison on permissible days. A strange sense of relief came over me when my mind had been made up on all these issues and I knew where I was going to end. People would no doubt sympathize with me, but always conclude with, 'Who asked him to encourage the man anyway? He brought it all on his own head. Let him not blame others.'

On the last day of my freedom, at dawn, I had gone as usual to the river for a bath and was returning to my house at five-thirty. As usual the adjournment lawyer was on his way to the river. An idea came to me: it had never occurred to me until now that he could be of use. I had only viewed him as a printing customer. Since I had printed his thousand cards, he had been avoiding me—because of the unpaid bill. The marriage was over, and the bill had become stale: after all I didn't charge him more than ninety rupees for the entire lot. These days I never saw him even on my morning walk back from the river. Perhaps he detoured and took a parallel road. But today, as my luck would have it, I came face to face with him.

A great feeling of relief came over me at the sight. 'Ah,

my friend,' I cried. 'Just the person I was hoping to meet.'

He looked panic-stricken. Luckily I cornered him at the bend of Kabir Street where the house of the barber abuts the street, and with the storm drain on the other side a man cannot easily slip out if his path is blocked. He said awkwardly, 'Just today I was planning to see you at the press. You know, with one thing and another, after my daughter's marriage . . .'

I felt overjoyed at meeting him, and asked him, 'How is your daughter? Has she joined her husband? How is your son-in-law? How do you fare in the role of a father-in-law?'

He said, 'Most people think that with the wedding all one's troubles are over. It's only half the battle! Ha! Ha!' I laughed in order to please him. I didn't want him to think that I had accosted him so early in the day for my unpaid bill. He said, 'It's only after a marriage that one discovers how vicious one's new relatives can be. How many things they demand and keep demanding! Oh, God.'

'That's true,' I said. 'Taking your daughter up and down to visit her mother-in-law.'

'That I wouldn't mind,' he said. 'After all she is our child; it's my duty to help her travel in comfort.'

'Yes, yes,' I said, wondering what it was that he really minded.

His answer was not long in coming. 'All sorts of things, all sorts of things.' The first rays of the sun touched up the walls of the barber's house with the morning glory. Sparrows and crows were flying already in search of grain and worms. As I watched them a part of my mind reflected how lucky they were to be away from Vasu's attic windows. The lawyer was talking, habituated to rambling on until the court rose for lunch. 'The presents demanded are enough to sink one,' he was saying. 'The new son-in-law must be propitiated all the year round, I suppose,' he went on with grim humour. 'He must be given a present because it's the sixth month after the wedding, because it's the month of Adi, because it is Deepavali, because it is this and that; every time you think of the great man, you must part with a hundred rupees in cash or clothes! It's all an old, silly custom; our women are responsible. I would not blame the young man; what can he do? It's his mother who demands these things and the bride's mother at once responds by nagging her husband. These women know that if a man is sufficiently nagged, he will somehow find the cash.'

'So,' I thought, 'can the good lady be made to take an interest in the payment of my bill?'

The lawyer, as if reading my thought, said, 'Now you know why I could not really come over to see you. In spite of one's best efforts, small payments get left out. In all I had to find about ten thousand rupees for the marriage— savings, borrowings, loans, all kinds of things. Anyway it is all over. I will not have to face a similar bother for at least a decade more. My second daughter is just six years old.'

'That gives you a lot of time,' I said, and I hoped he would now let me say a word about my own problem. But he added, 'I am sorry I kept your bill so long; it escaped my notice.'

'Oh, that's all right,' I said reassuringly. 'I knew you must have been busy. Some of my customers are like a safe-deposit for me; I can ask for my money whenever I want. Don't worry, sir, I would not mistake you. Don't trouble to come to my press. I can send Sastri to collect the amount from you.' This I added out of a sudden apprehension that he might think I was writing off the account. The sun had grown brighter now, and still I had not told him of my problem. I did not know how to make a beginning. He was on the point of moving off, having had his say, when I said quickly, 'I want to see you on a legal matter.'

He drew himself up proudly now. He was on his own ground. He asked brusquely, 'Any more problems coming out of your property matters? I thought they had all been settled once and for all.'

'No, no, it's not that,' I began.

'Or are you thinking of a partnership deed? A lot of business men are having them now, you know.'

'Oh, no, I am not such a big business man.'

'Or estate duty; have you any trouble on that account?'

I laughed. 'Fortunately I own nothing to bring the estate duty on my head.'

'Or Shop Assistants' Act or Sales Tax? You know, half the trouble with Sales Tax problems is due to a lack of definition in the phrasing of the Act. Today I could tweak the nose of any Sales Tax Official who dared to tamper with my client, with all their half-digested manuals!'

'I have a summons from the Rent Controller.'

'What for?' he asked. 'Do you know how many people . . .' he began, but I wrested the initiative from him and cut in. 'It is some fancy summons as you'll see. Can I meet you at home?'

'No,' he said. 'Come to my office.' His office was above a cotton warehouse, or rather a bed-maker's shop, and cotton fluff was always flying about. Clients who went to him once never went there again, as they sneezed interminably and caught their death of cold; asthmatics went down for weeks after a legal consultation. His clients preferred to see him as he lounged about the premises of the district court in search of business, and he tackled their problems standing in the veranda of the court or under the shade of a tamarind tree in the compound. But he liked his inexperienced clients first to meet him at his office and catch a cold. I tried to dodge his proposal, but he was adamant that I should meet him in the narrow room above the cotton shop.

I went sneezing up the wooden stairs. The staircase was narrower than the one leading to my attic devoted to dead wild life, and creaked in a way which dimmed the sneezings of a visitor. Although I was born and bred in the district, this was the first time I had trod Abu Lane, which was only four blocks away from my press, conveniently tucked away from the views and turmoil of Market Road. There you saw his signboard, bleached by time and weather—Mr . . ., Pleader—nailed to a pillar on which a more aggressive board announced Nandi Cotton Corporation. Inside you saw nothing at first except bales and bales of cotton, and then a heap in a corner with some women beating them into fluff bed-making. It was this process which spread tuberculosis and asthma among would-be litigants. Our lawyer's chamber was right on the landing, which had been converted into a room, with one table, one chair, and one bureau full of law-books. His clients had to stand before him and talk. The table was covered with dusty paper bundles, old copies of law reports, a dry ink-well, an abandoned pen, and his black alpaca coat, going moss-green with age, hung by a nail on the wall. Down below, the cotton-fluffers kept up a rhythmic beating. He had a very tiny window with wooden bars behind him, and through it one saw the coconut tree by a neighbouring house, a kitchen chimney smoking, and a number of sloping roof-tiles, smoky and dusty, with pieces of tinsel thrown away by someone gleaming in the bright sun.

'Allergy?' he cried on seeing me. My sneezings had announced my arrival. I stepped in, blowing my nose and rubbing my eyes. There was a beatific smile on his face, and his single tooth was exposed. He sat at the table and commented, 'Some people suffer from allergy to dust and cotton. But I never notice such things.' He seemed to feel that his superior physique had come about through a special arrangement between himself · and God, and he enjoyed the sight of allergy in others as if it gave him an assurance that God was especially good to him. 'Allergy, they say, is just mental, that's all,' he said. 'It is something you should overcome by your own resolution,' he added grandly. I stood in front of his table like a supplicant, and placed before him the brown document. He put on his spectacles, opened the paper, spread it out with the palm of his hand, put a weight on it (the inkless bottle), reared back his head in order to adjust his vision, and read. His unshaven jowl and chin sparkled as if dusted over with silver powder.

He sighed deeply. 'Of course, you have given him no sort of receipt?'

'Receipt? What for?' I asked.

'For the rent, I mean. I suppose you have been sensible

enough not to take a cheque from him?'

I was appalled. He was failing into the same pattern of thought as a dozen others, including my wife. I declared, 'I have not rented him the house.'

'Have you taken a lump sum?' he asked.

'Look here, he is not my tenant.'

'Whose tenant is he then?' he asked, cross-examining me.

'I don't know. I can't say.' I was losing my equanimity. Why were people so pig-headed as not to know or want to understand my position? My legs felt heavy with climbing the ladder, and he would not give me a seat. He seemed to delight in punishing people who came to see him. I could hardly recognize my own voice, it sounded so thick with cotton dust.

The man was pursuing his inquiry. 'If he is not your tenant, what is he?'

'He is not a tenant, but a . . . friend,' I said, almost unable to substitute any other word.

He was quick to catch it. 'Friend! Oh! Oh! What sort of friend is he to file a complaint against you! This is a fairly serious offence according to the present Housing Act. Why could you not have straightaway gone through the usual formalities, that is . . .'

'Stop! Stop!' I cried. 'I swear that I gave him the attic free, absolutely free, because he asked for it.'

'If I were a judge, I would not believe you. Why should you let him live with you? Is he a relative?'

'No, thank God; it's the only thing that is good about the present situation.'

'Are you indebted to him in any way?'

'No. On the contrary, he should feel himself in debt to me, and yet he doesn't hesitate to have me hanged!' I cried. I explained to him at length how Vasu had come in search of me and how it had all come about. Feeling that perhaps the lawyer was too sympathetic to my enemy, I tried to win him over by saying, 'You remember that day when you came to have the wedding invitations printed, and how he pulled me out and left you—that's how he does everything. Now you understand what he is capable of.'

That prejudiced him. He reflected with bitterness, 'And I had to sit there and waste a whole day to no purpose.' He spoke to me on many legal technicalities, and took charge of my summons. He pulled out of a drawer a sheet of paper and took my signature. Then he put everything away with relief, 'I'll deal with it; don't worry yourself any more about it. How much money have you now?'

'Not an anna,' I said, and emptied my pockets to prove it. He looked gloomy at this bankruptcy.

'I would not charge more than a minimum, you know. Some routine charges have to be paid—stamp charges, affidavit charges, and coffee charges for the bench clerk. He is the man to help us, you know.'

'Oh, how?'

'Don't ask questions. Now I'm wondering how to pay these charges, absolutely nominal, you know. Even if you can spare about five rupees . . .'

'I thought since . . . since you have . . . you might adjust your accounts.'

He threw up his arms in horror, 'Oh, no, absolutely different situations. Don't mix up accounts, whatever else you may do. It always leads to trouble. Can't you send someone to your press to fetch your purse, if you have left it there?'

I felt like banging my fist on his table and demanding immediate settlement of my account, but I felt humbled by circumstances; the lawyer must save me from prison. So I said, 'If you will manage it somehow, I will send the amount to your house as soon as I'm back at the press.'

'I am not going home. There is no time today for me to go to court if I go home, and so, I don't want to seem to trouble you too much, but one oughtn't to start out on a business like this without cash of any kind.'

'I came only to consult you,' I said.

'I hope you have found it satisfactory,' he replied ceremoniously.

'Yes, of course,' I said. I felt like a pauper petitioning for help. How long would he keep me standing like this? I could not afford to be critical. So I asked breezily, 'Now what is to be done?'

'First things first.' He studied the sheet of paper intently. 'The summons is for 11 a.m. Tuesday the 24th; today is Monday the 23rd. It is 10.30 now. I must file your application for non-appearance almost at once. The ruling gives twenty-four hours if a summons is to be non-responded. It would have been a different matter if you had dodged the summons. Did you sign that little paper the fellow had?'

'Yes, of course.'

'Ah, inexperience, inexperience,' he cried. 'You should have consulted me before touching it or looking at it.'

'I had no idea it was coming,' I said, putting into my voice all the shock I had felt at Vasu's treachery.

'That's true, that's true,' he said. 'You must have

thought it was some printing business from the district court, ha?'

'Now, is that all?' I asked.

'H'm, yes,' he said. 'I can always depend upon the bench clerk to help me. I'll do what I can. You must feel happy if you are not on the list tomorrow. I'll have to plead that you are away and need more time or notice.'

'But everybody can see me at my press,' I pleaded.

'Oh, yes, that's a point. But how can the court take cognizance if you are there? In any event, it'll be better if you don't make yourself too conspicuous during the hours of the court sitting.'

'Except when I am called out, I'm usually behind the blue curtain,' I said.

'That's good, it is always helpful,' he said.

'And what's the next step?'

'You will be free for at least four weeks. Rent court is rather overworked nowadays. They won't be able to reissue the summons for at least four weeks.' I felt grateful to the man for saving my neck for four weeks; but now he added a doubt. 'Perhaps the complainant will file an objection.'

'He may also say that I've not gone anywhere, as he lives right over my head.'

'But the court is not bound to take cognizance of what he says. It's not that way that your *mala fides* can be established.'

I didn't understand what he meant.

'I have some work now,' I said apologetically. I did not want to hurt his feelings with the least hint that I didn't like to be kept standing there while he talked; as a matter of fact my legs were paining me.

'You may go,' he said grandly. 'I'll be back home at three o'clock. I will manage it all somehow. If you are sending anyone at all to my house, send an envelope with ten rupees in it. Anyway I'll give you a complete accounting when it is all over.'

The proof of the lawyer's handiwork: I was sitting unscathed at my press, printing three-colour labels, on the day following my D-day. I gladly sent him ten rupees through Sastri. He would account for it all at the end. I was not to mix up accounts. Great words of wisdom they seemed to me in my fevered state.

CHAPTER SIX

FIFTEEN DAYS PASSED uneventfully. We left each other alone. I heard Vasu come and go. His jeep would arrive at the yard, I could hear that mighty fist pulling at the brake, and feet stumping upstairs. Amidst all his impossible qualities, he had just one virtue: he never tried to come to my part of the house; he arrived and departed as he liked. Only the stench of drying leather was on the increase. It disturbed the neighbourhood. I had a visitor from the health department one fine day—a man in khaki uniform. He was a sanitary inspector whose main business was to keep the city clean, a hard job for a man in a place like Malgudi, where the individual jealously guarded his right to independent action.

The sanitary inspector had the habit of occasionally dropping in at my press and sitting in a chair quietly when his limbs ached from too much supervision of the Market Road. He would take off his pith helmet (I think he was the only one in the whole town who had such headgear, having picked it up at an army disposal store), place it on the chair next to him, wipe his brow with a check-coloured handkerchief, sigh and pant and call for a glass of water. I could not say he was a friend, but a friendly man. Today, he leaned his bicycle on the front step of my press, and came in saying, 'There is a complaint against you.' He produced an envelope from his pocket and took out a sheet of paper, and held it out to me.

I was beginning to dread the sight of brown envelopes nowadays. A joint petition from my neighbours, signed by half a dozen names, had been presented to the municipal authority. They complained that on my terrace they noticed strange activities—animal hides being tanned; the petitioners pointed out that the tanning and curing of skins should be prohibited in a residential area as it gave rise to bad odour and insanitary surroundings. They also complained of carrion birds hovering around my terrace. One part of my mind admired my neighbours for caring so much for sanitation; the rest of it was seized with cold despair.

I requested the inspector to take a seat and asked what he expected me to do. He said, 'Can I have a glass of water?' I called Sastri to fetch water. The sanitary inspector said, after gulping it down in one mouthful (he was the most parched and dehydrated man I had ever seen in my life), 'By-law X definitely prohibits the tanning of leather indiscriminately in dwelling areas; By-law Y specifies exactly where you can conduct such a business. I did not know you were engaged in this activity. Why? Is your press not paying enough?'

I slapped my brow with my palm in sheer despair. 'I have not turned tanner!' I cried. 'I am still a printer. What makes you think I'm not?'

'Where is the harm?' asked the inspector. 'There is

dignity in every profession. You don't have to be ashamed of it, only you must carry it on at the proper spot without violating the by-laws.'

'All right, I'll do so,' I said meekly.

'Oh, good, you will co-operate with us! That is the difference between educated people and uneducated ones. You can grasp our problems immediately. Of course people will do wrong things out of ignorance. How can we expect everyone to be versed in municipal by-laws? I never blame a man for not knowing the regulations, but I'm really upset if people don't mend their ways even after a notice has been issued. May I have another glass of water, please?'

'Oh, surely, as many as you want. Mr Sastri, another glass of water.' I could hear Sastri put away the urgent job he was doing and prepare to fetch the glass.

The inspector emptied the second supply at one gulp and rose to go. He said in parting, 'I'll send off an endorsement to the parties, something to silence them.'

'What will you say?' I asked, a sudden curiosity getting the upper hand.

'We have a printed form, which will go to them to say that the matter is receiving attention. That is enough to satisfy most parties. Otherwise they'll bombard us with reminders.'

I saw him off on the last step of my press. He clutched the handlebars of his bicycle, stood for a moment thinking and said, 'Take your time to shift, but don't be too long. If you get a notice, please send a reply to say that you are shifting your tanning business elsewhere and pray for time.'

'Yes, sir,' I said, 'I'll certainly do all that you say.' I was beginning to realize that it was futile to speak about any matter to anyone. People went about with fixed notions and seldom listened to anything I said. It was less strenuous to let them cherish their own silly ideas.

The septuagenarian came along, tapping his stick; he stood in the road, looked up through his glasses, shading his eyes with one hand, and asked in a querulous voice, 'Is Nataraj in?' The usual crowd was there. 'Now is the testing time for Nehru,' the journalist was saying. 'If the Chinese on our border are not rolled back—' The poet had brought the next canto of his poem and was waiting to give me a summary of it. The septuagenarian asked again, 'Is Nataraj here?' unable to see inside owing to the glare.

'Yes, yes, I'm here,' I cried, and went down to help him up the steps.

He seated himself and looked at the other two. 'Your friends? I may speak freely, I suppose?' I introduced them to him, whereupon he expatiated on the qualities of a poet, and his duties and social relationships, and then turned to me with the business on hand. 'Nataraj, you know my grandson had a pet—a dog that he had kept for two years. He was very much devoted to it, and used to play with it the moment he came back from school.' I almost foresaw what was coming. 'Someone killed it last night. It lay under the street-lamp shot through the heart; someone seems to have shot it with a gun. Who has a gun here in these parts? I thought no one but the police had guns.'

'Why did you let it out?'

'Why? I don't know. It generally jumps over the wall and goes around the neighbourhood. It was a harmless dog, only barking all night, sitting under that street-lamp. I don't know what makes these dogs bark all night. They say that ghosts are visible to the eyes of a dog. Is it true? Do you believe in ghosts?'

'I haven't been able to see any,' I began.

'Oh, that's all right. Most people don't see them. Why should they? What was I saying?' he asked pathetically, having lost track of his own sentence. I was loath to remind him. I hesitated and wavered, hoping that he'd forget the theme of the dead dog and concentrate on the ghosts. But the journalist said, 'You were speaking about the dog, sir.'

'Ah, yes, yes. I could not bear to see its corpse, and so I asked the scavenger to take it away. I don't know what you call that breed. We called it Tom and it was black and hairy, very handsome; someone brought it from Bombay and gave it to my son, who gave it to this little fellow— quite a smart dog, very watchful, would make such a row if anyone tried to enter our gate, would wait for me to get up from my morning prayer, because he knew he would get a piece of the bread I eat in the morning. For the last three years doctors have ordered me to eat only bread, one slice of it. Before that I used to take *idli* every day, but they think it's not good for me. My father lived to be a hundred and never missed *idli* even for a single day.' He remained silently thinking of those days.

I was glad he was not asking to be reminded of his main theme. I hoped he would get up and go away. Everyone maintained a respectful, gloomy silence. If it had continued another minute, he would have risen and I'd have helped him down the steps. But just at the crucial moment Sastri came in with a proof for my approval. As soon as he entered by the curtain, instead of handing me the proof and disappearing he stood arrested for a minute, staring at the old man. 'What was all that commotion at your gate this morning? I was coming to the press and had no time to stop and ask. But I saw your grandchild crying.'

'Oh, is that you, Sastri?' asked the old man, shrinking his eyes to slits in order to catch his features. 'How are you, Sastri? It's many months since I saw you. What are you doing? Yes, of course I know you are working with Nataraj. How do you find his work, Nataraj? Good? Must be good. His uncle was my class-mate, and he had married the third daughter of . . . He used to come and play with my nephew. Where do you live, Sastri? Not near us?' Sastri mentioned his present address. 'Oh, that is far off Vinayak Street; ah, how many centuries it seems to me since I went that way. Come and see me some time, I'll be pleased.'

Sastri seemed pleased to be thus invited. He said, 'I must, I must come some time.'

'How many children have you?' Sastri mentioned the number, at which the old man looked gratified and said, 'Bring them also along when you come. I'd like to see them.'

Instead of saying 'Yes' and shutting up, Sastri said, 'Even this morning I could have come for a moment, but there was too much of a crowd at your gate.'

'Oh, idiot Sastri! What on earth are you becoming so loquacious for?' I muttered to myself. 'Leave him alone to forget this morning's crowd.'

But he had stirred up mischief. 'Didn't you know why there was a crowd?'

'No, I only saw your grandchild crying. I was in a hurry.'

The reminder of his grandchild nearly brought the septuagenarian to the verge of a breakdown. The old man almost sobbed, 'That boy is refusing to cheer up. I can't bear to see the youngster in such misery.'

'Why? Why? What happened?' asked Sastri.

'Someone had shot his pet dog,' said the journalist.

'Shot! Shot!' cried Sastri as if he had been poked with the butt of a rifle. 'When? Was it shot dead? Oh, poor dog! I have often seen it at your gate, the black one!' Why was he bent upon adding fuel to the fire? 'Do you know who could have shot it?' he asked menacingly.

'For what purpose?' said the old man. 'It's not going to help us. Will it bring Tom back to life?'

But Sastri insisted on enlightening him. He gave the old man the killer's name, whereabouts, and situation, and added, 'He is just the man who could have done it.'

The old man tapped his staff on the floor and shouted at me, 'And yet you said nothing? Why? Why?'

'It didn't occur to me, that is all,' I said hollowly. The old man tapped the floor with his staff and cried, 'Show me where he is, I'll deal with him. I'll hand him over to the police for shooting at things. What's your connection with him? Is he related to you? Is he your friend?' I tried to pacify the old man, but he ignored my words. 'In all my eighty years, this is the first time I have heard of a shooting in our street. Who is this man? Why should you harbour him? Tomorrow he'll aim his gun at the children playing in the street!'

Knowing Vasu's style of speech with children, I could agree with the old man's views. The old man's hands and legs trembled, his face was flushed. I feared he might have a stroke and collapse in my press—anything seemed possible in my press these days. I said, 'Be calm, sir, it will not do to get excited. It's not good for you.'

'If it's not good for me, let me die. Why should anything be good for me? Death will be more welcome to me than the sight of my unhappy grandson.'

'I'll get him another dog, sir, please tell him that, a beautiful black one. I promise.'

'Can you?' asked the old man, suddenly calming down. 'Are you sure? You know where one is to be found?'

'Oh, yes,' I said, 'the easiest thing. I know many planters who have dogs, and I can always get a puppy for our little friend.'

'Will you accompany me now and say that to him?'

'Oh, surely,' I said, rising.

Sastri chose just this moment to thrust the proof before me and ask, 'Shall I put it on the machine?'

I didn't want anything to stop the old man from getting up and going, so I said, 'Wait a moment, I'll be back.' But Sastri would not allow me to go. 'If you pass this proof, we can print it off, everything is ready. They are shutting off power at eleven o'clock today. If we don't deliver . . .'

'Oh, Sastri, leave everything alone. I don't care what happens. I must see the child first and comfort him.' I was desperately anxious that the old man should be bundled off before someone or other should offer to point Vasu out to him.

As Vasu became more aloof, he became more indifferent, and everything that he did looked like a challenge to me. I was, I suppose, getting into a state of abnormal watchfulness myself; even the sound of his footstep seemed to me aggressively tenant-like, strengthened by the laws of the rent-control court. He pretended that I did not exist. He seemed to arrive and depart with a swagger as if to say, 'You may have got an adjournment now, but the noose is being made ready for you.'

He brought in more and more dead creatures; there was no space for him in his room or on the terrace. Every inch of space must have been cluttered with packing-boards and nails and skins and moulds. The narrow staircase, at which I could peep from my machine, was getting filled up with his merchandise, which had now reached the last step—he had left just enough margin for himself to move up and down. He had become very busy these days, arriving, departing, hauling up or hauling down packing-cases, doing everything single-handed. I had no idea where his market was. In other days I could have asked him, but now we were bitter enemies. I admired him for his capacity for work, for all the dreadful things he was able to accomplish single-handed. If I had been on speaking terms, I'd have congratulated him unreservedly on his success as a taxidermist—his master Suleiman must really have been as great as he described him. He had given his star pupil expert training in all branches of his work. Short of creating the animals, he did everything.

Vasu was a perfect enemy. When I caught a glimpse of him sometimes when I stood at the treadle, he averted his head and passed, perhaps stamping his feet and muttering a curse. He seemed to be flourishing. I wondered why he should not pay me the charges for printing his forms and letterheads. How to ask him? I did not want to do anything that might madden him further and worsen our relationship.

I was beginning to miss his rough company. I often speculated if there could be some way of telling him that all was well, that he should not give another thought to what had happened between us, that he could stay in my house as long as he pleased ('only don't bring too many carcasses or keep them too long, this is a fussy neighbourhood, you know'). I could never be a successful enemy to anyone. Any enmity worried me night and day. As a schoolboy I persistently shadowed around the one person with whom I was supposed to be on terms of hate and hostility. I felt acutely uneasy as long as our enmity lasted. I was never more than a few paces away from him as we started home from school. I sat on a bench immediately behind him and tried to attract his attention by coughing and clearing my throat or by brushing against his back while picking up a pencil deliberately dropped on the floor. I made myself abject in order to win a favourable look or word from my enemy and waited for a chance to tell him that I wanted to be friends with him. It bothered me like a toothache. I was becoming aware of the same mood developing in me now. I was longing for a word with Vasu. I stood like a child at the treadle, hoping he would look at me and nod and that all would be well again. He was a terrible specimen of human being no doubt, but I wanted to be on talking terms with him. This was a complex mood. I couldn't say that I liked him or approved of anything he said or did, but I didn't want to be repulsed by him. My mind seethed with plans as to how to re-establish cordiality. I was torn between my desire to make a grand gesture, such as writing off his print bill, and my inability to adopt it—as I didn't like the idea of writing off anything. I liked to delude myself that I collected my moneys strictly and never let anyone get away with it. So I decided not to rake up the question of the bill with Vasu until a smiling relationship could once again be established between us and I could refer to the question in a humorous way.

While I was in this state of mental confusion, Sastri came up with a new problem. There was a hyena at the foot of the stairs, the sight of which upset him while he was composing the admission cards of Albert Mission High School. I was sitting at my usual place when he parted the curtain and cried, 'How can I do any work with a wolf and a whatnot staring at me? And there's a python hanging down the handrail of the stairs.'

'Sastri, I saw it; it is not a wolf but a hyena. Don't you think it surprising and interesting that we should have all this life around us in Malgudi? They are all from Mempi hills!'

The educational value of it was lost on Sastri. He simply said, 'Maybe, but why should they be here? Can't you do something about it? It's repulsive and there is always a bad smell around—all my life I have tried to keep this press so clean!'

I could see that Sastri was greatly exercised. It was no use joking with him or trying to make him take a lighter view. I feared that he might take steps himself, if I showed indifference. He might call to Vasu through the grille that separated us and order him to be gone with the wolf. I didn't want Sastri to risk his life, so I said placatingly, 'Sastri, you know the old proverb, that when your cloth is caught in the thorns of a bush, you have to extricate yourself gently and little by little, otherwise you will never take the cloth whole?'

Sastri, being an orthodox-minded Sanskrit semi-scholar, appreciated this sentiment and the phrases in which it was couched; he set it off with another propounder, one in Sanskrit which said that to deal with a *rakshasa* one must possess the marksmanship of a hunter, the wit of a pundit, and the guile of a harlot. He quoted a verse to prove it.

'But the trouble is that the marksmanship is with him, not with us. Anyway, he'll soon deplete the forest of all its creatures, and then he will have to turn to a tame life, and our staircase will be clear again.'

'He shows all the definitions of a *rakshasa*,' persisted Sastri, and went on to define the make-up of a *rakshasa*, or a demoniac creature who possessed enormous strength, strange powers, and genius, but recognized no sort of restraints of man or God. He said, 'Every *rakshasa* gets swollen with his ego. He thinks he is invincible, beyond every law. But sooner or later something or other will destroy him.' He stood expatiating on the lives of various demons in *puranas* to prove his point. He displayed great versatility and knowledge. I found his talk enlightening, but still felt he might continue with the printing of the school admission cards, which were due to be delivered seventy-two hours hence; however, I had not the heart to remind him of sordid things.

He went on; his information was encyclopaedic. He removed his silver-rimmed spectacles and put them away in his shirt pocket as being an impediment to his discourse. 'There was Ravana, the protagonist in Ramayana, who had ten heads and twenty arms, and enormous yogic and physical powers, and a boon from the gods that he could never be vanquished. The earth shook under his tyranny. Still he came to a sad end. Or take Mahisha the *asura* who meditated and acquired a boon of immortality and invincibility, and who had secured an especial favour that every drop of blood shed from his body should give rise to another demon in his own image and strength, and who nevertheless was destroyed. The Goddess with six arms, each bearing a different weapon, came riding for the fight on a lion which sucked every drop of blood drawn from the demon. Then there was Bhasmasura, who acquired a special boon that everything he touched should be scorched, while nothing could ever destroy him. He made humanity suffer. God Vishnu was incarnated as a dancer of great beauty, named Mohini, with whom the *asura* became infatuated. She promised to yield to him only if he imitated all the gestures and movements of her own dancing. At one point in the dance Mahini placed her palms on her head, and the demon followed this gesture in complete forgetfulness and was reduced to ashes that very second, the blighting touch becoming active on his own head. Every man can think that he is great and will live for ever, but no one can guess from which quarter his doom will come.'

Vasu seemed to have induced in Sastri much philosophical thought. Before leaving, his parting anecdote was, 'Or think of Daksha, for whom an end was prophesied through the bite of a snake, and he had built himself an island fortress to evade this fate, and yet in the end . . .' and so on and so forth, which was very encouraging for me too, as I felt that everything would pass and that my attic would be free. I hoped we would part on speaking terms, but Sastri did not think it necessary. I was glad he left me suddenly without asking me to throw out the hyena, having found a solution to his problem through his own research and talk. He vanished behind the curtain as he suddenly remembered that he had left the machine idle and that the ink on the plate was drying.

My aim now was to save the situation from becoming worse and gradually to come back to a hallo-saying stage with Vasu. I was glad I had warded off the danger emanating from Sastri, but this gratification was short-lived. Sastri himself seemed to take a detached, synoptic view of the hyena and other creatures on the other side of the grille. He got quite busy with the admission cards and left me alone, and I thought I had given a rest to the problem of Vasu and might some time be able to greet him. But it was not destined to be. One fine morning, the forester came to my press to ask if Vasu was still with me. I thought he had come to get his book of morals printed, and said, 'I have not forgotten my promise, but just as soon as I am able to complete all the work . . .'

He didn't seem interested, but said, 'All right, I am in no hurry about anything, but I am here on official work. Is Vasu still here? If he is I'd like to speak to him.' A sudden doubt assailed me whether it would be safe to be involved in this. The forester might have come as a friend, or he might not. So I said dodgingly, 'I'm not seeing much of Vasu nowadays, although he lives upstairs. He seems to be very busy nowadays . . .'

'With what?'

I became cautious. 'I don't know, I see him coming and

going. He has his own business.'

'Has he? That's what I want to find out. Would you answer some questions?'

'No,' I said point blank. 'I wish to have nothing to do with anything that concerns him.'

'Rather strange!' he said. He had seemed such a timid moralistic man some months ago when he visited me. It was a surprise for me to find him adopting a tough tone. He continued, 'He is your tenant, as everybody knows, and he claims your friendship, and yet you disclaim all knowledge of him? Is it believable?'

'Yes. You should believe what I say. Won't you sit down and talk?'

'No, I'm spending Government hours now. I'm here on official duty, and they are certainly not paying me to lounge in your chair. I must get busy with what I came for.' This thin cadaverous man, whose neck shot straight out of his khaki like a thin cylindrical waterpipe, was tough. He said, 'Any man who violates the game laws is my enemy. I wouldn't hesitate to shoot him if I had a chance. A lot of game has been vanishing from our reserves and even tigers disappear from the blocks. Where do they go?'

'Perhaps to other forests for a change,' I said.

He laughed. It was a good joke in his view. I hoped that humour would establish a bond between us.

'That shows your ignorance of wild life.'

I felt relieved that he recognized my ignorance. That would certainly induce him to view me with greater toleration and absolve me from all responsibility for what Vasu was doing. He recovered his composure, as if he realized that he ought not to spoil me by smiling too much, and suddenly compressed his lips into a tight narrow line and became grim. He said, 'Joking apart, I shall lose my job if I don't track down this mischief going on in the forests of Mempi. Somebody is busy with his gun.'

'Can't you keep a watch?' I asked.

'Yes, but in a forest of hundreds of miles you can't watch every inch of ground, especially if the thief operates at night. Some of our guards are none too honest. We rely in some places on the jungle dwellers, and they are not wholly dependable. I must first have a talk with your tenant.'

'He is not my tenant. I take no rent from him.'

'Then he must be your friend.' I recognized the pincer-movement in which this man was trying to trap me as all the others had done.

I said, 'He is not even my friend. I never knew him before he came here.' This sounded even worse—much better remain his friend or landlord than his business associate. I could see the cadaverous face hardening with suspicion.

He thought over the situation for a moment, and asked, 'Why don't you help me?'

'In what way?'

'I want to get at this man who is destroying game. Can't you give me some clues?'

We had come around to the same starting point, and I said, 'I wish to have nothing whatever to do with this business of yours. Leave me out of it. What makes you think I should have anything to do with it?'

'Since you are not his friend, why don't you help me?'

'I am not your friend either,' I said.

It seemed silly to carry on a vague talk on friendship like this early in the day, while the Market Road traffic was flowing by and the treadle was rolling nicely on the admission cards. I said with an air of finality, 'If you like to rest, come in and take a chair.'

'Do I go through here to reach his room?'

'No, it's blocked this way. He has his own door . . .'

He stepped down without a word and went away. I could read his mind. He was now convinced that I was a joint owner of the poaching and stuffing factory. He went out with an expression that said when the time came he'd round up the gang.

I heard him go up the staircase and knock on the door. Vasu was unused to having visitors. He shouted from inside, 'Who is it?'

I heard the other reply, 'I wish to see you for a minute. Open the door, please.'

'I asked who you are; what is your name?'

'I am Ramaswami. I want to see you.'

'Ramaswami, whoever you may be, go down and wait near my jeep. I will he coming down in a short time.'

'Why don't you let me in now?'

Vasu shouted from inside, 'Don't stand there and argue. Get out and wait.'

I heard the forester go down the stairs, pausing for a moment to study the hyena. Half an hour later, steps once again came tumbling down the stairs, and voices sounded from the yard where the jeep was parked. 'So you are Ramaswami, are you? To what do I owe the honour of this visit?'

I had to follow all the conversation through the wall at

my back and it filtered their exchanges into the lower octaves. I stood on a chair and opened a ventilator high up on the back wall in order to follow their conversation better. The cadaver was repeating his statement about the disappearance of game from Mempi Forest. All that Vasu said was, 'Why not?' The other merely remarked, 'Game in the sanctuaries is expected to be preserved.'

'Of course it will be preserved if you get help from a taxidermist who knows his job,' said Vasu jocularly.

The cadaver seemed a match for Vasu. 'Well, we may not get the taxidermist's services, but the taxidermist himself.'

By this time Vasu had climbed into his seat in the jeep, the forester standing beside it. What a contrast to the first day when he brought the forest official into my office and sat him down and flattered him as a noble writer!

'We will watch, and when we get at the man who is depleting the reserve, well, the law is pretty clear on that—'

'If your department needs my co-operation in any matter, don't hesitate to tell me,' said Vasu with that crude cynicism he was capable of. The forester ignored it, but said, 'How do you account for the hyena you have on the staircase?'

'The hyena came in search of me. I shot it right where you are standing now,' he said.

'What about . . .?'

'What about what? Nothing, that's all. I am not bound to say anything.'

'From which forest did you get them?'

'Not from your jungle. Go and look again and see if there is any trade-mark on them proving that they are from

Mempi. India is a big country with many jungles, and you can get everything everywhere. For your information, I've also some tiger-skins. Are they yours? Claim them if you can. I am hungry, and am going out for breakfast. No time to waste. Don't bother me unless you come with some more practical proposition. He drove off unceremoniously. The forester stood where he was for a second and moved away.

Nothing happened for two days. I was in my usual chair one afternoon when Vasu's jeep pulled up at my door. My heart gave a thump. He sat in his jeep and said, 'Nataraj, come here.' I had an impulse to drop whatever I was doing, rush up to him and seize the chance to make friends with the monster again. But my pride was stronger. I suddenly resented all the trouble he had caused me. 'Come and speak if you have anything to say.' I was amazed at my own temerity.

He grinned, 'Ah, you are showing some spirit after all, that's good.'

I didn't like the paternal tone he adopted. I asked again, 'What is your business with me? I'm rather busy.'

'Yes, yes,' he said mockingly. 'I see it, and it's good to see a man do an honest job at his office instead of chatting away the time with friends who treat the place as a club lounge.' This was a reference to my two friends who had come to see me after a long time. He went on shouting from his jeep, 'I appreciate your guts, Nataraj. I had thought that you were rather spineless. I now know that you have a spine. I'd never have dreamt that you would set that ghost in khaki on me! You were smart to think it up. So that's your move; you want to know what I'll do next?'

'No, I'm not interested. I'm busy.'

'You showed him the way to my room. He sees all the things there. What of it? Ask your friends to put a rubber-stamp on the backs of all the beasts in Mempi, so that he may identify them later and not make a fool of himself, and not make a fool of you either.' He drove off.

Sen said, 'I don't envy your luck in getting a man like that to live with.'

I wondered what Vasu's menacing words might mean. Legally he had trapped me at the Rent Controller's court, and the adjournment lawyer was handling the case, every now and then tapping me for a five or ten, but I found that he was satisfied even if I gave him just a couple of rupees, and made no mention of the money he owed me for printing his daughter's wedding card. I thought Vasu had done his worst, but now what did he mean? I hoped he was not planning to abduct my son and hold him to ransom. He might be up to anything. That evening I told my wife, 'If you have any urgent business to call me, wait till I come home. Don't send the little fellow across.'

She grew nervous and asked, 'Why?'

I just said, 'I don't want him to come there and make a fuss, that's all.'

'You see so little of him,' she complained, and added, 'You leave before he wakes, and come home after he is asleep, and if he wants to see his father he mustn't even come to the press, I suppose?' Then I had to explain and she grew really frightened.

She was in a panic. She kept the front door shut. She was completely demoralized if the boy did not come home at six. She behaved as if the monster would be unleashed and come rushing in to swallow up the family if the back door of my press was opened. My son seemed to enjoy the thrill of the situation as long as there was daylight. He spoke to his friends about the dangers that surrounded his life, and I saw batches of schoolboys standing around in knots in front of my press, looking up at the attic window during the afternoon recess at school. I became curious and beckoned to a couple of children to come in. 'What are you all doing here?'

'Nothing,' said one of them. 'We are going home from school.'

'What are you looking for?' I asked.

'Babu said there was, was . . . some giant here . . .'

'You want to look at him?' They nodded. 'Better not. Go home, boys. There is no such creature here.' I was anxious they should not see Vasu, as they might shout and circle round him and infuriate him. Knowing his attitude to children, I did not want to risk a meeting between them. One of them asked, slyly, 'Is it true that he eats dogs?'

'Oh, no,' I said immediately. 'He eats rice and other stuff just as we do. That's all false.'

'Then why did he shoot Ramu's dog?'

'Oh, that! It was shot by mistake. He was expecting a black bear and had his gun ready, but at the same time this dog came . . .'

'It was called Lily,' said one boy. The other contradicted, 'No, it was Tom.'

'No, it's Lily,' persisted the first. 'Yes, what'll you give me if it is Lily? Shall we go and ask Ramu?'

'Yes, come on,' and both ran off as if they were a

couple of birds that had alighted at the window and were flying off. Two other children who were watching the scene also ran off happily shouting, 'Let us ask Ramu.'

My son came up with Ramu one afternoon two days later. Ramu said, 'My grandfather asked me to see you.' My son added, 'He has come to ask for his dog.' Several weeks had gone by since I had promised the septuagenarian that I'd replace his grandson's dog. Although at that time it had seemed a perfectly feasible thing to find another dog, as days passed it began to look more and more difficult. I had promised in a moment of emotional stress, and now in the cold light of day it appeared to me an unreal, impossible task. I did not know how to acquire a puppy or where one was to be had. I had no doubt mentioned some planter with a dog. I had had in mind Achappa, a coffee planter on Mempi, for whose estates I used to do printing work at one time. I remembered his saying that he had a Great Dane pair with nine puppies. Did I need one? That was years ago. Achappa was not to be seen nowadays; occasionally his manager was observed at my neighbour's press.

I walked across to the Star and said, 'If you see anyone from Consolidated Estates, please call me.' He replied that it was months since he had seen anyone from Consolidated Estates and suspected that Achappa was getting his printing done at Madras. So there it was. The dog-sources were drying up. I needed some expert help in the matter. My sincerity was unquestionable, but my resources were poor. I had no time either. Every day the boy came to my press and said, 'My grandfather asked me to see you.' And every day I gave him some reply and sent him off. It was becoming a mechanical action. And the boy went away satisfied with any answer I gave. My intentions were absolutely honest, but the press work was heavy nowadays and I did not have a moment to spare. In addition to other work Sen was giving me manifestos to print and the poet was fetching his cantos with greater speed. With one thing and another my time flew swiftly each day. I had to work hard and make enough money at least to pay the lawyer whenever he held his hand out for cash! I had not given up hopes of recovering my dues from him, but I obeyed his advice not to mix up accounts.

I had no time actually to go out and seek a dog for the boy, but I had several plans in my head. I'd make a list of all my friends with dogs, tabulate each breed, note down their breeding time, make one of them promise to give one of the litter to me, make a round of visits every Sunday afternoon, and finally pick up a dog for the young fellow. My son asked me at nights while he nestled close to me (when night advanced the fear of the monster grew in him and he refused to sleep in a separate bed), as if he were a sharer of my dream, 'Get me a puppy too, Father, when you get one for Ramu.'

'Yes, yes,' I said. 'Why not?'

At the hyena's corner one day Sastri heard the jingling of bangles and turned to see a woman go down the steps and out of the building. He had been at the machine. I was in the front office, and presently the curtain parted and he peeped in. A look at his face and I knew something was wrong—some matter referring to Vasu. His face was slightly flushed and his spectacles wobbled as he raised and lowered his brow. There was no need for preambles and so I asked straightaway, 'What is the latest?'

He swallowed once or twice before saying, 'All sorts of low-class women are wandering around this press nowadays . . .'

'Where? Who are they?'

He flourished his arms upward, and I knew he was indicating not the heavens, but Vasu. I did not like to pursue the subject because I had a couple of visitors waiting to discuss a printing job. 'Sastri, I will be with you in a moment . . .'

He took my hint and vanished into the wings. After persuading my would-be customers to patronize the original Heidelberg, I went in to conduct the research with Sastri. He was printing the leaves of a bank ledger with a sullen face. I had never seen him so worried before. Even the first shock of finding a hyena beyond the grille had been nothing to what he seemed to face now. I stood beside him without a word except to sound bossy, 'There is too much ink. Watch the inking.'

He ignored my fussy advice and said, 'If this sort of thing goes on, our reputation in the town will be ruined. I saw Rangi going downstairs. Is she the sort of person we should encourage here? Is this a printing press or what?'

'Who is Rangi?'

He looked desperate, shy, and angry. I was enjoying his discomfiture immensely.

'Oh, you are asking as if you didn't know!'

'How should you expect me to know anything of Rangi, Sastri? I have so much to do!'

'As if I had nothing else to do.'

'I don't know anything about these people.'

'Best thing under the circumstances . . . We should not have this kind of person seen in a place like this, that's all.'

'I don't know what you are saying, Sastri. What is it all about?'

'That man has started bringing disreputable people here; where shall we be?'

I had no answer. Little by little I got it out of him. Rangi was a notorious character of the town. She lived in the shadows of Abu Lane. She was the daughter of Padma, an old dancer attached to the temple of God Krishna four streets off, our ancient temple. Padma herself had been an exemplary, traditional dedicated woman of the temple, who could sing and dance, and who also took one or two wealthy lovers; she was now old and retired. Her daughter was Rangi. Sastri darkly hinted that he knew who fathered her into this world, and I hoped it was not himself. His deep and comprehensive knowledge of the dancer's family was disconcerting. I had to ask him to explain how he managed to acquire so much information. He felt a little shy at first and then explained, 'You see my house is in Abu Lane, and so we know what goes on. To be frank, I live in a portion of the house, the other half is occupied by Damodar, who has a wholesale grain shop in the market. For many years he was keeping Padma, and after this daughter was born he suspected Padma's fidelity and gave her up, but she threatened to go to court to prove that he was the father, and finally he had to accept the situation and pay her a lot of money to get out of her clutches. He used to be a chum in our school days and he would never conceal his exploits from me.' Padma was now retired,

116

being old, fat, and frightening like the harem guards of Ravana, and her daughter Rangi had succeeded her at the temple. Before that she had studied in a school for a while, joined a drama troupe which toured the villages, and come back to the town after seducing all the menfolk she had set eyes on. According to Sastri, she was the worst woman who had ever come back to Malgudi. She was a subject of constant reference in Abu Lane, and was responsible for a great deal of the politics there.

Next morning I was at the machine, after sending away Sastri to the binders to look to something. I heard the sound of bangles and there she was—Rangi, stepping between the hyena and the mongoose and making for the door. She was dark, squat, seductive, overloaded with jewellery; the flowers in her hair were crushed, and her clothes rumpled; she had big round arms and fat legs and wore a pink sari. She evidently didn't care how she looked now, this was her off-hour, and I could imagine no other woman who would be prepared to walk along the streets in this *dishabillé*. I felt curious to know what she would look like in the evenings— perhaps she would powder her face, the talcum floating uneasily over her ebonite skin. Anyway whatever might be the hour, every inch of her proclaimed her what she was— a perfect female animal. How did she get home? When did she come in? When did she go out? She went about her business with such assurance, walking in and out of a place like a postman. My mind seethed with speculations. Did Vasu bring her in his jeep at the darkest hour? Not likely. What a man he must be who could turn his mistress out in cold blood when morning came!

My further speculations on the theme of lust were cut

short by the arrival of Sastri, who said, 'The binder says that one of his office boys is down with mumps, and that he cannot do the ruling until Friday.' He said this in a tone of utter fatalism.

'The sky is not going to fall because he holds it off till Friday,' I said.

'Unless the ruling is done, the bank ledger won't be ready and they'll come down on us.'

Why was Sastri always in a state of panic lest we should fail one or the other of our customers? He had no trust in my ability to manage things and no sort of confidence in me. I felt indignant. 'No need for panic! I have run this press for how many years? I've managed to survive and flourish, and so far not made a fool of myself. So why do you worry?' I could not conclude my sentence. There was no conclusion to it as there was no basis at all for beginning it. My mind was busy following the fleshy image of Rangi and perhaps I resented the intrusion.

I was mistaken in thinking that Rangi was the only woman. I had only to stand there between seven and eight in the morning, and it became a sort of game to speculate who would be descending the stairs next. Sometimes a slim girl went by, sometimes a fair one, sometimes an in-between type, sometimes a fuzzy-haired woman, some morning a fashionable one who had taken the trouble to tidy herself up before coming out. Most times Rangi came along also with one or the other of them, or by herself. Brisk traffic passed on the staircase. I guessed that after the challenge from the cadaver, Mempi Forest was being watched more carefully, and, his activities there neutralized, Vasu had turned his tracking instinct in another direction. I had had no notion that our town possessed such a varied supply of women.

CHAPTER SEVEN

IT TOOK ME time to make him out. His face was familiar. I had seen those slightly fin-like ears and round eyes somewhere. He stood on my threshold and brought his palms together and cried, 'Namaskaram.' On that voice, with its ring—I knew it. It was the afternoon hour. The Market Road was sleepy, a donkey was desultorily chewing an old newspaper at the fountain parapet, the black cow and its friend the free bull had curled up for a siesta right in the middle of the road, obstructing the traffic as was their wont. A couple of late schoolchildren were dawdling along the edge of the road, gazing with fascination into the gutter; a bright scalding sun was beating down; the woman sitting under the acacia selling a ripped-up jackfruit was waving a stick over its golden entrails, trying to keep off a swarm of flies; a *jutka* was rattling along on the granite metalled road; a sultry, sleepy hour. I had returned to my seat after lunch; Sastri had not yet arrived. My brain was at its lowest efficiency as I had to battle within myself to wrench myself away from a siesta. I had arrears of work to clear. I sat on the Queen Anne chair and stretched my legs on the ancient table as a compensation for forgoing my siesta.

'Come in, come in,' I said as a general courtesy to whoever it might be that said '*Namaskaram*'. He came in hesitantly, with an umbrella tucked under his arm, and lowered himself gingerly into the first chair.

'I came by the morning bus, not the one that brought you but the earlier one.'

Oh, yes, now it came like a flash. 'Oh, Muthu!' I cried, almost jumping up and hugging him. 'Whom have you left to mind the tea-shop?'

'Oh, the boys are there, they can manage it. I am returning by tonight's bus.'

'How is your business?'

'Doing very well, sir.'

'How are your children? Have you found a bridegroom for your daughter?' His face fell at the mention of it. I would normally not really have troubled him with any reminder of his daughter's marriage, but in order to cover my initial lapse I now tried to show off my knowledge of his problems. I could not be blamed for my lapse. At his tea-shop he had been bare-headed; now he had donned a white khaddar cap, a long *mull jibba* and a *dhoti*, and had a lace upper cloth over his shoulder—he had dressed himself to come to town, I suppose. I was very happy to see him. He had rescued me from Vasu that day. I had always anticipated another meeting with him at least in order to pay off the tea bill. I opened the drawer of my table and took out a rupee and held it to him. I was suddenly inspired by the lesson taught by my adjournment lawyer not to mix accounts.

He looked at the rupee with some surprise and asked, 'What is this for?'

'I have long wanted to pay you that bill for the tea and buns . . .' Even as I was speaking, I realized how silly it sounded. The lawyer had taught me a rather coarse lesson. Muthu looked rather hurt as he said, 'I have paid a bus fare of fourteen annas for coming and will pay fourteen annas for going back; do you think I am spending all that in order to collect—how much was it?'

I was abashed, but said, 'My duty, you know. Can I get you coffee or tiffin or anything?'

He shook his head. 'I never eat anywhere outside when I travel, and it keeps me fit. I like and enjoy a good meal when I go home.'

Now that all the awkwardness was gone, I asked, 'What's your command? Tell me what I can do for you.' A sudden fear assailed me lest he should ask me to go up to tell Vasu that his old friend was come. I said to test him, 'I saw Vasu go out in his jeep.'

'We see him at Mempi going up the hill now and then, but he doesn't stop to speak to us nowadays.'

I was pleased and relieved. 'What is the reason?' I asked.

'Why go into all that?' he said gently, tapping his umbrella on the floor. 'He is a man with a gun,' he said. 'Why speak of him? He doesn't care for us now.'

'He may have no more use for you,' I said, adding fuel to the fire.

'He has other people, who are more suitable to his temperament,' he said, hinting at a vast army of undesirable men, trailing behind Vasu, looking for mischief.

I didn't want to pursue the subject further. I merely said, 'He may drop them off when he finds someone more useful,' a sentiment on which we both immediately concurred. 'After all it may be for the best; it would be best to be forgotten by him and have nothing whatever to do with him,' I said, and then I tried to elaborate the statement with an account of all the happenings ever since he stepped over my threshold. I said in conclusion, 'He stood just where you stood; I welcomed him, he sat where you are sitting now. I make no distinction between men . . .'

Muthu sprang up as if he had occupied a wrong place, and said, 'I am not that kind.'

'I know, I know,' I said. 'Don't I know? You are a helpful man. You cannot see a man stranded. I know you.'

He was pleased and said, 'We helped that man so much. Now he thinks we have informed against him, and he came and created a scene at my shop and threatened us with his gun.' He laughed at the memory of it. 'As if we wouldn't know what to do, as if we would sit back and let him shoot us! We don't want to bother about him and so we leave him alone. He still passes up and down, but never stops for tea and doesn't seem to carry home much from the forests either—and he thinks we are responsible for it! Why, there are hundreds of people going up and down to the project on that road and anyone was bound to notice his activities.'

'It's all for the best if a *rakshasa* ceases to notice you,' I said and that put an end to our discussion of Vasu. I was very happy that he was no longer liked by Muthu. My enemy should be the enemy of other people too, according to age-old practice.

After all this preamble, he mentioned his business. 'You

remember our temple elephant I spoke to you about, though you couldn't see him that day? He had gone into the jungle for grazing? He's sick; and we want your help to see a doctor!'

Our doctor, Dr Rao of Town Medical Stores, how would he react to the presence of an elephant in his clinic? I said doubtfully, 'I don't know if our doctor knows enough about elephant-sickness.'

'Oh, no,' he said. 'We have heard of a Government hospital for animals recently opened. We want your help to get our Kumar treated there.'

I remained speechless—a new set of circumstances seemed to be approaching me in an enveloping movement. This was the first time I had heard of an animal hospital. I could have just said, 'I don't know anything about it,' and ended the matter there, but my nature would not permit it. I always had to get into complications. So I said, 'All right, let us see what we can do for poor Kumar. What is the matter with him?'

'He is not taking his food at all, nowadays. He shuns it.'

The enormity of the problem oppressed me. This was not something I could evade by suggesting that they looked over the Heidelberg. At the same time I felt flattered. That someone should think of me to tackle such a problem was itself an honour. I felt too proud to say that I knew nothing about elephant doctors; after all the man who had come all this way expected me to do something about it. Suppressing my astonishment at being involved, I asked, 'Is there any hurry? I mean, can't the elephant wait?'

He looked doubtful. 'I came to you because, more than

others, I knew you would be able to do something for me. You were kind enough to say I could ask you for any help. Poor Kumar, he used to be so lively, playing with all the children and now, for the last ten days, he is suffering, he accepts no food; I don't know, something is wrong with him. There is a fellow there in Top Slip, an elephant trainer, who looks after some of the elephants working in the timber yards, but he says that he cannot really judge what is the matter.'

'All right. I'll do my best. Now what are his symptoms? At least tell me that.'

'Oh.' He thought it over for a moment and said, 'He seems to get cramps—he lies down on his belly and howls. Have you ever seen an elephant lie down? I have never seen it; he has to be coaxed and cajoled to accept a ball of cooked rice.'

I felt genuinely concerned about poor Kumar now. I said, 'I'll go and meet this doctor you mentioned, and we will see what we can do. How shall I communicate with you?'

'Please drop a card, or send a note with any of the Mempi bus drivers, and I'll be here immediately.'

I noted down various details officiously. Before leaving he said, 'Nothing is more important to me than this, sir.'

I had to overlook the responsibilities on hand. Kumar's welfare became an all-important issue. The visiting cards that I was printing could wait, but not Kumar.

Later in the day I asked Sastri, 'Where is the animal hospital that was recently opened?'

'No idea,' he said. 'Lost interest in animals five years ago; after the death of my cow I vowed never to have another. I'm the first person in our whole family to buy milk from street vendors! My relations laugh at me for it.'

I inquired here and there. Two days were gone. I had the feeling of being a defaulter. As each hour and day passed I grew nervous and finally on the flash of an idea sought my friend Sen, who lived all alone in a converted garage in the compound of a house in Lawley Extension. I had to hire a cycle for this expedition. Sen was pleased to see me in his shed. He had surrounded himself with books and stacks of newspapers, which were all over the floor. He sat on a rush mat and worked by a small kerosene light.

I burst in on him at about seven in the evening. He had a sloping board on which was fixed a sheet of paper for writing. It had been a warm day, and he sat bare-bodied. He was delighted to see me. I sat on his mat.

'I can't give you coffee or anything, but, if you like, let us go to a restaurant. There is one not too far off.' He was visibly overwhelmed by my visit. He was used to visiting, but this was one of the rare occasions when he was receiving.

I said, 'I don't need coffee, thank you. I have come for some information; as a newspaper man, you'll be able to help me.' He liked to be called a newspaper man, and I hoped sincerely that some day he would see his views in print. He was always saying that he was about to secure the finances for a paper, he was on the verge of it, but something always happened, and he sat back, wrote his editorials and waited for the next financier. He was equipping himself for the task all the time. Part of his equipment was knowing what was going on in the town. I asked him about the animal hospital.

'Oh, yes, I remember something about it . . .' He frowned for a moment at all the accumulation of the past, got up, pulled down some stacks of old papers, turned them over, blowing the dust in my face. He thrust an old newspaper under my nose and tapped his finger on a news item. It gave a description of how a Deputy Minister had laid the foundation for a veterinary college and animal welfare hospital on the other bank of the Sarayu, for which ten acres of land had been gifted by the municipality; some foundation had given dollars and equipment for a start, and the Government had promised to take the hospital under its wing during the third Five-Year Plan and so on and so forth. A lengthy speech was reported in which the Deputy Minister dwelt on the importance of *ahimsa* and of animals in human economy, after which he was garlanded and made to tread the red carpet. I wondered how I had missed it.

'Do you know how you missed it?' Sen said. 'They mismanaged the whole thing. The printed invitations went out late and reached most people a day too late.'

'I wonder where they got them printed,' I said to ward off any suspicion that I might be responsible for the mess.

'The result was that no one turned up at the function except the organizers and the Deputy Minister—and he was furious. They had a platform, decorations, and an elaborate tea, but only a handful of audience; the Deputy Minister made his speech all the same. It looks dignified and impressive in print anyway,' he said fondly, looking at the printed column. 'However, the doctor is already on the scene, although little else is ready.'

Next afternoon I went in search of the animal doctor, crossing Nallappa's Grove on my cycle. It was about one o'clock and the sands were hot. A few bullock carts were crunching their wheels along the sand. The mango trees cast a soft shade and the air was thick with the scent of mango blooms. The river flowed on with a soft swish. It was so restful that I could have set my bicycle against the trunk of a tree and gone to sleep on the mud under the shade of a tree. But duty impelled me on. I cycled up the other bank across a foot-track, and suddenly came upon a bare field enclosed within barbed wire. The gate was barricaded with a couple of bamboo poles. A tablet on a bit of masonry commemorated the laying of the foundation. The south side of the barbed wire enclosure was bounded by one wall of the cremation ground, where a couple of funeral parties were busy around smoky pyres. A howling wind blew across the fields. There was a single palmyra tree standing up in the middle of this desert, although across the road, tops of green corn rippled in the air.

A signboard stood over the entrance. I left my bicycle at the gate and walked around to read, 'Department of Animal Welfare, World Q.R.L. (World Quadruped Relief League, Calif.)'. I saw the roof of a hut shining in the sky and sent a shout in that direction, 'Hi! Who is there?' I was enjoying the hunt. I shouted without any hope, expecting the Mempi hills shimmering on the horizon to echo back my call without an interruption. But 'Who is there?' a voice called back from the hut.

'I have come for the doctor,' I said.

It seemed absurd to be calling for a doctor out of empty space, but it worked. A man appeared at the door of the hut and gesticulated. He cried, 'Come along!'

'The gate is barred,' I cried.

'Come through the fence,' he called. I slipped through the fence, the barbed wire slightly gashing my forearm and tearing my *dhoti*. I swore at it, but it gave me a feeling of shedding my blood for a worthy cause.

The man stretched his hand. 'I'm Dr Joshi.'

'My name is Nataraj,' I said, as the wind howled about my ears.

Dr Joshi wore a shirt over white pants; he was a short man, with a small face and a brow knit in thought. 'Come in,' he said, and took me into the hut. A tin roof arched overhead; he had a bamboo table and a couple of folding chairs, a charpoy with a pillow, a few books in a small wooden rack, a kerosene lamp and a stove and pots and pans in a corner. Here definitely was a man with a mission. He seated me in a chair and drew the other close to me and said, 'Yes, Mr Nataraj? What can I do for you, Mr Nataraj?'

I looked around; there was very little of the hospital or dispensary or college about it. I told him about the elephant. He listened to me with the characteristic patience of a doctor and said, 'H'm, I would like to have it under observation and then I'll see what we can do.'

I had not visualized this prospect. I had thought that he would come over and examine the elephant. I suggested it. He said, 'It's impossible. The equipment for tests is here.'

'He is sick and keeps throwing himself down. How can we bring him so far?'

The problem looked frightening, but he had an absolutely simplified view. He brushed aside all my doubts and said,

'He has his mahout, hasn't he? Tell him that he must come here and prod him and prick him and make him walk. Animals, once they realize the pleasure of sitting will always sit down,' he added. 'It doesn't mean anything. It'll be our business to prod him and keep him on his feet. Unless I have him here, I shall have no means of handling him or testing him. You see there . . .' He walked over to a chest and threw it open—it was crammed with all kinds of shining instruments, tubes, bottles, and a microscope. 'This is the standard equipment that our League ships to every centre; it contains everything that a veterinarian can need, but you see, we are doing very little with it now.'

'Why so?' I asked.

'Our League provides equipment and a basic grant for a doctor like me, but the local organizations also have to do their bit. For instance the college and the hospital must be built before we can do anything.'

'When do you expect it all to be ready?'

'How can we say? The question is full of politics. People do not want it here, but somewhere else. Our Deputy Minister has no interest in the project and so it goes on at its own pace. The Public Works should give us the building and the sheds for the animals, but they are still in the stage of estimates and sanctions. I really cannot imagine when we shall start or what we can do. I alone am ready, because I'm being maintained by the League and there's a lot of equipment to guard. As matters stand, I'm just a watchman. I'm sticking on because I feel that if I leave even this will be gone. I have a hope that things will be O.K. some time. I'm not allowing things to rust, you know. All the time I'm bombarding the headquarters with letters and so forth . . .

I'm happy that you have heard about us and want our service.'

'It was in the papers,' I said knowledgeably.

'Bring your elephant over. I'll do what I can for the poor creature. I have always wanted to try my hand at an elephant.'

'What could be wrong with him?'

'Well, anything. Colic, or an intestinal twist, or he might have swallowed a sugar cane without chewing it and that sometimes causes trouble.'

'Do you know all about all animals?'

'Oh, yes, about most of them. Our League headquarters in California has one of the biggest collections of animals in the world and I went through a four-year course. Although our main job will be to treat the cattle of our country, we like to do our best for any creature. Most animals and men are alike, only the dosage of a medicine differs,' he said. He was a man completely serious, living in a world of animals and their ailments and diseases.

At Mempi the affair caused a sensation. The village elders gathered together in front of the tea-shop and a great debate started over the question of the elephant. Muthu was all for bringing the elephant over. After carrying on their discussion in front of the teashop, everybody trooped to the little temple. Lorries and cars passed by. I marched with them to the little shrine at the cross-roads; the four-armed Goddess watched our proceedings serenely from her inner sanctum. Within the yard of the temple the elephant was tied by his hind leg to a peg under a very large tree. He had flopped himself down like a dog, with his legs stretched out. His trunk lay limp on the ground; his small eyes looked at us without interest; his tail lay in the dust; his tusks seemed without lustre. Muthu patted his head and said, 'He has been like this for three days now.' He looked unhappy. A few boys stood outside the ring of elders and watched the elephant, and commented among themselves in whispers.

Everyone looked at me sourly as a man who had come to abduct their elephant and make things worse for them. I said, 'If you do not send the elephant along, what is the alternative?'

'Bring the doctor here,' said the tailor, who kept his machine next to the tea-shop and who was one of the trustees of the temple. There was a schoolmaster in their gathering who was not sure what he wanted to say but kept interrupting everyone with his reminiscences. 'There was once,' he began, 'an elephant,' and he narrated a story which was considered rather inauspicious as by the end of it the elephant had become incurably ill. 'Oh, master!' appealed Muthu. 'Should I teach a wise one like you what to speak and when, and what not to speak?' He looked sadly at the teacher.

I began afresh to outline the whole proposition by stages. 'Our main business will now be to see that the elephant Kumar gets well.' This was the only part of my statement which received universal and immediate accord. 'And so,' I began, 'what is most important is that we should see that he gets on to his feet and moves freely.' It was the same sentiment in another form; they hesitated for a moment, examined it critically, and accepted it also as one without a trap. Now I mentioned something really dangerous. 'And so he should be made to get up and move in the direction of the doctor.'

'No,' said the obstinate tailor. 'The doctor must come here. Have you no pity? How can a sick animal tramp fifty miles? It'd be cruel.' For a moment, everyone made noises of sympathy for the tailor. This brought the question back to its starting point. The tailor had won his point; he looked triumphantly obstinate, and moved away.

I felt desperate among an immobile elephant, an equally immobile doctor and a mentally immobile committee; there seemed little to do except pray for the elephant. I realized that in a committee there was likely to be no progress, and so I didn't press the point. I knew that the tailor would not go on standing there for ever; sooner or later someone would come to his shop and demand his clothes back. So Muthu and I spent the time morosely watching the recumbent elephant, suppressing the suggestions which occurred to our minds, but which we knew would be thrown out in no time. The ring of children grew smaller as they had grown bored with watching the gloomy elders and had exhausted themselves in suppressed giggles (for fear of the elders who were constantly turning to them and ordering them to shut up). There were really five on the committee of the temple, but except Muthu and the tailor the rest were men of no consequence. All they did was to simper and evade any commitment.

I had not too much time to waste today; I had come by the first bus in the morning and the last bus was leaving at six. At four o'clock there was still no sign of an agreement. I was still hoping that the tailor would be called off, and as if some customer of his had been hit by a thought-wave from me, an errand boy from the shop came up panting with the statement, 'The trouble-maker is back, and won't go until he can talk to you.'

The tailor lost his head at the mention of the trouble-maker, whoever that beneficent soul may have been. 'Has he no other business than bothering me for those miserable jackets of his wife's? This is the fifth time he has visited me!'

'Perhaps his wife has barred the house to him until he brings home the jacket,' I commented under my breath.

'Throw his pieces out. Fling his pieces in his face,' cried the irate tailor.

'But you have locked them up,' said his errand boy seriously.

'That settles it. I'll be back soon,' the tailor said and rushed out in a rage. I felt relieved, lighter in my chest. This was my chance. Now I had the committee in my pocket. I told Muthu hurriedly, 'Before my bus leaves, I must see this elephant on his feet. We will discuss the other things later.'

'But how to get him up? Kumar,' he appealed, 'please, please stand up!'

One of the stragglers, a young urchin who had been watching us with a thumb in his mouth, took out his thumb and said suddenly, 'I know how to make an elephant get up.'

'How? How? Come on, do it!' I said eagerly, pulling his hand from his mouth and propelling him forward.

He grinned, showing a toothless gum, and said: 'If you get me a frog, I can make him get up.'

'What! How will you do it?'

'When a frog is put under an elephant, it'll jump, and

the elephant will jump with it,' he said.

I was even prepared to dig a crowbar under Kumar and lever him up if necessary, but a mahout arrived at the crucial moment. He was attached to the timber yard five miles up in a mountain jungle. They had sent a desperate summons to him four days ago by a lorry-driver who passed that way, and only today had the man found time to turn up. He arrived just when we were hesitating between applying a jumping frog or a crowbar, wanting to do something before the tailor should return. The mahout wore a knitted vest and over it a red sweater and a white *dhoti* coming down to his knees, a combination calculated to strike terror into the heart of any recalcitrant elephant. He pushed his way through the ring of watching loungers, and looked us all up and down questioningly. 'Why is he lying down?' he asked.

'That is what we would like to know,' said Muthu. 'He has been like this for four days.' The mahout looked at Kumar questioningly, put his face close to the elephant's and asked, 'What is your secret?' in a soft murmur. He told us, 'Keep away. He doesn't like a big audience for his speech, you understand? Move off, and he will tell me.' We moved away. He put his face close to the large trunk of the elephant, murmuring something, and after a while we turned to look as we heard a swish proceeding from a very thin green switch in his hand, which lashed the underside of the elephant within his reach. He repeated it at intervals of a second and the elephant was on his feet. He flourished the green switch (it looked no different from any trailer of a plant), and said, 'This is . . .,' he gave us the name of some obscure plant grown in mountain thickets. 'This is more

135

serviceable than one's own brothers emanating from the same womb,' he explained. 'I have still to see an animal that does not respect this stick.' As he flourished it the elephant blinked and gave a loud trumpet. I only hoped that it would not bring the tailor scrambling in. The trumpeting was loud and prolonged.

The mahout leaned on the side of the elephant as if posing for a photograph and smiled at the gathering. He seemed to fall into a mystic trance as he drew the switch across his nose. 'Now get me a broken coconut and a little jaggery and a piece of sugar cane.'

We sent a youngster running to fetch these. While waiting for his return, the mahout leaned on the elephant and regaled us with his memoirs; he recounted the tales of all the elephants that he had coaxed and taken to the various zoos in the country and he spoke of a chance that he once had of taking an elephant to Tokyo or New York, which was frustrated by his brothers who did not like the girl he had married and wanted to punish him for not marrying according to their own arrangements. From Kerala, far-off Kerala, this mahout had brought a girl to marry, but his brothers advised him to pay off the woman and raised among themselves two hundred rupees. The mahout went up to her with the money and asked her to go back to Kerala. She quietly said, 'Keep your money, only tell me if there is any deep well or tank nearby where I can drown myself. I want you to know that I have come to you not for your money. If I can't be worthy of being your wife, I shall be quite happy to be dead at your feet, rather than go back to my village with two hundred rupees.' He explained, 'Two hundred rupees, not just two rupees, and she did not

want it. I immediately told my brothers that I did not care
for them, told them to do their worst and married the girl.
You think that I married her on the money from them? Not
me. I returned it to them. I actually threw it out of the door
and told them to pick it up, and borrowed a hundred rupees
on which I am still paying interest of five rupees a month,
and married her. Such a wonderful woman. She won't eat
her food unless I am back home, even if it is midnight.
What can I do? Sometimes I have to be out for days and
days, and what does she do? She starves, that is all,' he said,
and added, 'A dutiful wife.'

He never finished his narrative to tell us how it prevented
his going to Tokyo or New York, for at this moment the
elephant coiled his trunk around his back, and he patted it
and said, 'Now we are friends, he wants me to sit on his
back.' He tapped the elephant's knee, and took hold of its
ear, and pulled himself up even as he was talking. By this
time the youngster had brought the coconut and jaggery.
The mahout stooped down to take them, and held them out
to the elephant, saying something. The elephant just picked
up the bamboo tray, raised it and sent it flying across the
field. Muthu was crestfallen, 'See, that's what he does to
food!'

'Never mind,' said the mahout. 'He is not hungry, that
is all. I would myself fling the dinner plate at my wife's face
if I did not feel hungry and she persisted. Now I am ready,
where is he to go?'

'Ride him to the town,' I said promptly. 'I will meet you
at the toll-gate outside the city.' And before we knew what
was happening, he had flourished his green switch and was
off, all of us trooping along behind. All the children let out

a shout of joy and ran behind the elephant. I was not very happy about the amount of public notice the whole business was receiving. It might stir the tailor up once again. Muthu walked with a look of triumph beside the elephant. I felt triumphant too in a measure.

To put our ideas in proper perspective the mahout leaned down to say, 'Because he is trotting don't imagine he is not ill. He is very sick. I have my own medicine for his sickness, but you want to see an English doctor; try him and come back to me. I never stand in anybody's way of doing something, although I know what English doctors can do. They will sooner or later call me . . .'

This made Muthu once again thoughtful. He suddenly remembered that he had come out without thanking the Goddess. He ran back to the temple, lit a piece of camphor before the Goddess and rejoined the procession. At the Market Road, when the procession passed in front of the tea-shop, he invited the mahout to stop for a moment, and ran into his shop.

The mahout said, 'If you can, reach me a glass of tea here, otherwise I can't get down. If I get down, Kumar will also sit down immediately, that is his nature.' Kumar seemed to understand this, I could detect a twinkle in his small red eyes, and he swayed his head in appreciation. Muthu brought out a tray covered with buns and a tumbler of tea, and held it to the mahout. The flies that swarmed in his shop sought a diversion by settling in a mass on the back of the elephant for a ride. The mahout sat comfortably in his seat, set the tray before him and started to drink his tea. And now the tailor came flouncing out of his shop, demanding, 'Everyone get out of the way and tell me what is happening.'

The mahout thought the remark beneath his notice and looked down from his eminence with indifference. This irritated the tailor. He repeated, 'This is our elephant. Where are you taking him?' The tailor's sense of ownership was comical, and everyone laughed. Muthu, who had gone back to his seat at the counter, now said, 'He knows how to handle the elephant, don't worry. He is taking it out for its own good.'

'What? To the city? I will never have it, never, never . . .' He stamped his feet like a petulant child.

The mahout was confused. He looked puzzled and asked, tying a towel around his head as a turban, 'What does it mean? Am I stealing an elephant?'

Muthu came out of his shop, put his arm around the tailor, and said, 'Come and have tea,' and managed to say at the same time to the mahout, 'Yes, yes, you go, it is getting late, remember where you will be met . . . We will look to other things.'

The mahout flourished his green switch ever so gently and the elephant was on the move again, with the trail of children behind it. Soon his green turban vanished from the landscape around a bend.

The tailor was disconsolate until Muthu poured oblatory tea into him, unwashed glass after unwashed glass. 'At this rate,' I said to myself, 'Muthu will be a bankrupt, if he has to treat all his elephant associates to tea. He will close down his business, and then who will pay for the elephant doctor at the other end?'

I sat on the plank bridging two empty kerosene tins in front of Muthu's shop, watching the scene with detachment. Now that the elephant was gone, a big worry was off my mind. I didn't care what the tailor thought or said. Refreshed by tea and buns, he came out of the shop, wiping his mouth with the sleeve of his shirt, and passed me without a word. But his look, the brief one that he cast in my direction, was enough to indicate what he thought of me—an abductor of elephants. He was soon out of view in his own shop four doors off. I could hear him say to someone, 'Take away those pieces if you cannot wait. I promised you the jackets only at the end of this week.'

I could not hear the rest of his sentence as the dreaded jeep drew up in front of me on the road. Vasu had come down the hill. He looked at me from his seat and said, 'Coming along? I am going back to the town.'

I hesitated for a moment. The bus had been due any time the last ninety minutes. Still there was no sign of it. But how could I go with this man? We were facing each other for the first time after months. I didn't like to tell him about myself or my mission here. I would be at his mercy if I climbed into his jeep. I said, 'I am not coming back yet.'

'Why not?' he asked persistently. 'What do you want here? You want to spend the night here?'

He was blocking the road; a lorry was trying to pass, the driver sounding his horn impatiently. Vasu merely waved his arm, 'You have enough clearance, get along.'

'There is a ditch.'

'All right, get into the ditch. Don't disturb me now. Don't you see that I am talking to a gentleman?'

The lorry-driver edged close to the drain and passed. Vasu said to me, 'I will take you back home.'

'You may go,' I said.

He indicated the back seat. 'I have nothing there today.

I knew that you would swoon at the sight of a dead creature. That is why I came without any today.'

How did he know my movements? Perhaps he had been watching me all the time. In any case I did not like to talk to him about it. I merely said, 'I have another conveyance. You may go, thank you.'

'What other conveyance?' he persisted. 'Your bus has broken down at the tenth mile up, axle gone. Men, women and children are sitting by the roadside. They will have to be there until . . . I don't know. If anyone has a gun there he may shoot a tiger or a rogue elephant that may prowl around tonight. If you are keen on catching the bus, I will take you there and leave you with that crowd.'

I wondered for a moment if there might be truth in his report. As I hesitated he commanded, 'What are you waiting for? If you want to spend the night with that tea-shop crowd, go ahead, please yourself. I have things to do, if you don't mind,' he said cynically.

He had irritated me at first, but I suddenly realized that this was a good chance to establish contact with him again. He spurned me and picked me up again as it suited his fancy: this was a galling thought no doubt, but it was better than being continuously ignored. So I climbed into the jeep without a word. He drove off. We remained without speaking for some time; he drove at his usual reckless speed, swearing at bullock carts, threatening to smash them up and calling insults at passers-by. He was disappointed when they accepted his bullying unprotestingly, but when one or other of the cartmen turned round with a frown or a swear-word, he was delighted, and he nudged me and confided, 'That is how I like to see my countrymen. They must show better spirit; they are spineless; no wonder our country has been a prey to every invader who passed this way.'

I could not accept his view, and so I asked, 'Do you want everyone to be a blustering bully in this country?'

'Yes,' he said simply. He was in an extraordinarily good humour. I wished he would continue thus. It was becoming dark and the lights were on in the homesteads on the way. He said, 'How busy are you nowadays?'

'Well, the usual quantity of work.'

'And the usual quantity of gossip-mongering?'

'What do you mean?' I asked rather sharply.

'No offence, no offence,' he said with mock humility. 'Just my fun, that is all. I meant those chair fixtures in your press.'

'Why can't you leave them alone?' I asked. 'They hardly ever think of you; why should you bother about them?'

'No offence meant, no offence meant,' he said with a great display of humility. 'I just wanted to know. I am their well-wisher, and I just wanted to know how they are faring, that is all.'

'Look here, Vasu,' I said, with a sudden access of foolhardiness, 'you should leave others alone; it will make for happiness all round.'

'I can't agree with you,' he said. 'We are not lone dwellers in the Sahara to live self-centred lives. We are members of a society, and there is no point in living like a recluse, shutting oneself away from all the people around.'

There was no use arguing with him. I once again became aware of my mounting irritation and wanted to guard against it. I said, moderating my tone, 'After all the poet has done a remarkable performance with his life of Krishna. He is completing *Radha Kalyan*, that is the marriage of Krishna with Radha, and his book will be out soon.'

'H'm,' Vasu said with a half-interest, 'and what about the other?' He was referring to his favourite target, the journalist.

'Well,' I said, with considerable pride, 'his plans are almost ready for starting a small news-sheet in this town; he is already issuing printed manifestos.'

He remained thoughtful for a moment and said, 'I like people to do something, whatever it may be.'

So the journalist and poet had secured this man's approval, I reflected. I wanted to tell him, but could not, that it was impertinence on his part to think that the world waited for his approval. He was pleased to think that humanity could move only after securing a clearance certificate from him. There was no use arguing with him as he was one of those strong men who had no doubt at all about their own conclusions. He asked suddenly, 'I want to know if you are willing to print a book I am writing. I have been busy with it for some weeks now.'

'Aha!' I cried unable to restrain myself. It was unthinkable that he could be busy with a literary composition. He brightened up on hearing my interest and said, 'It is a monograph on wild life. Every day our papers are full of speeches and meetings on the problem of preserving wild life, and most people don't know what they are talking about. I have some very important points to make on the subject. What has happened in this country is that amateurs have invaded every field. People just talk their heads off. I have made many important points in my

book, and I want it to be ready for the conference on wild
life at the end of this year.'

'But that conference will be for the preservation of wild
life?' I asked.

'What if it is? My book is also about better methods of
preserving wild life. This cannot be achieved by refusing
game licences to honest folk, or by running behind animals
with cries of sympathy.'

I restrained my interest. I did not want to get involved
in his affairs again. I dreaded the prospect of having him
again in my parlour, sharpening his wits against the poet
and my other visitors. I maintained my reserve and silence
for the rest of the journey as the jeep sped along the dark
highway.

CHAPTER EIGHT

THE POET WAS in a grand exalted mood. He had completed the portion of his poem where Krishna meets his future wife Radha, and their marriage is to be celebrated. He had written off several hundred lines of crystal-clear monosyllables; he had evolved his own prosody and had succeeded. His manuscript was ready, several little exercise books stitched by himself and wrapped in brown paper, closely filled with writing in green ink. He had written till late on the previous night. His eyes were red with sleeplessness, but his face glowed with triumph. With the marriage, the book would make about ninety-six pages. Sastri had printed the book at the rate of four pages a month over a space of countless months and it had now assumed the shape of a volume. Sastri himself was excited at the completion of the volume with the marriage episode. He brought in the proofs of some pages, and hesitated for a moment. When Sastri stood thus I always knew he had something to say, and I hoped that if I did not turn round and meet his eyes he would be gone. As I bent over my paper, I was aware of his shadow behind me. 'What is it,

Sastri?' I asked sharply. He looked at the poet and both of them smiled. So I knew it was a good piece of news, and felt relieved. 'When a poet has arrived at the stage of the marriage of a god, it would be auspicious to celebrate the occasion.' He went on to explain how the celebration was to be conducted. I was fond of the poet and anything that was going to give him a place in our society was welcome to me.

Enormous preparations began. Once again, my normal work of composing and printing was pushed to the background. The fruit juice man had prospered more than ever and wanted four thousand more of the three-colour labels, but I was not prepared to give him his labels yet. I had only time to print the first basic grey. I put it away to dry and said so every time the messenger came from Fruit Juice. Let him try and print it elsewhere and I should not object. But where would he get the magenta, that thirst-creating shade which drew people in a rush to wherever his bottles were displayed? The sixth time when I turned back the boy, K.J. himself came thundering in, and shouted at Sastri beyond the curtain. He did not know I was also there, helping Sastri to compose an appeal for our celebrations, for which we needed funds. We were also in conference with an astrologer in the composing room. We did not want to be disturbed. There now hung a thickly-woven bamboo mat which screened us off from whatever might be on the other side of the grille. Vasu might have all the dead animals in creation on the other side, but it was not going to affect us. All the prostitutes in the town might be marching up and down the steps, but that was not going to distract either me or Sastri. We could hear footsteps moving, but that didn't distract our attention. We went on with our jobs, although if I felt too curious I could always peer through a pin-hole in the bamboo curtain and get a lovely circular vision of a hyena's snout or the legs of some woman or the hefty feet of Vasu himself stumping upstairs. But it was a luxury I permitted myself only under very special or extraordinary conditions, never when Sastri was around, as I did not want him to get into the habit. I don't think he even knew of the existence of the peep-hole.

The astrologer was sitting on the floor beside the treadle. He had a page of an almanac open before him, held far away at arm's length for better focus, and was explaining, 'On the full moon, the moon is in the sixth house, which is the best place we can have for the moon, and the presiding star that day is . . ., which means—' he shrunk his eyes to catch the figure in the column and muttered, 'I've left my glasses at home,' whereupon Sastri took his own glasses off his nose and handed them to him. He put them on and said, 'You see this here . . . What's the number?' It was now Sastri's turn to snatch the almanac from the other man's hand and hold it at arm's length. Still not being able to see, he held his hand out for the glasses, which the other removed from his nose and handed back. Now Sastri saw the number and said something, and the other, wanting to verify it, held his hand out and thus they bandied Sastri's silver-rimmed glasses back and forth. The conference proceeded on these lines—I'd not much to do, a veritable ignoramus among the stars. The idea was to fix a day suitable to the poet, also coinciding with the spring festival at the Krishna temple.

A loud voice called through the curtain, 'Sastri!' I was

offended by the commanding tone. I signalled to Sastri to
find out who it was, but before Sastri could take a step
forward the voice continued, 'Are you delivering the labels
or not? If you can't, say so, instead of making our boy run
to you a dozen times.' Now I knew who it was. He went
on in a big way cataloguing his grievances, our lapses, and
threatening us with dire consequences. Sastri and the
astrologer looked intimidated. I could notice on Sastri's face
a slight satisfaction too at the realization that I had not
heeded his warning.

It was time for me to show myself. I said, 'Who is it?
Is it K.J.?'

There was a pause and the man said from the other side
of the curtain, 'Mr Nataraj, you are letting me down. How
can you expect us to deliver our bottles when . . .'

I could have spoken for him. I knew all his points. So
I cut him short with, 'Why don't you take a seat, my friend?
I'll be with you in a minute.' I had hesitated for a moment
whether I should tell him to come through the curtain as a
special gesture, but abandoned the idea for fear it might
create a bad precedent. People respected the curtain, and it
was better so. Vasu alone had pierced its privacy and this
had turned out to be a nuisance in every way. I did not
want it to happen again, and so I said to the angry fruit-
juice seller, 'Sit down comfortably in that big chair, and I'll
join you in a moment.'

He made no reply. A silence ensued and I heard the
movement of a chair and guessed he must have acted on my
advice in a mood of sullen compliance. I allowed him to
wait, giving him time to cool off. We resumed our conference
with the astrologer, who sat carrying on his investigation

among the planets, unruffled by the happenings round him. After half an hour's silent calculations, with Sastri's spectacles perched over his nose, the man lifted his head slightly but would not yet speak. He behaved like one still in a trance. I knew that the man in the other room was impatient. He was kicking the floor and clearing his throat in order to attract my attention. I felt satisfied that I had cowed him. The astrologer sat beside the treadle and still said nothing. Sastri stood respectfully looking down at him. I asked, 'What are we waiting for?' The astrologer merely looked up. The visitor in the other room again cleared his throat. Sastri said, 'He may take another fifteen minutes.' I thought it would be best to dispose of the visitor. I passed through the curtain.

The drink-seller sat cross-legged in the Queen Anne chair, his sandals abandoned on the floor under the chair. He was an old-type orthodox, who wore a red caste-mark on his forehead. It was clear that he was there to see this thing through and to have it out with me. Initiative was half the victory in a battle, and so before he could open his mouth I remarked, wearing a look of grievance, 'What's the use of my friends losing their temper here? I never delay anyone's business without a reason.'

'What's it this time?' K.J. asked cynically, and added, 'Blocks not ready? Ink not available? That's why I made sure of sending with my order that can of ink which I got from Madras.'

'And your can of ink is perfectly safe here,' I said, producing it out of my drawer. I turned the can in my hand, scrutinized the label and gave it to him. 'This is unsuitable. If I had used it, people would have run away from your bottles. Do you know what it looks like when it dries? It assumes the pink of an old paper kite picked out of a gutter.'

'I got it from Madras, the same brand as you suggested.'

'But I use only the imported variety. This is canned in Delhi, did you know that?'

This was good, as it made K.J. look so ignorant, wrong, and presumptuous that he remained dumb. I said, 'I wouldn't use stuff like this on your work even if you forced me at the point of a gun. I have my responsibility.'

He asked like a child, 'So what shall we do about it now?'

'Well, I won't let you down, an old valued customer. If you have trust in me, I'll never let you down,' I said as if I were a god speaking to a sinner. 'Sastri!' I shouted. 'Please bring that magenta ink.' Turning to K.J. I said, 'You can see the difference for yourself . . .'

There was some vague movement of response inside the curtain. I knew Sastri would not pay any attention to my call unless I called him again. K.J. grew interested and asked, 'Is Sastri in?'

'Why?' I asked.

'He never answered, although I called him.'

'He is a very busy man,' I said. 'He carries a hundred things in his head.'

'Except my work, I suppose,' K.J. said with a sort of grim humour.

'Don't blame him. He has a hundred different things to do.'

'May I know the nature of his hundred activities?'

I could easily have snubbed him, but I said quietly, 'A

poet is going to be launched on the world soon, and he is busy with the arrangements connected with it.' I realized that in the last resort truth was more convincing and effective than any fabricated excuse.

K.J. looked stunned on hearing it, and asked, 'Does it mean that nothing has been done about our labels?'

'Yes,' I said, 'the main reason being that we could not use your ink and had to wait for our usual brand. The other reason was that this poet's business came up suddenly. We are in search of a good day for the function; as soon as the date is settled, we'll approach you. It's a good cause for which everyone should do his best.'

'How? How? What do you expect me to do? Give money?'

'Yes, that'd be best, but we leave it to you. The only thing is that a good man like you must share the honour with us in doing this noble task; in what way, we leave it to you.'

He was afraid to ask further questions for fear of involvement, but still he was curious to know. 'How am I concerned? What do you want me to do?' he asked.

I could see that he was scared. He was not one who gave a donation cheerfully, or mustered the courage to say so straightaway. He was an in-between type. So I said, 'Some people give a hundred rupees, some have promised to give more. How can anyone set a limit on these things?'

He mumbled faintly, 'A hundred rupees! I'm not so big, sir . . .'

'What is a hundred rupees to you?' I asked. 'You make it every hour. Don't I know how you sell?'

He looked forlorn. He felt sorry that he had walked

151

into this trap, and wished that he hadn't ventured out of his orbit. He looked as if he were facing the Income Tax Commissioner.

'No compulsion, no compulsion,' I said. 'Whatever is given must be given out of free will, otherwise the money will be worth nothing. Another thing, even in accepting donations we are selective. We don't care to take money from all and sundry. Money is not our main consideration. I mentioned the matter to you because your name is first in our list, and you came just when we were discussing you.'

He began to fidget in his seat: he was eager to get up and get out of sight. I was unwilling to let him go. I practically held him down and enjoyed it immensely. I said, 'What do you propose to do for us? It's always easy to adjust these things, and I'd hate to trouble you unnecessarily. What exactly would you like to do for us?'

'I'm very busy just now. I am going round organizing our sales in the surrounding country, where we are facing a certain amount of competition. A host of imitators have come into the field . . .'

'It's perfectly all right. We are not suggesting that you should disturb yourself. All we want is encouragement from people like you. After all you are an important citizen of this town, and we feel honoured when people like you are associated with us.' I laid it on thicker and thicker till he became panic-stricken. He got up suddenly and dashed out, muttering that he would see me again.

After he was gone the astrologer and Sastri emerged from their seclusion. The astrologer clutched a sheet of paper and the open page of his almanac in his right hand, and in his left dangled Sastri's silver spectacles. 'I have a date for you . . . No, actually I have three dates: good, not so good, and half-good,' he said. 'You may make your choice according to your convenience. Each man should choose what is convenient.'

The good date was five months hence; the poet would never survive such a delay. I knew him. He was impatient to launch his work within the next twenty-four hours. We rejected the half-good date, so there remained only the not-so-good day, which was four weeks hence, when the full moon came up a second time over the municipal tower and, more important, coincided with the festival at the temple. The astrologer said, 'This is as good a date as the best one, but do you know why it's classed not so good? You see, there is a slight aspecting of Jupiter, and the poet's ruling star is . . ., and it might not prove so beneficial after all. Jupiter's aspects remain for four and a half hours; that will be until 5.25, and it may mean a slight setback in one's efforts, that's all.'

'What sort of a setback?' I asked, rather worried.

'Well, it's hard to describe. It may be nothing more serious than a stubbed toe. Or the milk kept for coffee may turn sour. Are you going to give coffee for all the guests that day?'

'Certainly not,' I said.

He was wondering how he should describe the impending setback. 'Or the water in the tap might suddenly stop flowing.'

'Or flow into K.J.'s bottles a little too much,' I said. 'K.J. was here and he may probably offer to serve drinks to all the visitors and fill up his bottles with just water and nothing more.'

'Oh, that's possible,' the astrologer echoed. 'Or anything else in a general way.'

Sastri now interpreted, 'You see in astrology anything is a setback. If a fly settles on your nose at a crucial moment and annoys you, you may treat it as one astrological setback worked off.' He laughed, and the astrologer laughed, and both of them said more or less simultaneously, 'When it comes, it comes; when it goes, it goes; but it is useful to know ahead approximately.' 'Or the ink in the pen may not flow,' added the astrologer. 'Or it may be . . .' They were now at the game of drawing up a list of minor annoyances. The list grew. Jupiter's aspecting seemed to bring about a set of minor worries. The astrologer probably felt that he was belittling the planet too much, and suddenly drew himself up to explain, 'He could be very vicious, left to himself—bring enough harm to a man's life itself or to his limbs; but when the presiding planet is Saturn, he yields place to him. You understand me? Saturn has more powers, although Saturn will not actually interfere with Jupiter's activities.'

I had to send people to be served by Heidelberg, as neither myself nor Sastri had any leisure to attend to our profession. I sent my printing customers in a steady stream next door. Sastri and I had a hundred things to do, morning till night. I kept walking in and out of my office. I saw very little of my wife and child. I went home for dinner late every night. We printed appeals for donations in the form of a letter, setting forth our cultural heritage and so forth. We had to gear up our press to compose the final forms in readiness for the great day. I went out to meet the townfolk and get their subscriptions for our function, by no means an easy job as everyone of our citizens had the same temperament as K.J.—affluent, afraid to reject an appeal, but unwilling to open the purse. We needed a lot of money. We were planning an elaborate ritual, a procession, and a feast for a thousand. A few of the people we approached asked point blank why we wanted to do anything at all if we had no money in hand—a reasonable question, but we did not contemplate a retreat. We had to keep going on, and the city was flooded with my notice. Sen was good enough to compose it for me. He wrote a few hundred words, beginning with the origin of the world; then he went on to the writer's duty to society, the greatness of the tale of Krishna and our cultural traditions, the merits of monosyllabic verse, concluding with some spicy remarks on the Nehru government's attitude to creative writing. These were totally erased by Sastri himself before he set up type. 'Let Sen write a separate book on Nehru, if he chooses. Why should he try to display his wisdom at our cost?'

Our appeals were scattered far and wide and its effect was to draw Vasu into our fold again. He caught me late one evening as I was opening the door of my press in order to pass through to the back door. His jeep stopped at my door and he followed me in. I hadn't even switched on the lights. I was for passing straight in. He followed, asking, 'Are you in a hurry?'

'Yes . . . I'm . . .'

'Then slow up. Such frenzy will do your heart no good. Slow down, or slow up. Why stand in the dark and talk? Switch on the light. Where is the switch?' He fumbled along the wall and found the switch. He sat in his usual chair and ordered me to be seated too.

I said, 'I'm hungry, I've to go in and have my dinner.'

'I too am hungry,' he said. 'You are not the only man who eats, are you?'

I sat down reluctantly on the edge of my table. 'Well, what is it?' I asked.

'Look, Nataraj, I'm trying to be good to you. Don't be naughty. I don't like anyone to talk to me in that tone.'

'Can't we meet some time tomorrow? I am very tired, that's all,' I said.

'What has tired you? Being a busybody? Do you think I don't know what's going on?'

'What do you know?'

He produced one of our notices from his pocket and flourished it. 'I'm as good a citizen as any, and even if you don't send me one I can always get one. You print it right under my floor (I winced at his expression 'my floor') and yet no one has the courtesy to send me a copy! Strange world!'

I had no answer. While we had posted several hundred envelopes, I had deliberately avoided sending him one. Though our cold relationship was slightly improved, I could not bring myself to send him an invitation. There was an uneasy thought at the back of my mind that something might go wrong if this gunman was called in. But he was not the kind who would wait to be called. I merely said, 'I knew you would get it, and so I did not think it was particularly . . .'

'Important?' he said while I was fumbling for an expression. 'Why? Did you think I'd not be good enough to

156

give you money, that I have no money?' This was really crushing. Why was he trying to have a fight with me?

'Do you want to find a reason for a fight with me?' I asked.

He said, 'I'm not going to fight with anyone. If I had to fight, there'd be no half measures and it would not be at all good for the man who asked for it. You want to fight?' he asked solicitously as if he were asking, 'Would you like to wash or take a cup of coffee?'

I adopted diplomacy and said, 'I thought of coming to you late, because I knew you would be here.'

'That's better,' he said. 'Now you sound better. H'm. I had no notion that the poet had gone so far. A hard-working fellow!' he added with a sort of appreciation. He took out his purse and held out to me a ten-rupee note, holding it carelessly at the tips of his fingers. 'Well, this is my contribution, although you wouldn't ask for it.'

I stared at the note uncomprehendingly for a while and then said, 'Is this all? I was going to ask you for a hundred.'

'A hundred! H'm, that's interesting. If my business were as good as it used to be . . . Those bastards are trying to lock away the animals, very unhelpful,' he said, thinking of the big army of forest guards. 'Still, they can't put me down, you know. It only makes my business a little complicated, that is all. Who are they to tell me how to shoot or when!'

'You are right in a way,' I said in order to sound agreeable, without bothering to think what I meant— without thinking of the river of animal blood which would have flowed if he had had his way.

He looked at me for a moment. 'Nataraj! You really

think so? I don't really need anybody's support or encouragement. I can get on very well by myself.' The ten-rupee note still fluttered at his fingers' ends. 'Well, do you want this or not?' he asked with sudden aggressiveness.

My mood began to match his. 'I said I want a hundred from you, not less.'

'Okay,' he said and put the money back into his pocket. 'Now you can tell me how much you have collected in one hundred rupees.'

It was a challenge and I said, 'So far I have got fifty donors of the hundred-rupee class.' That made him thoughtful.

'So! Five thousand rupees! How much of it is in your hands?'

That was a point. I said, 'I don't want to take it yet. Nearer the time of the function. Why should we burden ourselves with the custody of so much cash?'

He made a sound of deprecation with his tongue and said, 'Such a lot of cash! After all it's five thousand rupees, not five lakhs!'

'It is big enough from our point of view,' I said, 'Someone else's money is always a burden to carry.'

'That's an unphilosophical way of looking at things. Money is only a medium of exchange and has no value by itself, and there can be no such thing as your money and my money. It's like the air, common to mankind.'

'Then why not let me take your purse?'

'Why not indeed!' He took it out of his pocket and dropped it on my lap, rose, strode away to his jeep, and drove off. I sat transfixed. It was a large, well-stuffed purse, the size of a lady's handbag. I sat for a while wondering what to do with it. I couldn't guess where he was gone. I had never expected that I would be charged with the custody of the man's purse. Its flap was buttoned with an old-type metal head which could be pressed in. If you applied your thumb in the gap under the flap and lifted your finger, the flap snapped open. It had several compartments. It was stuffed with letters and currency. There was a photograph, plastic-covered, of a brawny young man with wavy hair standing up like a halo ear to ear, and bushy eyebrows. If you scrutinized it for a few minutes, you could easily recognize the face—Vasu at eighteen or twenty; you could recognize him by his bull-neck. There was a larger side-flap into which were stuffed currency, some letters, bills to be paid, and one letter in a blue envelope. The colour blue always aroused my curiosity. I pulled it out, toyed with the idea of going through it, but put it back. I lacked the courage to read it. If he came back suddenly and caught me reading, he might perhaps break my spine or hold me upside down and rattle my teeth out of my skull. I also wanted to know urgently how much money he had in his purse and what were the unpaid bills standing in his name, but I lacked the courage to undertake the research now. I folded back the purse, pressed down the metal buttons, and put it carefully in my drawer and locked it. I shut the front door and went in for the night.

Three days later Vasu came to claim his purse. He peeped into my roll-top desk when I was looking through a list of persons who had promised us funds, snatched the list from my hand, glanced through it, and asked, 'How much money do you expect to collect?' I opened a green folder in which all the papers relating to accounts, receipts and cash already collected were kept. I examined the account and mentioned a figure. 'Give it here,' he said, snatching away the green folder too. 'I will double it for you. You mind the other things.'

I stammered, 'But . . . but . . .' and stretched my hand out for the folder. He pushed away my hand. 'Leave this to me, and attend to other matters.' I tried to argue with him, but he didn't stop to hear me. He walked briskly to his jeep and drove away.

A week later he came into my office with a triumphant look. He flourished the green folder and asked, 'Can you guess how much I have managed to get out of all the tight-fists in your town?' I mentioned a figure. He said, 'You are wrong. Try again,' and went away.

After that, during my round of visits I met people who remarked, 'What a money-gatherer you have engaged! One will have to sell the vessels in the kitchen and find the money, only to be rid of him! What a specimen!' There could be no doubt that he was extremely active.

I had to know exactly what he was up to. I waited patiently. When he came in one afternoon I asked him straightaway, 'Where is the green folder?'

'It is locked up in an iron safe,' he replied.

I ceremoniously showed him the Queen Anne seat, and began, 'We are all grateful to you for your help. You know a poet is . . .'

'Oh, no!' he cried. 'I can't stand all this thanksgiving rigmarole.'

'You are doing so much,' I said ignoring the insult. 'Part of the collections will be utilized for expenses connected with the festival, and then whatever is left over . . .'

'Why do you tell me all this?' he snapped.

I said, 'We need funds now for making a few advance payments.'

He thundered, 'So what?' He cooled suddenly and asked, 'How much do you want anyway?'

'At least five hundred rupees,' I said.

'All right, you shall have it.' He made no movement to fulfil his promise.

I asked, 'When? When shall we . . .?' He was trying to swat flies with a piece of cardboard.

He said, 'Why do you let these flies swarm here? Have you stored sweets in your desk for your favourite poet?'

'It is important we should know how much you have been able to collect and from whom,' I said firmly.

'All in proper time,' he said. 'Meanwhile, observe proper manners, keep your expenses down. Don't imagine you are millionaires!' He rose abruptly, glared at me for a moment, and was off.

CHAPTER NINE

WE WERE A grim and silent trio that night. I had never worked harder as a printer. Details connected with the celebration had kept us so busy that I had had to neglect the most important item—the book to be dedicated on the day of the spring festival at the temple. I had to have at least one copy of the first volume ready in a special binding of hand-woven cloth. We still had a thousand lines of verse to be printed to bring it up to the end of the marriage of God Krishna with Radha. The poet had given us the last instalment of the manuscript weeks before, but it had lain in storage. I found no time even to open the cover. The poet was patient. He could not hustle me as this was practically a free service I was doing. He had always said that if the whole of it could not be got ready, they could always make use of the manuscript for the ceremony. But it was a matter of prestige for me as a printer to get through it and have at least one bound copy ready.

So we were working on this desperately tonight—myself, Sastri, and the poet: Sastri to compose each page, the poet to pass the proof, and I to print off the page as it came through. We had between us a large flask of coffee. We were weary and tired. All speech between us had ceased. During the earlier part of the night we had discussed the various aspects of the function and cracked a few jokes, but an hour before midnight we were irritated by each other's presence. My legs ached, my eyes smarted and I longed for bed. There were moments when I wondered why I had involved myself in all this, when I could have spent the time profitably printing K.J.'s fruit-juice labels. The poet sat in the Queen Anne chair and nodded; the sight of him provoked wild thoughts; I felt like flinging a tumbler of cold water over his head; I felt furious at seeing him nod, as I sat in the chair opposite him. 'We are doing all this for your sake. How dare you sleep?' was my thought. And I took a pleasure in shouting in his ear, 'Here, should it be— or—?' a doubt, a query, any excuse to pull him out of sleep. Looking at his mild face one would never imagine that he was a fanatic, but he was an implacable foe of all disyllables, and this drove him to attack and pulverize polysyllables so that they might fit into his scheme. A new syntax had grown from this, which caused Sastri endless headaches. Every few minutes Sastri called out to me from the composing room to clear his doubts and I in my turn prodded the poet to give me an answer. Strange problems faced us. The poet had used too many K's and R's in his composition, and the available poundage of K and R in our type-board was consumed within the first twenty lines; I had to ask him whether he could not use some other letters in order to facilitate our work. Sometimes he was obliging and sometimes he refused point blank. At these moments we managed to put in a star in place of K or R and continue.

Whenever he saw a star, the poet went mad and asked, 'What does it mean?' I answered pugnaciously, 'Don't worry, we will take care of it while printing. Otherwise we may add a footnote to readers to say that whenever they see a star . . .' All this upset the poet very much, and kept him awake.

When I threw on the poet's lap a particular complicated, star-filled galley, I watched him from my chair with calm satisfaction for a while. I always told him, every time, monotonously repeating myself, 'Proof-correcting is like child-bearing. It is to be performed by you and you alone; no one else can step in and help you,' and I sat down and rested my neck on the high back of the Queen Anne chair and watched him. He was a man of few words, probably because most expressions are polysyllabic, and he just glanced at me and got absorbed in proof-correcting. He held between his fingers a very small, white-handled pencil, and often nibbled its tip and brushed it against his cheek. The sight somehow annoyed me and made me say, 'Is your cheek a pencil-sharpener?'

'I do that whenever I think.'

'Stop thinking when you correct a proof. Let only your eye watch the word, letter, punctuation. If you start thinking, we shall have to go on with corrections and proofs till eternity.' I suddenly felt that I sounded like Vasu, and added softly, 'If we had had more time I would not have minded anything, you know.'

'That's why I said . . .' he began and I cut him short with, 'Let's not waste the midnight hour. Go on, go on with

the proof. Only when you have passed it can I print it.'
Watching him working under the twenty-five-watt bulb, my
eyes swam. I ceased to notice anything. A radiant light
gathered around him and isolated him as if he were within
an illuminated capsule or cocoon. His frayed *jibba* and
dhoti, and the silly jute bag on his lap in which he carried
his papers, were no longer there; they became smudgy and
vague. I could see only his face—unshaven (he was saving
up a blade for the great day); the light fell on his nose-tip
and the rest receded in shadow.

The policeman's whistle sounded far off somewhere,
and everything conduced to a dopy state of mind. I felt light
and floated and sank into sleep, forgetting everything for
the moment—Sastri, the temple, the poet, the celebrations,
and the funds locked up with Vasu, the pipe and drum, the
feeding arrangements and garlands. Like a dagger-jab, I
heard the words, 'Shall I stop with this line on this page?'
Sastri stood over me and bellowed his question, and all the
fine fabric of my oblivion was completely torn and messed
up. Evidently Sastri got jealous when he saw me asleep and
invented a doubt in order to pull me out of it.

Then it was Sastri's turn to seek a corner chair. He
arranged it perfectly; after turning a chair to face the wall,
he curled up in it. His deliberate preparations to sleep upset
me, but I could do nothing about it, as he had an
unchallenged right to doze. It was my turn to work, for
until I printed off the formes he had no types left to
compose; for the poet's work had swallowed up all the
contents of the type-case and left them blank. Until I
released the types there was nothing for Sastri to do but
sleep, and of course the poet was entitled to sleep because

until Sastri gave him a galley . . . I wished I could make them do something instead of letting them sleep, but my devilish brain was too dead at this hour to devise anything, and so I stuck the types on the treadle, adjusted, and operated the pedal. I could hear them snore in the other room beyond the curtain, but there was nothing I could do about it. Perhaps I might have splashed a bucket of water over them, had I felt able even to contemplate the lifting of a loaded bucket. The sound of the treadle parts came in a series, *chug*, *gluck*, *pat* and *tap*. I was trying to classify their sounds. I poured out a little coffee in the thermos lid, and paused ever so slightly to sip it.

Now over the *chug*, *gluck*, *pat* and *tap* I heard a new sound: a repeated tap on the grille that separated me from Vasu's staircase. I hoped that the stuffed hyena had not come to life. I tried to ignore it and go on with my printing. *Tap*, *tap*, on the steel mesh. I applied my eye to the private pin-hole and saw a vague outline stirring. 'Oh, the ghost of the hyena has come back!' I cried. A thrill of fear lifted the hair on my scalp and forearm. I wondered if I should wake up the other two—it was a perfect excuse—and make them share my fright.

'Sir, sir,' whispered the animated hyena, 'this is urgent—listen.'

I lifted the edge of the bamboo curtain. The light from the treadle fell on the other side and illuminated the face of Rangi. My hair stood on end. Rangi! The woman to avoid.

My first reaction was one of thankfulness that Sastri was on the other side of the curtain, facing the wall. It was impossible—that woman whom I saw going down the steps every morning with the flowers crushed in her hair, the awful fleshy creature whom Sastri considered it a sin to look at! Was it possible that I was a prey to hallucinations? Perhaps overwork and the strain of the last few weeks had done their trick. I turned away to my treadle, smiling indulgently at the pranks my mind was playing. But the phantom sounded husky as it called again, 'Listen to me.' Was the woman trying to seduce me at this hour? I looked around. If my wife happened to come in, it would be the end of my domestic career. Although Rangi was black as cinders and looked rugged, there was an irresistible physical attraction about her, and I was afraid that I might succumb to her charms. But there was the safety of the grille between us. I asked, with needless sternness in my voice, 'Why do you disturb me at this hour of the night? Have you no . . .?'

'Sh! Sh!' she said, gesturing with her fingers to cover her mouth. 'You will wake him up if you talk so loudly. Listen to me, sir,' she said. 'I have very urgent news for you.'

'What is it? Couldn't you have spoken to me earlier in the day?'

When I saw her nearer, she wasn't so rugged. The light touched her high cheekbones, and I found myself saying to myself, 'Not bad, not bad. Her breasts are billowy, like those one sees in temple sculptures. Her hips are also classical.' I resented the attraction she exuded from a personality so rough. She wore a thin reddish sari. She interrupted my midnight dreaming with, 'I must get back before he awakes. Listen: he is talking of shooting your Kumar tomorrow. Be careful.'

I took a little time to grasp the sense of her information. The name Kumar stirred up in me all the necessary memories, from the first day when we had made him get up on his legs, through all our effort to restore him to health, to this day, when he was peacefully swaying and crunching all the sugar cane that the children of the neighbourhood brought him.

During his convalescence Kumar had become our own temple elephant and was living in the compound. He was to be a main feature of our festival, and afterwards he would be returned to Muthu.

'I am also a woman of the temple and I love that elephant. It must not be shot. Sir, you must somehow see that he doesn't do it. Please save the elephant.'

'How? How can I shield the elephant? What sort of an armour can we provide for him?' I asked. And then on a sudden doubt I whispered, 'Are you in your senses? Or have you been taking opium or something of that kind?'

She glared at me angrily, 'Sir, I am only a public woman, following what is my *dharma*. I may be a sinner to you, but do nothing worse than what some of the so-called family women are doing. I observe our rules. Whatever I may do, I don't take opium.'

I felt apologetic for uttering so outrageous a remark and said, 'What you say is so unbelievable.'

She looked nervously up the stairs, as there was a slight stirring noticeable above. 'If he wakes up . . .' she whispered. 'Wait here, don't go away,' and she ran up the steps. My blood tingled with an unholy thrill. I let my mind slide into a wild fantasy of seduction and passion. I was no longer a married man with a child and home, I was an adolescent lost in dreams over a nude photograph. I knew that I was completely sealed against any seductive invitation she might hold out for me, but, but, I hoped I would not weaken . . .

My mind speculated on how I was to neutralize the grille between us if it came to that; the grille had a lock, and the key was in the drawer of my table in the other room. I stepped up to the curtain, parted the edge of it, and was relieved to see Sastri continuing his sleep, his position unchanged. The poet slept equally soundly, but he had drawn up his legs and curled himself in the Queen Anne. If I approached the desk for the key, it was bound to disturb the sleepers. Anyway, I left the problem alone, resolved to tackle it somehow at the right moment.

When I tiptoed back to my place beside the grille, there she was, ready as it seemed to swallow me up wholesale, to dissolve within the embrace of her mighty arms all the monogamous chastity I had practised a whole lifetime.

I found her irresistible. She stood on the last step, a goddess carved out of cinder. The shadows cast by the low-powered lamp were tricky and created a halo around her. I pressed my hands on the grille and put my face close, and, adopting the appropriate tone of a man about to succumb to seduction, I said, 'Oh, you are back!' I tried to put into the sentence all the pleasure I was anticipating.

She looked at me indifferently and said, 'I only went up to see if he was sleeping; he was just rolling over, he won't get up till five, I know him.' She sat down on the last step, took out of the folds at her waist a pouch and from it a betel-nut and leaf and two inches of tobacco, put them into her mouth and started chewing. She looked completely relaxed. In my fevered state I wanted to ask her if she was aware that the grille was locked and the key was where Sastri was sleeping.

She asked, 'Are you going to save that elephant or not?'

'Why do you ask? Tell me all about it.'

'He will kill me if he knows I have been talking. But I don't care. He has been telling me his plans. Tomorrow night, what time does your procession pass this way?'

'You should know, you are in it.'

She was to perform her original function of a dedicated woman, and dance in front of the God during the procession, although her dance would consist only of a few formal flourishes of her arms. She was perhaps the most indifferent dancer in India, but no one expected anything else of her. People were used to seeing her before the God and no one cared how she performed. Her place would be right between the decorated chariot and the group of pipers and drummers.

'He doesn't want me to go in the procession tomorrow,' she said, 'because he says it'll not be safe for me.' She giggled slightly, and threw the end of her sari over her face, feeling shy at the thought of Vasu's considerateness.

I asked in a panic, 'Aren't you joining the procession?'

'Yes, I'll be there. It will be my duty.'

'But, but, what about Vasu?'

'Oh, let him say what he pleases; no man so far has stopped my doing what I like,' she said proudly.

'Why doesn't he want you there?'

'He doesn't want me there when it happens.'

'What happens?'

'When he shoots the elephant from his window.'

'I never thought Vasu cared for anyone so much.'

'He cares for me very much, although sometimes he is completely mad and picks up all kinds of women and expects me to quarrel with them—but not me. Let any man do what he fancies. I don't care what anyone does, so long as he doesn't dictate to me what I should do.' She chewed her tobacco contentedly. 'He wants to take me with him to Bombay—that's why he doesn't want me to get lost in the crowd.'

'What will you do in Bombay?' I asked, my curiosity roused.

'Cook for him. He likes the *pulav* I make, so he wants to take me along with him. I want to see new places too when the time comes. In a year or two who will care to have me?'

'Oh, you will have your charms,' I wanted to say in my impassioned state, but I restrained myself. She treated me with much respect, always addressing me as 'sir', and she would have been shocked if I had spoken to her like a lover. Even at that mad hour, I am glad to think, I kept my head and tongue. 'Good man,' I said, 'he cares for you so much!'

'He is tired of his restaurant food, he says, and he doesn't want me to risk my life in the crowd when he shoots the elephant from his window.'

'Why shoot the poor thing?' I persisted. 'Does he think I will let him do it?' I asked heroically. 'I will tell the police.'

'Oh, sir,' she begged, 'don't do that. How will it help? The police themselves may ask him to shoot it. They may want someone able to shoot.' And then she explained, 'When the elephant is passing here, it may go mad and charge into the crowd.'

'Oh, God. Why?'

'Well, elephants are easily excited; and then he will take aim from his window and shoot it. He is certain that he can finish it. His aim is always accurate, you know,' she said.

I said, angrily, 'If he is such a good shot, the place for him to demonstrate it is elsewhere, not here.'

'Master,' she implored, 'don't be angry. Think calmly what you should do, and act before it's too late.'

'Anyway, why does he want to shoot the elephant?' I asked.

'He says it's more useful dead. He may kill me for speaking, but I don't care. I want to save poor Kumar.'

'Neither you nor Kumar need have any fear. The time has come for me to hand him over to the police, the devil!' I said with a lot of passion but little idea of what I could do about it.

I finished printing the formes, woke up Sastri to do more, woke up the poet to proof-read, printed four more pages, and it was nine o'clock in the morning when I saw the last page off the machine and one set of formes was assembled ready for the binder. The sacred copy was to be bound in Benares silk and kept in the temple. I said to the poet, 'It's all right, go home and wash and be here in time. We have to be at the temple before three.'

He yawned, scratched the back of his head and went down the road muttering, 'I'll be back soon. Tell me if there is anything more I can do.'

I sent Sastri with two copies to the binder. Sastri hesitated for a second. 'Can't I go home for half an hour— for a wash?'

I was irritated. 'Why not me? I also would like to go home and sleep and wash and relax.' As I was talking my little son came running down the road. 'Father, Mother says . . .' Even before he finished his sentence, I said, 'Tell your mother not to call me for the rest of the day. Tell your mother that even Sastri is not going home today. We are all very busy.' I handed him a bunch of coloured notices. 'Give one of them to your mother and the rest to your friends or anyone you like—let them all turn up at Krishna's temple. We'll all meet there. Tell Mother I'll come home, but I don't know when.' Even as I spoke I remembered Rangi, and for a moment I wondered whether to ask my son and wife to keep out of the crowd. 'Damn it!' I said to myself. 'Nothing shall happen. I shall have Rangi and that paramour of hers in the police lock-up.' This thought gave me strength although I had no notion how I was going to achieve it practically. The police would not listen to my orders if I said, 'Lock up that man.' Why should they?

Every hour of that day was like a tenth of a second to me, it was so compressed and so fleeting. After sending everyone away I sat down to take stock of all I had to do between now and the grand function. I found my head in a whirl. I didn't know where to make a start in drawing up a schedule. Every item appeared to be important and clamoured for immediate attention. I could now understand why Government officials liked to stack up on their desks trays marked Immediate, Urgent, and Top Priority. Everything today was on the top-priority level.

Although we had been working madly for weeks, everything seemed to be crowded into the last minute. First I must remind the flower-dealer to get us the first supplies for decorating the chariot by eleven. We had engaged two specialists, brothers from Talapur, who were in demand all over south India. Given the foliage and the quantity of chrysanthemums they demanded, their decoration of a chariot was a masterpiece, but they needed a clear eight hours to arrange the flowers. The chariot must be ready for the procession at eight in the evening, and they would have to begin their work at eleven in the morning. I had paid a visit to them at Talapur ten days before. They accepted the engagement only because the police inspector with whom I had influence interceded; otherwise they had a much bigger job to do at Madras. I gave them an advance of fifty rupees and noted down their indent: seven thousand yellow chrysanthemums, four thousand of a certain green plant, two thousand red oleanders, two hundred thin bamboos splintered according to their specification, which they'd loop around the pedestal of the God, working the flowers into them, and seventeen bundles of banana fibres thinly torn off for binding the flowers. In addition to these basic requirements they had asked for a thousand roses, twenty measures of jasmine buds, and bouquets and garlands ready-made to be strung according to their specifications. These latter items could arrive after six, but the first supply of chrysanthemums must be there before eleven. The brothers were arriving by the bus at ten o'clock behind the market depot, and they were stars who expected to be received on arrival. I was the only one who had seen them, and it meant that I would have to wait for them at the market stand. Also I had to visit the florist who had his shop at the farthest corner of Market Road, a man amenable only to my influence. He waited in his turn on the suppliers from the surrounding gardens. We were taking all the flower supplies coming into town that day, and the price of flowers for common folk shot up.

I had also to make sure that our piper and the drummer, who lived not too far away, would arrive in time. Our chief piper blew through a silver-covered pipe, and the drummer had gold beads around his neck and beat his drum with ivory-tipped fingers; they were stars in their own line, and so expected personal attention from the organizers as represented by me. They were in demand all over south India for marriage and temple festivals, but they had condescended to accept a local engagement because it was the first of its kind in our town. They lived right on the edge of the town, the last house in Ellaman's Street, but, since they were cousins of our barber whose house abutted Kabir Street, we were able to exert pressure on them through him and set him to bring them to the temple at three in the afternoon.

We had an enormous programme of feeding the public too. We had planned to offer the God rice cooked with jaggery and spiced with cardamom and coconut and distribute it to the crowd following the procession. One of the rice merchants had donated us all the rice that would be needed together with the coconut and jaggery. All that he wanted in return was that, in any public speech, his shop should be mentioned. We had a kitchen in the temple, and an enormous cauldron was fetched and mounted over a fireplace with half a ton of chopped wood burning under it. Four professional cooks were engaged, and several thousand little receptacles made of banana bark would be filled with sweetened rice and distributed. And then there were the Kitson lights and pitfall lamps for the illumination of the temple and the procession, in addition to torches soaked in oil. And above all fireworks.

The whole town was at it. The Chairman of our Municipal Council had agreed to preside over the function, the advantage in that being that the municipal services were easily secured for us! When it was known that the Municipal Chairman would be there, the roads were swept and watered, and the licence for a procession was immediately given. Along the corridor of our Krishna temple we had erected a *pandal* and a dais, on which the Mayor (he liked to be called Mayor) would stand and harangue the gathering before the dedication.

All the public relations and the general arrangements at the temple were undertaken by Sen, who never left the temple precincts for seven days, working at it night and day. He had managed to get a band of young volunteers from Albert Mission College and High School to assist him and run small errands; he had managed to erect a *pandal* with coconut thatch and bamboo; he saw to the decorations, and kept a hold on the Municipal Chairman by writing his speech for him. He had also arranged to keep in readiness hand-outs and photographs for newspapers. K.J., our aerated-water specialist, had set up a booth at the temple gate and had offered to open a thousand bottles free of cost and thereafter charge only half-rate to the public gathered at the temple. There were three donors who had offered five hundred rupees each, and they expected me to fetch them by car, although one had to be brought from New Extension, the other from Gandhi Park and a third from Lawley Road. I had fortunately the assistance of Gaffur, who ran his 1927 Chevrolet as a taxi. It was always available around the fountain. 'Any time, anywhere, this car is yours,' he had declared. I had only to fill the petrol tank, ask him to drive and give him ten rupees at the end of the day.

'First things first, and I have to be at the temple at three,' I told myself. There was Dr Joshi, the elephant doctor beyond Nallappa's Grove, who wanted a car to be sent for him. 'I must remember to take with me six bottles of rose water and the sandalwood paste, and then . . .' Items kept coming to mind, like the waves beating on a shore. 'Oh, when Muthu and his party arrive, I must leave a guide at the bus-stand to take them to the temple.' Everything was important and clamoured for first attention.

I dropped what I was doing, dashed through the press, opened the back door and stepped across to my house. I'd have no time to visit the river today. I went straight into the bathing-room, saw that there was cold water ready in a brass cauldron, undressed and poured the cold water over my head, shouting through the door to my wife, 'Bring me my towel and a change of clothes.' She thrust the towel through the half-open door, and I cried, 'I forgot to shave; bring me my safety razor and mirror. I'll shave here.' She ran back to fetch these, and presently my son entered, bearing them in his hand. I shouted, 'You should not handle razor blades.'

'Mother asked me to carry them.'

I called his mother urgently and told her, 'After this never let the young fellow handle razor blades.'

'He insisted upon fetching them himself.'

'That's no excuse,' I said, 'You must watch him.'

'What else do you think I am doing?' she asked. 'But now I have your breakfast on the fire, and I know how you will dance for it and make us dance who serve you, the moment you come out of the bathroom.'

'No time for arguments today.'

Within fifteen minutes I was leaving home again, completely refreshed by my bath and food. I took leave of my wife. 'Try and manage to come to the temple at five with Babu. I'll give you a good place for watching the show, then you can go back home and come again before the procession. The decoration will be the finest. Come with some of our neighbours.' I was off.

Across the street, back at my press, I was troubled with a secret uneasiness that perhaps I should have asked her to stay at home in view of Rangi's warnings. 'First things first . . .' If I devoted four minutes to each task, I could get through everything and reach the temple in time before the Chairman arrived. But, but, I had to get this affair of Vasu straightened out; I braced myself to face him. I did not want to give myself any time. If I began to think it over, I'd find an excuse to go ahead with all the other tasks, while the lives of thousands of men and women might hang by a thread depending on my interview with Vasu, not to speak of the survival of poor Kumar who had proved such a delight to our neighbourhood!

I dashed home for a minute to ask my wife to pack up and give me some eatables that she had prepared, and then turned to go to Vasu. I went around to the yard. Until I turned the corner I had a hope that the jeep might not be there. But there it was. My steps halted for a second at the bottom of Vasu's staircase, where I noticed the plaster on the walls peeling off. 'I must attend to this,' I said to myself, and immediately felt a pang at the thought of how little I had to do with this part of my property. At the foot of the stairs the hyena was still there. 'There seems to be no demand for stuffed hyena nowadays,' I said to myself. The python was gone, but a monitor lizard, a crocodile, and a number of other creatures, looking all alike in death, cluttered the staircase. I went up to the landing, making as much sound as I could. It was about eleven and I knew Rangi would not be there. I stood on the landing and called, 'Vasu, may I come in?' I didn't knock on the door as I felt it might upset him. 'How can I find time today for this?' I thought. 'I hope they'll remember the rose-water bottles.' I stood brooding, waiting for Vasu. The door opened.

'What an honour!' he cried ironically. I passed in, took my seat on his iron chair, and settled myself for a talk with him, although one part of my mind went on repeating, 'Where is the time? Rose-water, sandal-paste, New Extension, Gandhi Park . . .' We had avoided each other since the day I asked for my accounts and thus entered a second phase of our quarrel. Last time it was he who had come with peace overtures; this time I was initiating them. My heart swelled with pride; I was performing a mighty sacrifice on behalf of God and country. By approaching him and humbling myself I would be saving humanity from destruction . . .

I said, 'Vasu, I have no time today for anything, as you know, but I've come to invite you personally to our function this evening.' He received my words coldly, without even thanks, and made no reply. I looked around; the room was once again cluttered with hides and stuffed creatures and packing-sheets and materials. I noticed a small tiger cub in a corner. I tried to win him by saying, 'A pretty cub that!'

He picked it up and brought it closer, 'Someone picked it up right in the centre of a road while coming from . . .'

'Its mother?'

'Will miss her, of course. I was busy with other things, and could start on it only last week.'

'You could have kept it alive and brought it up,' I said, trying to discover ways of pleasing him.

'Me? No. I've spent a lifetime trying to make you see the difference between a zoo-keeper and a taxidermist,' he said with weariness, as if I'd been trying to place him among an inferior caste of men. 'Anyway it's easier to rear a dead animal. For one thing it saves complications with a landlord.'

I felt proud that he still recognized me as the lord of this attic. Vasu without a live tiger was quite a problem enough, and I had made the suggestion only to please him. In the hope of pleasing him further I added, 'Of course, a baby anything is a beauty. I'd have loved to have him around.'

'It was a she,' he corrected.

'What is the safe age?'

'What do you mean?'

'Up to what age can a tiger be kept as a pet?'

'Until it starts licking the skin off the back of your hand,' he said, 'Anyway, how should I know? I am not a zoo-keeper.'

I tried to find something nasty to say about zoo-keepers, that odious tribe of men whom he loathed, but failed. I merely said, 'Most peculiar profession. I would not be a zoo-keeper for all the wealth in the world.'

He set the tiger cub before me on a stool. I shivered slightly at the thought of anyone taking so young a life.

'Doesn't she look cute? I have had more trouble shaping this than a full-grown one. Guess what I am charging for it?'

This was really a problem for me. If I undervalued it, I might antagonize him. If I mentioned a fantastic figure, he might despise me, seeing through the trick. While my mind was working fast, I stole a glance through the little window over the street. Yes, the fountain would be within his range. From the fountain, down the road, branching off to Lawley Road—he could aim anywhere within the perimeter.

'What are you watching?' he asked suddenly.

'Nothing. I always look at far-off things when I have to do a calculation. I've been thinking over your question. If you charge five thousand rupees, as you told me once . . .'

'Oh, the question is unimportant, leave it alone,' he said. He carried the cub off and put it back, covering it over with a piece of cloth.

I was not to be quenched so easily. I said, 'About two thousand? The labour of shaping it must have been equally great.'

'You are right. It's slightly less. I never charge a round sum. My bill for it would be eighteen hundred and twenty-five, packing extra.'

I gave appropriate cries of admiration for his cleverness, and after talking a little more on the same lines we came to business. 'Why don't you come along with me at three o'clock?'

'To your wonderful function? I have had enough of this tomfoolery.'

'Well, you were enthusiastic about it once!'

181

'That's why I want to keep away. Let me alone, enjoy it yourself.'

He had still to render us an account, but this was not the time to tackle him about it. There was enough time ahead—after tonight, after the elephant was safely returned to Muthu. I wanted to assure him now that I had not come about the accounts. I said, 'Everyone is bound to ask why you are not there. You have done so much for us already.'

'I have had to spend over two thousand rupees out of my pocket. You have no idea how much of my business I have had to set aside. Time is money. I can't be like some of your friends.'

'Let us not talk of all that,' I said.

'Who are you to ask me to shut up!' he cried.

We were coming dangerously near another clash. I did not want to lose my head and lose the chance of keeping him with us and saving the elephant. This was the only tactic I could think of. He spurned me again and again as I repeated my invitation, and finally said, 'Your whole crowd sickens me! You are a fellow without any sense. Why you are so enthusiastic about a poetaster obsessed with monosyllables I don't know. And then that local Nehru. Who does he think he is? All of you joining to waste everyone's time and money! If I had any authority I'd prohibit celebrations of this kind as a waste of national energy.'

I did not want to say that he could keep out if it didn't suit him. I wanted to stretch my capacity for patience to the utmost in the cause of God and country. He was abusive and angry. I wanted to assure him that I was not going to mention accounts for a considerable time to come. So I said, 'Vasu, I have come to you as a friend. I thought it would be fun to have you around. We could see things together and laugh at things together. Perhaps you are worried we might ask about those collections . . .'

'Who? Me, worried!' He laughed devilishly. 'A hundred of you will have to worry before you can catch me worried.'

I laughed pretending that he was joking. I looked at the time. I had wasted nearly three-quarters of an hour in the *tête-à-tête*, and still I had not come to the point. How was I to ask him for an assurance that he would not shoot the elephant?

I now took the rice cake and sweets out of my bag, and placed the packet before him. 'Ah, I forgot about this,' I said. 'I have brought you something to eat. I found it at home and thought you might like it.'

'What is it?' he asked. He opened the packet and raised his brow. 'You want to practise kindness on me! All right. This is my first experience of it from you. All right, all right, while it lasts.' He put a piece in his mouth, chewed it with critical seriousness and said, 'Not bad, but tell the person who made it to fry the pepper a little more before putting it in. Anyway better than nothing.' He transferred the whole of it, and swallowed it at one gulp, accepting it as something rightfully due to him. I was a little upset to see him take it so casually and critically, and was especially hurt to think that he couldn't pay a compliment to my wife even for courtesy's sake. He merely said, 'If you want to find this stuff at its best, you must taste it at . . .' and he mentioned some exclusive place of his own.

'This was prepared by my wife,' I said, trying to

forestall any nasty statement he might make. But he merely said, 'Modern women are no good at this. Modern women are no good at anything when you come to think of it.' I did not want him to elaborate the subject as I feared he might say something nasty about my wife, so I desperately changed the subject to the real issue. I said, 'Vasu, I have come to appeal to you not to harm our elephant tonight.'

'How can anyone harm an elephant, of all things? Don't you know that even if you drive a bodkin into its skin, it will only break the point? Anyway, what are you trying to tell me?'

This was challenging. He had risen from the cot, which showed that he was agitated by my question. He tried to look calm, but I found that he was roused. 'Who has been gossiping, I wonder.' He paced up and down, then stood for a moment looking out of the window—as I guessed, at the market fountain. 'Has that bitch been talking to you?'

'Which bitch?' I asked.

'That woman Rangi,' he said with heat.

'Who is Rangi?' I asked.

'You pretend you don't know her!' he cried. 'Why all this show? I'll wring her neck if I find . . .' He didn't finish the sentence. He asked suddenly, 'Well, suppose I decide to shoot that elephant, what can you do about it?'

I had no answer. I only asked, 'What has the poor elephant done to you?'

'Has it occurred to you how much more an elephant is worth dead? You don't have to feed it in the first place. I can make ten thousand out of the parts of this elephant— the tusks if my calculation is right, must weigh forty pounds, that's eight hundred rupees. I have already an order for the legs, mounted as umbrella stands, and each hair on its tail can be sold for twelve annas for rings and bangles; most women fancy them and it's not for us to question their taste. My first business will be to take out the hairs and keep them apart, while the blood is still hot; trunk, legs, even the nails—it's a perfect animal in that way. Every bit of it is valuable. I've already several inquiries from France and Germany and from Hong Kong. What more can a man want? I could retire for a year on the proceeds of one elephant.'

'Why don't you go and shoot one in the forest?'

'Forest! I want to show them that I can shoot anywhere. I want to teach those forest men a lesson.'

A strange way of teaching a lesson to foresters. I said weakly, 'Shoot a wild one, and no one will blame you.'

'This will be wild enough, don't worry.'

'What do you mean?'

'You watch out,' he said. 'You will thank me for my services. That Kumar is mad already; none of you have noticed it. Have you ever observed his eyes? See the red streak in his little eyes; that means at the slightest provocation he will fly off . . .'

'What sort of provocation?' I asked.

'How can I say? Elephants are really crazy animals. Anything, any slight . . .' He did not explain.

I felt worried. What was he planning? How was he going to excite it? 'Have you plans to excite it?' I asked point blank.

He laughed diabolically. 'You want to know everything, my boy. Wait, and you will know. Whatever you have to know will be known one day,' he said in a biblical manner.

185

I said, 'Whatever horrible plans you may have, remember there will be thousands of people around—men, women, and children dragging the chariot.'

'Let them go home like good citizens before midnight. They can have all the fun they want until midnight.'

'Who are you to say when they should go or come?'

'Now, now, don't try to be nasty. Let them stay or go, that's their business. If the elephant runs wild . . .' He ruminated.

'A few will be trampled and choked in a stampede,' I said.

'You are saying things I don't say. You have a morbid mind.' He said a moment later, 'The elephant has been promised me when it's dead. I have it in writing here.'

'Who has promised?'

'Why should I tell you everything? As far as I'm concerned, you have no business with me at all. How are you concerned with the elephant? It's not yours. I'm not bound to tell you anything. I'm an independent man. You keep it locked away, if you like; that's not going to bother me. Why come and talk to me? Get out of here and mind your morning's work.'

I trembled with excitement and helplessness. I dared not say anything more, lest he should hit me. I pleaded, 'Vasu, you are a human being with feelings like any of us. I am sure you are only pretending to be so wild.' He laughed. He seemed delighted at the way he had brought me down.

'All right, keep your own view of me. I don't mind. You are . . . Shall I tell you what's the matter with you? You are sentimental. I feel sickened when I see a man talking sentimentally like an old widow. I admire people with a scientific outlook.'

186

'What's scientific about the terrible plans you have?'

'Ah, you see! You use the word "terrible" and are carried away by it. You allow your mind to be carried away by your own phrases. There's nothing terrible in shooting. You pull your trigger and out goes the bullet, and at the other end there is an object waiting to receive it. It is just give and take. At one time I was squeamish like you. It was Hussein who broadened my outlook. He used to tell me the way to be broad-minded is to begin to like a thing you don't like. It makes for a very scientific outlook.'

'It may be science, but the object at the other end does not deserve to be brought down. Has that occurred to you?'

'How can you say? What do you do with an animal which goes on a rampage? Should the public not be protected?'

'This is not that kind of animal,' I said weakly. It was idiotic to try to change his mind, but I wanted to try to the last.

'Unscientific! Unscientific!' he cried. 'What's the premise for your conclusion? Normal behaviour is one thing and the abnormal behaviour of a beast is another. Exactly when a beast will cross the frontier is a matter that's known only to those who have studied the subject. If you had printed my book on wild life, you'd have found it profitable. I've devoted two chapters to animal behaviour. But you chose to busy yourself with monosyllables.'

I said placatingly, 'I'll take it tomorrow and finish it,' carefully avoiding a mention of the original Heidelberg which was rising to my lips.

'I don't believe your promise,' he said. 'Did you think I'd wait on your pleasure indefinitely? It's already being printed.'

187

I felt jealous. 'Here, in this town? Who could do it?'

He laughed at my question and said, 'Now I've given you all the time I can. You'll have to leave me. This is my busy day.'

I shuddered at the implication.

The interview knocked out all the joy I had felt in the festival. I had looked forward to it for weeks, and now I felt like a man working towards a disastrous end and carrying a vast crowd with him. I'd have willingly stopped the entire celebration if it had been practicable. But we had started rolling downhill and there was no way of checking our momentum.

It was four o'clock when I managed to reach the temple at Vinayak Street. Men, women, and children thronged the street and the courtyard of the temple. Sen had put up a few bamboo barriers here and there to allow some space for the Mayor and his entourage. He had dressed himself in a *dhoti* at his waist and had wrapped a red silk upper cloth around his shoulder and his forehead was blazoned with sacred ash, sandal-paste, and vermilion. He was nearly unrecognizable in his holy make-up. The poet had donned a pink bush-coat for the ceremony, and it hurt my eyes. It reminded me of the labels for K.J.'s drinks. K.J. had spread out his coloured water on a wooden platform, and was doing brisk business. Since he had not specified when the free drinks would be supplied, he was freely plying his trade. The babble of voices was deafening. A few shops had sprung up—paper toys, fried nuts, and figurines in red and green sugar, on little trays at the temple gate. The back of the temple was filled with smoke rising from the enormous cooking. Some of the temple priests were busy in the inner sanctum, decorating the God and lighting oil lamps.

Kumar was chained to a peg at the end of the temple corridor, under a tree. A crowd of children watched him; and he was briskly reducing to fibre lengths of sugar cane held out to him by the children. The mahout from Top Slip was perched on his back, painting his forehead in white, red and green floral patterns, to the huge delight of the children, to whom he was appealing, 'Don't make so much noise, give us a chance, give us a chance. Kumar can't hear me if you keep making so much noise.' He had scrubbed and cleaned Kumar's tusks so that the ivory gleamed in the sun. He had decorated the tusks with bronze bands and rings; he was very happy because someone had promised him the loan of gold head-ornaments and brocades. The elephant seemed to enjoy it all immensely and was in a fine mood. My heart sank at the sight of the happy animal.

I found Dr Joshi standing near him, stroking his trunk. In all the rush of work, my promise to fetch him had gone out of my head, but he had somehow arrived. I approached him, pushing my way through the crowd of sightseers. I wanted to apologize for my lapse. But the moment he saw me, he said, 'Sorry I couldn't wait for you. I had to come to the town on business and have stayed on.'

'Oh, that's all right, Doctor, I'm happy to see you. How do you find Kumar?'

He said, 'He is in good shape, I think.'

'Will he stand all the crowd and excitement?'

'Surely. What else do you think he is good for? You will find him at his best in such surroundings.'

'I was wondering whether he would tolerate the fireworks and the band?'

'Why not? But don't let sparks fall on him from the torches or the fireworks. Some elephants get a fright when a flare is held too close. Keep an eye on the torch-bearers, and that should be enough.'

'Do you think he'll go wild if something happens?'

'Why do you ask?' asked the doctor.

'I've heard some people say that an animal can suddenly charge into a crowd.'

He laughed at my fear. 'Don't talk about such ideas. People might get into a panic and that would be really bad in a crowd like this.' We surveyed the jam of humanity. Any rumour might ruin the occasion, and create a stampede. The distribution of the offerings was planned for the end of the procession, when we returned to the temple. That meant that most of the crowd would wait for it. One way of reducing the crowd would be to distribute the sweet rice as soon as possible. I sought out the chief priest of the temple to ask if it could be managed. He said immediately, 'No. The offering is for the eleven o'clock service. How could we distribute anything before that?'

I was obsessed with plans to save the lives of the people who had come out for enjoyment: little girls had dressed themselves in bright skirts, women wore their jewellery and flowers in their hair, and men had donned their best shirts and bush-coats and *dhotis* and silks. My wife and son were somewhere in that crowd. I had no way of reaching them either. The air was charged with the scent of the jasmine and roses which decorated the chariot.

The Mayor's speech was drowned in the babble in spite of a microphone and loudspeaker. This was the journalist's domain, and I kept away from the dais. I saw from far off the pink bush-coat of the poet rising. He was respectfully presenting the silk-bound copy of the book to the priest. The crowd demonstrated unmistakably that they hadn't assembled there to listen to a speech. The piper and the drummer were providing a thunderous performance. The priest was busy placing offerings at the feet of Krishna and Radha, and Rangi was dancing and gesticulating before the golden images. She had draped herself in a faded brocade and wore a lot of tinsel ornaments on her head and around her neck. I wanted to speak to her—it was urgent—but it would be improper to be seen engaged in a talk with the woman, and the enormous crowd might boo me. I toyed with the idea of sending an emissary to her, any young urchin, but if the fellow was bent on mischief he could expose me and make me the laughing-stock of the crowd. The crowd was in a mood to enjoy anything at anybody's expense.

What did I want to see her for? I wasn't very clear. It seemed vulgar to share a secret with her. If Sastri came to know of it, he would denounce me and leave my service. All the same I wanted to attract her attention, why I couldn't say. I could glimpse her only over several heads and through gaps between shoulders. She was agitating herself in such a way as to make it impossible for anyone to catch her eye. All the same I edged closer, pushing my way through the crowd. The incense smoke and camphor, the babble of the priest's recitations over, the babble of the crowd suddenly proved too oppressive. All night I had sat up working on the formes, and after all this trouble the whole business seemed to be unimportant. I found it strangely irritating to think of the pink-coated poet and all the trouble he had caused me.

The God was beautifully decorated. He wore a rose garland, and a diamond pendant sparkled on his chest. He had been draped in silk and gold lace, and he held a flute in his hand; and his little bride, a golden image draped in blue silk and sparkling with diamonds, was at his side, the shy bride. The piper was blowing his cheeks out, filling the air with 'Kalyani Raga', a lovely melody at this hour. The temple was nearly a century old, built by public subscription in the days when my grandfather and a few others had come here as pioneers. Beyond the temple had been a forest extending to the river; today all the forest was gone; in its place were only a number of ill-built houses, with tiles disarranged by time and wind, straggling houses, mainly occupied by weavers who spread out their weaving frames all along the street. But the temple, with its tower and golden crest and carved pillars, continued to receive support.

The story of Krishna and Radha was now being recited in song form by a group of men, incoherently and cacophonously, while they acted as vocal accompanists for Rangi's dance, as she swayed and gesticulated. With all the imperfections, the effect of the incense and the chants made me drowsy and elated, and I forgot for a moment all my problems. Vasu was like an irrelevant thought. He should have no place in my scheme of things. People I had never seen in my life acted as a padding to my right and left and fore and aft. I had lived a circumscribed life and had never thought that our town contained such a variety of humanity—bearded, clean-shaven, untidy, tidy; women elegant, ravishing, tub-shaped and coarse; and the children, thousands of them, dressed, undressed, matted-haired, chasing each other between the legs of adults, screaming with joy and trying to press forward and grab the fruit offerings kept for the Gods. Half a dozen adults had set themselves the task of chasing the children away and compelling them to keep out of the main hall of the temple, but when they overflowed into the corridor and the veranda, half a dozen other people set themselves a similar task of keeping them out of the assembly listening to the Chairman's perorations. They chased them back into the hall with equal vigour, and the gang of children came screaming in, enjoying immensely the pendulum swing back and forth.

Through all this babble, the music went on. But I had withdrawn from everything and found a temporary peace of mind. The sight of the God, the sound of music, the rhythm of cymbals and the scent of jasmine and incense induced in me a temporary indifference to everything. Elephant? Who could kill an elephant? There came to my mind the tale of the elephant Gajendra, the elephant of mythology who stepped into a lake and had his leg caught in the jaws of a mighty crocodile; and the elephant trumpeted helplessly, struggled, and in the end desperately called on Vishnu, who immediately appeared and gave him the strength to come ashore out of the jaws of the crocodile. 'In this story,' I told myself, 'our ancestors have shown us that an elephant has a protected life and no one can harm it.' I felt lighter at heart. When the time came the elephant would find the needed strength. The priest was circling the camphor light before the golden images, and the reflections on the faces made them vibrate with a living quality. God Krishna was really an incarnation of Vishnu, who had saved Gajendra;

he would again come to the rescue of the same animal on whose behalf I was . . .

Unknowingly I let out a terrific cry which drowned the noise of children, music, everything. 'Oh, Vishnu!' I howled. 'Save our elephant, and save all the innocent men and women who are going to pull the chariot. You must come to our rescue now.' Unknown to myself, I had let out such a shout that the entire crowd inside and outside the hall stood stunned, and all activity stopped. The Chairman's speech was interrupted as my voice overwhelmed the loudspeaker. Rangi stopped dead in her dance. I was soon surrounded by a vast crowd of sympathizers. I felt faint and choked by the congestion.

'Did you shout like that? The Chairman's speech . . .' It was Sen speaking, to whom the only thing that mattered was the Chairman's speech. He was angry and agitated. I heard someone remark, 'This man is possessed, listen to him.' My shout had brought round me all the friends I had been looking for in the crowd. Muthu, the tea-stall keeper, was very tender. He said, 'Are you feeling well?' I felt not unwell but foolish to have brought on myself so much attention. 'Where have you been all along? I've been looking for you.' I had now lost the initiative in my affairs. A number of busybodies carried me out to the veranda under the sky and fanned my face. The veterinary doctor felt my pulse and injected a drug into the veins of my arm. The poet had my head on his lap. 'Doctor, don't give me an elephant dose of anything. I have never seen you curing human ills.' The crowd that stood over me was enormous. Faces everywhere, to my right, left, above and aside. A glut of breathing, sighing, noisy humanity, packing every inch of space. The journalist suddenly lost his head and charged madly into the crowd crying, 'If you don't leave him alone, he'll die of lack of air,' and people made way. The incomplete speech of the Chairman seemed to have given an edge to his temper.

The Chairman sailed in with a lot of dignity. He stooped over to ask, 'Are you feeling better?' 'I'm absolutely well, nothing is the matter with me. Please go and continue your speech. Don't stop it on any account.' The Chairman looked pleased at the importance given to his speech. He cackled like a shy adolescent. The Chairman of the Municipal Council was actually a man who owned a sweetmeat shop and had risen to his present position through sheer hard work. He was supposed to have started life as a servant and ultimately became the owner of the sweetmeat shop. He always wore (even in his sleep, so people said) a white Gandhi cap as an unwavering member of the Congress Party; a chubby, rosy-cheeked man, who evidently consumed a great deal of his own sweets. Seeing his face so close to mine, I felt reassured. Here was a man who could save the elephant. I said, 'You must protect the elephant.'

'Which elephant?' he asked, rather startled.

I explained. I took my head off the lap of the pink coat and said to the poet, 'Take him to where the elephant is kept.' The poet demurred, the Mayor dodged the suggestion, but I was adamant. The Mayor was being watched by a big circle of the crowd; he did not want to be embroiled in a scene with me and so left. The poet was glad to be out of the spotlight too. I could now sit up. I realized that I had an odd commanding position. People were prepared to do anything I suggested. I felt better. At this moment my wife entered the scene, accompanied by my little son. Both of them rushed to me with agonized cries. I didn't like such a dramatic show, so I told my wife, 'Why are you behaving like this? I only felt a little choked in there and so came out to sit here.'

'You were lying flat on Uncle's lap,' said my boy.

'Only because they would not let me rise to my feet.' My wife burst into tears and remained sobbing. 'Now, now, don't be ridiculous; people will laugh at us for creating a scene and spoiling their day for them. Now, now, go and enjoy yourselves.'

I was on my feet again, and went out of view of the crowd, so that they might carry on normally. I felt rather foolish to have drawn so much attention to myself. I left the temple swiftly by a back door and went home through the lanes. My wife and son accompanied me. I felt bad about depriving them of the pleasure they had come to enjoy at the temple. My son was openly critical. 'Why should we go home so soon? I want to stay and watch the fun.' On our way we saw the schoolmaster going towards the temple, and I handed over the boy to him with: 'Please don't let him join the procession, he must come home for supper.'

'I'll bring him back,' said the teacher.

We were not gone long before we heard the piper resume his music, and the loudspeaker's mumbo-jumbo over the babble of the crowd, and that made me happy. Life had become normal again at the temple.

CHAPTER TEN

AT HOME MY wife unrolled a mat, spread a soft pillow and insisted upon my lying down to rest, turning a deaf ear to all my pleading that I was in a perfectly normal condition. She went in to make coffee and nourishment for me. She grumbled, 'Not eating properly, not sleeping, not resting. God knows why you wear yourself out in this way?' How could I tell her about Rangi? It would be awkward and impossible. But if I tried to explain it would be impossible to talk of the matter, leaving out Rangi. And if my wife should ask, 'When and where did Rangi meet you?' I would be unable to reply. I thought it best to accept the situation and rest my weary body on the mat and consume whatever was placed before me. Anyway no one was going to miss me, and nothing in the programme was going to be altered because I wasn't there. The whole programme was so well organized that nothing could be halted. That was the chief trouble now; neither Vasu nor the temple authorities seemed prepared to relax their plans ever so slightly. Each was moving in a fixed orbit as if nothing else mattered or existed.

After the refreshment she had provided me, I fell into a drowse. What had really been the matter with me was lack of food and sleep; now I was having both and benefiting by them. I enjoyed the luxury of floating off through the air on drifting cotton-wool immediately I shut my eyelids. My wife sat at my side, fanning me. She was very anxious about me. I don't know what she had heard. I myself had no notion what my state had been before I let out the shout about the elephant. My wife had dressed herself in her heliotrope silk sari, which she reserved for special occasions; it showed that she considered the temple function a most important one, and it depressed me to see her forgo it. I had implored her, 'Please go and enjoy yourself at the temple. I can look after myself quite well. Don't worry about me.'

She ignored my advice and replied light-heartedly, 'I went there only because you were there,' which pleased me. She added, 'Not that I care for these crowds. Babu was crazy about it, and has taken out all the savings in his money box for sweets and toys.'

'Oh, I should be with him. I could give him such a nice time,' I said remorsefully.

'You will do us all a favour if you keep away from the crowd,' she said, and added, 'Now sleep a little.'

'Why am I being treated like a baby?' I protested. She did not answer and I fell asleep, until I heard soft hammer-strokes on the walls of cotton-wool which had encased me. When the hammerstrokes ceased, I heard voices, and then my wife stood over me. A ray of evening sun thickened with iridescent specks of dust came in through the ventilator of our dining-hall. It used to have a red glass pane when we were young, and made me sick when the evening sun threw a blood-red patch on the wall. Luckily the red pane had been smashed by a stone thrown by a street urchin one mango season, who had actually aimed at the fruits ripening on the trees in our garden, and the pane was never replaced.

My wife said, 'Someone to see you.' She did not like any visitor to disturb me. Her tone was hostile. She added, 'His name is Muthu. Seems to be from a village.'

Immediately I was on my feet. 'Ah, Muthu! Muthu! Come in, please.'

He had his umbrella hooked as usual to his forearm. 'I wanted to see you and so came. I told the mistress of the house that I would wait until you were awake. Why did you disturb yourself? Go back and rest. I will wait.'

I resisted his suggestion, but he was so firm and insistent that I had no alternative but to go back to my mat. He followed me and sat down on the edge of the mat, carefully laying his umbrella on the floor beside his feet. He looked round appreciatively and cried, 'What a big house you have! Do you live in the whole of it or have you rented out a portion?'

I lay back on my pillow, and hotly repudiated the idea. 'I never want to be or ever wanted to be a rent-collector. We have always entertained guests rather than tenants.' I put into my sentence all the venom I wanted to inject into the memory of Vasu.

'It all depends,' Muthu said. 'There is no harm in making a little money out of the space you really do not need.'

'It depends,' I echoed. 'My wife would never permit me, even if I wanted to.'

'Then you can do nothing about it,' he said. 'It's best to

listen to the advice of one's wife—because sooner or later
that's what everyone does, even the worst bully. Take my
own uncle, such a bully for forty years, but at sixty he
became a complete slave to his wife. If people are not slaves
before sixty, they become slaves after sixty,' he said. He
was trying to amuse me—a sick man. It was obvious that
he was trying to steer away from the topic of the procession
and the temple ceremony. 'He waits for her command every
moment, and even stands and sits according to her direction,'
he said and laughed. It really amused me, this picture of the
bully fawning on his wife at sixty, and I cried to my wife,
'Coffee for my friend!' at which he shouted, 'Good lady,
no, don't trouble yourself, no coffee for me.'

'Don't listen to him, but bring the coffee or make it if
you haven't got it ready,' I cried. He called in turn, 'Good
lady, if you must be troubled, let it be just cold water, a
glass of water.'

'Is it impossible for me to offer you anything?' I cried.

'Yes, yes, I never need anything. I have told you I never
take anything outside my home.'

'And yet you want everyone to come and ask for tea in
the village!' I said complainingly.

'I never force it on anyone,' he said.

There was another knock on the door, and presently my
wife ran across to open it and came back, followed by Sen.
'Another cup of coffee,' I cried as she went back to the
kitchen. Sen cried, 'So good to see you again in this state;
the speech went off very well in spite of the interruption.
You really gave a shout which could have gone to heaven,
you know.'

'Why talk of all that now?' said Muthu.

'Why not?' cried the journalist aggressively. 'He is all right. And he was all right. Why shouldn't a man let out a shout if it pleases him? This is a free country in spite of all the silly rules and regulations that our Government is weaving around us.'

By the time my wife was ready with two cups of coffee, there was a third knock on the door, followed by another one a moment after: the pink-coated poet, followed by the veterinary doctor. So there was a full assembly on the mat at my house. My wife had to prepare coffee again and again. She accepted the situation cheerfully; the important thing was to keep me in good humour at home. The veterinary doctor felt my pulse and cried, 'You are in perfect gear, you must have had some temporary fatigue or something of the kind, a sudden attack of nerves . . .'

'I have never felt better,' I said, although the thought kept troubling me that the veterinarian was trespassing unwarrantedly into human fields.

'Haven't you noticed a dog let out a sudden howl, or an elephant trumpet out for no known cause? It's the same mechanism in all creatures. In our institute we spend a course of six months on comparative anatomy and psychology. Only the stimuli and medicinal doses differ between human beings and animals.'

As we were talking the beam of light on the wall had disappeared and a dull twilight was visible above the central courtyard. It seemed absurd that after the preparation of weeks we should all of us be gathered tamely on the mat in my hall instead of bustling about in the temple. What a difference between the picture of the situation as I had visualized it and as it turned out to be! I said with a sigh,

'All of us should be there at the temple.'

'There is nothing very much to do at the moment,' said the journalist. 'This is a sort of intermission. The main worship is over—the poems have been read and dedicated.'

'I missed it,' I said ruefully.

The poet said, 'You didn't miss much. I felt too nervous, and I don't think anyone understood anything.'

'It was quite good,' said Sen encouragingly. 'Some people came round to ask where they could get copies.'

'Probably they expect free copies.'

'Free or otherwise, the world will have to wait until I am ready to print,' I said.

Muthu said, 'Please give me also a copy.'

I said, 'Yes,' although I was not sure if he read anything.

The poet was by nature silent and retiring, and beyond sniggering a little he said nothing. The journalist had him in complete charge. 'Oh, I am sending review copies to thirty newspapers first thing tomorrow, and a special copy to Sahitya Akademi at Delhi. They are wasting funds giving an award to every Tom, Dick and Harry. This is the first time they have had a chance to recognize real literature. Our Government has no lack of funds, but they don't know how to spend properly, that's what is the matter with them. I am going to show them a way to redeem themselves. I put this into the Chairman's speech, pretty strongly, and he just recited it as I wrote it, although he is a Congressman.' He laughed at the memory of his trick.

Night fell. Lights were switched on. My wife began her work in the kitchen. I could hear the clinking of vessels. I said, all my responsibilities coming back into my mind one by one, 'Did the flower supplies, did the . . .' I fretted until they assured me that everything was going well. And then one by one they came round to asking what really had upset me. I had to tell them about Vasu's plans. They were incensed.

'Who is this upstart to come and disturb us? We will get the police to seize his gun.' 'We'll throw him out of the town.' 'I'll knock him down with a hammer, if it comes to that.'

I suggested, 'Why not change the route of the procession?'

'Why should we? We will change nothing for the sake of this man! We will twist his neck so that he faces the other way.'

'It's not possible. The route has been fixed and the licence taken for it. It's impossible to change anything.'

'Why not drop the procession altogether?'

'Thousands of persons to be frustrated because of this fool, is that it?'

'No—never. We'll deal with him. We have been too tolerant.'

'Or why not leave the elephant out?'

'Impossible. What's a procession without an elephant? You know how much we've spent on the elephant.'

'I'll be with Kumar myself, and let's see what happens. He is more sound in mind than any human being in this town.'

'No, no, let's change nothing,' Sen said. He swore, and the others agreed, 'We'll route the procession as arranged. Nothing shall be changed. Let us see what happens.'

Muthu became extremely nervous about his elephant. He lowered his voice and said, 'I knew something had been going on. It started long ago. Do you remember that tailor?

He is a friend of Vasu, fancies himself a part owner of the elephant. And I heard he has already received money from Vasu and has given him a document transferring to him his share of the elephant. I heard also a rumour that it was Vasu who tried to poison Kumar.'

'Aha,' said the doctor. 'I suspected something like it.'

They sallied out in a great rage, determined to tackle Vasu in a body. I could not stop them.

They were a determined lot. In their numbers they felt strong. First, led by the journalist, they started out to find the District Superintendent of Police at his home in Lawley Extension, for which purpose they hired Gaffur's taxi at the fountain. They found that he had just returned from a long journey, had put up a reclining chair and was resting on the terrace with a paper in his hand. Sen was his friend. He went straight to the terrace and spoke to him.

He listened to their complaint and said, 'How do you know that he is going to create a disturbance? How do you know that he will employ his gun in the manner you suggest? He has an arms licence, hasn't he?'

'So any man with an arms licence can shoot at anything, is that it? A wonderful law!'

The DSP was annoyed at the contemptuous reference to the law, and retorted, 'That depends; we cannot simply snatch away a licensed weapon because someone thinks it will be fired.'

'So you want to wait until the damage is done?'

'We cannot take action unless there is concrete evidence or a consequence.'

'Can't you do something to prevent possible damage to life and property?'

'That only a magistrate can do, but even he cannot bind anyone over without a proper cause.'

The Superintendent was a police officer, seasoned in jargon and technicalities. He refused to accompany them to Vasu's room, but telephoned to the Town Inspector, 'Have you made proper arrangements for this evening's procession? Have enough men to handle the crowd along the route. There must be no trouble or complaints anywhere. I've some people here who apprehend a breach of the peace. I want you to go with them and tackle a man who is threatening to create a disturbance. Meet them at the market fountain in five minutes.'

At the fountain, a police officer in uniform was there to receive them. They jumped out of the taxi, and surrounded the officer and gave an account of the impending trouble. He was a tall, lean man, with a lot of belts and cross-belts, a very serious-looking man with lines on his forehead. One look at him, and they were satisfied that here was a man who would stand no nonsense from anyone, a grim, determined man.

He simply repeated the doubts that the Superintendent himself had mentioned. 'If the man possesses a licence, he can keep his weapon wherever he likes. Who can question him?'

'But can he shoot from the window?'

'Why should he do that? What's your basis for saying it?' They had no answer to give and he said, 'All right, we'll see what we can do.'

The Inspector stayed downstairs. Led by Sen, supported

by the veterinary doctor, the pink-coated poet bringing up
the rear, they boldly went up the staircase and knocked on
Vasu's door. They were considerably emboldened by the
fact that a real live Inspector of Police was down below,
waiting to appear at the lightest summons. The door
opened, and Vasu's head appeared with its dark halo of
hair, set off by the light from his room. 'You people want
to see me now?'

'Yes,' said the journalist. 'Rather urgently.'

Vasu raised his brow. 'Urgent! All of you to see me?'
And then he counted, 'One, two, three, four people to call
on me! I don't want to see anyone now. So try again
tomorrow.' With that he turned back and tried to shut the
door in the face of his visitors. Since the door opened
outwards, the journalist seized the knob and held it back.
Vasu looked amused. 'Do you know, I could easily pick up
all four of you and toss you downstairs? When I plainly say
I don't care to talk, how can you persist? All right. I will
give you each a minute. Be brief. What is it?' He was not
disposed to admit them. He blocked the doorway, and they
were ranged on the landing.

The journalist stated point blank, 'We have a report
that there is likely to be a disturbance while the procession
passes down this road.'

'If you know that, why don't you take the procession
around somewhere else?'

'That's not your concern. We will not tolerate any
disturbance.'

'Oh, iron-willed men! Very good. I agree with you.
Don't tolerate any disturbance.'

'That elephant belongs to no one but the Goddess on

206

the hill road. If anyone tries to harm it . . .' began Muthu and Vasu cut in, 'Why don't you mind your tea-shop and keep off the flies, and leave these issues to others? Don't try to speak for any elephant.'

'We know what you have been trying to do, and we aren't going to stand any nonsense,' the veterinary doctor said. 'I have examined Kumar and know him inside out. He is in perfect health, more sober than any human being here.'

'So what?' asked Vasu.

'If anyone wishes to drive him crazy, he'll not succeed, that's what I wish to say.'

'Doctor, you may have an American degree, but you know nothing about animals. Do they have elephants in America? Try to get into a government department, count your thirty days and draw your sinecure's allowance. Why do you bother about these matters? Poet, say something in your monosyllables. Why are you silent? Don't be smug and let others fight your cause. Sell me a copy of your poem as soon as it is ready. That's all? Now be off, all of you.'

The journalist warned him, 'We are not bothered about you. We'll leave you alone. You leave our procession alone. This is a sacred function. People are out there to be with their God . . .'

'If God is everywhere, why follow Him only in a procession?'

The journalist ignored this remark and said, 'Hundreds of men and women and children with the chariot . . .'

'What's this special point about women and children? You are all practising chivalry, are you? If men are to be caught in a stampede, why not women and children also? What's the point in saving women and children alone?

What will they do after their men are stamped out? If you are a real philosopher and believe in reincarnation, you should not really mind what happens. If one is destroyed now, one will be reborn within a moment, with a brand-new body. Anyway, do you know why we have so many *melas* in our country? So that the population may be kept within manageable limits. Have you not observed it? At *Kumb Mela*, thousands and thousands gather; less than the original number go back home—cholera, or smallpox, or they just get trampled. How many temple chariots have run over the onlookers at every festival gathering? Have you ever paused to think why it's arranged thus?'

Vasu's philosophical discourse could not proceed further as the Police Inspector showed himself at this moment. He pushed the others aside and accosted Vasu.

The Inspector asked, 'You have a gun?'

'I have two,' replied Vasu.

'I want to see your licence.'

Vasu opened a cupboard, produced a brown envelope and tossed it at the Inspector. The Inspector went through it and asked, 'Where are your arms?' Vasu pointed to his rifle on the chair, and his revolver on the table. The Inspector went over, picked them up, and examined them. 'Are they loaded?' he asked.

'Of course they are loaded. They are not toys.'

'Where is your ammunition statement?'

'In that envelope.'

'When did you discharge your last shot?'

'Shut up, Inspector, and get out. I don't have to answer your questions. What's your authority for coming and questioning me?'

'Our DSP's order.'

'It's my order that you clear out, with this bunch of men who have no business here.'

The journalist protested. Muthu jumped up and down in rage. Vasu said, 'Inspector, you are trespassing in my house. Where is your warrant to enter private premises? Come on, produce a warrant. Otherwise I will complain against you for trespass and these men will be my witnesses. I'll wire to the Inspector-General and the Home Minister. You think you can fool me as you fool all these wretched bullock-cart drivers and cobblers and ragamuffins whom you order about. Whom do you think you are talking to?'

'Be calm, be calm. I came here only as your friend.'

'Nonsense. You my friend! I have never seen you.'

'I came to ask something of you, that's all.'

'What is it? Be brief.'

'I just want to suggest, why not let me hold your weapons for you in our Market Station. You may take them back tomorrow.'

Vasu said, 'I see that you are still toying with that gun of mine. Put it down where you took it from. Come on. Don't play with it.'

'I'll arrest you for disorderly behaviour and lock you up for the night or for any length of time under the Public Safety Act.' He took out his whistle, and was about to blow it and call the men who were patrolling the road below. Before anyone could realize what was happening, Vasu plucked the whistle out of the Inspector's mouth and flung it away. It sailed over the landing and fell with a clatter down below amid the pythons and all the other stuffed creatures. The Inspector was enraged. He raised his arm

209

and tried to slap Vasu's face. Vasu reared his head back, shielding his face with his hand, then gave a sweep with the back of his hand and brought it down with a slicing movement on the Inspector's wrist and dislocated it. The Inspector screamed and recoiled as if he had touched fire. He still held the gun in the other hand.

'I told you to put that gun back where you took it from. Will you do it or not?'

'You are trying to order me,' cried the Inspector. Tears welled up in his eyes through pain. Vasu took him by the shoulder and propelled him to the cot, then pushed him down, saying, 'Take a rest, you poor fish. You should not venture to do things without knowing what's what.' He snatched the gun from his hand and put it away. The police officer wriggled with pain. Vasu looked at him for a while, and said with cynical laughter, 'You have hurt yourself. I did nothing. I never hit anyone. Years ago I made that vow. If I had hit you with my hand—do you want to see what would have happened?' He brought his palm flat down on the iron frame of the cot and cracked it. The Inspector watched him mutely. Sen asked, 'Do you know what the penalty is for assaulting a police officer in uniform?'

'Do you know what the consequences could be for trespass? Anyway my lawyer will deal with it. Now all of you leave me. I do not want to hit anyone, you now know why. Inspector, you should not have hurt yourself like that!' He mocked the man in pain.

The veterinarian approached the Inspector and said, 'Let's get this dressed immediately. Come along, we'll go to the hospital.' They were all for leaving. Sen said, 'If anything happens to the people or the procession . . .'

210

Muthu said, 'We know what you are trying to do with that elephant. If anything happens . . .' which only provoked Vasu's mirth. The Inspector got to his feet, glared at Vasu and said, 'I'll get you for this . . .' The poet alone tried to sneak downstairs without a word. Vasu just held him by the scruff, turned him round and asked, 'Where is your patron saint? Send him up next. He's the one who has sent you all up on this fool's errand, I know.'

While all this was happening (as narrated to me by Sen later), at home my wife was arguing with me to stay put on my mat. I had got a passing notion that I ought to visit the temple and take charge of the procession. My wife was aghast at the idea. She repeated several times, 'The doctor has said you must not . . .'

'What doctor! He is only an animal doctor!' I said. 'We can't pay serious attention to what he says.'

But she was adamant and pleaded with me, 'Can't you stay in at least one day in a year!' She had prepared a feast for me. She knew all my preferences: potato and onion mash, rice patties fried in oil, chutney ground with green chili, sauce with brinjal and grated coconut, cucumber sliced, peppered and salted. She was so full of enthusiasm that I had to prevent her by my rude remarks from exceeding ten courses. Our house was fragrant with the frying in the kitchen. All this felicity was meant to be a compensation to me for missing the magnificent flower decorations, the music, the lights and the crowd. My son came home with his schoolteacher and was full of descriptions of what he had seen. He said, 'The chariot is made of jasmine buds, and they have fitted small electric bulbs all over it. Father, Father, I bought a sugar cane for the elephant. He snatched it from my hand, and you know how quickly he ate it! I bought him another one, and that left me with only six annas. I bought this whistle.' He produced from his pocket a reed whistle and blew shrilly. 'The mahout has promised to give me a ride on the elephant's back. My friend Ramu says that the elephant is borrowed and that it'll go away tomorrow. Is it a fact, Father? Let us have our own elephant for this temple. The mahout has taught him how to take a garland from a basket and present it to the God. He is very intelligent. Father, Father, please let me go and watch the procession.' His mother added from inside, 'If our neighbours are going and if you promise to stay in and rest, I would like to go and see the start of the procession and come back immediately. The child will love it. We can't say when we may have another chance.'

'All right, why not let me take you both?'

'No, no, in that case I don't want to go,' she said. 'It's not so important.' I enjoyed the status of being more important than the procession. To be fussed over like this came only once in a decade when one fell ill or down a ladder; it was a nice change from protecting and guiding others and running the household as its head.

I lay back on the mat, picked up a picture book and read Babu a story, much against his will as he only wanted to talk about the elephant and the procession. But we had exhausted the topic of the procession. He had been talking of nothing else; whom he met, who fell off the steps leading to the tower of the temple, why the drummer suddenly ceased in the middle of an enraptured performance because he found a grasshopper crawling down his spine—Babu knew who had perpetrated the joke because he had assisted him in tracking and trapping the grasshopper; how he and another friend snatched away from under the nose of the chief priest the plantains which had been kept on a plate for offering to the God, and to this minute no one could guess what had happened to the fruit. He looked at me triumphantly in appreciation of his own exploits. He narrated how he and his gang had devised a game of hide and seek between the legs of the devotees assembled in the hall and how, as they all stood in prayer with eyes shut, his friends had crawled between their legs and roused them by tickling their calf-muscles. I realized how he must have multiplied the task of those men who had been busy since morning chasing the urchins out. Then he went on to tell me how one of his friends was waiting for a chance to poke a needle into the elephant's side. At this I remonstrated, 'Never do that. An elephant will always mark such a fellow down and . . .' I thought I might turn his ideas from these dangerous paths and picked up one of his picture books and tried to read him a story. 'Once upon a time . . .' I began, but he was not interested. The activities of the temple were so immediate and real that the images of fiction were uninteresting. He got up and ran to the kitchen on the plea that he felt hungry.

Presently my wife called me in to dinner. She had spread out a large plantain leaf and had served my food on it as if I were a rare guest come to the house. She had placed a plank for me to sit on. She watched me with satisfaction as I made preparations to eat with relish. I suggested, 'Why don't you also put a leaf for yourself and let us serve ourselves?' She turned down my suggestion. She had decided to play the hostess and serve me ceremoniously. Nothing I suggested was going to be accepted today.

I enjoyed my dinner, and kept paying her compliments on her excellence as a cook. There was a knock on the door. Babu, who had finished his dinner, ran out to open it. He came back to say, 'A *mami* has come.'

'*Mami!*' cried my wife. She was busy serving me. 'It must be our neighbour come to see if I'm ready for the procession. Tell her to come in and take a seat. I'll see her in a moment.'

The boy said coldly, 'She is not asking for you. She is asking for Father.'

'What! Who is she?' asked my wife with a sudden scowl on her face.

I trembled within myself and muttered with a feeble, feigned surprise, 'Asking for me. Ha! Ha! It must be a mistake!'

My wife set the vessel down and went out of the room, saying under her breath, 'Let me see.'

The boy tried to follow her. I called him back. 'Boy, fetch me that water-jug.' When he came close to me with the jug, I asked in a whisper, 'Who is she? What is she like?'

'I don't know. She was in the temple dancing.'

I knew now. My worst fears were confirmed. All the fine moments of the evening, the taste of exquisite food, everything was turning to gall on my tongue. I knew my wife. Although I had had no occasion to test it, I knew she could be fiercely jealous. Before I had time to decide what to say or how to say it, she stood before me.

She said, 'That woman wants to see you. What's your connection with her?'

'What woman?' I asked with affected innocence. I got
up from my dinner, went out to rinse my hand and wipe it
on a towel, and came back to the hall. 'Bring the betel leaf
and nut.' I put on a deliberate look of unhurrying
indifference, though all the time I knew that Rangi was
waiting at the door. I chewed the betel leaves and went
back to the kitchen. My wife had settled down to her
dinner, serving herself. She did not look up. I said, 'Have
you any food left, or have I eaten everything up? If there is
nothing left, it's your own fault, you should not have
excelled yourself in that way!'

She tried to smile; my praise, very sincere of course, had
its effect. She was transferring food from the dining leaf to
her mouth with her head lowered. Now she looked up to
say, 'I have asked her to wait in the passage. I didn't want
the neighbours to see her at our door.' She had to lower her
voice in order not to be heard by the woman concerned.

I whispered back, 'You did right, you did right,' and
then, 'You could have asked her why she had come.'

'Why should I? If it's your business, it's your business,
that's all. I am not interested.'

I made a noise of vexation, and said, 'What a nuisance!
It must be something connected with the temple. Can't I
rest even for a day?' So muttering, I made my way towards
the dark passage. There she was standing in the passage.
She had taken off her gaudy dance ornaments and costume
and was dressed in a plain sari; even in the dark I could see
the emphatic curves of her body. I stood away from her, at
a safe distance, right by the inner doorway, and asked
rather loudly, 'What is the matter?' I did not want to carry
on a whispered dialogue with her.

215

But she replied in a whisper, 'I wanted to know how you were, master?'

I was touched by her solicitude. 'Oh, I'm all right. Nothing was really the matter.'

'I saw everything, but could not come over because I was on duty before the God.'

'Oh,' I said, feeling rather pleased. 'Are your duties finished for the day? What about the procession?'

'It's at nine o'clock. I shall have to get back.'

'Oh,' I said.

'Won't you go with the procession, sir?' she asked.

My son, who had stood around uneasily, feeling rather shy in the presence of a dancing woman, went away and hid himself in the kitchen. Rangi assumed an even softer and hoarser whisper to say, 'He came to my house in the afternoon when I was at the temple, and left orders that I should see him.'

I grew apprehensive, 'Don't go. Get back to the temple. Be with the crowd.'

'He may come to my house again and set fire to it. Only my old mother is there—deaf and blind.'

'Why should he set fire to your house?'

'He is wild with me and wants to talk to me!' she said with a sigh.

'Talk to you! He will probably murder you!' I said. She brooded over my words. I told her, 'Why don't you tell the police?'

She shook her head. 'He won't be afraid of the police. He is afraid of nothing. The police will laugh at me. What can they do? He is not afraid of anything or anybody. That's how he is.'

216

'Don't go to him,' I implored her.

My wife had finished her dinner and was passing up and down on various minor errands, casting sly, sidelong looks at the two of us in the dark passage. Rangi was sobbing at the prospect before her. 'I don't know what he will do to me! He has summoned me. He confided in me. I betrayed his trust. I had to . . . I hope, hope, you have taken precautions.'

'Oh, surely,' I said with a grand show of confidence and aggressiveness. 'We won't let a fellow like that get away with his ideas.'

'You don't know him well enough. He is afraid of nothing on earth or in heaven or hell.'

'We have our own methods for dealing with such fellows. We are a match for him,' I said.

'He is so strong and obstinate. If he thinks of something, he has to do it; no one on earth can change his mind.'

The woman seemed obsessed with the grandeur and invincibility of the man. I was not going to tolerate it. 'Rangi, don't be carried away by the notions you have of him. He is just an ordinary common bully. We know how to tackle him.'

'Now, what shall I do, sir? I have come to you because I don't know what to do. I thought of going to him to see if I could get him into a good mood to listen to my words. I have cooked his favourite *pulav* and have it here.' She indicated a hamper of food she had brought along.

'But you said yourself that it's impossible to make him change his mind.'

She whispered seductively, 'I'll try. A woman in my position has her ways.'

217

I didn't know what she meant, but it sounded mysterious. I said, 'He may not let you go back to the procession. Don't go to him. Go home.'

'If I don't obey his summons he may set fire to my house, with my blind mother not knowing what is happening.'

'I'll arrange for people to guard your house. Don't let him blackmail you into visiting him. He'll hold you back. He may even tie you up hand and foot. I'll send the proper people to guard your house.' I spoke grandiosely, without the shred of a notion how I was going to arrange it. She brought her palms together in a salute and left me, and vanished down the moonlit street.

I went back to my wife. I found her tidying herself up in the dark ante-room, before a mirror. I said expansively, 'You know what's the matter with that woman?'

'Why should it interest me?' she asked. I was struck by the cold, indifferent tone in which she spoke. 'I don't know who she is, and I don't care.' She readjusted her sari and called, 'Babu!' In a moment he was at her side. 'Coming to the temple?'

'Yes, of course.' He had already gone ahead, to the outer door. I asked her, 'Are you going to the temple?'

'Yes,' she said monosyllabically.

'But you said you would not go!' I said.

'Now I say I'm going, that's all there is to it.' I could see even by the dim light that her ears were red.

'I wanted to speak to you. I thought you might rest here and talk over things.'

She turned a deaf ear to what I was saying. I followed her mumbling, 'You wanted me to stay at home, now you are going!' I sounded pathetic.

'Stay or go, it's all the same to me,' she said and was gone down the steps. She went on down the road, with Babu prancing beside her. She had not given me a chance even to pick a quarrel with her.

I didn't like to go in. I sat on the *pyol*, looking in the direction in which she had gone. What was the use? There was a silly little hope that she would repent her brusqueness and come back to make amends. My only other companion for the night was a street-dog curled up in the gutter. All the other living creatures of that area had gone to the temple. Not a soul remained at home—except the asthmatic in the sixth house, whom I could hear cough and expectorate. Sitting there and brooding, I had time to take stock. The trouble with me was that I was not able to say 'no' to anyone and that got me into complications with everyone, from a temple prostitute to a taxidermist. I repeated to myself all the stinging rejoinders I should have hurled at my wife. I should have behaved like one of my ancestors (the story was often told by my great-aunt), who used to bring home his concubine and have her dinner served by his wife. So when my wife asked, 'What is your business with her?' I should have instantly said, 'I want to seduce Rangi or be seduced by her.' If my wife had said, 'Of all women!' I should have replied, 'Yes, of course, you are blinded by jealousy. No doubt she chews tobacco and looks rugged, but she has it—it comes through even when she whispers to you. How can any man resist her? I'm sorry for you. You should take more trouble to keep me in good humour. It's no good losing your temper or sulking or snapping a reply. If I followed the same procedure, you'd not be able to stand it for a second. As a man I have strength no doubt to stand all your nonsense. But you should not strain it too much. That's all now, don't do it again.'

The moon came over the roof-tiles of the opposite row of houses, full and brilliant. I could hear the hubbub of voices from the temple half a mile away. It saddened me to be detached from all this activity. I felt like a man isolated by an infection. I almost formed, as a sort of revenge on my wife, a plan to appear at the temple precincts and take a hand in the conduct of the procession. Without creating a panic, I would gently navigate the chariot into a different route. That is, of course, if I rushed around a bit, met the DSP and changed the permit for another route. There was not a single person in that whole throng who could organize and guide a procession as I could. I swelled with pride. I was the one man who could still achieve results.

But then I remembered I was an outcast. I felt nervous of appearing before the crowd again. I was not certain what I would do. Under the pressure of the crowd, if I let out a cry again, that would be the end of me. It might have the desirable effect of making my wife regret her petulance, but it was also likely to have me bundled off to the Madras Mental Hospital by the next train. I remembered a boy, a brilliant fellow, who had strode up and down Kabir Street singing all Tyagaraja's compositions for three days and nights continuously and had covered most of the compositions of that inspired saint. If he had been left alone for another day, he would have completed the repertory, but they seized and bundled him off by the five o'clock express to Madras. He came back a year later with a shaven head, but sober and quiet in all other respects. He was a friend of mine in my school days, and he confessed that he had sung Tyagaraja's compositions only because he was keen on letting the public get an idea of the versatility of that great composer, but now he was afraid even to hum the tunes in his bath. Our Kabir Street citizens had exacting standards of sanity. I didn't want to be seized and put into the Madras train. Even if I didn't create a scene, the crowd would look at me as if I had recovered from a fit of epilepsy. They would not let me go with the procession.

All my old anxieties, which had been falsely lulled, suddenly rose to the surface. I took stock of the situation. What cause had I for smugness? I had done nothing to divert the procession, I had done nothing to disarm or dissuade Vasu; God knew what trick he might have up his sleeve. He might do nothing more than fling a firecracker from his window or bribe one of the torch-bearers to hold the torch close to the leg of the elephant. All evening we had done nothing but discuss the various methods of maddening an elephant—a needle stuck into a coconut or banana and given it to swallow, an ant dropped in its ear, or a grain of sand in its eyes; it would be the easiest thing to drive an elephant mad. If people were lucky they might get out of its range or if they weren't a few might be caught and trampled to death, particularly if there was a stampede at that narrow bend in the Market Road, with the broad storm-drain on one side and the small mountain of road-metal heaped on the other (it was meant for the improvement of Market Road, but had remained untouched since 1945). People would thank anyone who shot the elephant at that moment. That poor elephant! He was enjoying all the fun today, decorated, happy, playing with the children, starting the day so well. Somehow he must return to the Goddess on the mountain road and graze in the forests on the blue hills and continue to delight the children in all those villages. Muthu hoped by hiring out the elephant for processions to earn enough money to build a tower for the temple of the Goddess, which would be visible for fifty miles around. It was impossible to conceive of Kumar stuffed and dissected and serving as an umbrella-stand or waste-basket in some fashionable home in the Eastern or Western world.

I had to do something. My wife had gone out, expecting me to act as the watchman of the house. It would be good to abandon the house and let her discover that after all she could not presume on my goodness. A better plan still would be to lock the door and take the key away so that when she came back after midnight she would wonder how to get to her bed. It was nearing ten, and the procession should be starting any minute now. No one could judge when it would arrive at the fountain. While on the road, the piper might start a big *alapama*, and until he attained certain flights and heights in a particular melody and returned to earth the procession would not move, even if it took an hour. So by stages it might take hours to cover the distance between the temple and the fountain.

There was no sign of the music yet. Only the hubbub of voices indicated that the crowd was still waiting for the procession to start. If it had started, I'd have heard the voices and music moving nearer, and above all my wife would have come back home. However temperamental she might be, I knew she would not go with the procession along with that crowd. She had enough sense to return home in time.

I felt angry at being chained to the house. I would go into the outer fringes of the crowd unrecognized and study the situation. I shut the door behind me and stepped down. I walked to the end of the street. Two men were coming in my direction. I stopped them to ask, 'Has the procession started?'

'No, they are waiting for ornaments for the elephant. Someone has gone to fetch them from the Talapur temple, head-ornaments of real gold.'

Ten miles up and ten miles down, and perhaps an hour getting the ornaments out of the temple vaults. No chance of the procession starting before two a.m. What madness! Did it mean that my wife was going to stay at the temple till two? With the boy? I was in a measure relieved; every hour's delay seemed to me an hour's reprieve. I went back home; if the procession was starting late, then there was no purpose in my loitering at the temple gate. I went back home and laid myself down on the *pyol*. If I was to be a watchman, I'd better be one thoroughly, not a haphazard one! I didn't want the house to be looted; this was just the chance thieves waited for, when every householder would have gone out to the festival.

Lying on the mat on the *pyol*, as I kept gazing on the moonlit street, I fell asleep. I woke up hours later as I heard drums and pipe music approaching—I knew that the procession was in Market Road, parallel to our house. I grew worried about my wife and son, thinking that they were still out. On second thoughts I went in. I saw her asleep in her bed, with the child also asleep. I must have been soundly asleep indeed not to have known when she arrived. She must have come in long ago and gone to sleep.

She ought to have wakened me, but she had preferred to go on practising her coldness towards me. In order to mete out the same treatment to her, I went back to my mat on the *pyol*.

I lay tossing on my mat. Far off the piper's music came from the procession. I followed it, visualizing all the stages of its progress. Now it must be passing the elementary school conducted on the top storey of the Chairman's sweetmart, a rickety terrace which would come down any day, but no one could prevent it being there because it was the Chairman's building and was certified to be safe. Some day when it fell it was going to imperil the lives of a hundred schoolchildren and six or eight teachers. But so far it had lived up to the optimistic estimate of the municipal authorities and most of its ex-pupils were now adults working and earning a living in various walks of life all over India; I preferred to send Babu to another school, however. The drummer made enough noise to shatter the foundations of this precarious building, but it was a matter of courtesy for the procession to stop there, and the piper had saved his breath for his masterpiece—'Bhairavi'. He was beginning an elaborate, intricate rendering of this melody, and that means the crowd would gather round him, the God would repose in his chariot, the elephant would stand ahead of the procession with the mahout asleep on his back. People would crowd around the piper and behave as if they had no further way to go.

It was much better that the procession halted here than at the fountain. The time was around midnight now, and it would take at least an hour for the procession to approach the market fountain. I had plans to join the procession and

mix with the crowd an hour hence, and till then there was
no harm in sleeping. 'Bhairavi' could be heard as well here
half asleep as anywhere, and so I allowed myself to be
lulled by it, my favourite melody in any case. It brought to
my mind my childhood, when visiting musicians used to
come as our guests; there was a room in our house known
as the musician's room, for we always had some musician
or other staying with us, as my father was very proud of his
familiarity with all the musicians in south India and
organized their recitals in our town. (One of the charges
levelled against him by the opposing lawyer was that he had
squandered the family funds in entertaining musicians.)
This room was also used as a storing space for old bottles.
The great joke in those days was to answer, when anyone
questioned why old bottles were kept so safely, that if my
uncles sued for them, they could be given their due share.
The room contained about seventy philosophical works too;
the entire philosophical library collected by my father or
someone before him in Sanskrit and Tamil, along with
bronze images used for worship. They had been willed to
the third uncle, but they were left in our custody as my
uncle was in the railway department and never stayed in the
same place for more than three months. He was never
known to have opened a book in his life after leaving
school, but still he occasionally sent us a postcard to inquire
if the volumes of philosophy were safe. Whenever my
mother got into an argumentative mood, she would arraign
my father for being a custodian of other people's property,
and demand to know why he did not throw the articles out
and get rid of all the responsibility. But my father was fond
of his brothers, whatever they might do, and told her not

to peep into that room as there was sufficient space in the rest of the house for her to mind.

I must have fallen asleep. When I woke up 'Bhairavi' was no longer being played but some other tune, and the music was coming from close quarters across the row of buildings on Market Road. If my judgement was right the procession must now be near the silkware house. The next stop would be the fountain. I was seized with anxiety. The procession was nearing the range of Vasu's window. What reason had I for my inactivity? What right had I to presume that Muthu and the rest would have succeeded in restraining Vasu? Suppose they had done nothing, and a torch-bearer scalded the toe of the elephant and drove it mad? My duty now was clear. I must go and divert the procession away from the fountain and turn it into a side-street. But this might itself start a panic, and if Vasu really meant no mischief I should become responsible for a lot of panic and confusion.

There was no use lying here and cogitating while every minute a vast assembly was moving towards its doom. I had to do something about it. I got up briskly. I could hear my wife stirring, awakened by the pipe and band; she would probably come out to watch from the end of Kabir Lane, in which case I did not want to meet her. I walked across the road, opened the back door of my press and shut the door behind me. I was going to make a last-minute attempt to stop Vasu. He was not such a bad fellow after all. He would listen to me. He was considerably mellower than he used to be. I looked up at the attic. There was no light in it. Of course he would put out all lights. He was the prince of darkness, and in darkness his activities were to be conducted.

226

Suddenly I was inspired by all sorts of wonderful and effective plans. They were not shaped very clearly in my mind yet, but I was positive that all would be well. If you had asked me to see a blueprint, I would perhaps have fumbled, but deep within me the plans were ready, I felt sure. I would first steal up to his room, walk softly to his side; he was sure to be watching the window. Why not stun him from behind and save everyone all the worry and trouble of argument? Not practicable. One might talk of finishing off a cobra with a staff of bamboo, but it was always more likely that the cobra would prove smarter. Vasu might after all not be facing the window, but facing the door. Non-violence would be the safest policy with him. Mahatma Gandhi was right in asking people to carry on their fight with the weapon of non-violence; the chances of getting hurt were much less.

I had to squeeze myself through a little fence between my press and the staircase; the jeep was there all right. He was undoubtedly upstairs. It might be a good idea to set its petrol tank on fire. That would keep him busy until the procession passed. Of course he might make pulp of me if he discovered me doing it, but why not? No one was going to miss me. My wife was separated from me, there was none to bemoan my loss; true, Babu was likely to miss me for a few days, but children adapted themselves to new circumstances with surprising ease. It was pleasing to reflect that my wife would after all learn a lesson, that sulking did not pay. When Rangi spoke to me on an important matter, the thing for a rational being to do was to ask what exactly it was all about and approach things in a scientific frame of mind . . . No wonder Vasu was bitter against the whole world for its lack of scientific approach. If people were scientific-minded they would not jump to conclusions when a man spoke to Rangi in a half-dark passage.

I was at the foot of the staircase. The hyena was still there but pushed away to the side; it must have been a wasted labour for Vasu. It was surrounded by a few other odds and ends of dead creatures, nothing outstanding among them, but a miscellany of small game, such as a wild squirrel, a fox, a jungle dog, a small cheetah, and several reptiles. Vasu seemed to have turned his attention to small things in keeping with our Government's zeal for small industries. The smell of hide and packing-cases overwhelmed me.

I climbed the stairs. I had presumed all along that the door would be open. What if it should be shut? I would knock on it and allow events to develop. I was going to stop him from disturbing the procession; that was certain, but how was a question I still could not answer. I was going to depend upon my intuition. I was prepared to lose my life in the process.

I found the door open. I gave it a gentle push and peeped in. There he was as I had visualized him, beside the window, on a long easy chair. The lights, the Kitson vapour lamps and the torches of the procession were already illuminating the walls of the room, and there were moving shadows on them. The band and the pipe and the shouts of the men pulling the chariot could be heard from below. I could see his silhouette at the window, where he seemed to have made himself comfortable, with a pillow under his head. He had stretched his leg on a stool, he had his timepiece on another small table, and his gun lay on the floor within his reach. I could see so much by the flares flickering along the wall through the narrow window. Other silhouettes, of the small tiger cub and a few animals, stood out in the semi-darkness. He didn't move. That was a good sign. He had probably fallen asleep waiting for the procession to come along. All the drumming (they could at least have had the sense to pass the spot noiselessly, as a precaution) had apparently made no impression on him. He was obviously a sound sleeper, thank God.

My decision was swift; I would make a dash for his gun and seize it. My heart palpitated and my breath came and went like a bellows as I crawled towards the gun. If he woke up before I reached it, that would be the end of me. I started crawling like one of those panthers of the Mempi jungle, the distance between me and the gun being only a dozen feet; I covered half of it, the other half seemed interminable. My knees were sore, but I felt that it was for a good cause that I was skinning them. He was still asleep. As my fingers reached the cold butt of his gun, I could have swooned with excitement. I had never touched a gun before and felt scared. I rose to my feet and covered him with the gun. Below the window the procession was passing rather quickly, as I thought. I wished I could go up and take a look at it, but he was between me and the window, and if he slept through it that would be the best arrangement possible. If he woke up, well, I had the gun with me at point blank range. I would follow the method they used in films and command him not to stir until the procession passed. If he made the slightest movement, I would pull the trigger. My finger was on it already. Although I had had no practice with guns, I knew if I fiddled with the trigger the shot was bound to go off. I held the muzzle directly at his head, keeping it away, just out of his reach, in case he attempted to snatch it from my hand. I would hold him until the procession passed our road . . . and then how was our encounter to conclude? I couldn't say. I felt rather worried about it, although I was triumphant at my success thus far. I couldn't keep my eyes off him, although I was curious to watch the procession. From my place I could see the flower-decked top of the chariot and the little bulbs sparkling on it, the head of the elephant brilliant with the gold plates from Talapur, and the hunched form of the mahout. While passing he cast a look through our window. I supposed he had been advised to drive fast. In a moment he was out of view, and soon the procession itself was gone. The reflections on the walls vanished and the drums and pipes sounded far away, leaving a faint aroma of jasmine and roses in their wake. Just at this moment I was startled by the alarm bell of the clock going off. I gave a jump, the gun dropped from my hand, and I made a dash for the landing out of Vasu's reach.

CHAPTER ELEVEN

LIFE RESUMED ITS normal pace on the Market Road next morning, although the day started late. It was as if our town were waking up from a fantasy full of colour, glitter, crowd, and song. After this, it was difficult to wake to a dull workaday world. The Market Road was covered with litter, banana peels, coconut shells, leaves, and flowers. Municipal sweepers were busy. Sastri came only at nine o'clock and went straight to the type-board; he seemed determined to complete K.J.'s labels today. Muthu and the rest had left by an early bus for their respective homes. I sat at my desk and placed a pad and a pencil in position in order to make a note of payments to be made, cash in hand and cash promised. My head was still very unclear about the practical aspects of everything.

Our postman, Thanappa, whom we had known as children, old enough to have retired twice over but somehow still in service, was my first visitor for the day. I remembered seeing him in the days when postmen were given a red turban and a shining belt, a leather bag and khaki uniform. He had passed from that to the latest stage of donning a forage cap—a portly old man who not only knew the address of every citizen in the town but also the ups and downs of their fortunes. He was a timeless being. At his favourite corners, he spread out his letters and bags and packets and sat down to a full discussion of family and social matters; he served as a live link between several families, carrying information from house to house. All this took time, but nobody could hustle him, and we accepted our letters when they came. He was welcome everywhere. His habit when he came to my press was to stand in the doorway, rest his shoulder on the doorpost, and spend at least half an hour exchanging information with me. Only before leaving would he remember to give me the letter or book-packet. Today he stood on my door-step and looked serious, blinking through his inch-thick glasses. There was a frown on his face, and he breathed hard with excitement. He held up a letter without a word. I said, 'Come in, Thanappa,' and asked, 'How did you like the procession last night?' He mumbled something and moved in as if he were in a trance. He placed the letter on my desk. 'This receipt has to be signed.'

I saw it was addressed to Vasu. 'This is for him, Thanappa. Take it upstairs.'

'I went up, but, but,' he wetted his lips with his tongue, 'he is dead.' He spoke softly, he looked scared. 'I usually take his mail to his bed, though I hate to go to his room. I thought he was sleeping in his chair. I went up with the letter. I almost touched him,' he said with a shudder. The man looked desperate with the disgust he felt at the memory of that icy contact.

I said, 'Thanappa, go and deliver those letters and try to

get this thing out of your mind. Don't speak about this to anyone. I will go up and see things for myself and come back.'

Thanappa hesitated for a second and decided to follow my advice. He asked, 'So this registered letter goes back? Has no one else authorization to sign for him?' He picked up his bag and stepped out.

I went down the steps, around the side street and through the yard, and stood for a moment at the foot of the stairs, with the hyena shoved aside and mouldering in a corner, its glassy stare fixing me at the foot of the steps. I hesitated for a moment in the desperate hope that I might hear the stirrings of feet above. But there was the unmistakable silence of death. I reluctantly took myself up.

There he was as I had seen him last night on his canvas chair, with his arm dangling at his side. I went near and peered closer to see if he was really dead. For the moment I was not bothered with the mystery of his death but only with the fact. He had accustomed us so much to a still-life view that he seemed logically to be a part and parcel of his own way of life. The alarm-clock which had screeched in the dark on the previous night was now ticking away modestly. Its pale pink face must have watched the process of Vasu's death. I looked around. The frame of his bed was smashed; that was probably the reason why he could not sleep there but only on the easy chair. Somehow at that moment I took it very casually and felt no bother about how he might have met his end. I folded my arms across my chest, remembering that I had better not touch anything and leave a fingerprint. Anyway, Thanappa's fingerprints were bound to be there, so why add mine to the confusion and complicate the work of the police? My desire to search for Vasu's purse and read the blue letter in it was really great, but I didn't want the police to conclude that I had killed him and taken his purse. I peered closer to see if there was any injury. His black halo of hair was rumpled and dry. His eyes were closed. I could see no trace of injury. 'Where is all your bragging,' I thought, 'now, and all your pushing and pulling and argument? Are you in heaven or hell? Wherever you are, are you still ordering people around?' I noticed on a low stool the jute bag containing food which I had seen in Rangi's hand on the previous night at my house. I wanted to see if he had eaten it, but the lid of the brass vessel was covered tight and I did not like to give it my thumb impression. His clothes lay, as usual, scattered on his cot and on every available space. The lid of his trunk was half open, revealing his familiar clothes, particularly the red check bush-shirt and the field-grey jacket he affected when he went out on his depredations. I stood over his trunk and kept looking in; if I could have rummaged in it without touching anything I would have done so. I wished I had gloves on, but this was not a part of the world where gloves were known. Not all my precautions to leave things alone could keep me from giving a jump when I saw the green folder peeping from within the folds of his clothes. What an amount of trouble he had given us over it! He had said, 'An orang-utan has carried it up a tree and gone back to the jungle. If I see it again, I shall ask it to return it to the rightful owner, namely Mr Nataraj. I know he will oblige us, he is a very reasonable orang . . .' and laughed at our desperation. All I had been able to muster was, 'We didn't know orang-utans existed in

India.' 'You want to teach me wild life?' he had asked
aggressively. That was before our last break, after which he
walked out of my office and I never saw him again until I
swallowed my pride and went up to the attic to plead with
him for the elephant. The green folder peeped out of a linen
bushcoat and a striped Singapore *lungi*. I brooded for a
moment about how to extract it without disturbing the
arrangement. I went out to the terrace to see if I could find
some handy stick with which to grasp it and pull it out. I
became desperate, as I realized that I must hurry now. The
voices of people in the street frightened me. I was afraid
that Sastri might suddenly come up and scream for the
police. It was essential that I should take charge of the
green folder before anyone else saw it here. I fervently
hoped that Thanappa had the sense to keep his mouth shut.
The alum solution, moulds and various odds and ends and
nails were there, but not a cleft stick with which I could pry
the green folder out. I thrust my hand under my shirt,
worked my fingers through the end of my shirt, and gently
tugged the folder from his clothes. A couple of angry
mosquitoes buzzed around my ears, but I could not wave
them away as my hands were engaged. I now had the folder
in my hand. This would solve, more than the mystery of his
death, the mystery of the festival accounts. I could give the
poet details of the moneys collected on his behalf, though
perhaps not the cash. I hurriedly opened the folder and
looked in; the papers were intact, the printed appeal and a
list of the donors and the receipt book; but cash? Not much
to be seen, except a bundle of one-rupee currency notes. I
tucked it under my arm and was leaving when I caught
sight of the tiger cub on the small table, covered over with

a handkerchief. He had valued it at two thousand rupees. I seized it with the covering and quiely went down, leaving the door ajar. I passed into the side street; the cub, his masterpiece, was small enough to be hidden under my arms along with the files. A couple of pedestrians were passing along. I walked bravely with my articles, dreading lest someone should be in my office waiting for me. Luckily there was no one. I quickly opened the roll-top desk, pushed the tiger cub and the file in, and locked it.

My office became an extension of the Town Police Station. The District Superintendent of Police set himself up in the Queen Anne chair. They had found the grille I had put up between the treadle and the staircase irksome, as it made them go round every time by the side street. It was unlocked and the place was thrown open for the entire city to walk about in. All kinds of people were passing in and out, going upstairs and coming downstairs. It became so crowded that I found it impossible to do any work in the press, and Sastri had no space to stand and set his types. The sanctity of the blue curtain was destroyed, gone for ever. Anyone could push it aside and go up; I dared not ask who he was; he might be a plain-clothes police officer, the Coroner's Committee man (there was a body of five to find out and declare the cause of Vasu's death), a newspaper correspondent, a hanger-on, or the thin-legged policemen sent up for sentry duty on the attic landing to watch that no one tampered with evidence. Vasu dead proved a greater nuisance than Vasu alive. Anyone who had had anything to do with him for the past six weeks was summoned to my press by the police. Muthu was there, away from his tea-shop, the poet was there, the journalist was, of course, there, and the elephant doctor and the tailor (who was bewailing all along that he had promised clothes for a wedding and ought to be back at his sewing machine). A police van had gone and brought them all. Sastri proved to be the shrewdest. The minute he heard of the corpse upstairs he planned his retreat. He hesitated for a moment, smiled to himself and remarked, 'I knew he would come to some such end; these people cannot die normally.' He had been preparing to work on the fruit-juice labels. He just put his work away, wiped his hand on a rag, and took off his apron; I watched him silently. He went through his process of retreat methodically. He said, 'These things happen only in the expected manner. Only I didn't think it would happen so soon and here. What a worry now! Our press has had such an untarnished reputation all through.' He sighed and remained silent as if I had been responsible. Confirming this hint, he said broadly, for the hundredth time within the last few months, 'On the very first day he came here you should have turned him out. You didn't.'

I asked, 'What's your plan now?'

'I am going home and then I am catching the afternoon train for Karaikudi. I have to attend my wife's niece's marriage.'

'You never told me about it!' I said in surprised anger.

'I'm telling you now,' said the imperturbable Sastri. 'You were so busy the whole of yesterday that I couldn't get a word with you.' He pulled out a yellow wedding invitation and showed it to me as evidence.

'When will you be back?' I asked.

'Well, as soon as the marriage is over,' he said and prepared to go. 'Our train leaves at one o'clock.'

'The police may want you here,' I said viciously.

'I have nothing to do with Vasu or the police,' he said with a clarity of logic rare under the stress of the present circumstances. It was true. He had resolutely kept away from contacts with Vasu. While all of us were running around him, Sastri alone had maintained a haughty aloofness. No one could ever associate Vasu with Sastri. I had no authority over Sastri. I could not stop him. He went out by the back door to Kabir Street. At the doorway he paused to say, 'Anyway, what is the use of my staying here? There is no space for doing any work here.' With that he was off.

As I said all my friends were there as if we were assembled for a group photo. Rangi . . . oh, I have forgotten Rangi. After the night's endless gesticulations before the God, she looked jaded in a dull sari, with unkempt hair, and stood in a corner. She would not sit down before so many. The lean man, the Town Inspector, was among those who had to be provided with a seat. The DSP from his seat of honour kept glancing around at us. He had demanded a table and I had to request my neighbour with the Heidelberg to spare me one from his office. He was only too willing to do anything. He looked overawed by the whole business—a murder at such close quarters. He gave me a teak table which the burly DSP heaped with a lot of brown papers and drew up before the Queen Anne chair. To this day I do not understand why he held the inquiry in my office rather than at the police station. Perhaps they wanted to hold us until the body was removed to the mortuary, which was a small tin shed at a corner of the compound of the District Hospital. Under this hot tin roof, there was a long stone table on which Vasu would be laid. I was depressed to think that a man who had twisted iron rods and burst three-inch panel doors with his fist was going to do nothing more than lie still and wait for the doctor to cut him open and examine his insides to find out what had caused his death.

At the mortuary, the wise men, five in number, had stood around the stone-topped table, read the report of the pathologist, and declared, 'Mr Vasu of Junagadh died of a concussion received on the right temple on the frontal bone delivered by a blunt instrument. Although there is no visible external injury to the part, the inner skull-covering is severely injured and has resulted in the fatality.' In addition to this they had also taken out his stomach contents and sent them for examination to Madras Institute, there to be examined for poisoning. The wise men reserved their final verdict until they should have the report from Madras. Meanwhile they ordered the burial of the body according to Hindu rites in order to facilitate exhumation at a later stage if necessary. At this one of the five demurred, 'How can we be sure that the deceased would not have preferred to be cremated?' At this they looked at each other, and since there was no way of ascertaining the wishes of the person concerned, they hesitated for a moment until the foreman said, as if on a sudden revelation, 'We shall have no objection to a final disposal of the body in the form of cremation; the present step is only an interim arrangement until we are able to ascertain the causes of the death of aforesaid Vasu with certainty.' Everyone grabbed this sentence as a way out.

Assembled at my press, they desperately tried to discover the origin of the brass food-container found in Vasu's room. They kept looking round and asking, 'Can anyone throw light on who brought this vessel? Can anyone say to whom it belongs?' They turned the vessel round in their hands, closely looking at it for any signature of ownership. They failed. I could see Rangi squirming in her corner, twisting and untwisting the end of her sari around her finger. She kept throwing anxious glances in my direction and fidgeting; if the police officer had not been so hectically busy writing, bent over his papers, he might have easily declared, 'I charge you with being the owner of this brass utensil,' and led her off to the lock-up. When I opened my mouth to say something she almost swooned with suspense. But I merely remarked from my seat on the edge of my desk, 'I often noticed his food coming to him in that vessel.'

'Where was he getting his food from?' An excellent chance to confuse things by making the nearest restaurant busy defending their innocence. I thought over the name of restaurants I might mention. What about the Royal Hindu Restaurant? The owner used to be my customer and had walked out after creating a scene over a slight delay in the delivery of his printed stationery. I dismissed the thought as unworthy, and said, 'I've really no idea. The deceased must have been getting his food from various quarters.' I spoke breezily. The Superintendent looked up coldly as if to say, 'Don't talk more than necessary.' But I was in my own place and no one had the right to ask me to shut up. I added, 'It doesn't seem as if its lid has been opened.' The Superintendent made a note of this also, and handed the vessel around for inspection to the Committee. They all examined it and said, 'Yes, the lid does not seem to have been opened.' The Superintendent made a note of this again, and then asked, 'Shall we open this to see if it has been touched?' 'Yes,' 'Yes,' 'Yes,' 'Yes,' 'Yes.' He took a statement from the five to say that the lid had been opened in their presence. They watched with anxious concentration as the lid was prised off. It was placed on the table. The smell of stale food hit the ceiling. A strong-smelling, over-spiced chicken *pulav*, brown and unattractive, was stuffed up to the lid. Everyone peered in, holding his nose. 'It has not been touched.' The verdict was unanimous. 'Shall a sample be sent to Madras?' 'No.' 'Shall we throw this food away?' 'No.' 'What shall be done with it?' 'Keep it till the report from Madras is received. If there is suspected poisoning, the food can be analysed.'

The Superintendent wrote this down and took their signatures. He passed the container to be sealed in his presence to an orderly, and then the five men appended their initials on the brown paper wrapped around it. The DSP worked like an impersonal machine. He did not want to assume any personal responsibility for any step and he did not want to omit any possible line of investigation, always laying the responsibility on the five wise men chosen for the purpose. If they had said, 'Put this Nataraj in a sack and seal him up; we may need him in that state for further investigation,' he would have unhesitatingly obeyed. Sealing up was the order of the day. Vasu's room was sealed, the food-container was sealed, and every conceivable article around had been sealed.

The Superintendent's writing went on far into the night; he must have written several thousand words. Each one assembled there had to say when he saw Vasu last, why, and what were that worthy man's last words. While Rangi totally denied baving seen him last evening, the others were not in such a lucky position, the whole lot of them having gone there in a body after seeing the Superintendent. They gave a sustained account of what he had said to them. It was computed that he must have died at about eleven at night, and where was I at eleven?—at home sleeping on the *pyol* after seeing my wife off to the temple. My wife was brought in by the back door to corroborate me, my son too. Fortunately no one knew of my last visit to the attic. I bore in mind our adjournment lawyer's dictum, 'Don't say more than you are asked for.'

The only satisfaction I felt was that our Town Inspector was treated as one of us, made to sit in our group and answer questions before the Committee. Normally they would have let him handle the investigation, but the situation was no different; he was also one of us, an aggrieved party. His hand was in a sling and his finger was encased in a plaster cast, having suffered a slight fracture. He had to clear himself first—a most awkward thing. When his turn came to make a statement, he began bombastically, 'I was ordered to supervise the peace and security arrangements on the Market Road on —— at —— when I had a call at the control room from our District Superintendent of Police ordering me further to investigate a complaint of threat to the safety of the crowd from one Mr Vasu of Junagadh. When I went up to question the said person and take charge of his licensed weapon, he assumed a threatening attitude and actually assaulted the officer on duty, causing a grave injury.' He held up the bandaged part of himself as an exhibit. And then, according to him, he went away to take all reasonable precautions for the peaceful conduct of the procession. He intended to file a complaint as soon as they were free in the morning, and proceed against the same person officially for assaulting an officer on duty. He failed to mention that he had told Vasu before leaving, 'I will get you for it.'

I and Muthu discussed it later, when the incident was officially closed. If anyone had breathed a word then, it might have complicated the Inspector's version and placed him definitely on the defensive. But everyone was considerate. Still, the Inspector had to prove where he was at the time of Vasu's death, which occurred two hours after he had been visited by the Inspector. He explained that he had left the security arrangements in the hands of his assistant while he had gone in the police car to the District Superintendent's residence to report to him, and then to the District Headquarters Hospital to secure medical attention. He could cite both the District Superintendent of Police and the medical officer on duty at the casualty section as witnesses. But still Muthu felt, as he confessed later, 'What prevented the man from sending someone to do the job? A number of them might have gone and overpowered the man. I don't say it is wrong, but they might have done it, and hit his skull with a blunt instrument.'

During the following days the air became thick with suspicion. Each confided to the other when the third was out of earshot. Sen, who walked down the road with me for a breath of fresh air after the police left us, said, 'That tea-shop man Muthu . . . I have my own doubts. People in rural areas are habitually vindictive and might do anything. How many murders are committed in those areas! I won't say in this instance it was wrong. Someone has actually done a public service. I wouldn't blame anyone.'

'What would be Muthu's interest in murdering Vasu?'

'Don't forget that the elephant was his and that he was anxious to save its life at any cost. He could have just sneaked up. Where was he at eleven o'clock?' He cast his mind back to remember if Muthu had by any chance slipped away from the procession. He gave it up, as they had been too engrossed in the procession to note each other's movements.

The poet came to me three days later all alone. 'I was with Sen this afternoon in his house in New Extension, and, do you know, I noticed in a corner of his room, amidst a lot of old papers, a blunt thing—a long iron bolt which they use on railway sleepers. He looked embarrassed when I asked why he had it. Easiest thing for him to have slipped upstairs, gone up from behind . . . I don't blame him. He had stood enough insults from that man. I knew that Sen would do something terrible sooner or later . . . I wouldn't blame him.'

I knew that they were all unanimous in suspecting me when I was not there. I could almost hear what they were saying about me. 'Never knew he could go so far, but, poor fellow, he had stood enough from him, having made the original blunder of showing him hospitality. Whether he took him in as a tenant or just as a friend, who can say? Who will let his house free of rent to another nowadays? Whatever it may be, it is none of our business why he gave him his attic. But how that man tortured poor Nataraj! Poor man, his patience was strained. Deft work, eh? What do you say? Smashed the vital nerve in his brain without drawing a drop of blood! Never knew Nataraj could employ his hand so effectively! Hee, hee!'

My wife said the same thing to me that night when I went home. Our friendly relations were resumed the moment she heard that there was a dead body in the press and that the police had assembled in my office. Since the Rangi episode, the first words uttered between us had been my urgent invitation to her to come and say where she had seen me at eleven o'clock on the previous night. She hesitated, wrung her hands in fear and despair. 'Oh, why should you have got mixed up in all this affair? Couldn't you have minded your own business like a hundred others?' I was very humbled now, and very pleased that at least over Vasu's dead body we were shaking hands again. I had been gnawed by a secret fear that we might never resume friendly relations and that all was over between us. She rubbed it in now. 'That woman, and all sorts of people—what was your business with them really?'

I had no satisfactory answer for her, and so said, 'I have no time to explain all that now; the DSP is waiting; you will have to come and say where I was last night at eleven o'clock.'

'How could I know?' she asked. 'I will tell him that I didn't see you.'

'Yes, say that and see me hanged, and then you will probably be able to collect a handsome insurance on my life.' She screamed and covered her ears. 'You could also describe how you deserted me on the *pyol* to guard the house and went out. It will do you good to speak the truth. And if you remember your visit to the temple, you will probably also remember having seen Rangi there, so that you will not be tempted to say I had gone out with her.'

'I didn't see her at the temple,' said my wife simply. She had got out of her suspicious mood of yesterday but had not decided to let go of it fully.

I said, 'While we are bantering here, the police . . .'

'Why should they believe what I say? Won't they think you have tutored me?'

'Oh, it is only a formality, they are not analysing evidence of any sort. They will record whatever you say or I say or anyone says, and that is all that they want at this stage, so you had better come along.' She was very nervous at coming before the Superintendent, but she would not hear of the public recording her statement at home. She said, 'After all these years of honest and reputable living, we don't want the police marching in and out. Even in the worst days when the property was partitioned no one dreamt of asking the police to come. We don't want to do that now.' She preferred to walk across the street when the neighbours were not looking and slip into my press by the back door and face the police.

That night I went home at eleven o'clock. Babu had gone to sleep. My wife said, 'Hush, speak gently. Babu wouldn't sleep. He was too excited about everything. I managed to send him to sleep by saying that it is all false and so forth. But he is terribly excited about everything . . . and, and, feels proud that you killed a *rakshasa* single-handed! At least you have Babu to admire you.'

'For God's sake don't let him spread that sort of talk. The noose may be put around my neck.'

She sighed deeply and said, 'A lot of people are saying

that. After that rent control case . . .'

'Oh, shut up,' I cried impatiently. 'What nonsense is this!'

'You may close the mouth of an oven, but how can you close the mouth of a town?' she said, quoting a proverb.

I saw myself as others saw me, and was revolted by the picture.

CHAPTER TWELVE

AT FIRST I resented the idea of being thought of as a murderer. Gradually it began to look not so improbable. Why not? It had been an evening of strange lapses. I could remember nothing of what I had said or done to cause the fuss around me that evening at the temple hall. Later was it quite impossible that I had battered someone's skull and remembered nothing? Going over my own actions step by step, I remembered I had gone up the staircase stealthily, opened the door on the landing. So far all was clear. The procession was passing in the street below. Vasu lay in a long chair beside the window. I had crawled towards his gun and run out when the alarm-clock screamed. Between my entrance and exit I remembered holding the gun at Vasu's head until the lights of the procession vanished. Perhaps while he slept I had rammed the butt of the gun into his skull. Who could say? But what about the time of his death? The doctor had declared that the man must have died at eleven, long before I had sneaked up the attic stairs. But the doctor might have hazarded a guess; it was one more item in a long list of conjectures!

I had clung to the hope that Rangi had poisoned Vasu and then smashed his head, but the chemical examiner at Madras reported, 'No trace of poisoning.' With that the last trace of hope for myself was also gone. While I sat in my press all alone I caught myself reconstructing again and again that midnight visit to the attic, trying to gain a clear picture of the whole scene, but each time I found it more confounding. When people passed along Market Road and looked at me, I averted my head. I knew what they were saying, 'There he sits. He ought really to he hanged for murder.' My friends of Mempi village never came near me again. They had had enough trouble with the police as the result of knowing me and visiting my press. 'That press! Lord Shiva! An accursed spot! Keep away from it!'

There was not a soul with whom I could discuss the question. Sen avoided me. The poet was not to be seen. He took another route nowadays to the Municipal School. During my morning trip to the river and back no one stopped to have a word with me. The adjournment lawyer and the others hurried on when they saw me in the distance. All the same one morning I accosted the adjournment lawyer at the bend of the street where the barber's house abutted. He pretended not to see me and tried to pass. 'Sir,' I cried, stepping in front of him.

He was flurried, 'Ah, Nataraj! Didn't notice . . . I was thinking of something . . .'

'I want to ask you . . .' I began.

'What about? What about?' he asked feverishly. 'You see I am out of touch with criminal practice. You should really consult . . .'

'Consult? For what purpose?' I asked. 'I have no problem.'

'Oh, yes, yes, I know,' he cried, fidgeting uneasily. 'I remember that they left an open verdict, nothing was imputed or proved. After all who can be sure?'

'Oh, forget it,' I said with the casual ease of a seasoned homicide. 'It is not that. I am more worried about the collection of dues from my customers. When did you celebrate your daughter's marriage? Months ago! Why don't you pay my charges for printing those invitation cards? What are you waiting for?'

'Oh, yes, by all means,' he said, edging away.

'I have no one in the press to help me. Even Sastri has left me. You had better send the cash along instead of waiting for me to send someone to collect it.' A touch of aggression was creeping into my speech nowadays. My line of thinking was, 'So be it. If I have rid the world of Vasu, I have achieved something. If people want to be squeamish, they are welcome to be so, but let no one expect me to be apologetic for what I have done.' I hardened myself with such reflections, and suffered at the same time. The press was silent. I kept my office open at the usual hours. Visitors were few. I spent my time attempting to read Tolstoy's *War and Peace* (discovered among the seventy philosophical volumes in the family lumber room) and diverting myself by following the complex fortunes of Russian nobility on the battlefields of ancient Europe.

I caught sight of the poet one morning beyond the fountain. Before he could avoid me and take another route to his school I ran forward and blocked his way. I implored him to come into the press and seated him in the Queen Anne chair.

'What has happened to you all?' I asked.

'They have given me eight more hours of work a week, with so many teachers absent!'

'Ah, innocent poet!' I thought. 'What clumsy guile you have cultivated within these last weeks!' I asked aloud, 'What about Sen?'

'I don't know, he was expecting a call from a Madras paper.'

'Don't lie!' I cried, suddenly losing my temper. 'Haven't I seen him sneaking in next door to get some work done on the Heidelberg? You people are avoiding me. You think I am a murderer.' He remained silent. I checked myself when I noticed the terror in his eyes. He glanced anxiously over his shoulder at the doorway, interpreting the glint in my eyes as maniacal. I wanted to speak to him about the accounts entombed in the green folder, about the moneys collected on his behalf and spent by Vasu, and to explain to him about the tiger cub I had seized, but all I could produce was a shout of abuse at the world in general. I realized that I was frightening the poet. I modified my tone to a soft whisper, smiled, and patted his back. I said, 'I want to give you a present out of the money collected for your benefit. Something in kind, something salvaged.' I fixed him with a look lest he should try to escape, flicked open the roll-top desk, and brought out the stuffed tiger cub. I pulled off the kerchief covering and held it to him. He looked transfixed.

'A tiger! What for?'

'It is yours, take it,' I said. 'He valued it at two thousand. Something at least . . .'

He gazed back at me as if noticing in my eyes for the

first time unplumbed depths of lunacy. He pleaded
desperately, 'No, I don't want it. I don't need it. I do not
want anything. Thanks.' He suddenly shot out of the Queen
Anne chair, dashed out, and was soon lost in the crowd on
Market Road.

'Poet! Poet!' I cried feebly. In addition to thinking me a
murderer, perhaps he thought I had embezzled his funds
and was now playing a prank on him. This was the greatest
act of destruction that the Man-eater had performed; he
had destroyed my name, my friendships, and my world.
The thought was too much for me. Hugging the tiger cub,
I burst into tears.

While I was in this state Sastri parted the curtain and
entered. 'I came by the back door,' he explained briefly.

'Ah, Sastri!' I cried in sheer joy. 'I thought you would
never come back.'

He was business-like, and turned a blind eye on my
emotional condition. 'After the marriage at Karaikudi, my
wife insisted on going on a pilgrimage to Rameshwaram,
and to a dozen other places. A couple of children fell ill on
the way. I was fretting all along to get back, but you know
how our women are! Sickness or not, my wife insisted on
visiting every holy place she had heard of in her life. After
all, we get a chance to travel only once in a while . . .'

'You could have dropped me a postcard from
somewhere.'

'True,' he said, 'but when one is travelling it is impossible
to sit down and compose a letter, and the idea gets
postponed.' He took out of his pocket a tiny packet
containing a pinch of sacred ash and vermilion and held it
out to me, saying, 'Offerings from all the temples mixed

252

together.' I daubed the holy dust on my forehead.

He noticed the tiger cub on my lap and exclaimed, 'Ah, what a tiny tiger!' as if humouring a child. His silver-rimmed spectacles wobbled and his face was slightly flushed. I knew he was shuddering at the sight of the stuffed animal, but still he pretended to be interested in it and stretched out his hand as if to touch it. He was trying to please me. He said, 'It must have been a pretty baby in the forest, but what a monster it would have become when it grew up! Did *he* give it to you?' he asked after a pause. I couldn't explain that I had stolen it from the dead man, and so I remained silent.

'I meant to give it to the poet,' I said, 'but he spurned it and went away.' I was on the point of breaking down at the thought. 'He may not come again.'

'It is natural that a poet should feel scared of a tiger. In any case what could he do with it?'

'He may never come this way again.'

'So much the better for us. Anyone who refuses to come here and waste our time must be viewed as a well-wisher. K.J. is our customer, and you may be sure he will always come to us.'

'Naturally. Where else can he get the magenta, even if he wants to leave us?'

'People who have business with us will always come and keep coming.'

'Everyone thinks that this is a murderer's press,' I said gloomily.

He gently laughed at the notion and said, 'They are fools who think so, but sooner or later even they will know the truth.'

253

'What truth?' I asked.

'Rangi was with him when he died. You know I am on the temple committee,' began Sastri, 'and she came to see me on business last evening. I had a feeling all along that she was hiding some information. I refused to listen to her problem unless she told me the truth. Much against my principles, I called her inside the house, seated her on a mat, gave her coffee and betel leaves to chew, and induced her to speak. My wife understood why I was asking this woman in and treated her handsomely on the whole.'

'What did Rangi say?' I asked impatiently.

'It seems that evening she carried a hamper of food to him. He refused to eat the food, being in a rage over many things. Rangi had perhaps mixed some sleeping drug with the food, and had hoped that he would be in a stupor when the procession passed under his window. That was her ruse for saving the elephant that night. But the man would not touch the food!'

'He might not have felt hungry,' I said, remembering the eatables that I had plied him with earlier that day.

'It may have been so, but it embarrassed the woman because she had duties at the temple that night. She was really bothered as to how she was going to get out of the place. When he understood that the procession might start late, he set the alarm-clock and sat himself in his easy chair. He drew another chair beside his, and commanded the woman to sit down with a fan in hand and keep the mosquitoes off him. He hated mosquitoes, from what the woman tells me. He cursed the police for their intrusion, which had made him break his cot-frame to show off his strength and now compelled him to stretch himself in an easy chair instead of sleeping in his cot protected by a mosquito-net. Armed with the fan, the woman kept away the mosquitoes. He dozed off. After a little time she dozed off too, having had a fatiguing day, as you know, and the fanning must have ceased; during this pause the mosquitoes returned in a battalion for a fresh attack. Rangi was awakened by the man yelling, "Damn these mosquitoes!" She saw him flourish his arms like a madman, fighting them off as they buzzed about his ears to suck his blood. Next minute she heard a sharp noise like a thunder-clap. The man had evidently trapped a couple of mosquitoes which had settled on his forehead by bringing the flat of his palm with all his might on top of them. The woman switched on the light and saw two mosquitoes plastered on his brow. It was also the end of Vasu,' concluded Sastri, and added, 'That fist was meant to batter thick panels of teak and iron . . .'

'He had one virtue, he never hit anyone with his hand, whatever the provocation,' I said, remembering his voice.

'Because,' said Sastri puckishly, 'he had to conserve all that might for his own destruction. Every demon appears in the world with a special boon of indestructibility. Yet the universe has survived all the *rakshasas* that were ever born. Every demon carries within him, unknown to himself, a tiny seed of self-destruction, and goes up in thin air at the most unexpected moment. Otherwise what is to happen to humanity?' He narrated again for my benefit the story of Bhasmasura the unconquerable, who scorched everything he touched, and finally reduced himself to ashes by placing the tips of his fingers on his own head. Sastri stood brooding for a moment and turned to go. He held an edge of the curtain, but before vanishing behind it he said, 'We must deliver K.J.'s labels this week. I will set up everything. If you will print the first colour . . .'

'When you are gone for lunch it will be drying, and ready for second printing when you return. Yes, Sastri, I am at your service,' I said.

NOVELLA

Talkative Man

TALKATIVE MAN

NARAYAN WAS A voracious reader of British magazines of the late 1920s, most of which had stories narrated by someone in a club, or by the fireside after dinner. One assumes that these gave Narayan the idea of using the literary device of a narrator, who was not Narayan, the bard of Malgudi, but a storyteller in his own right. The result was the Talkative Man who tells, in first person, several of the early stories Narayan wrote, which usually deal with some minor catastrophe that occurred to him. *Talkative Man* is the first full-length story in which the character appears. 'They call me Talkative Man. Some affectionately shorten it to TM. I have earned this title, I suppose, because I cannot contain myself. My impulse to share an experience with others is irresistible, even if they sneer at my back. I don't care.' In this novella, the TM meets Dr Rann, who claims to be a United Nations specialist, and unable to find a place for the strange visitor—who, as they used to say, was suited and booted—takes him to his own house. The TM's troubles start now. Being a journalist he manages to take a photograph of Rann and publish it in his paper. Trouble starts soon enough for the TM. Dr Rann displays a real interest in the local female population, and one day, a large and powerful looking woman, who introduces herself as Commandant Sarasa, flourishes his news story about Dr Rann and demands to be taken to him as she is his deserted wife.

Talkative Man is really an extended short story, but it is as full of Malgudi as any of Narayan's longer novels. The minor characters come to life at the magic touch of Narayan—the bewildered railway station master, the photographer, the librarian are all true citizens of Malgudi. Hilarious as the book is, and manic things happen in the usual Narayan style, the book was described by the *New York Times* as 'the kind of tragicomic storytelling that can make the exotic seem familiar'.

THEY CALL ME Talkative Man. Some affectionately shorten it to TM: I have earned this title, I suppose, because I cannot contain myself. My impulse to share an experience with others is irresistible, even if they sneer at my back. I don't care. I'd choke if I didn't talk, perhaps like Sage Narada of our epics, who for all his brilliance and accomplishments carried a curse on his back that unless he spread a gossip a day, his skull would burst. I only try to interest my listener or listeners, especially that friend Varma who owns the Boardless Hotel. (He is considerate, keeps a chair for me inverted in a corner so as to prevent others from occupying it, although from the business point of view I am not worth more than a cup of coffee for him, whenever I stop by.)

My chair was generally set facing a calendar portrait of that impossible demon Mahishasura with serpents entwining his neck and arms, holy ash splashed on his forehead and eyeballs bulging out through enormous side-whiskers, holding aloft a scimitar, ready to strike. I never liked that picture . . . too disturbing. It was a seven-year-old calendar, ripe to be discarded, but Varma would not hear of it. He would boast, 'I have never thrown away any calendar for thirty years. They adorn my walls at home, sometimes four on a nail, one behind another. All our Gods are there. How can anyone discard God?'

It was no use arguing with that man Varma; he was

self-made, rising from a menial job to his present stature as the proprietor of the Boardless, which fact proved, according to him, that he knew his mind and could never be wrong. I never tried to correct him, but listened, even appreciatively, to his spasmodic reminiscences. Fortunately he was not much of a talker, but a born listener, an ideal target for a monologist: even while counting cash, he listened, without missing a word, as I sat beside his desk and narrated my story.

The story that enchanted Varma was the one about Dr Rann, which I told him off and on spread over several weeks.

Dr Rann was actually, as I discovered later, Rangan, a hardy Indian name which he had trimmed and tailored to sound foreign; the double N at the end was a stroke of pure genius. One would take him to be a German, Rumanian or Hungarian—anything but what he was, a pure Indian from a southernmost village named Maniyur, of the usual pattern: tiled homesteads and huts clustering around a gold-crested temple that towered over an expanse of rice fields and coconut groves; similar to a hundred others, so commonplace that it escapes the notice of map-makers and chroniclers.

From this soil arose Rann of double N. He had blonde hair, a touch of greenish-blue in his eyes, and borderline complexion—unusual for an Indian of these parts. My private view on his ethnic origin might sound naughty, but is quite an historic possibility. A company of British, French or Portuguese soldiers must have camped at Maniyur or in its vicinity in the days when they were fighting for colonial supremacy and, in the intervals of fighting, relaxed by philandering among the local population.

I met him for the first time at the Town Hall reading room. Those were the days when I was struggling to establish myself as a journalist. They used to call me Universal Correspondent since I had no authority to represent any particular publication. Still, I was busy from morning till night, moving about on my bicycle or on my neighbour Sambu's scooter. I was to be seen here and there, at municipal meetings, magistrates' court, the prize distribution at Albert Mission, with a reporter's notebook in hand and a fountain pen peeping out of my shirt pocket. I reported all kinds of activities, covering several kilometres a day on my vehicle, and ended up at the railway station to post my despatch in the mail van with a late fee—a lot of unwarranted rush, as no news-editor sat fidgeting for my copy at the other end; but I enjoyed my self-appointed role, and felt pleased even if a few lines appeared in print as a space-filler somewhere.

I did not have to depend on journalistic work for my survival. I belonged to one of those Kabir Street families which flourished on the labours of an earlier generation. We were about twenty unrelated families in Kabir Street, each having inherited a huge rambling house stretching from the street to the river at the back. All that one did was to lounge on the *pyol*, watch the street, and wait for the harvest from our village lands and cash from the tenants. We were a vanishing race, however, about twenty families in Kabir Street and an equal number in Ellamman Street, two spots where village landlords had settled and built houses nearly a century back in order to seek the comforts of urban life and to educate their children at Albert Mission. Their descendants, so comfortably placed, were mainly occupied in eating, breeding, celebrating festivals, spending the afternoons in a prolonged siesta on the *pyol*, and playing cards all evening. The women rarely came out, being most of the time in the kitchen or in the safe-room scrutinizing their collection of diamonds and silks.

This sort of existence did not appeal to me. I liked to be active, had dreams of becoming a journalist, I can't explain why. I rarely stayed at home; luckily for me, I was a bachelor. (Another exception in our society was my neighbour Sambu, who, after his mother's death, spent more and more of his time reading: his father, though a stranger to the world of print, had acquired a fine library against a loan to a scholar in distress, and he bequeathed it to his successor.)

I noticed a beggar-woman one day, at the Market Gate, with Siamese twins, and persuaded my friend Jayaraj, photographer and framer of pictures at the Market Arch, to take a photograph of the woman, wrote a report on it and mailed it to the first paper which caught my attention at the Town Hall reading room; that was my starting point as a journalist. Thereafter I got into the habit of visiting the Town Hall library regularly to see if my report appeared in print.

The library was known as Lawley Memorial Library and Reading Room, established on a bequest left by Sir Frederick Lawley (whose portrait hung from a nail high up near the ventilator) half a century ago. An assortment of old newspapers and magazines was piled up on a long table in the middle of the hall, mostly donated by well-wishers in the neighbourhood. Habitual visitors to the reading room sat around the table on benches, poring over newspaper sheets, not noticing or minding the dates on them. An old man sat at the entrance in a position of vantage and kept an eye on his public. He had been in service from time immemorial. He opened the doors precisely at nine in the morning and strictly closed them at five in the evening, shooing off the habitués, who sometimes stepped in the opening and stayed on. 'Fortunately,' said the old man, 'the Committee won't sanction candles or lanterns, otherwise those loungers would not leave till midnight.' He was intolerant and suspicious of most people, but tolerated me and, I could say, even liked me. There was a spare seat, a wooden stool at his side, which he always offered me. He admired my activities and listened to my city reports, and hoped I'd find some donors to subscribe for current newspapers. I managed to get some money from Varma himself, though he was resistant to all approaches for money, that enabled us to get two morning papers from Madras.

Today when I entered the Reading Room, I found my usual seat occupied, and the librarian looked embarrassed. A man dressed in full suit was sitting on my stool. He looked so important that the librarian, as I could see, was nervous and deferential, which he showed by sitting forward and not leaning back with his legs stretched under the table as was his custom. He looked relieved at the sight of me, and cried, 'Here is a man waiting for you.' The other made a slight movement, acknowledging the introduction. I threw a brief glance at him and decided he was an oddity— dressed as he was in a blue suit, tie, and shining shoes, and holding a felt hat in hand. He sat without uttering a word. Somehow, I resented his presence and suppressed an impulse to say, 'Why do you sit there dumb? Say something and above all quit my seat. I am not used to standing here.' The newspaper addicts at the long table were watching us, so unused to seeing anyone in a blue suit and hat in the Town Hall. The old librarian was fidgeting, unable to attend to his routine work.

I fixed my look rather severely at the stranger and asked, 'You wish to talk to me?'

'Yes,' he said.

'Then come out,' I said. 'We must not disturb the readers.' I felt triumphant when he rose to his feet and followed me to the veranda. I surveyed the prospect before me with authority and declared to my companion, 'Not an inch of space for us to sit,' and then glanced at him from head to foot, and realized that the fellow was short— though while seated he looked imposing. 'Not an inch,' I declared again, 'everybody is everywhere.' Vagrants were stretched out on the lawn, fast asleep; idlers sat in groups cracking peanuts and popping them in. The cement benches scattered here and there were all taken.

'Let us step down and see,' he said, looking about, trying to conceal his disgust at the spectacle of Malgudi citizenry. 'How is it so many are asleep at this hour?'

'They must have spent a busy night,' I said.

I began to enjoy his discomfiture and said, 'Why don't we go over and sit in that shade?' indicating the southern corner where a spreading banyan tree stood with its aerial roots streaming down. He threw a glance in that direction and shuddered at the sight of more loungers in addition to a couple of donkeys standing still like statues, and mongrels curled up in the dust. He looked outraged at my suggestion. I added, 'The grass is soft there,' asking myself, What, did this man expect Spencer's Furnishing Department to provide him cushioned seats?

He simply said, 'I am not used to sitting down. Lost the habit years ago.'

'How long ago?' I asked, trying to draw him out. Hoping he would become reminiscent. He ignored my question and asked suddenly, 'Is there a bar or a restaurant where we may possibly find a quiet corner?'

I really had no idea still why he sought me, out of the hundred odd thousand populating our town. The librarian must have given him a golden account of me. Why was that old man so fond of me? I suspected that he might be a match-maker and have his eyes on me as eligible for his granddaughter, me a bachelor with not a care in the world, owning property in Kabir Street.

'No bar or a good enough restaurant,' I said and added, 'nor do we have an airport or night club except Kismet in New Extension, not very good I hear. If you are interested I could give you a long list of things we don't have—no bars, sir, we have only toddy shops, which serve liquor in mud pots, which one has to take out.'

'Not interested, thank you. I am a TT. I only order orange juice at a bar and seek a quiet corner for a chat.'

'Nor are apples and oranges known here. We only come across mango, guava, gooseberry, all cheap fruits,' I said, getting into a devilish mood and resenting more and more this man's presumptuous presence in our town. I was exaggerating its shortcomings, avoiding mention of Pasha's

Fruit Stall at the northern end of the market, which displayed on its racks every kind of fruit. He was said to get his apples directly from Kulu valley, grapes from Hyderabad, dried fruits from Arabia, and so on. He won prizes every year for the best display of fruits at the market.

'When did you arrive?' I asked Rann when we had managed to find a vacant space on the fountain parapet. Two men had just moved away, and I grabbed their seats as if jumping out of a queue. He had no choice but to stoop down, blow off the dust, spread his kerchief, and sit beside me on the parapet. After all these preambles I now left it to him to begin a conversation. He remained silent waiting for me to question him. After a few minutes, I remarked on the weather and went on to a lot of political titbits to prove that I wasn't taken in particularly by his blue suit.

'What did the old man tell you about me?' I asked.

'That you were the one person who could help me.'

'What sort of help? I had no notion that I was so important.'

'Don't say so, one can never judge oneself. You are a journalist, active and familiar with this town, and certainly would know what's what.'

That won me over completely, and I asked, 'Where are you from?'

'Timbuctoo, let us say.'

'Oh, don't joke.'

'No joke. It is a real place on the world map.'

'Oh!' I said. 'Never expected any real person to come out of it. You are the first one.'

He became serious and said, 'A lovely place on the west coast of Africa. A promising, developing town—motor cars in the streets, skyscrapers coming up—Americans are pouring in a lot of money there.'

'May I know what took you there and what has brought you here?'

'I was on a United Nations project.'

I didn't ask what. Project is a self-contained phrase and may or may not be capable of elaboration. I come across the word in newspapers and among academicians, engineers and adventurers. One might hear the word and keep quiet, no probing further. Sometimes a project might involve nothing more than swatting flies and sending reports to the headquarters.

He volunteered an explanation as if catching the trend of my thoughts. 'I have to send a report to my headquarters out of the voluminous data I have collected. I am also writing a book on a vital theme. I learnt that this is a quiet town, where I may collate my material in peace. Here I have been the last three days, practically living in the little waiting room of your railway station. Oh! the bed-bugs there! I sit up all night for fear of them. Tell me, who is the railway minister now, and help me to draft a letter to him.'

His presumptuousness annoyed me. Ignoring his question I hallooed to the peanut vendor hovering about with a bamboo tray on his head. When he came up I engaged myself in a game of haggling, disputing his measure and quality, before buying a handful of nuts which I kept on the parapet beside me. My friend looked rather shocked. I explained, 'Full of protein, you know, packed and hermetically sealed by nature, not the minutest microbe can sneak in: you may pick the nut off the road dust, crack it open, and eat it without fear of infection. Don't you consider the arrangement splendid?'

I demonstrated my observation by hitting a nut on the cement surface to crack it open, and held it out to him. He shrank from it, mumbling an excuse.

The next duty he imposed on me was to bring him out of the railway waiting room. The station master was distraught. He was a diminutive person whose job was to flag in and out two passenger trains at wide intervals, the non-stop express, and the goods wagons. After each performance he re-rolled the flags, tucked them under his arm, and turned into his office to make entries in a buff register while the Morse keys tapped away unattended. After the passengers left, he put an iron lock on the platform gate and retired to his 'quarters', a small cottage fenced off with discarded railway sleepers, besides a Gul Mohur tree in whose shade his children, quite a number, swarmed, playing in the mud. He was a contented man, one of the thousands apparently forgotten by the Railway Board in far-off Delhi. He still had two years' service before retirement, and then he would go back to his village a hundred miles away. It was a life free from worries or hurry until this stylish passenger alighted from Delhi. His blue suit and manner overwhelmed the little man, as he stepped out of a first-class compartment majestically.

The old porter thought, with some pride, Someone from London, and hoped for a good tip. The train moved. The porter tried to lift the big suitcase. The visitor said, 'Waiting room,' at which the porter looked embarrassed.

The diminutive station master noticed the scene and

came running after completing his duties in his little office.

'You are in charge?' inquired the visitor.

'Yes, sir, I'm the station master,' replied the man with a touch of pride but restraining himself from adding, I've still two years to go and then will retire honourably, back to my village where we have our ancestral land, not much, four acres and a house.

'Where is the waiting room?'

'Over there, sir, but please wait, I'll get it ready for you.'

He himself took charge of the suitcase from the porter, although he was only a few inches taller than what was really more like a wardrobe trunk, and hauled it along to the station veranda.

'Don't drag it, I'll carry it,' implored the visitor.

'Never mind, sir,' said the station master and would not let go his grip till he reached the veranda. The porter was gone to fetch the keys of the waiting room and also a broom, duster, mop and a bucket. Opening the door, the station master begged, 'Don't come in yet.' With the porter's help he opened a window, dusted and swept the room, and got it ready for occupation. He kept saying, 'I've requisitioned for carpet and furniture at headquarters.'

'After a couple of days, he realized that the grand visitor had no intention of leaving. Dr Rann went out in the morning and came back only at night. It was against the rules to let anyone occupy the waiting room for more than two nights, but the station master was afraid to say so to the present occupant. Next time I visited the railway station with my letter for posting, the station master said, 'The Railways Act is very clear as to rules for occupancy of waiting rooms, but there is this man who wants to stay permanently. I fear I'll get into trouble—for thirty years I've served without a single adverse note in my service register—if the DTS ever stops for inspection, it'll be the end.'

'How can he know how long the occupant has been—'

'Entries in the register.'

'Don't make the entry.'

'For thirty years I have lived without a remark in my service records.'

'I'll ask him to buy a ticket for the next station, while waiting for the train. He can buy a ticket for Koppal, which will cost after all two rupees,' I said. But, he looked miserable at the prospect of a doom after thirty years of unblemished service.

'Don't worry about it,' I said finally. 'Keep him for another day or two till I find him a place. I'm sure your DTS won't come in the near future. Even if he does, mention my name, and he will say OK.'

I had the journalist's self-assurance although I did not have any paper or news editor to call my own. (The station master, I noticed, was too timid to ask my full name, knowing me only as a journalist.) He was busy fingering the telegraph keys.

'7 Down will be at the outer signal in a few minutes.'

He got up and directed the porter to run up to the yard and release the signal. The train arrived, and a group of villagers returning from the weekly market fair at Koppal got off with their baskets, bags, bundles and children. I ran up to the mail van and handed in my despatch for the day, with the late fee. The mail sorter said, 'Why do you waste money on the late fee, when you could post normally at the HO?'

'You may be right,' I replied, 'but I have to wait till the last minute for news. Anything might turn up at the last minute.'

He stamped the envelope and the engine whistled and moved, while the station master stood flourishing the green flag. The porter went up to lock the signal lever.

I chose this moment to take out a five-rupee note and present it to the station master, with, 'Just a goodwill token for the festival.' I could not specify a festival, but there was bound to be one every day in the Hindu calendar. 'We have 366 festivals for 365 days,' said a cynic once. The station master was used to receiving such goodwill tokens from businessmen, who did not want their parcels to be held up in the goods yard and loaded on a later train. The station master looked pleased as he pocketed my five-rupee note.

I whispered, indicating the waiting room, 'The one in there is no ordinary soul—he is from Timbuctoo.'

The station master was duly impressed with the manner in which I delivered this news. He asked, 'Where is Timbuctoo?'

I did not know myself, so I said: 'One of those African countries, you know . . . interesting place.'

Between the bugs and the station master, Rann felt uncomfortable continuing as a resident of the waiting room. And for me the daily visit to the railway station for mailing my despatch was becoming irksome. The moment he flagged off the 7 Up, the station master would turn his attention to me; luckily, he would not immediately be free, as he always had something to write on those hideous buff-coloured forms, or had to give a couple of taps to the telegraph key in his office, all this activity taking less than five minutes. When he dashed into his office for this brief interregnum, I could dash out and escape, but when he found me trying to slip away, he gripped my arm and led me into his office. I fully knew his purpose—to talk about his waiting room occupant.

'Sir, you must think of my position—you must do something about that man there—he can't make this his home.'

'Why do you tell me?'

'Whom else am I to tell?'

'How can I say? I'm not his keeper. Why don't you speak to him yourself?'

'I don't know how to speak to such gentlemen.'

'A pity! I don't know how to speak to such gentlemen myself. I have not been taught.'

He wailed, 'I don't know how to approach him. He goes out, and when he comes back, he shuts himself in and bolts the door. Once Muni knocked on the door and was reprimanded severely. When he comes out he moves so fast, I can't speak to him at all.'

'That's how they live in foreign countries—they always move fast and won't tolerate any disturbance except by previous appointment.'

'Oh, I didn't know that,' he said seriously.

Another day he wailed, 'That gentleman was angry this morning. He said he is going to report to the Railway Board about the upkeep of the station—you think I care? I have served for thirty years—I can ask for retirement any moment if I like. What does he think? Am I his father-in-law to look after him?'

'Definitely not,' I said and he looked pleased at my concurrence.

'He is grumbling about bugs and mosquitoes as if the railways were cultivating them! The notions some people have about railways!'

Rann would buttonhole me in the Town Hall, where he knew my hours of visit. He also browsed among the musty ancient volumes in the back room, having gained favour with the librarian.

'I say, my friends—the bugs are eating me up every night. Do something. That funny man at the station says that it is not his business to keep the waiting room free of bugs and mosquitoes.'

'May be that is the Railway Board's policy to discourage the occupants from staying too long.'

'Should I write to the Railway Board?'

'No use, the bugs being a part of our railway service— they are service bugs actually.'

'Oh, I didn't realize,' he said, taking it literally.

'Anyway, why should you stay on there?'

It was the wrong question. 'Where else can I go?'

I shook my head, trying to evade any responsibility he might thrust on me. But there was no escape. He said, 'I can leave the railway station only when you find me another place.'

I ignored this proposal but could not suppress my curiosity. 'How long do you have to be here?'

'I don't know,' he said, 'till my work is completed. I have to make a field study, collate and organize my material and write. I have found some rare reference volumes in the stack room of the Town Hall library—some early nineteenth-century planters' experiences and their problems, which give me priceless data for my study.'

At my next visit to the station, the master cornered me again: 'Impossible situation. This is the third week, your friend must go. He can't make the waiting room his father-in-law's house.'

'Why not?' I bantered.

'I have told you a hundred times, rules don't permit more than eight hours' stay between trains, may be extended by a couple of hours at the discretion of the station master. Not more. I'll lose my job at this rate!'

'Why don't you throw him out? What have I to do with him?'

'Don't go on in this strain, sir. How can I treat roughly a big man like that?'

'Rules are rules and he may not be so big, after all.'

'I have never seen anyone dressed like him!' the station master said reflectively. 'I feel afraid to talk to him. I asked Muni to go up and tell him, but when Muni peeped in, that man turned round and asked, "What do you want?" and Muni withdrew in confusion. Please help me get him out of here somehow.'

I thought it over and said, 'Keep him for a week or ten days on a ticket to the next station each day and I promise to pack him off or find him a room.'

The station master looked doleful and began, 'Thirty years' service—'

I held out twenty rupees and said, 'You will buy him a ticket for Kumbum every morning and punch it for ten days and you will say he arrived by 7 UP or something, waiting to catch the 17 Down or whatever it is.'

This proved effective. Whether he pocketed the money or bought the ticket each day was not my business to probe. That gave Rann ten days' extension.

I utilized the time granted to search for a room. It was proving an impossible task; Rann could not specify what he wanted. I took him around all over the town—east, west, north and south. I had no confidence to have him on the pillion of Sambu's scooter, so I thought it best to engage an autorickshaw. One had to make an advance booking for it—it was gaining such popularity among the citizens. One morning I set aside all my other business and went to Nalli's Hardware, owned by Gopichand, an astute businessman who had migrated from Sind during the partition. He said, 'Take the auto at the stand if you find it. I never can say where they may be found until they return at night to give me the day's collection.'

I drew myself up and asked haughtily, 'Why should I come to you if I can find it at the stand?' My tone was indignant. I had served him in my own way—helped him to print his handbills when he started his autorickshaw business, brought him customers for his hardware, and also enlisted subscribers for a crazy financial scheme. He remembered my help and at once relaxed, 'Anything for you, my friend. You are my well-wisher,' and summoned his boy and said, 'Go at once and find Muniswamy and come with the vehicle.'

It was an idle hour for hardware business and he seated me on an aluminium stool and discussed politics. When we exhausted politics, I watched the crowds milling about the market, leaving Gopichand to read a newspaper reclining on a bolster amidst his hardy environ of nails and rods and chains and clamps.

The boy came back to say, 'Muniswamy is away, can't be found.'

Gopichand proclaimed grandly, 'Tomorrow morning the vehicle shall be at your door. Very sorry to disappoint you today.' As a compensation he drove the boy out to the next stall to fetch a sweet drink for me which came in an opaque unwashed glass. I declined at first, but had to pretend to drink in order to please him.

Next morning the autorickshaw was at my door.

'Ah, you have also started using an auto!' commented my immediate neighbour Ramu, who had grown so fat and immobile that he could do nothing more than sit on the *pyol* leaning on a pillar morning till night enjoying the spectacle of arrivals and departures in Kabir Street. I looked on him more as a sort of vegetation or a geological specimen than as a human being. He loved to play rummy, provided the company assembled around him.

Now he remarked from his seat that an autorickshaw ride was heating to the blood and also disjointed the bones. The autorickshaw driver Kari was upset at this remark and retorted haughtily:

'People are jealous and create such rumours. Simpson Company at Madras have built the body and they know what is good for our bones.'

And he stepped out and approached Ramu to explain his point with vigour. I didn't like this development and summoned him back to his seat, hurriedly shut and locked the door of my house, and got into the rickshaw.

'Railway station,' I commanded.

He started the auto and over its rattle said, 'Did you hear what that fatty said, as if—'

I didn't encourage him to go on. 'Don't you pay any attention to such things. They are all an old-fashioned, ignorant lot in our street.'

'People are better informed in Lawley Extension. More enlightened men there.'

'Naturally,' I said, which agreement pleased him, and by the time we reached the station he was quite at peace with the world. I left the auto in the shade of the giant rain-tree outside the station, went up and found Rann half asleep in a chair in the waiting room. He stirred himself and explained: 'Not a wink of sleep—what with bugs and mosquitoes and the rattling goods wagons all night.'

'Get ready, we'll inspect the town. I'll wait outside.'

While I waited, the station master sidled up to me and whispered, 'DTS is coming . . .'

'You have already said that several times.'

He lowered his voice and asked, 'Does he drink?'

'How should I know?'

'He was wild last night, threatened to kick Muni for some small fault of his—'

'Never mind,' I said indifferently.

'Please take him away before bad things begin to happen.'

Rann was wearing olive-green shorts with his shirt tucked in at the waist, and crowned with a solar topee as if going out hunting in a jungle or on a commando mission. Actually, as we proceeded through the crowds in the Market Road he looked as if watching wild-life, with eyes wide open in wonder, and over the noise of the vehicle, he kept saying, 'Never been in this kind of vehicle—a bonerattler really . . .' (I prayed to God that Kari would not hear) and kept asking, 'Where are you taking me?'

I felt irritated and ignored his question.

First stop was at Abu Lane, which was off the East Chitra Road. We pulled up in front of an old building. He cried, 'Seems like a downtown area—not suitable.'

'What's your downtown? Anyway we are not placing you here—stay in the auto . . . I'll be back.'

He sat back sullenly while a small crowd of downtowners, old and young, stood around staring at the autorickshaw decorated with a pouncing tiger painted on its sides, and at the fantastic passenger. I dashed up a wooden stair in the veranda to a little office of a young real-estate agent, and picked up from his desk a list of available houses in the town, returned, and ordered Kari, 'First drive to North-end.'

'North-end? Where?'

'Across Nallappa's Grove, other side of the river.'

'Oh, there! No houses there,' said Kari.

'Twenty North-end, come on,' I said with authority.

'Cremation ground there , . . no houses.'

I flourished the list before his eyes. 'That chap there who gave me this list knows the city better than you. Just drive on, as I say.'

Rann seemed to be affected by the term cremation and began to fidget. 'Let us try other places . . .'

'Don't be scared. Hey Kari, don't talk unnecessarily . . . go on.'

One of the men watching obliged us with the statement, 'The cremation ground was shifted further off.'

'But the corpses are carried that way, the only way to cross the river—even two days ago—' Kari began.

But I said, 'Shut up, don't talk.'

'I don't want to live on that side of the river,' said Rann.

'Why are you sentimental?' I asked.

It was getting stuffy sitting in that back-seat and getting nowhere, with time running out. Rann began to narrate something about his days when he had to carry on his field studies with dead bodies strewn around. 'One gets used to such things . . .' he concluded grandly while the crowd stood gaping at us. I said determinedly, 'Driver, North-end. Are you going or not going? We have not set out this morning to parade ourselves in this street wasting our time . . . Rann, come out.'

He edged his way out and both of us stood in the street unused to so much publicity.

'Follow me,' I said. 'We'll find some other means of going.'

'Now where are we going?' he asked.

'Follow me, don't go on asking questions like a six-year-old urchin.'

He was cowed by my manner, and followed me meekly, with the locals forming a little procession behind us. I really had no idea what my next step was going to be. I had a general notion to go to the Market Place and complain to Gopichand about his driver or seek the help of Jayaraj to get a vehicle. Perhaps a *jutka*, but I was not sure if Rann could crawl into it and sit cross-legged. I was so grim that no one dared talk to me while I strode down the road without any clear notion of where I was going. The autorickshaw followed at the tail end of the procession. He honked his horn and cleared a way through the crowd and drew up alongside.

'Who pays the meter charges?' Kari asked.

I glared at him and said, 'Your boss Gopichand. I'm going on foot so that he will know what sort of a service he is running in this city with you as his driver. And with this distinguished person, whose feet have never touched the street!'

There was a murmur of approval from the assembly moving with us.

Someone came forward to confront Kari and say, 'You fellows deserve to be . . . to make a foreign gentleman trudge like this . . .' That settled it. Kari felt humbled and contrite.

'I never said anything to upset those masters. They themselves got out of their seats.'

And the busybody said, 'Forget and forgive, sirs. Get into your seats.' I took this chance and accepted his advice and pushed Rann into his seat, sat down, and said grandly, 'North-end first.'

An hour later we reached North-end over a broken causeway at Nallappa's Crossing. I had the satisfaction of noting water splashing off the wheels on the green uniform. Rann looked disconcerted but said nothing, bearing it all with fortitude. We arrived at North-end: a few thatched huts and, beyond them, an abandoned factory with all the windows and doors stolen, leaving gaping holes in the wall. Away from the factory four cottages built of asbestos sheets with corrugated roof, meant for the factory staff, stood in various stages of decay, and all passage blocked with anthills and wild vegetation.

I was a little shocked that the real-estate agent should have this first on his list. The young agent must have taken someone's word on trust and placed it on his list. Not a soul anywhere. We didn't even get down. Dr Rann smiled wanly. I said, 'These things happen, you know. Now Kari, turn round. The next on our list is . . .'

Kari looked quite battered by the strain of driving his rickshaw. Our eardrums were shattered, so were our joints. The man from Timbuctoo began to droop and looked bedraggled in his safari olive-green, which had now lost its original starched neat gloss, and revealed damp patches at the armpits and at the shoulders; the jacket was unbuttoned, exposing a grey vest underneath. If our expedition had gone on further, I'm afraid he would have stripped himself completely. This was the second day of our search, with no time left for tiffin or lunch. Yet I saw no end to our quest. We had our last trial at New Extension, a bungalow bearing the number 102/C. The auto stopped at the gate. The house looked fresh and promising. Rann surveyed it through the gate railings and declared, 'It'll be a nuisance to maintain the garden—and what should I do with a big house?' He shook his head without even waiting to inspect it. A caretaker came running, opened the gate and said, 'I've the keys.'

Rann was unmoved: 'I don't want a big house.'

'Not a small house, nor a medium-sized one, not on the East or West, North or South, neither downtown nor uptown,' I said singsong, carried away by the rhythm of the composition. I tried to sound light-hearted but felt bitter, and hated the whole business of house-hunting.

We got into the carriage. On the way back, I saw the Kismet, and stopped.

'Come in, I want to celebrate the non-conclusion of our expedition with ice-cream and coffee. Normally I'd have preferred the Boardless, but it is miles away at the other end—and I am not sure of being able to bear up that long.'

Rann brightened up. We refreshed ourselves. I ordered coffee and snacks to be sent out for Kari too, who had borne the brunt of our house-hunting and was waiting patiently outside. When the bill was brought Rann's fingers fumbled about his safari pockets. But I held up a warning sign grandly and paid down, although it was four times what it would have cost me at the Boardless. I belonged to the Kabir Street aristocracy, which was well known for its lofty, patronizing hospitality, cost what it may.

The moment we reached the railway station, the station master came up to tell me, while Rann had gone in, 'Message has just come that the DTS arrives at 17.00 hours tomorrow for the day's inspection. Your friend must positively vacate right now. I have to tidy up.' There was no choice. As soon as Rann appeared, I asked, 'How many pieces have you, your baggage, I mean?'

'Not many. Why?'

'Pack them up at once. You have no time to lose. If the DTS arrives anytime now, you will have to live in the open. Pack up and be ready and come out in thirty minutes. That's all the time you have.'

'Outrageous. Where is that funny man the station master? Where are you taking me?'

'Don't become difficult or questioning, unless you want your baggage thrown out. The DTS has authority to throw out things you know.'

The station master stayed out of sight, but I was sure he was listening. I said to Rann finally, 'I'll leave now, but send the rickshaw back for you and your bags . . . I'm too tired to answer more questions. You have no choice—unless you want to take the next train to Madras.'

'Oh, no, that can't be done . . .'

When he arrived at my door with his heavy suitcase and an elegant roll of sleeping bag and other odds and ends, the whole of Kabir Street was agog. People stood at their doors to watch the new arrival.

Malgudi climate has something in it which irons out outlandish habits. It was not long before the blue Oxford suit was gone—perhaps embalmed in moth-balls; and the doctor began to appear in shirtsleeves and grey trousers, almost unrecognizable. In due course even that seemed odd and out of fashion in a street where everyone was seen in a *dhoti* from waist down edged with a red border over a bare body, or at most in a half-sleeve shirt on occasions. For a few weeks Rann used to come out only in his three-piece suit puffing and panting in the heat. At home he would never emerge from the privacy of his room except in pyjamas and a striped dressing gown tasseled at the waist. Luckily I had inherited a vast house, no stinting for space as I have already mentioned. So vast and uninhabited, you'd be in order even if you wore no clothes when you emerged from your room; but here was this man, who never opened his door without being clad in his robe, his feet encased in slippers and a heavy towel around his neck.

We were not familiar with this costume. On the first day, the old sweeper who had been coming to clean and dust since the days of my parents gave one startled look at the gowned apparition emerging from the front room, dropped her broom, and fled to the backyard, where I was drawing water from the well, and said, her eyes wide open, 'A strange man in that room!' And the stranger was equally startled, and retreated like a tortoise into its shell, shutting the door behind him. He could not shut himself in indefinitely, however; he had to visit the toilet in the backyard.

I had to tell him that I could not change that century-old architecture in any way. He was aghast at first that he would have to travel all the way from his front room through two courtyards and corridors to wash and perform his ablutions at the well. But I gradually trained him, repeating every time, 'Where there is a will . . .' The latrine was a later addition, with a septic tank which I had installed after coming into possession of the property. On the very first day I had to explain to him a great deal, rather bluntly:

'You will have to accept this as it is. I cannot change anything—I can't bother myself with all that activity even if I find the time, money and the men.'

Following it, I gave him a tour of inspection of the house. When he saw the flush-out latrine he said:

'This is impossible. I have no practice—I need a European type—'

'In that case you have come to the wrong place. Our town has not caught up with modern sanitary arrangements, even this is considered a revolutionary concept. The Modern

Sanitaryware man on Market Road is going bankrupt—sitting amidst his unsold porcelain things. Our ancestors bathed and washed and cleansed themselves at the well and the river. With the river running down our door-step, they didn't have to make special arrangements, did not let themselves be obsessed with washing all the time, which is what Western Civilization has taught us. Considering that the river flows almost all the year round, although thinning down a bit in summer—' I waxed eloquent and left him no choice.

'What do I do with the bathrobe?'

'Oh, don't worry about too many details. Things will sort themselves out. I'll drive a peg into the wall, where you can hang down your robe.'

'What does that word Timbuctoo sound like?' I began an article. 'It's a fairy-tale or cock-and-bull setting. Sometimes a word of disparagement or . . .' I went on for about a hundred words in the same strain, and finally came down to the statement, 'Hereafter we must pay more respect to that phrase. For I realize today that Timbuctoo is very real, as real as our Malgudi. I have actually shaken hands with a man from Timbuctoo. You will be right if you guess that I poked his side with my finger to make sure that he was real . . . He has come on a vital project on behalf of the UN and it's an honour for Malgudi that he should choose to work here. From his description of the place, Timbuctoo is a paradise on earth, and you feel like migrating, abandoning our good old Motherland.' And then I composed a word picture of Rann in his three-piece suit.

Every journalist has his moment of glory or promising glory—the brink of some great event to come, a foretaste of great events. A knock on my door, and my neighbour stood there outside, the fat man who rarely stirred from his seat on his *pyol*. This massive man held out a telegram.

'This came when you were away . . . I signed the receipt.'

While I tore it open, he waited to be told of its contents. I looked at him, murmuring a word of thanks, and wishing mentally that he would take his massive self off. Oh, big one—be off! I said mentally. I had much to think and dream over the message in the telegram, which was from my editor: 'News item interesting—but useless without a photograph of the Timbuctoo Man. Get one soonest.' For the first time in my life I was receiving encouragement. Normally whatever I mailed would be lost sight of, like flotsam on the current of Sarayu in flood. Or if it was printed, it would be so mutilated and presented in such minute type that you would have to search for it with a magnifying glass; and of course, no payment would be expected for it, not that I needed any, thanks to the foresight of my forefathers, who did not believe in spending but only in hoarding up endlessly. Here was the telegram in my hand, and this enormous man would not leave so that I might dream on it.

I turned to go in and he said, 'Hope all's well? Good news?'

'Oh yes, excellent news—from my news editor who wants something written up—routine stuff.' I sounded casual and tried to turn in, even as the fat man was saying, 'I'm very nervous when a telegram arrives. Otherwise I'd have opened it to see if it was urgent, and then of course, I'd have gone in search of you.' The picture of this paunchy man with multiple folds shuffling along Market Road barebodied in search of me was too ridiculous, and I burst out laughing, and shut the door, murmuring, 'Very kind of you.'

I gloated over the message secretly—not yet decided how far I could share the feeling of journalistic triumph with others. I went about my day feeling that I was on the brink of a mighty career. I don't aspire to become a so-called creative writer, I kept saying to myself, but only a journalist who performs a greater service to society, after all, than a dreamy-eyed poet or a storyteller. The journalist has to be in the thick of it whatever the situation—he acts as the eye for humanity.

Sitting in my corner at the Boardless lost in thought, my coffee was getting cold, which was noticed by Varma in spite of his concentration on the cash flow in the till. He suddenly ordered, 'TM's coffee is getting cold. Boy, take it away and bring hot.' I woke from my reverie to explain:

'A telegram from my editor, important assignment—but it depends very much on a photograph . . .'

'Whose?' he asked.

'I'll tell you everything soon.' I left it at that. Didn't want to make it public yet. I brooded over it the rest of the day and decided on action—since it was urgent and could be a turning point in my career—I must be ready to go anywhere if ordered, even if it meant locking up my home in Kabir Street. But I had misgivings about Rann, doubts about his reaction to a photo. Some instinct told me that it would not be so simple. And my instinct proved reliable when I faced him with the request. He was in his room. When I sounded him out, he became wary, and asked: 'Why?'

'Just for the fun of it . . . You have lived in many countries and must have interesting photographs.'

He brushed aside the suggestion with a wave of his hand, and resumed the study of the papers on his desk. Remarkable man. Though I had given him an unfurnished room, he had furnished it with a desk and chair and a canvas cot. I hadn't entered his room till now—he always locked it when leaving for his bath. He had been getting about evidently.

'How did you manage to secure a desk?'

'On hire. I found a shop on Market Road . . . for the four pieces they will be charging fifteen rupees . . . not bad, less than a dollar and a half, that's all very cheap . . .'

Rather disconcerting. He was entrenching himself while I had thought of giving him only a temporary shelter. I asked in a roundabout manner:

'How much advance for the whole period?'

He was evasive, 'Well not much really by world standards. He'll collect the hire charges from time to time, and no time-limit.'

He was too clever for me. I left it at that, looked around the walls and said, 'No photographs?'

'What sort of photograph?' He shook his head. 'I don't like photos of any sort.'

'I thought you might have an interesting collection, having lived in so many parts of the world . . .' I sensed this man would not give me his photograph. Today he was wearing a Japanese kimono and looked grim and busy.

'I must get these reports off—already overdue—all this amount of travelling is unsettling and interferes with one's schedule.'

I rather resented his continuing to be seated while I stood. I was consumed with curiosity to know what the report was about; there was a pile of typed and handwritten sheets. Where were the reports going? But I let the queries alone. My immediate need was for a photograph of this man. Some instinct told me not to mention it now.

I consulted Jayaraj later. 'I want a photograph of the man . . .'

'Put him before my camera and you will have it.'

'But he seems to shy away from the camera—I do not know why. Otherwise I could invite him to have a group photo with me as a mark of friendship.'

'I'd charge twenty-five for photographing two figures . . .'

Following this I got into a pointless debate which in no way concerned the present problem. 'So does it mean that if you take a group photo of fifty school children you will count the heads and charge *pro rata*?'

'Naturally.' he answered. 'How else? I have to survive. If you find another photographer, you are welcome to go to him. Can't get rolls, either 35 or 120, no developer, no printing paper—hopeless situation. I think our government is trying to suppress photographers, and they draft their import rules accordingly. The little supply I have is thanks to that helpful breed called smugglers, who come regularly to that coastal village at Kumbum, their country craft loaded with things—where I go once a month to buy materials. The bus fare is five rupees each way, and I have to recover it in the charges to my customers. The Councillor came for a frame of a wedding group. I told him point blank that he was welcome to bring anything to frame, but no photo business please. Nowadays I am concentrating more and more on framing pictures and the painting of signboards—but even there . . .' He went on haranguing an imaginary audience about the conditions; frames that were flimsy, cheap wood, dyed and passed off as gilt frames by the suppliers, which once again was due to government policy. He was obsessed with the wiles of a hostile government out to do him in. I always allowed plenty of time for his speech, while sitting comfortably on the bench which jutted out of his shop at the Market Entrance. The authorities did their best to remove the bench, as it obstructed the public passage, but could do nothing about it, and Jayaraj always boasted that he would go to the Supreme Court if necessary to keep his long bench where he chose. His fundamental right could not be questioned.

He talked on squatting on the floor, his hands busy nailing and cutting frames; in a recess at the back wall he had his photographic department, that mysterious darkness where he professed to have treasures of photographic equipment through the grace of his friendly smuggler. After allowing him as long a speech as he desired, I said:

'Be a good chap. My whole career depends on your help now. I'll manage to bring that man this way, and you must manage to snap him, front or side, without his knowledge, and enlarge it. We want only a bust.'

'Done,' he said readily. 'My camera is the old type, on a tripod, but the best ever made, I can't take a snap with it, but I'll get the Japanese one from the Councillor who got it from the smuggler recently, which I can hold in my palm, and work wonders with the telephoto lens and superfast film.'

He got into the spirit of adventure and stood up at the entrance of his dark room and said, 'I can stand here and click when you step into that arch. But tell me the precise date and hour when you propose to bring him. I'll do anything for a friend who remains undiscouraged by what I may say.'

'Of course, I know that—otherwise wouldn't I try the Star Studio?'

'That wretched fellow! Don't go near him. He is a photographer of propped up corpses—no good for live subjects.'

He approached his task with a lot of seriousness. He brooded over the logistics. He held a sort of dress rehearsal next morning with me understudying for Rann. In this season sunlight fell aslant at a particular spot under the Market Arch for about twenty minutes, but as the sun rose higher there was a shade . . .

'I must catch him in full light while it is available—otherwise I may have to use a flash, which is likely to put him off. Five minutes, that's all. You must see that he faces the market and stands still for a moment. I'll see to it that no one crosses in at that time. I'll post my boy to keep people away, only for a few minutes and no one will mind it either, not a busy hour . . . It'll be up to you to see that he doesn't pass through without stopping. Perhaps you should hold him and point at something. Don't worry that you may also be in the picture—I'll mask you and blow up the other.'

293

He leapt down, marked the spot for me under the arch, directed me to look straight ahead, hopped into his shop, concealed himself in the dark room, and surveyed through the viewfinder. I'd never expected he would plunge so heartily into the scene.

'You should be a film director,' I said.

I fell into an anxious state. The rehearsal was very successful but the star would have to cooperate without knowing what was going on. And he could be manoeuvred only once, there could not be a retake. I was pressed for time—the newspaper might lose interest if the photograph was delayed. Jayaraj could borrow the smuggled Japanese camera only for a day from the Councillor. I'd have to catch hold of Rann and manipulate him through. It was nerve-racking. In order to think I had to retire, to what used to be known in our family as a meditation room, a sort of cubicle in the second court, away from the general traffic routes of the family where you could retreat. It was dark and musty with a lingering smell of stale incense, a couple of pictures of gods faintly visible in the sooty wall. There I retired so that Rann might not intrude. A blue glass pane among the tiles let in a faint sky light, enough for my purpose. I sat down on a wooden plank, cross-legged, and concentrated on my problem, with a scribbling pad on my lap. I jotted down a script for the scene ahead.

Evening today: I. Meet Rann and describe the Swami's Cottage Industries at the market as worth a visit. Talk him into it. (*Earlier* prepare Sam to be ready with a souvenir for Rann.) Explain to Rann that Sam is one who respects international personalities, and always invites them to honour him with a visit, and that he has collected and treasured letters of appreciation from outstanding men. Rann must spare a little time for my sake. *10.10 a.m.* Leave Kabir Street and walk down. *10.25 a.m.* Market Arch. Stop and push him gently towards the foundation tablet now covered with grime. Encourage him to scrutinize the inscription. *10.30 a.m.* Leave Arch.

Rann fell into the trap readily. I knocked on his door and saw him lounging in my canvas chair, my heirloom, and wool-gathering. He was probably feeling dull. So it was a propitious moment for me to make the proposal.

'Can you spare half an hour for me tomorrow morning?'

'Well, of course, what for?'

'You have been here and not known the peculiar treasures of this town.'

'I'm so preoccupied with my work . . .'

'I know, I know, but still you must look around. You will find it worthwhile . . . I want to take you to meet a friend of mine in the market.'

'Market! It'll be crowded.'

'Not always. I'll take you at a time when it is quiet. I want you to see a handicrafts shop—a very small one, managed by a chap we call Sam—absolutely a genius, dedicated. He makes lacquerware and sandalwood stuff which are famous all over the world. So many awards at Leipzig and other international fairs. He has distributors in Africa, Europe, the US and everywhere. He is well known all over the world; mainly foreigners come in search of him and place orders. He is less known here as usual. No visitor from a foreign land ever misses him. Their first question will always be, 'Where's *Sam's Crafts*?' Ten o'clock tomorrow morning we will walk up; spend half an hour at his workshop and then you will be free. He will feel honoured by a visit from an international figure.'

The scheme worked according to timetable. At the Market Arch I paused, he also paused. I stepped aside. I pointed at the fading tablet on a pillar facing us and as he stood gazing at it, I was aware of the slight stirring of a phantom at the threshold of Jayaraj's dark chamber. I kept talking.

'It's mud-covered, but if you are keen we may scrape the mud off and see the date of the foundation stone . . .' He stood gazing at it and said, 'Thanks, don't bother about it,' and we moved on to Sam's.

I had gone as usual to post my news at the mail van when my friend the station master came to see me, all excited, saying, 'There is a large woman who came by 7 Down, staying at the waiting room and won't leave, just like the other fellow, that London man whom you took away—perhaps you should take away this woman too.'

'None of my business, whoever she may be,' I said.

'Not my business either,' he said. 'The waiting room is not my ancestral property to be given to every—'

Before he could complete the sentence, the subject of his complaint was approaching—a six-foot woman (as it seemed at first sight), dark-complexioned, cropped head, and in jeans and a T-shirt with bulging breasts, the first of her kind in the Malgudi area. She strode towards us, and I knew there was no escape.

'You must be the journalist?' she asked menacingly having observed me at the mail van. She took out of her handbag a press-cutting of 'Timbuctoo Man', with the photograph of Rann I had managed to get.

She flourished the press-cutting and said, 'You wrote this?'

'Yes madam,' I said meekly.

'No one can fool me,' she said.

The diminutive station master tried to shrink out of sight, simpered and stayed in the background. I felt rather intimidated by the woman's manner, but still had the hardihood to retort, 'What do you mean by it?'

'I mean,' she said, undaunted, 'if you know where this so-called doctor is, you will lead me to him.'

'Why?'

'For the good reason that I am his wife—perhaps the only one wedded to him in front of the holy fire at a temple.'

I took time to assimilate the idea.

'Of his possibly several wives I was the only one regularly married and the first. You look rather stunned sir, why?'

'Oh no,' I said clumsily. I had no other explanation. The whole picture of Rann was now assuming a different quality if this lady was to be believed. The station master looked embarrassed but, held by curiosity, hovered about with the rolled flags under his arm, and behind him stood the porter. We were the only ones on the railway platform. She eyed them for some time without a word and then asked, 'Station master, is your work for the day over?'

'Practically—9 Up is not due until 20.00 hours.'

'What's 20.00 hours? Now the bother of addition and subtraction,' she muttered. 'Why don't you railway people use a.m.-p.m. as normal civilized beings do?'

'Yes madam,' he said sheepishly.

'Is that your only porter?' The porter, on being noticed by the queen, came a few paces forward.

'I've served here for thirty years, madam,' he said. The queen accepted his statement without displaying any special interest, whereupon he withdrew a few paces back, but within hearing distance. She swept her arms about and said, 'Normally, they'd have a couple of cement benches on any railway platform, but here nothing. Come on, let us go into the waiting room anyway, there at least are a couple of chairs. Come! Come!' she said beckoning me authoritatively. Sheepishly I followed her. She had a commanding manner.

The station master followed discreetly at a distance. She carried two chairs out of the waiting room. 'No, no,' I persisted, 'let me—'

But she would not pay any attention to my gallant offer and said, 'You have seen him, tell me all about him.'

'I cannot say much . . . Ours was a brief meeting. I was interested because—' She did not let me complete the sentence: 'It is more important for me to know where he is rather than anything else.'

She looked so fixedly at me that I said, 'Not in my pocket,' and tried to laugh it off. 'We met for less than fifteen minutes at our Town Hall library where he had come for a reference work and did not like to be interrupted.'

'So studious indeed! How marvellous! Good to know that he is still bookish.' And she laughed somewhat cynically. Then she became serious and said, 'All that I want to know is where is he at the moment. If you will only give me a hint I'll give you any reward.'

I felt slightly upset and said righteously, 'I'm in no need of a reward. I can survive without it.' The station master, who was following our dialogue from a respectable distance, added, 'He is rich, madam, comes from a big Kabir Street family really.'

She said, 'Station master, perhaps you would like to attend to other things?'

The station master shrank out of sight, and the porter too melted away. I got up saying, 'I must go now, you must excuse me. The only novelty about him was his mentioning Timbuctoo, and as a journalist I thought it had news value. After that I lost sight of him, never asked him where he was going—that's all. He was inquiring about some long distance buses . . . That's all madam, all that I can say is that if he is staying in this place, he cannot remain unnoticed.' I had given full rein to my imagination. 'I'd suggest you look for him at Madras or a place like that instead of wasting your time here.' And I rose, carried my chair in and said, 'Goodnight.' I felt uncomfortable in her presence with a constant dread lest I should betray myself. And so I hurried away, glancing back over my shoulder to make sure she was not following me. She stuck to her chair without a word and watched me go.

Rann was in his kimono when he opened the door, on my knocking repeatedly, with a scowl on his face. I resented his attitude: in my own house he was a visitor to whom I'd offered asylum for no clear reason. It had just been an impulse to help him, nothing more, and to rescue him from bed-bugs flourishing in the railway station waiting room.

Yet he behaved as if I were a hotel steward violating the privacy of a guest.

'Why don't you hang a "Don't disturb" board on your door? I thought you might have brought a souvenir from one or the other of the hotels in your travels—'

He was taken aback. 'Why do you say that?'

'I see that you are busy—' I said cynically. He wasn't. I could see that he had been lounging on the canvas easy chair (my heirloom) which I had let him have out of idiotic kindness. Yet this man dared to shut the door and look too busy to open it. There were no papers on his table, nor a book at his side in the canvas chair or anywhere. He must have been lounging and staring at the ceiling and wool-gathering, and he chose to scowl at me—me, his saviour from bed-bugs. Soon my anger was mitigated as I anticipated the pleasure of shocking him with news at which I knew his flamboyance and foreign style would be punctured. I simply announced, from the door, like the opening lines of a play, 'A lady to see you,' and turned round, shutting the door behind me (a piece of deliberate good manners). I went down to the backyard and shut myself in the bathroom and stayed there, although I had heard him open his door and follow me. I took my own time.

When I opened the bathroom door, he stood there, his face full of questions, and he seemed to have become a little paler and shrunk a few inches into his Japanese kimono. I had not needed a wash, but I had splashed water over my head for no better reason than to taunt him. 'Oh!' I cried with feigned surprise. Then I raced along the back courtyard to my room, while he followed me. My clothes and things were widely scattered in various rooms in different blocks of that house, and I never found at any time what I wanted, towel in one room, kerchief in another, trousers at another corner, and so forth. Now I was dripping, water running over my eyes, and wet all over—very annoying. I cried, 'Where is the damned towel?' At which Rann vanished for a minute and fetched a fresh towel from his room. I felt pleased with my show of authority, murmured a thanks indistinctly, and wiped my face and head. We were standing in the passage.

'I'll return it washed tomorrow—' I said.

'Oh, that's all right,' he said. 'No hurry.'

'So soft and strong,' I said admiringly and stretched it and held it to the light from the courtyard. I noticed an embroidered corner and spelt out 'Neville'.

'What's that?' I asked.

'Hotel in Rhodesia—it's a souvenir.' Perhaps he had stolen it.

'How long were you there?'

'Oh, quite a few times in connection with the project—'

'But they say, it's difficult for coloured people—'

'Oh, it's all exaggerated. Don't you believe it. For me, no problem, the UN Passport can't stop you anywhere.'

I felt inclined to provoke further elaborations on the subject, while I knew he was dying to ask questions about the lady but feeling rather awkward about reviving the subject. I felt a sudden compassion for him—his bewilderment and awkwardness as he shrank into his fancy kimono. I asked suddenly, 'You want to ask about that lady?'

'Yes, yes,' he said meekly with a sigh, 'I don't understand

it at all. Who is she?'

'The station master says that he saw a photograph in her hand, looking like your good self.'

'Ah!' he cried involuntarily.

'It matches the picture in the *Telegraph*.'

'How did my photo get in anywhere?'

'Newspapers have their sources, you know.'

He asked, 'What sort of a person is she?'

'Well, a long time ago I gave up staring at women and studying their worth, so I'm not able to provide a good description. Anyway, I'll dress and come to your room, please wait there.'

He was waiting impatiently in his room. I had taken my own time to look for my clothes, to groom myself before my mirror, the ornate oval in a gilded frame with a vine pattern carved on it, perhaps a wedding present for my grandmother: it was full of spots and blank areas. Now fresh from an unnecessary bath and dressed in my *kurta* and a laced *dhoti* and a neatly folded upper cloth over my shoulder, I felt ready to face the emperors of the earth. I strode into his room, where he had had the good sense to leave the door open. I had a glimpse of him fidgeting impatiently in his chair. The moment he saw me he rose and offered me the seat, and lowered himself into it only after I had sat elsewhere. Now I looked as if ready to go on with our conversation and give him a hearing.

'I told you about a lady at the railway station where I had gone to post my evening despatch.'

I knew that Rann was dying to have a description of the lady as he sat squirming and fidgeting.

'Was she tall?' he asked, trying to draw me out.

302

'Could be,' I replied.

'Medium height?'

'She did not seem short,' I said. 'I could see her only from a distance.'

'How far away were you?' he asked stupidly.

I felt irritated. 'I forgot to take a measuring tape with me,' I said, and tried to laugh it off. He looked miserable and I had to ask:

'Why are you bothered?'

He said, 'Because—I don't know. You are right. Dozens come and go at the railway station, do I care?'

'Bravely said,' I remarked. 'Let us go to the Boardless. You will feel better.'

He shrank from the idea. He had, apparently, a fear of being waylaid by the woman. I persuaded him, but before coming out, he spent much time to decide how to dress for the visit. I advised, 'the Boardless is a special place, where you could go in your underwear or in royal robes, it's all the same to the crowd there. No one will question or notice.' Still, he took his time to decide and came out in a pink slack shirt and grey flannel trousers.

We walked up. I took him to my usual corner, facing the Mahishasura calendar, had another chair put up. The habitués turned round to study him for a moment and then resumed their coffee and talk. I ordered *dosai* and coffee, but he couldn't enjoy it; he seemed overwhelmed and self-conscious. Varma, the proprietor, said 'Hallo' to him formally and looked gratified that the Boardless should be attaining an international touch with this man's visit. I briefly explained, 'He is a scholar, come on business', avoiding Timbuctoo because of its phoney sound. I thought

I should do something to integrate this stranger in our society and cure him of his kimono and carpet-slipper style and alienation, and so had persuaded him to walk along. Of course, it had not been an easy passage though, people stared at us—it was inevitable.

The lady's haunting presence at the railway station somehow drove Rann closer to me. He seemed to depend on me in some obscure manner for any information I might spring on him. He looked on me, I suppose, as a possible harbinger of some good news such as that the lady had left suddenly by some train or that she had thrown herself under the midnight goods train. So he watched my movements eagerly with almost a questioning look to say, 'Any good news? How good is the goods train? Anything under it?' Formerly, he had always shut himself in his room and bolted the door. These days he kept a door open so that he might not lose glimpse of me; while I moved about he watched me surreptitiously from his chair, which was an excellent position for spying. My forefathers must have used that same strategic position to keep an eye on the household, particularly the army of servants, so that no one could slip out unnoticed. Rann found this advantageous. As I passed in and out he greeted me with casual ease. 'Good day to you, TM. Starting on your interesting rounds for the day?' Sometimes he just smiled and nodded, without obviously questioning, feeling perhaps: 'If he has anything—he is bound to tell me—not the sort to keep mum—'

On the whole, he seemed to have limbered up, and was slightly more relaxed. It suited me, too. I took advantage of his leniency and the half-open door policy to step into his room informally for a chit-chat now and then. I'd walk in and make straight for the easy chair without any preamble.

I lounged in his canvas chair comfortably. He sat in his hired chair uneasily, pretended to be looking through some papers on his desk, put them away, and got up and paced the narrow room up and down like a bear in the cage. After a pause and silence for fifteen minutes I just pronounced:

'You seem very agitated, why?'

'Oh, no. I am sorting out some problems in the paper I'm writing.'

'Very well then, let me leave you in peace . . .'

'No, no, stay,' he said. It seemed to me that he wanted to say something but was reluctant to begin or rather unable to find an opening line.

'I do not mind relaxing and lounging here all day, but you will have to do something about it, about the lady in question,' I said.

'What do I care? Hundreds of persons come and go at a railway station.'

'Not everyone carries your photo asking questions—'

'What the hell!' he cried, red in the face. I enjoyed the annoyance he displayed and added, 'Also calls herself your wife.'

'Nonsense!' he cried, and paced up and down. I had never found him in such a mood or using intemperate language. The thought of this woman seemed to loosen the bolts of his mental framework.

'What's he to Hecuba or Hecuba to him?' I asked light-mindedly.

'Does she call herself Hecuba? I knew no one of that name.'

I had to explain to him that I was quoting Shakespeare.

'Ah, Shakespeare. I had almost forgotten. Long time ago, of course. Would you believe it? Once I sat down and read the Oxford Edition from the title page to the last.'

'Yet, thou varlet weakeneth at the mention of a perfidious female!'

'I say, this is maddening! Please do something and send her away.'

'Why? This is a free town for anyone to come and go or stay. How can I arrogate to myself any right to expel anyone! I don't think I'll see her again. . .'

'What's she like?' he inquired suddenly. I couldn't continue in a mood of levity—if she was really his wife. So I just said, 'Well, an impressive personality—slightly dark, but a commanding personality, rather large build, I should say. Perhaps exaggerated by the blue jeans and T-shirt and bobbed hair. The station master was quite cowed by her manner and opened the waiting room promptly when asked . . .'

'Though he made such a fuss when I wanted it! That funny character. Did she mention her husband to him also?'

'I don't know,' I said, 'but he was the first to be shown your photograph.'

'Outrageous!' he cried. 'You have done me a disservice!'

'On the contrary I was doing you a service without being asked. Do you know the number of men who curry my favour to get their names in print?'

'You could have at least consulted me!'

'It'd be against the journalists' code. Freedom of the

Press and all that. Even the PM cannot say "Yes" or "No" to a Journalist when he is out to make his copy,' I said grandly.

'Photograph! How did the photo get in?'

'I can't say—you have been in so many places, anyone might have snapped you.'

After about an hour's rambling talk he begged, 'Don't betray me. You have been hospitable right from the beginning, just help me now by leaving me alone and without mentioning me to that person, whoever she may be, in jeans and T-shirt. Is she Indian? I'll explain everything when the time comes. Not now. Don't ask questions.'

'After all,' I said, pitying his plight, 'she is not going to live permanently in the waiting room. She will have to leave some time. Don't be seen too much for some time,' I said encouragingly.

'I need a lot of mental peace at least till I complete my work. That's why the shelter or asylum you have given is doubly valuable. I must have no sort of distraction till I complete the writing of my book. Anyone who helps me to work in peace will be my benefactor. To me nothing is more important than the book. It's going to be a sensation when it comes out. It will shake up the philosophers of today, the outlook will have to change. It's in this respect that I value your hospitality and shelter. When I publish I'll acknowledge your help surely.'

'Ah ha, my name too will be in print. Excellent! While my profession is to get a lot of people's names in print, that is the first time it will be happening to me. Great! Do you know my name? You have never gone beyond calling me TM or UC as those people at the Boardless do—why not we adjourn to the Boardless for refreshments, after all you have visited it only once. I'm hungry.'

He resisted the suggestion.

'Are you afraid to come out?' I asked and left it at that.

'Why should I be afraid? The world's full of evil things. I have seen all sorts of things, everywhere in this world. I'm not afraid of anything. Any airline hostess or a waitress in a restaurant might turn round and blackmail you if you were foolish enough to have said "How do you do?" in a friendly tone. These are situations which develop unasked. I won't be disturbed too much by these things.'

'So, a man of experience! Come out with me and if you are accosted, draw yourself up and say, "Begone phantom wretch! I know you not."'

'You are very Shakespearean today,' he commented. I was happy to see him thawing. 'I've also as I told you read Shakespeare with genuine pleasure,' he added.

I decided to protect him from wifely intrusions.

How she found her way to Kabir Street must forever remain unexplained. There she stood on my threshold one afternoon. The neighbours viewing her from their *pyols* must have been startled; her dress and deportment were so unusual in our setting. She was attired like a Punjabi woman, *kurta* or *salwar kameez* or whatever they call it, which seemed to exaggerate her physical stature, which was already immense. She was a large woman by any standard.

In our street where women were used to glittering silk sarees, gold and diamonds, she looked like a visitor from another planet. She wore around her neck white beads in a string, like a gypsy, and had around her shoulder a pink muslin wrap—the total effect was startling, really. No wonder the spruce tailor's dummy called Rann quailed at the very thought of her. I was happy that the fellow had gone out, and I only prayed that he would not blunder in and stumble on her. I seated her with her back to the window opening onto the veranda as you came up the steps so as to prevent her catching sight of Rann if he happened to come.

I didn't know where he was nowadays. I thought he went out to do research, but later learnt from our gossip sources what he was actually doing. I'll come to that later.

Now the big lady was settled squarely in the hall. I had placed her strategically so that she could have a view of the second courtyard and the crows perched on the roof-tiles and the drumstick tree looming beyond, and not notice Rann if he should appear on the other side of the window.

'I'm sorry, I've nothing to offer . . . this house is just a shell, I go out to eat—not a soul anywhere.'

I refrained from questioning how she had managed to come. I guessed the station master must have given her directions.

She said, 'I don't expect anything from you except help to get at that man.'

I remained silent, not knowing what to say, dreading that she might turn her head at the sound of footsteps. She was there to investigate thoroughly.

'That station master is helpful . . . good man. But for him I'd have taken the next train back instead of continuing in this wretched place—Oh, the bugs in the waiting room!'

'Yes, yes, others also run away on account of it . . .'

realizing how similar Rann's experience was. That seemed to be their only common bond. (Bug-bond was the phrase that kept drumming in my head.)

'I gave him five rupees and he has been so helpful—even got a spray pump and eliminated the bugs almost fifty per cent! Now it is tolerable. He has also arranged to send me food from his house,' she said.

Why is that fool of a station master so helpful, I wondered. Must warn him.

'He must be having special regard for you. Usually he applies the rules and won't let anyone occupy the waiting room for more than a few hours.'

'Yes, he mentioned something, but five rupees goes a long way; first thing in the morning after 7 Up or 6 Down or whatever it is passes, I slip the five-rupee note before he can mention the rules and his unblemished service record in the railways. Also a couple of rupees to the porter, who sweeps and cleans the room and does not let anyone approach it—and so there I am. No one except yourself has set eyes on the so-called Rann for years. You must help me get at him . . . a strange character. Sometimes I have felt like wringing his neck but on the whole I'm very very fond of him, although I am not sure what I'll do if I set eyes on him. Anyway, first show him to me and then I will decide.' She tightened and bit her lips—her expression was so forbidding that I shuddered at the picture of slippery Rann in her grip.

'How did you get his photograph? He was always shying away from photographs. Even our wedding photograph he tried to destroy but I saved it. I have it with me in my box at the station.'

'Why so?'

'Because he was a crook and wanted to remain invisible, that's all.' She said this without hesitation. I didn't explain how I got the photograph because I feared she might call me a crook too, being so uninhibited and loose-tongued. She suddenly went on, 'Now tell me all about him. Though I loathe him, I like to hear about him.'

I didn't see why I should oblige her with information and so just said, 'I too met him only at the Town Hall where I had gone to look at a paper. I stopped by because he was rather strange-looking in his three-piece suit and all.'

She laughed at the mention of his suit. 'Oh, three-piece suit. Three-piece suit! What a gentleman! Once he was one hundred per cent Madrasi—only *dhoti* and *khaddar* half-arm shirt.'

'One could easily take him for a London banker now.'

'Three-piece suit indeed! What shade?'

'Blue—all blue or near blue,' I said, getting into the spirit.

'Tell me about him, I'm dying to hear all about him . . . ages since I saw him, years and years, what does he look like? Has he grown stout? Your photograph doesn't say much.'

'Newspapers won't print more than a bust or the head as on a coin or postage stamp, and that seems to have brought you down.'

'If you had published a full photograph, that might have brought quite a crowd to your railway station, enough to drive the station master crazy.'

'Must have been a popular man,' I said.

311

'A regular lady-killer, sir; the only one who could survive was myself. I've been to the capitals of the world, hunting for him with the help of the Interpol and met only the poor wrecks he left behind when he vanished. What does he look like these days? Has he put on weight?'

I realized presently that like the Jesting Pilate, she would not wait for an answer. If I remained silent, still she would go on—

'He was quite attractive in those days. Does he have a moustache?'

'Yes, a thin line—reminds one of—reminds one Adolphe Menjou, a film actor in the thirties—'

'Must be greying, surely . . . or does he colour? I wouldn't put it past him.'

I remained quiet, letting her talk on. It looked as though I'd have to surrender my title of Talkative Man and take a second place in the world of talkers. My constant fear was that the fellow might arrive. I was apprehensive as to how they would react to each other, also about my position as his keeper. The lady would unhesitatingly call me a liar and might even assault me, which would create an unprecedented sensation in Kabir Street. She looked as if she might make a move. She must have heard rumours of my hospitality toward Rann—again from the station master.

On an idea, I got up with an excuse to go out: 'I'll be back in ten minutes, suddenly remembered something . . .' I went down the steps to the fourth house in the same row, Sambu's. As usual, he was reading in his small study.

'Look, when Rann comes back to return your scooter, keep him here, lock him away if necessary till I sound the all-clear. Tell him someone is waiting for him—he'll understand.'

312

After that I hurried down to the corner shop and bought a dozen bananas, a packet of biscuits, and a couple of soft drinks, went home, and set them on a plate before the lady.

'Ah, you are a thought-reader. Very welcome.'

She must have been starving. She ate three plantains, half a packet of biscuits and washed it all down with a soft drink that claimed to be pure orange juice. Revived, she remarked, 'Husband-hunting is a fatiguing business.'

'Are you sure we are referring to the same person?' I asked.

'No doubt about it. The photograph is unmistakable: he might make himself into Adolphe Menjou or whoever, or grow a beard or a horn on his head, but he can never change. Eyes and nose betray a man unmistakably. They cannot change or cheat. I have done nothing but gaze on his wonderful countenance for months and years out of count, and I know.'

She paused and wept a little. I tried to look away, and did not know what would be the right statement to make in this situation. It was awkward. I did the best I could under the circumstances, looking away through the window—hoping and hoping that the man would not come back suddenly, bypassing Sambu or because the bookworm Sambu should forget to hold him, as was likely with bookworms. I contemplated this possibility while glancing at her mopping her tears with a minute handkerchief which she had to fish out of her bag each time, and wondered if it would be appropriate to lend her the 'Neville' towel Rann had given me. Suppose she was settled here for the day?— since my parlour was as good as the waiting room for her.

In a voice thickened with nose blowing, she said, 'If I had the slightest clue that he would act like this . . . At Madras, I was reading at St Evans in Egmore, and lived with my parents in one of those sidelanes nearby. My father had a furniture and carpentry shop and this man you call Rann would often come in on a bicycle; he was a delivery boy for a circulating library, delivering and collecting magazines, mostly film journals, charging a daily fee. He was also a student at Loyola College, supplementing his income through his job, which he seemed to enjoy, as it suited his wandering temperament. The library had a few journals of a serious kind in addition to film magazines, which appealed to my youthful taste in those days. He enjoyed his job because he could read all sorts of things, some of the serious journals too like the *National Geographic*. Occasionally he would recommend a special article in a journal to improve my mind. He reserved his visit to us as the last on his rounds— bringing us the cheap magazines we liked as well as the serious ones which he would recommend to us. In addition to delivering magazines his boss would send him to get racks and stools and benches for his shop from my father's workshop, which was a small shed in the backyard, though he employed many hands and turned out a lot of furniture for the shops around. A stone bench under a mango tree in our compound was very convenient for us. We sat close to each other, while he read out of a journal something that he felt I should know and understand. You know how it is when two young persons sit close to each other and discuss intellectual matters in soft whispers! Inevitable, inevitable . . .'

At this moment I noticed Sambu coming up my veranda steps. I excused myself for a moment and went outside.

314

Sambu whispered: 'That chap is come—about an half-hour ago—and is restless. What shall I do?'

'Kick him up a ladder to that loft in your hall and remove the ladder. He had better stay out of view for a long time. There is someone in there waiting to dismember him; I'll tell you the story later. She shows no sign of moving, but I'll do something about it soon. Please wait, and tell the idiot not to peep in at the window.'

Sambu, an ever obliging neighbour, threw a brief glance at the window and withdrew.

I had to explain to the lady, 'I'm afraid I've a meeting to report. My friend is waiting. I suggest that you go back to the railway station. I'll meet you in your room later when I come to post a letter in the mail van—after that I'll be free. You must also want to eat and rest. I'll definitely see you?'

She narrated her life story further, after ordering a couple of chairs to be placed under a tree on the railway station platform. She ordered the station master about and commanded the porter unreservedly until they supplied all her needs. I had posted my despatch dutifully—a court case and a municipal meeting, in the 7 Up to Madras. The platform was deserted; only the station mongrel lay curled up on the signalling platform. The lady had rested and looked refreshed and had now changed to a cotton saree, which made her look larger than she seemed in the morning. A mild breeze was blowing from the mountains, some birds were chirping in the tree.

'The waiting room must have been a dungeon at one

time where prisoners were cooped up. I'd not want even my worst enemy to come in there. This tree is my shelter all through the day. I watch the travellers come and go and would willingly sleep under it during the night, but for my sex—still the world is not an easy or safe place for us.'

I resisted the impulse to blurt out, Who would dare to come near you? As if reading my thoughts she said, 'I always carry a little pistol—of course licensed, because I'm an officer in the Home Guards at Delhi, though I have never had to shoot even a fly. I took a rifle-training course the police once organized at Madras, and I know which is the right end of a gun.' And she laughed. She seemed to be in a benign mood now, having probably got it off her chest in the morning. 'There is no train till 21.00 hours, to use the master's language—I think it is the 11 Up, a lumbering goods train which is so noisy that you can't sleep till it has passed the outer signal. You see, I'm picking up the railway language quite successfully.'

After a few more pleasantries of this kind, she paused to look at the station master and the porter, standing respectfully a short distance away, and said, 'That'll be all for the present, master. Tell your wife not to go to any trouble tonight. All I'll need is a glass of buttermilk if she can manage it.'

'Definitely, madam,' said the master and withdrew, followed by his porter. 'I'll be away to do some marketing, madam, not more than an hour.'

'Away till 17.30 hours?' she asked with a laugh.

'Very much earlier,' he said. 'Muni will be here and will attend to any important messages . . . he's experienced.' At which the porter looked pleased.

'I don't wish to bore you,' she said to me, 'but I have to tell you. In addition to our meetings in the evening at my home, he used to waylay me on my way to or from school and take me on his bicycle. I began to miss my classes happily, and spend the time with him at a coffee house or ice-cream parlour. He was very liberal in entertaining me. I was charmed with his talk on all sorts of subjects. Our discussions on the cement bench under our mango tree became infrequent since we were together in other places. We went to the museum, where he would take me through, explaining all sorts of things. I liked his voice and felt thrilled to be told about the eleventh-century bronzes or in another corner about the nomads or forest tribes and their cowrie-shell ornaments, and so on. And of the stuffed animals, their habits and character, whatever he said would just charm me. I couldn't decide how much of what he explained was genuine—but it held me, his voice lulled my senses. The museum was the nearest rendezvous for us, and I could go back home from there unnoticed, but sometimes we took the bus to the beach and enjoyed the ozone in the air, the surf and sand: he held my arms and dragged me knee-deep into the waves. A thrilling experience—made me forget my home and parents. Of course, a matinee at the Elphinstone on Mount Road occasionally. At Egmore, I had felt hemmed in, the horizon was restricted—but now this boy was opening my eyes to the wide world. I was not yet eighteen, but I possessed all the craftiness needed to save my skin. When my father demanded to know why I was late, I would always say that I had had a special class or was on an excursion with the teachers or doing joint study with a friend in some difficult subjects. My father, battling all day with carpenters to execute his constantly overdue orders, would not probe further. Fortunately, I was passing my exams and that was what he was particular about. But my mother, who had possessed sounder instincts, took me aside while I was leaving for school and said, 'I can hear your evening school bell quite clearly, remember. If you are not here within ten minutes of the bell, I'll tell your father. You know what he will do if he is upset. He will chip the skin off your back with his tools.'

'The next few days I came home punctually at the end of the school, avoiding the young man's company. When he cycled up and brought us magazines, my mother told him, "We don't have time for magazines. You may stop."

' "Why? Why?" he asked. And I could hear my mother's answer, "That's so, that's all, go . . . ."

'He hesitated, "Perhaps uncle may want to read."

' "Uncle! He is not your uncle! Begone!" she shouted, while my father kept himself deliberately in the shed, away from the scene. Listening to it all, I felt a sudden pity for the fellow and for all the kindness he had shown me, and I dashed out to say. "Why should you be so rough?" At which my mother slapped my face and I ran in crying.

'I became a virtual prisoner in the house—allowed only to get to my school and back under strict surveillance, escorted by Thayi, our old servant maid. My mother seemed a terrible woman in those days. I stopped talking to her, answered her questions in monosyllables, and whenever I thought of the boy, my heart bled for him. Leaning on his bicycle bar, he was bewildered by all the rudeness he was encountering in the world. I missed the warmth of his company and his enlightening talk, and above all the timid pecking on the neck and hugs when no one was looking.

'Though we were apart, we still found a way to communicate. Little notes or bits of paper passed between us through the agency of the woman chaperoning me. At the circulating library she dropped my note on his desk and brought back an answer. Thus I saved my head from being sawn off. To that extent, I respected, or rather we respected my parents' command. My final examination was due in a few months. I was not going to do anything that might disrupt my studies. So I acted the model child at home, and my parents looked very happy and pleased, and plied me with their kindness and trust. I concentrated on my studies and did well in my examinations in March. Although I felt desperate sometimes for his company we kept up our show till the May of that year when the results were announced.

'Occasionally we did meet when my parents were away. My mother's family lived at Avadi, fifty miles away. My father would escort her in the morning and they would come back by the evening train, which would leave me free for a full day. They would always warn: "Don't leave the house, take care of everything. Take care." The old servant would be told to stay to guard me from intruders (which was my mother's indirect way of indicating the young man). But I bribed the old lady to guard the house and that left us free to visit the circulating library. This would be our happiest moment. He would lock up his little office and take me out. We would go out to the farthest place possible, most times Elliot's Beach in Adyar, which was another planet as far as Egmore citizens were concerned. Elliot's Beach has one or two shacks where sea-bathers could dress—ideal retreats for lovers. All afternoon we stayed in a shack: they were happy hours. We were recklessly happy. I took care not to go beyond a certain limit in caresses, cuddling and fondling—though within that limit, we attained supreme happiness. We discussed plans for our future—many alternatives. We stayed in the shack watching fishermen go out to sea on their *catamarans*. Sometimes they would peep into the shack, smile and leave us alone. Sometimes they would demand a rupee or so for cigarettes—and then leave us alone. Thus the hours passed—while we stayed in the pleasure of each other's company listening to the waves splashing on the shore, blue sea and blue sky and birds diving in and the breeze. All of it made him say: "Let us go on and on here, why should we go back? Let us stay here till we die."

'But we had to scramble to our feet when the six o'clock chimes were heard from the San Thome cathedral. My father's train was due at seven at the Egmore Station and he would be home in fifteen minutes walking down the railway track. The old lady showed me the utmost sympathy and cooperation, seemed to get a vicarious thrill out of my romance. If my father threw a searching look around and asked the old woman: "Is everything all right?" she would answer, "Yes, of course, the child went on reading the whole day. Oh! how much she reads!"

' "Book? What book?" my father would ask suspiciously, on the alert to find out if it was from the circulating library.

' "I want to prepare for a correspondence course in accounting and borrowed a book from Shanta," I said.

'He was relieved and happy and commanded my studious habits, but also warned me against overdoing it, "because you have just worked hard for your Matriculation Exam."

'This kind of deceitful existence did not suit us. I felt rather dirty and polluted. When the results came and I was successful, I made up my mind. The next time my parents left for Avadi, my lover brought an old car, borrowed from one of his well-wishers, to the carpentry shop and took me away. He gave the old woman, my chaperone, ten rupees, and before we drove away told her: "You must bless us." I bundled up a change of clothes, while the old woman shed tears at the parting. In a voice shaking with emotion, she placed her hands on my shoulder and said, "May God bless you with many children!" the only blessed state that she could ever imagine.

'He stopped at a flowerseller's on the way, bought two garlands of jasmine and chrysanthemum, and drove straight without a word to a temple on the outskirts of the city: he seemed to have been busy earlier preparing for our wedding. A priest had lit oil lamps all around the image of some god. He presided over the exchange of garlands, asked us to prostrate before the god, lit a heap of camphor, got a couple of his friends to witness, in addition to God, distributed fruits to the gathering, lit a little flame which we circled, and sounded a bell. He then gave the bridegroom a yellow thread, and told him to tie it round my neck, charged us fifty rupees for his service, issued a rubber-stamped receipt, and we were man and wife.'

The lady's volubility overwhelmed me. I felt like the wedding guest whom the Ancient Mariner held in a spell of narrative, preventing his entry into the reception whence the noise of festivities was coming. He wailed that it was late and he should go in, but the Ancient Mariner held him with his eyes, ignoring his appeal and just said, 'With my cross-bow I shot the Albatross' and continued his hypnotic narration while the wedding guest beat his chest. I didn't go so far, but went on punctuating her speech with 'I think it's time for me . . . college socials to attend and report . . .'

She brushed off my protestations and hints and continued her narration as if only her tongue functioned, not her ears. She was quite carried away by her memories.

'We found an outhouse, a cozy one with a kitchen and bed-sitting room in Poonamalle High Road, and lived there happily, as happily as we could. Both of us worked. He continued in his library, which was now bigger, and he held a senior position with a lot of responsibilities. I was a receptionist at a travel agency. Both of us left at nine every day after breakfast and with a one-item simple lunch to pack and carry. I got up at five a.m. and cooked the food for the day. We returned at different times in the late evening and most days, being too tired to do anything else, ate some cold leftovers and went to bed.

'Occasionally I visited the carpentry to see my parents who had become friendly, perhaps taking a realistic view that they had acquired a son-in-law without spending money on dowry, feasts or celebrations.'

When she found me fidgeting and, trying to get up, she waved me back to my chair and said, 'Spare me some more time please, I'll finish as briefly as I can, though it's a long story. We may not meet again. While I can hold you, I'm anxious you should know the full story—I've not given up hopes you'll see him again, and you must have the full picture of your hero.'

'Oh no, not my hero and I'll not,' I protested.

'Please don't interrupt,' commanded the Ancient Mariner. 'If you don't keep interrupting, I'll finish my story quickly . . . otherwise you may make me forget and I've to go back and forth. Already, I think I missed an important episode. It's a vital link. Have I told you what happened on the day of my wedding and my father found me missing when he came home from Avadi?

'When he found me missing, the man seems to have lost his head completely. The old woman Thayi defended herself by explaining, "A car came into our gate suddenly: Roja (my name at home) was standing at the door, two young men seized and pulled her into the car and drove away . . . I don't know anything more . . . I ran down crying but the car was gone." After that my father went to the Egmore Police Station and gave a written complaint that I was missing and that he suspected kidnapping. Inspector Natesh was a family friend. Many were the table legs and rickety stools that my father had mended for him. He seems to have said with gusto:

"Leave this to me. I'll recover your lost daughter. These are days when young persons try to imitate the cinema stories."

'He spread his net wide and surprised us at a remote place called Fisherman's Hut, beyond Adyar, where we were hiding but living a beautiful existence. Two policemen came in a jeep with Inspector Natesh. We were just enjoying our lunch on the sea-shore, trying to live all the romantic poetry one has read in one's life. It was awkward when Natesh seized my husband's wrist and put the fetters on. However, he said to me, "Don't cry—you are all right."

'We drove back—a long, silent drive back to the city. First halt at the penitentiary, where the young man was dropped and handed over to a sergeant at the office, and then I was taken home and handed over to my parents—the worst kind of homecoming for anyone.

'The young man was charged with abducting and kidnapping a minor under eighteen years of age. A lawyer who was a customer of the circulating library and known to my husband came into the picture at this stage and said: "This is nonsense. I'll get the young fellow out, first on bail." Three days later the young man went back to his library as if nothing had happened. After that the case came up, off and on at the Presidency Magistrate's court, adjourned again and again. I went through hell, and so did my husband. The validity of our marriage was questioned, and I had to bear the hostility of my mother and relatives. I felt outlawed and miserable. In addition to all this misery, my father's lawyer coerced me to sign a document to say that I had been abducted and forced into a marriage. Said the legal luminary, "She is a minor and it cannot be a valid marriage." They bullied and browbeat me to sign a document charging him with abduction.

'This was the most painful part of the whole drama and I could never forgive myself for doing it. Signing a long story based on the old lady's report. How I had been snatched up from our house when I stepped out to get a couple of bananas from the shop across the street. How suddenly a car pulled up, the door opened and I was bodily dragged into the back seat, and the car sped away. The rest of the story was that I was first taken somewhere and kept a prisoner, locked up and watched, and also tortured until

I agreed to go through the exchange of garlands at the temple. My parents and their lawyer stood over me to sign the document, the old woman was asked to put her thumb impression as a witness to the kidnapping part of the story. At first I threw away the pen and wept and went without food, but my parents were firm. They kept saying: "No girl will be safe in this country unless we act. Young scamps like him must be taught a lesson." All my pleading was to no avail. Finally they broke my spirit, but assured me: "Nothing will happen to that scamp. Our lawyer will recommend clemency. All this is just to give him a fright, that's all."

' "Why?" I asked, "What has he done? He is my husband."

' "Husband! Husband!" they laughed, "Don't keep saying it. You'll be ruining your future! Some rascal—don't mention it outside."

'Then the lawyer added, "That sort of marriage is not valid my dear child . . . you are under eighteen."

'At every session of the hearing, the boy had to stand in the box and face the cross-examination. Being on bail, he could go back to his room or to work after attending court. His lawyer was, however, determined to save him. He got busy investigating and going into old records, located the Government Maternity Hospital where I was born and took extracts from the old registers to prove the hour and date of my birth. He proved that we were married at 3.30 in the afternoon of 18 May 1978, and my birth date and hour according to the hospital register was 11.30 a.m. and so it confirmed that at the time of my marriage I was eighteen years and three hours old, I had become a major with full power to decide my own course of life, and at the time of the so-called abduction, I was thirty minutes past eighteen years. Our lawyer demolished the prosecution's time scheme in a series of cross-examinations. I don't want to go into those details now as I may take time. To be brief, the court declared us properly married husband and wife.

'After the case I joined my husband and we established our home as I have already explained. In the course of time, forgotten were the police case and all the earlier bitterness and the feud. My parents once again doted on me. But the son-in-law could not accept the compromise. He refused to visit them or meet them—one point on which he would never yield, although he never interfered with my visiting my parents. He not only refused to visit them, but kept aloof and silent when they happened to come to see us at Poonamalle Road, always bringing some food or delicacy— but he never touched it in spite of my pleadings. I noticed a new development in him—he had become rather firm and hardened in his outlook. He brooded a great deal and seemed to have undergone a change of personality. It was not the trial and prosecution but my sworn statement read out at court that seemed to have shattered his faith. I could never forget the expression on his face when the lawyer read it out and I had to confirm it in public. Our wedded life had now acquired the dull routine of a fifty-year-old couple. I put it down to physical fatigue on his part, and did my best to cheer him and draw him out but only with partial success.'

I kept murmuring that I had to attend a function. but the Delhi woman continued. I almost expected her to say, 'With my cross-bow I shot the albatross.' Instead of that

she simply said, 'He didn't come home one evening—that
was the end.' Her voice shook a little, and again she
fumbled in her handbag for the tiny handkerchief. It was
not a moment when I could leave. She could not stop her
narration. Even if I left she would still be talking to the
stars, which had come out, with the pale lantern of the
railway station throwing an eerie illumination around. The
goods train had arrived and lumbered along, but still she
went on.

At some point when she paused for breath I resolutely
got up murmuring, 'I'll have to go to a wedding reception,
having missed the college socials.' She concluded, 'A man
from our travel agency noticed him at the airport at the
Kuwait Air counter. Through our associates at Kuwait I
tried to get information about him, but they could not trace
him. God only knows what he calls himself now. I seem to
have lost him forever.'

The lady left the next day for Delhi. The station master
became maudlin at the parting—a man who was used to
seeing off hundreds of passengers each day in either direction,
in a cold businesslike manner, had tears in his eyes when
the engine pulled up.

'Great woman! She was welcome to stay any length of
time—even if the inspector came, I'd have managed without
disturbing her.'

His wife and children were there to bid her farewell.
First time I noticed what a lot of children he had produced
under his little roof. I suspected that the Delhi woman must
have distributed liberally gifts and tips—not overlooking
Muni.

When the engine whistled the lady took out of her handbag her card, and gave it to me remarking, 'Most important—I almost forgot it in this *mela* of leave-taking—although I suspect the masterji held up the train for full ten minutes.'

I accepted her card and promised, 'If I get the slightest clue I'll reach you by every means of communication possible.'

I found Rann moping and felt sorry for his lonely alienated existence. I declared with extra cheer, 'Time to be up and celebrate.'

'What?' he asked without much enthusiasm, thinking that it was a bit of a joke.

I said, 'The lady has left for Delhi by the 7 UP.'

'Are you serious?' he asked.

'Absolutely. Just an hour ago. My hands are still warm with all the handshakes. We all broke down at the parting.'

'Oh, where, where is she gone?'

'I've told you, Delhi. Not to the next station but far-off Delhi.'

He nearly jumped out of the easy chair. I said, 'Let us go out for a walk after a visit to the Boardless.'

'Where?' he asked without moving.

'To the river.'

'You have it at your backyard.'

'This is no good now; much better at Nallappa's Grove, beyond Ellamman Street.'

He hesitated at first. I talked him out of his reluctance. Finally he agreed. 'How should I dress?' he asked.

'Better tie a *dhoti* around your waist and wear a half-sleeve shirt.'

He had bought these recently at the Khadi Stores, made in handspun material.

'If you wear khadi, they'll respect you, take you for a nationalist, a follower of Mahatma Gandhi.'

'He was a great man,' he exclaimed irrelevantly.

'That's all right. Get ready, let us go.'

'I'm not used to a *dhoti*. I can't walk. It keeps slipping down to my ankles, can't make it stay around the waist.'

'All right, come in any dress you like . . . I'll wait outside.'

I sat on the *pyol* and waited for him. He had the sense to appear in a shirt and grey trousers, but still, when we went down Market Road, people looked at me, as if questioning, 'What is this oddity always keeping you company?'

'I feel uneasy when they stare at me.'

'No harm, better get used to it. I don't know what it is like in Timbuctoo, but here we don't mind staring, actually encourage it. It gives people a lot of pleasure. Why not let them please themselves that way? It costs nothing.'

He wouldn't say anything but fixed his gaze on the far-off horizon, looking at no one in particular.

I said, 'No one will mind if you stare at them in return. You miss a great deal by not staring. It's a real pleasure and an education, really.' He said nothing but took it as a sort of perverse quipping on my part, probably saying to himself, Cranky journalist. We reached Ellamman Street which dissipated into sand, beyond which the river curved away gently. People were sitting around in groups, students,

329

children, old men, ancient colleagues and pensioners, young men hotly arguing, and of course also a peanut vendor going round crying his ware. On the main steps, people were washing clothes and bathing in the river, or reciting their evening prayers sitting cross-legged. I found a secluded spot near Nallappa's Grove where bullock carts and cattle were crossing. I selected a boulder for a seat so that Rann could be perched comfortably, while I sat down on the sand. The hum of Market Road reached us, but softly, over the chatter of birds settling down for the night in the trees. I realized that he was responding to the quality of the hour—the soft evening light with the rays of the setting sun touching the top branches of trees, the relaxed happy atmosphere with children running about and playing in the sand. He said all of a sudden, 'Have you noticed the kinship that seems to exist between sand and children? It's a feature that I have noticed all over the world—in every part of the globe, in any continent.'

I was happy to note his sudden eloquence. 'It's one of the things that unites mankind and establishes the sameness. Sand and children and this . . .' he said all of a sudden stooping and pulling out a bunch of some tiny obscure vegetation from the ground. A plant that was hardly noticeable under any circumstance . . . a pale tuft of leaves and a stalk with little white flowers. His eyes acquired a new gleam—unseen normally. 'This is the future occupant of our planet,' he said in a tone of quiet conviction: 'This is a weed spreading under various aliases in every part of the earth—known in some places as Congress weed, don't know which congress is meant, Mirza Thorn, Chief's Tuft, Voodoo Bloom, the Blighter and so on. Whatever the name,

330

it's an invader, may have originated out of the dust of some other planet left by a crashing meteor. I see it everywhere; it's a nearly indestructible pest. Its empire is insidiously growing—I have surveyed its extent and sent a memorandum to headquarters.'

I refrained from asking, Which headquarters? Like the word 'project' it's a tabloid word which needs no elucidation. He went on as if inspired: 'No one has found a weedicide capable of destroying it. They seem to go down at the first spraying, we tried it in Uganda, but a second generation come up immune to it . . . I have calculated through computers that, at the rate of its growth, the entire earth will be covered with it as the sole vegetation by about AD 3000. It'll have left no room for any other plant life; and man will starve to death as no other growth will be possible and this has no food value—on the contrary, it is a poison. You will notice that cattle don't touch it. In addition to other disservices, it sucks and evaporates all the ground water. We should call it the demon grass. My notes on this are voluminous—and the book, when it comes, will be a sensation.'

'What's your field of study?' I could not help asking. I suspected he was egging me on to do so, why not oblige him? I was feeling kindly toward him. I was softening. His outlandish style of living and dressing was fascinating. Why should I grudge him a little attention, a fellow who was giving me so much entertainment?

He seemed pleased at my query. 'Call it futurology—a general term which involves various studies. We have to make a proper assessment of all our resources and dangers; human as well as material. All kinds of things will have to

331

go into it. We must get a scientific view and anticipate the conditions and state of life in AD 3000. To know whether we shall, as the human species, survive or not.'

I could not help bursting into a laugh. 'Personally, I wouldn't bother—what, ten centuries hence, none of us, even the most long-lived, will not be involved . . . so . . .'

'How do you know?' he asked. 'Present developments in biology and medicine may prolong life endlessly.'

'You crave for immortality. I don't care.'

'Whether you crave for it or not, that's not the question. We are moving in that direction willy-nilly, and it's important to assess how much of present civilization is going to survive . . . taking into consideration various conditions and symptoms.'

'You remind me of our psychology professor who used the words "tensions", "symptoms", and "trends" at least once every nine seconds, when I was a student.'

He didn't like my frivolous attitude and suddenly became silent.

The reason why I wanted to puncture this pompous fellow was this: the old man at the town hall library had a granddaughter who brought him a flask of coffee and some tiffin in a brass container at about three in the afternoon most days. The old man, who came after an early meal to the library before 10 a.m., faded progressively in his chair until the tiffin came, and if any of the readers at the library asked a question at that time, he barked out his reply and looked fierce. 'My fate has not decreed me a better life than sitting here guarding dusty volumes. Don't add to my

troubles. If you don't see the book, it's not there, that's all
. . . Go, go take your seat; don't stand here and block the
air, please.' This would be his mood on the days when the
girl came late, but generally she was punctual. At the sight
of her, his face would relax. He would welcome her with
a broad smile, and say, 'Baby, come, come! What have you
brought me today?' The sight of her brought him endless
joy. He would get up from the chair and say: 'You sit here,
child—I'll come back.' He carried the little plastic handbag
with the flask and tiffin packet to a back room, beyond
which was a washroom with a tap. While he was gone the
girl occupied his seat, and listened to the water running in
the washroom and then stopping and, after an interval,
running a second time, and she would know that he washed
his hands before touching the tiffin and washed again after
eating, and she would get up and vacate the seat for him as
he returned, timing it all perfectly. As expected by her, he
would reappear wiping his lips with a checked towel and
beaming with contentment.

'Was it all right?'

'Yes, of course, can't be otherwise . . .'

'Grandmother got sugar from the neighbour. We had
run out.'

'Tell her, I'll buy some this evening on my way home.'
The girl was about seventeen years old. He called her 'baby'
and derived a special joy in thinking of her, watching her
come and go, and talking to her. She was at Albert Mission
in the BA class. Tall, and though not a beauty, radiated the
charm of her years.

Rann came into the library one afternoon when the girl
was occupying the chair. Just then I was rummaging in the

old newspaper sheets on the central table, searching for some information, what it was I forget now. I was at the newspaper end of the hall and he didn't notice me, but I could see him as he approached the table and halted his steps, with all his faculties alert and tense like a feline coming upon its unsuspecting prey.

Ah! he seemed to say, I didn't know that the Town Hall library possessed this treasure! Is that old fellow gone and my good fortune has put you in his place? He greeted the girl with an effusive, ceremonious bow, and put on an act— of the most winsome manner. I wanted to cry out, Keep away, you—I don't know what to call you! She is young enough to be your daughter. You are a lecherous demon and wouldn't mind even if it were a granddaughter! Keep off!

The girl said something and both of them laughed. I wished the old man would come back from his lunch, back to his seat. But he was in the habit of reclining on an easy chair and shutting his eyes for fifteen minutes. It was generally a calm hour at the library and he left the girl to take care of things for a while, which seemed to be a god-sent chance for Rann. I felt it was time to apply the brake. I folded the newspaper, put it away, got up, and approached the table. The girl cried from the table, 'Uncle, here is an interesting gentleman from Timbuctoo. I didn't know there was such a place! Where is it?'

'Ask him,' I said, not ready to be involved in a geographical problem.

Rann rose to the occasion. He took a few steps to the table and demanded, 'Get a piece of paper. I'll show you.' On the blank sheet, with a stylish slim gold pen, he drew a map. When he said, 'You see this is where we are. Timbuctoo is—' the girl brought her face close to his. I'm sure he was casting a spell at that moment, for it seemed to me that the girl was relishing the smell of the after-shave lotion and hair-cream, which, I suspected, made him irresistible to women. He knew it and turned it on fully. With his palm resting on the map, he manoeuvred and agitated his forefinger and middle finger as if playing on a musical instrument, to indicate places, volubly explaining historical, topographical, economic matters of Timbuctoo in detail; he looked up from time to time to ask, in a sort of intimate whisper, now do you understand? I feared that he was going too far, rather too close to her, when the old man reappeared with the plastic bag in hand, the very picture of contentment, and threw a kindly look at the visitor. He was not overwhelmed by the other's personality as on the first day since Rann was no longer in a three-piece suit but had adapted himself to a normal Malgudi executive costume, cotton pants and shirt-sleeves. The girl rose to give up her seat to her grandfather, who lowered himself m the chair saying, 'Long time since we met, how have you been, sir?'

'Thanks,' Rann said with a bow. I noted how accomplished an act he was putting on. He was versatile— one moment to impress the girl and patronize her and take her under his wing—so solicitous, kindly in tone—the world of the fairytales, the next moment the international scholar academician adopting his manner to impress the old man—on whose goodwill he would have to depend in order to get closer to the girl.

And there were other reports I was getting about Rann

from here and there that I did not like at all. At the
Boardless, Gundu Rao, a horticulturist (in municipal service
and responsible for maintaining the nominal park around
the Town Hall, the struggling lawns at the Central Police
Station and the Collector's Office, and for seeing that the
fountain sprayed up and rose to the occasion on national
festivities such as Gandhiji's birthday and Independence
Day), approached my table to whisper: 'Want to tell you
something . . .'

Varma who was watching us said, 'What secret?'

Rao simpered and replied, 'Nothing important.'

Varma having to listen to so much all day left us alone.
When I had finished the coffee, I found the horticulturist
waiting in the street, leaning on his bicycle. He said, 'That
man in your house. Who's he?'

'Why?' I asked, resenting his method of inquiry.

'You see . . . you know the Protestant Cemetery far out
on Mempi Road?'

'Yes, though I have had nothing to do with it.'

'I have been asked to trim the hedges and some of the
border plants. The Collector called me and told me to take
it up—I don't know why this interest in the cemetery, not
my business, really, but I must obey orders.'

'Naturally, but you were trying to say something else?'

'Ah, yes, about that man who is living with you. I notice
him often there, sitting on a far-off bench in a corner—
always with a girl at his side. I know who she is, but I
won't tell you. That place is at least five miles out—it's my
fate to cycle that distance everyday—such a strain really—
but if I don't go the old gardener who lives in a shed won't
do a thing and the Collector will come down on us, though

I can't understand what the Collector has to do with the cemetery!'

'All right, tell me more about that man.'

'Well, I wondered why they had come so far and how; but then I noticed a scooter parked at the gate—and he rides down with the girl sitting at his back—as they do nowadays. Not my business really, when a man and a woman sit close to each other, I generally stay away—it makes me uncomfortable—'

And then Nataraj, manager of the Royal Theatre, met me at the magistrates' court veranda and said, 'You don't come to my theatre at all, why? I have improved the seating and upholstered the sofas, with foam rubber cushions and nylon covers—why don't you drop in some time and write a few words about our improvements? We are showing a picture with a karate expert acting in it. Full house, every show, I tell you. Your guest reserved two sofas in the balcony a couple of days ago. He appreciated the new designs and furnishing—coming from one who has seen the world—'

And Jayaraj, the photographer at the Market Arch, who is really the main reservoir of local gossip (with several tributaries pouring in about people and their doings), where I generally stop to know what's happening everywhere, said, 'Your guest is very active nowadays. He used to hire a cycle from Kennedy, but that poor fellow has lost the regular customer. You know why? Because Sambu seems to have surrendered his Vespa scooter to him freely. You know why the scooter for the gentleman?'

'Because he has a pillion rider?'

'You know who it is?'

337

'Yes, yes, I guess.'

'And so that's that! He is very attentive to the girl,' he added with a leer. He was in his element with gossip of this stature in hand. 'You know what his routine is? At 10.30 he is ready behind the Town Hall compound, as 10.35 the girl materializes on the pillion of Sambu's Vespa, 10.45 Kismet Ice-Cream Stall at New Extension, 10.58 at the level-crossing so that she may walk up to the Albert Mission College gate as if she had come walking all the way. After the college she is met again at the level-crossing—and where they go after that is their business, don't ask me.'

Others also mentioned the subject—each in his own way. The old man at the library, during one of my morning visits, said, 'I see very little of Baby nowadays. She used to bring my tiffin, but I walk home for my tiffin nowadays, leaving the watch to some known person in the reading room. Obliging fellows really—some of the old library users. I even take a few minutes' nap after tiffin and come back. But Baby never comes home before eight nowadays—final year for her and special classes and joint studies every day, I suppose. Nice to think she will be a graduate soon. Then what? Up to her parents to decide. But you know my son-in-law is not a clear-headed fellow—too much of a rustic and farmer and his wife, my daughter, has developed almost like her husband although I had visions of marrying her to a city man in Madras or Calcutta, but this fellow was rich and was studying at Madras and I thought he would pass a civil service exam, but the fellow settled in their village when his father passed away—and now his mind is full of cowdung and its disposal, and a gobar gas plant which utilizes it. He and his wife can talk of nothing else—but gas, gas, gas, which lights their stoves and lights everything. Baby, when she goes to her parents for a holiday, cannot stand that life though I insist upon her spending at least ten days with her parents—I brought her away when she was ten so that she could have her education. After she finishes her college, what? That's the question that bothers me day and night. I'd like her to become an officer somewhere—but not too far away. Also I want her to marry and be happy—and again stay not too far away from me. I'm so accustomed to her presence—my wife too says we should not live too far away from her. Anyway let us see what God proposes.'

At this point an old reader approached us to ask, 'The tenth page of the *Mail* is missing.'

'What's special in it?'

'Crosswords,' the man said.

The old man replied, 'I suspected so.' He took it out of his drawer and gave it with the warning, 'Copy it down, don't mark on the paper.'

I bottled up my uneasiness at these reports. I had no clear notion what I could do about the situation or why. It was not my business, I said to myself, but then I began to have suspicions about Rann's background. Before tackling him, I wanted to arm myself with facts. I had no other recourse but to act as a spy. These days he went out after breakfast and kept away till lunch, came in and went out again. I realized that his movements were based on Girija's timetable. When he left in the afternoon I could count on his absence all evening till eight o'clock or longer. I opened his room with a duplicate key. When I stepped in I felt like a burglar in my own home. I felt excited and hard-pressed for time. I quickly examined his briefcase and a portfolio of letters— quite a handful. Envelopes addressed to different names— only two to Rann—and the address was always Poste Restante in different towns and countries. Like our gods, he seemed to have a thousand names—Ashok, Naren, D'Cruz, John, Adam, Shankar, Sridhar, Singh and Iqbal and what not. The letters were all from women: imploring, appealing, and accusing and attacking in a forthright manner; some of them were intensely passionate, from Mary, Rita, Nancy, Manju, Kamala, and so on. One or two had been addressed to Dubai or Kuwait, and forwarded from place to place. And there were some from Roja herself, who somehow managed to reach him. There was a common feature in every letter: the cry of desertion. A few blackmail attempts, some threats to inform the police and set Interpol on his track. You would have needed a world map to mark his movements as deduced from the postmarks and the various postage stamps—quite an album could be made with stamps from his envelopes. No wonder he had so many pursuing him, but unable to get at him. 'You are heartless—a monster, don't you have a feeling for the child you pampered, who is crying for you night and day? How can he understand the perfidy of your action in melting into the night without even a farewell kiss?' Another letter said, 'Come back, that's enough for me. I'll forget the money.' In another, 'You need not come—if you appear at my door, I'll throw you out. Only return the share due to me—at least 20,000 pesos and you may go to the devil. If you ignore this, I'll

340

write an anonymous letter to the Interpol.' This last made
me wonder if he was a drug trafficker too. He had a way
of slipping away from address to address: it puzzled me
why he left any postal addresses at all, and was not afraid
of being discovered while collecting mail. He must have had
a pathological desire to collect letters and preserve them.
This was rather puzzling. Why would any man treasure
such correspondence?—enough to damn him and send him
to prison. Extraordinary man! I admired on one side his
versatile experience, indifference and hardihood. What was
the great driving force in his life? I picked up a fat bound
book, which seemed to be a journal written from time to
time. I was nervous about going through it. If I sat reading
it, I might not notice the time passing and he might come
back. And so I hurriedly gave it a glance, opening a page
here and there. Why this man perpetuated his misdeeds in
chronicles was beyond my understanding. On one leaf he
noted, 'No use hanging on here. S is proving impossible. No
woman supposes that a man has any better business than
cuddling and love talk.' Another entry said, 'My project is
all important to me. I am prepared to abandon everything
and run away if it is interrupted. Again and again I seem to
fall into the same trap like a brainless rat. It is difficult at
this stage to make others see the importance of my book—
which has to go side by side with the project even if it is
only an offshoot. The world will be shaken when the book
is out. The highest award in the world may not be beyond
my dream.' He noted on another sheet, 'Your Majesty,
King Gustav and Queen, Members of the Nobel
Committee—I'm receiving this award, I feel you are
honouring my country. India and Sweden have much in

common culturally.' I heard the hall clock chime five, and quickly put all the letters and diary back in their original place in the drawer, shut the drawer, locked it as before and quickly and quietly withdrew, leaving no thumb impression on anything.

'What do you think of that girl?' I asked him innocently one day.

'Which girl?' he asked.

'Girija—the librarian's granddaughter, whom he calls Baby.'

'I don't know,' he said, 'I don't know her very well—though I see her here and there—especially at her school whenever I go there to see one of the professors. Now that you ask, she is quite smart, and will go far with proper training. But this place is no good for her. She must get out of this backwood, if you don't mind my saying it.'

I was rather irked. 'But you seem to prefer this to a lot of other places in the world.'

'My job is different—but for a young mind starting in life, a more modern, urban, cultural feedback will help. My private view is, don't quote me, from what I have seen, she shouldn't grow up with her grandfather. A hostel would be preferable—where she can compare and compete with her age-group. Anyway after her final exam in March, she should decide her future.'

'Marriage?'

'Oh, no, not necessarily, though I would not rule it out. A girl can be married and still pursue intellectual and social values. But the important thing is she should get out of this—'

'Backwood.' I completed his sentence. He only smiled. Impossible to fathom his mind's workings.

The old librarian said, 'Girija is lucky. That man has agreed to coach her through. He seems to be an expert in certain subjects. What do you think of it?'

I hesitated. It was a complex situation. I did not know how far the old man was aware of the situation. In his zeal to see his granddaughter well placed he might welcome Rann's proposal. I couldn't understand anything until I could speak to Girija, but it had become impossible to get at her, though formerly I always enjoyed a little banter with her at the library. Now I remained silent while the old man waited for my comment. One or two at the reading-room table paused, looked up and turned in our direction expectantly. I said to the old man to put the eavesdroppers off the track, 'It's getting unusually warm these days—' and left, at which the inquisitive souls at the long table looked disappointed and resumed their reading.

I returned to the library at closing time with the definite objective of talking to the old man when others would not be there. The old man was closing the windows, pushing the chairs back into position, and giving a final look around before locking the door.

'What brings you here at this hour?' he asked.

'I was passing this way and I thought I might as well stop by. I'll walk with you.'

He tucked his old umbrella under his arm, its bamboo handle dark yellow with the age-old contact with his fingers, and strode off. I pushed my bicycle along. He lived

343

nearby—fifteen minutes away—at old Palm Grove, in a small house with its broad cement platforms overlooking the street. All the way down he was talking of Girija and her future, which seemed to be very bright. I dropped the idea of warning him about Rann. I felt I'd be making myself unpopular if I spoke against Rann.

He invited me in. I leaned the bicycle against a lamp post and sat down on the *pyol*. He excused himself and went in for a wash, and came back drying himself with a towel and bade me come in, and settled down in the easy chair. He had hung up his upper cloth on a nail and the shirt over it, his bare body covered with the towel.

'Only two of us in this house—and Baby, you see that's her room. You may peep in if you like.' To please him, I went in and dutifully peeped. She had a small table on which were heaped her books and papers, and clothes, on a little stand, again in a heap. On the wall she had pasted up some portraits of film stars and one or two gods also; on the latter she had stuck flowers. A small window opened on the next house; there was only a small bulb throwing a dim light. 'She always studies in the hall, sitting on the floor with her books spread about,' complained the old gentleman. 'Not a soul in the house to disturb her. When she is reading I tiptoe around, and her grandmother doesn't dare raise her voice. Our only interest is to see her pass with distinction, and she must get a Government of India scholarship too.'

Meanwhile his wife who had gone to a neighbour's came back. He introduced me to her as the host of the distinguished foreigner, and added, 'He is a Kabir Street man. They are not ordinary men there.' He gave a grand account of my ancestors.

The venerable lady added her own knowledge of my family members, traced various relationships, and also claimed kinship with one of my aunts, whom I had never heard of. She said: 'You are really fortunate to have a guest of such distinction. Good guests really bring us honour. There was a time when I used to cook and feed with my own hands any number of men and women, not here but in our original home at Gokulam. Well, we had to move here—that was God's will. My daughter was not married at that time—Girija was born in this house when we lost that house—'

'Why do you tire the gentleman with that old tale?'

None the less she continued: 'My husband was the registrar of the District Court—'

'Don't be absurd. I was only a sheristedar, not the registrar. I've corrected you a hundred times.'

'What if! You had so much money coming in every day and so many visitors—no one would come bare-handed. We had no need to go to the market for anything: vegetables and fruits or rice—'

'Friendly people all round in those days,' he explained.

I understood what this meant: a court sheristedar had favours to dispense in the shape of judgment copies, court-orders and so on, and he favoured court-birds in his own way.

The old man did not feel comfortable and tried to change the topic.

'Only after I retired did I take up the library work—convenient, being close to this house. When I hesitated, the judge who started the reading room, whose portrait is on the wall beside Sir Frederick Lawley's, compelled me to accept it, as a sort of social service. On the opening occasion—it was a grand function—he also referred to me in his speech.'

I suspected the judge accepted bribes chanelled through the sheristedar. 'I must have been in high school at that time,' I added.

The lady said, apropos nothing, 'Dr Rann came here a couple of days ago. Girija brought him. He is such a simple man—absolutely without conceit—considering his status. He has held such great posts in so many countries—knows so much! I could have listened to him all night! His conversation is so absorbing, but my husband felt sleepy— I insisted the distinguished visitor have food here, and he enjoyed it, though our fare was simple and we couldn't give him porcelain dishes or a spoon. He ate with his fingers! Only thing, he could not sit on the floor like us.'

When I got back home, I saw the light in Rann's room. I had an impulse to go and demand an explanation as to what game he was trying to play, to warn him to keep off, and not to add one more desperate correspondent to his files. But I felt doubts about my own understanding of the situation. I might be misreading the whole scene. After all, he must have seen enough women, and Girija might mean no more to him than a niece of whom he was growing fond and whom he would like to see develop academically so that she might have a worthy career. The old couple seemed to have developed a worshipful attitude to Rann. They might misunderstand if I said anything contrary to their views; it might seem as if I had evil motives or was envious of the girl's good luck. They might turn round and say, None of your business . . . we know. And I could not very well reveal Rann's private affairs. If he walked out of my house it might give rise to public talk, and perhaps compromise the girl and cause an innocent family embarrassment and scandal. I might be misreading the whole situation. After all, a child whom I had been seeing for years, since her Albert-Mission-Nursery-School-uniform days, but now too tall for her age, dressed in perfectly starched and pressed cotton saree and looking quite smart, this wouldn't mean that she was an adult woman capable of devious and dubious adventure. She might well still be a child at heart, like most womanly-looking girls. But if so why the Protestant Church rendezvous? That didn't seem so innocent. If he was only helping her studies and general knowledge, it was not necessary to go so far . . . Lying in bed I kept sifting and analysing and finding justifications and overcoming doubts and suspicions about Girija and Rann, till I fell asleep well past midnight.

Our Lotus Club was twenty-five years old, and we decided to celebrate its silver jubilee with a grand public lecture at the Town Hall by Dr Rann of the United Nations, on a brand new subject, 'futurology'. Rann somehow accepted the proposal when I mentioned it. He said, 'Normally I have an aversion to public speaking. I am a writer, not a speaker. However, you have been good to me, and I can't say no to you. I must oblige you.' This was on the day following our evening on the river sand when he had expounded to me his theory of the cosmic extinction of all life through the Giant Weed.

The Lotus Club was desperately in need of a show to

boost its prestige, but more than prestige, the Lotus Club had sufficient funds to spend on an occasional burst of activity, and a rich man, decades before, had left an endowment and special fund for the silver jubilee. The President, who had been rusting, readily agreed. He was proud to have an international personality to deliver the jubilee lecture and on a subject that was so mysterious: 'futurology'. 'Everyone knows what astrology, physiology and zoology are, but no one knows about "futurology". I am agog to hear this lecture.'

He wanted me to print a brochure entitled 'Lotus Twenty-five Years of Public Service' and distribute it in the hall, also several thousand handbills announcing the meeting, and five hundred special invitations printed on decorated cards to be mailed to India's President, Prime Minister, the editors of national newspapers, every VIP of the land. Nothing could appeal to me more than this activity.

At the Truth Printing Works, the printer Nataraj cleared a corner of the press for me. I sat there in the morning writing up the pages of the jubilee brochure, arranging the invitations and notices; hot from my desk, the matter was passed to the printer. Nataraj had set aside his routine work and devoted all his energy and time to this task. I felt happy and fulfilled, being so active, and was already worried at the back of my mind as to how I would stand the dull days ahead when all this activity should cease.

The President of the Lotus Club was one Mr Ganesh Rao, a pensioner now but at one time a judge of the Supreme Court at Delhi. My day started with a visit to his bungalow at Lawley Extension. A gracious elder of the community who looked like Lloyd George or Einstein with

white locks falling on his nape, he was a prized possession
of our town—the citizens remarked with awe and gratitude
that after decades of distinguished service at Delhi, Kashmir,
and even at some international courts, he should have
chosen to return to the town of his origin.

Gaffur the taxi driver, whose Ambassador always occupied
a position of vantage beside the Fountain Wall on the
Market Road—except at train time when it could be seen
under the Gul Mohar tree at the railway station—was the
man I was desperately searching for before the big meeting.
I had to go round town distributing invitations and notices
and on various other errands in connection with the meeting.
I had so much to do that I felt the need for a transport
quicker than my bicycle or Sambu's scooter, if available.

Gaffur was not to be seen. I had to go in search of him
here and there. No one was able to guide me. I was pressed
for time; the day of the jubilee was drawing near. As ever,
Jayaraj came to my rescue. He said, 'He lives in Idgah—one
of those houses. I'll find out and leave word on my way
home tonight.'

Gaffur's Ambassador was at my door the next morning.
He left the car at the street corner and came to my room
while I was shaving before my ancient mirror. 'Madhu, you
want me?' he asked, being one of the boyhood associates
who called me Madhu instead of TM. My face was still full
of soap. I spoke to him looking from the mirror.

'Gaffur! Where have you been all these days? You have
become scarce—and I want you so badly for the next
week.'

'Madhu, your tenant is the one who keeps me busy. I have to be at his call every morning. I don't call for him here, he doesn't want it that way, but he hails me at the fountain almost at the same hour each day at about ten-thirty, and then he leaves me at five o'clock, after I have returned tht girl.'

'Which girl? Where do you take her?'

'I think they are going to marry—the way they are talking in the backseat and planning, he is taking her to America . . . though it is none of my business, I can't help listening.'

'Oh, God!' I cried, involuntarily blowing off the soap on my lips.

'Why do you worry, Madhu? Is it that you want to marry her yourself?'

'Oh, God!' I cried a second time. 'I've known her since she was a baby, and she is like a daughter to me.'

'So what?' he said. 'You must be happy that she found a nice man for a husband. Otherwise you'd have to spend so much money to get her a husband. After all, in your community, unlike ours, girls are free to go out without a veil and talk to men—and so what is wrong?'

'He is old enough to be her grand-uncle.'

'I won't agree with you. He is very sweet, looks like a European . . . Good man, pays down by the meter without a word, a gentleman. If there were more like him, I could buy a Rolls Royce or a Mercedes Benz.'

I left it at that. I learnt a great deal from Gaffur that morning. I had also noticed the past two days that Rann was packing up; and had settled with the furniture company to cart their pieces away after the Jubilee meeting. The plot was revealed by Gaffur: after the meeting at the Town Hall he was to pick up Rann's suitcases from my house, meet Rann at the Town Hall, then drive away to Peak House on Mempi Hills the same night, with the girl, who would be waiting some place. From Peak House they would descend on the other side of the mountain to Mempi Town, and then leavé by bus to God knows where. I was shocked by the smooth manner in which Rann was manoeuvring to elope with the girl.

Gaffur's report was invaluable. I had to base my future action on it, but I realized I was facing a delicate situation. I had to avoid upsetting anyone on any side. The old librarian must be protected from shock or a stroke, Girija from a public scandal and an eventual desertion in some far-off place and all the frustration and tragedy that befell every woman captivated by Rann's charms. My mind wandered over morbid details as to how far the girl had admitted him; when it was all over, one must somehow take her to Dr Lazarus, the lady doctor at the Government Hospital, to get her examined for a possible abortion, a lesser evil than being burdened with a fatherless child. While the other women in Rann's life were perhaps hardy and sophisticated, capable of withstanding the tragedy, this girl was innocent, her mind in a nascent state, unless already complicated and corrupted by association with Rann. It was not a good sign that she was lying to her simple-minded grandfather. I doubted if she cared for her studies at all nowadays; Rann might have promised any degree she chose from any university on earth. I could well imagine his boastful assurance, 'Oh, you leave it to me—I'll speak to Turnbull, president of . . . when we get to the

United States.' His voice rang in my ears with this sort of assurance, and the picture came before me of this girl looking up at him adoringly. I luxuriated in a passing vision of slapping this girl for her stupidity and shutting her up in a room and kicking out Rann, but on the other hand Rann had to be kept in good humour. If he was upset and backed out and vanished, I'd be hounded out of Malgudi by its worthy citizens for being fooled with all that trumpeting about the Town Hall lecture. Sitting in the meditation room after Gaffur left, I brooded and brooded and came to the conclusion not to speak about anything till the meeting was over. I would pretend not to notice Rann's packing up either.

It was an inspiration. I moved out of the meditation room and rummaged in my desk till I picked up the pocket diary in which I remembered placing the address card of the lady from Delhi. At first it eluded my search—all kinds of other cards, addresses and slips of paper fell out from between the leaves. I almost despaired, then gave a final shake and her yellow card fell out—'Commandant Sarasa, Home Guards Women's Auxiliary, Delhi', with her address, telephone, and telex numbers. I hurried to the post office and sent off a telegram.

COME IMMEDIATELY. YOUR HUSBAND FOUND. COME BEFORE HE IS LOST AGAIN. YOUR ONLY FINAL CHANCE TO ROPE HIM. STAY RAILWAY WAITING ROOM. I'VE FIXED IT. TAKE CARE NOT TO BE SEEN IN TOWN. WILL MEET AND EXPLAIN FURTHER PROCEDURE.

The strategy was perfect.

I had to soften the station master again with a five-rupee note, and he promised to entertain the lady royally in

the waiting room as before. I expected her to arrive on the
eve of the jubilee meeting at the Town Hall, when Rann
would be preoccupied with both his romantic plans and his
preparations for the lecture, now of course facilitated by
having Gaffur's taxi at his disposal. I was in suspense while
I waited for the train from Madras, but it did not bring the
lady in. The second train, from Trichy, also disappointed
me. No sign of her. However, she arrived late that night by
road from Trichy, where she had flown from Delhi. Her car
was parked in the station compound. She woke up the
station master and got the waiting room opened.

Having been busy the whole day with a hundred things
to do before the meeting, I found time to go to the station
master's house only at midnight and was relieved to learn
that the lady had arrived. I didn't want to spend any more
time at the station. I gave him another token of esteem in
cash, as well as a sealed envelope addressed to the
Commandant to be delivered to her without fail in the
morning. I also gave him a VIP invitation card to attend the
Lotus Club meeting, which pleased him tremendously.

My letter, which I had composed under great strain,
gave the lady precise instruction as to what she should do
next.

The extraordinary publicity generated by the Lotus Club
brought in a big crowd. On the day of the meeting, the
Town Hall auditorium was packed. The organizers were
plucky enough to have organized a Deputy Minister to
preside, which meant that the local officials could not stay
away. The police and security arrangements were spectacular.

The Deputy Minister was in charge of Town Planning, Cattle Welfare, Child Welfare, Family Planning, Cooperation and Environment, Ecology and other portfolios too numerous even for him to remember. In Delhi he had six different buildings for his offices and files.

The President of the Lotus Club had written a letter to him requesting him to grace the occasion, and he had readily agreed. Being the most ubiquitous minister one could think of, every day the newspapers carried reports of his movements. Malgudi had been rather left out of his official circuits, but now it was coming on the official map, much to the satisfaction of the towns folk.

When the meeting began, the foot-lights came on. The minister was seated at the centre of the stage in a high-back gilded chair; Rann was seated on his right in a not so high and less gilded chair; and three other chairs were occupied by the President of the Lotus (ex-judge of the Supreme Court) and two other factotums. I was given a seat at right angles to this main row as became the press and also because I was really the creator of the entire function. Behind the minister sat his secretary and behind him a uniformed orderly in a high-rise glittering lace-edged turban.

The hall was packed, as I noted from my position of vantage; students, lawyers, businessmen and a motley crowd of men and women, mostly wives of government officials. A lot of noisy children ran around chasing each other. The organizers were kept busy trying to catch and immobilize them, but the little devils were elusive and ran behind and between the chairs. The distinguished men seated on the dais looked away and tried not to notice, but the ex-judge beckoned to an executive and whispered, 'Can nothing be

354

done to quieten these children?'

Whereupon the man went up to the women and said, 'Please control your children.'

A woman retorted haughtily: 'Tell their mothers, not me.'

'Where are the mothers?' No answer came. The man was helpless and felt foolish and lost. He caught hold of a boy and whispered to him: 'They are distributing sweets over there,' pointing outside, and the boy turned round and ran out gleefully, followed by all the other children. 'Children from the neighbourhood, not ours,' explained someone.

The ex-judge rapped on the table with a paperweight, took a gulp of water from the glass, and began, 'We are honoured by the presence of the Honourable Minister.' He elaborated the minister's role in building up a first-rate nation. This presentation took twenty-five minutes. He devoted two minutes to Rann the main speaker today, about whom he did not have much to say, and hurried on to call upon the Hon'ble Minister to speak. The minister, a seasoned orator, clutched the microphone expertly, drew it to his lips, and began:

'My respected elders, the noble mothers of the land, and the distinguished brethren here, we have in our midst a distinguished scholar who has come from afar and has dedicated his life to . . .' He fumbled for the right word and paused for a second to look at a piece of paper. 'Futurology,' he went on. 'You may ask what is futurology. The speaker of this evening is going to tell us about it. I should leave it to him to explain his subject. I'll only confine myself to what Jawaharlal Nehru said once—' He somehow twisted the context of futurism and whatever meaning it might have, to an anecdote centring around Jawaharlal. And then he explained Mahatma Gandhi's philosophy. 'In those days,' he reminisced, 'I was a *batcha*, but serving our motherland in some capacity, however humble, was my only aim in life, inspired by our leaders and encouraged by them. I was always in the presence of Mahatmaji wherever he camped, and of course Jawaharlal was always with him and so were many of our distinguished patriots and leaders. Though I was a *batcha* Mahatmaji and Nehruji encouraged me to be with them, and if I count for anything today, I owe it to their affection and if I have served our motherland in any capacity, it's through their grace.' He managed to add a mention of Lord Mountbatten also as one of his gurus, and then he came back to Mahatmaji and explained how two days-before his death, Gandhiji had said to him, 'My inner voice tells me that my end is near,' and how he, the future Deputy Minister, broke down on hearing this and implored him not to say such things, whereupon Gandhiji said, 'Yesterday at the prayer meeting at Birla's house: were you present? Didn't you notice a group at the gate? I could infer what they were saying . . .'

At this point I noticed a couple of old men nodding in their seats, lulled to sleep by the minister's voice. I looked at our well-groomed Rann in the full regalia of his Oxford blue three-piece suit—he, too, was bored with the minister's rambling talk. He kept gazing at the typed sheets as if wondering if he would have a chance at all to lecture. The minister had gone on for an hour without a scrap of written material, sentences spewing out without interruption. Those who were familiar with his speeches would have understood that as a routine he narrated the Mahatma Gandhi episode at the conclusion. But most of the assembly was unaware of this and now despaired whether they were fated to listen to this man until midnight.

From out of the student group was heard a voice saying, 'We want to hear the speaker of this evening.' Undaunted by this request, accustomed as he was to hecklers in parliament, the minister retorted cheerfully, 'You are right. I'm also anxious to hear our friend on the subject of—' He had to refer again to the piece of paper. 'But let me finish what I was saying. You'll find it relevant to the subject today.' And he went on to talk about the importance of rural handicrafts. After fifteen minutes, while his hecklers looked resigned to their fate, he sat down. Then he whispered to Rann at his side: 'I'd like to read your speech in the papers tomorrow, I'm sure. Now I've another meeting at Bagal, people will be waiting. Have to finish and drive to Trichy airport—must be back in Delhi tonight. So you will excuse me . . .' When he half inclined his head, his aide stood up and took charge of the minister's garland, bestowed earlier by the ex-judge, and they left abruptly.

Rann came to the microphone after a formal introduction and abruptly began: 'As you are all aware how near disaster we are—'

'No, not yet,' said a heckler in the audience. 'Not heard the worst yet. Do go on.'

Unperturbed, Rann read on, holding up a warning finger all through. 'Man was born free and everywhere he is in chains, Rousseau said.'

'No, Voltaire,' said the heckler.

'One or the other, it doesn't matter. It's time we noticed our chains, invisible though they may be, these chains are going to drag us down to perdition unless we identify them in good time, and those chains and fetters which are imperceptible now will overwhelm—'

'That's all right, we'll call the blacksmith to file them off. Now go on with your story.'

From another group a man shouted, 'Throw this wag out. He is disturbing the meeting. Don't mind sir, please go on.' At this point a scuffle ensued, and the heckler was dragged out of the hall by a couple of strong men. They came back and said generously to Rann: 'Please go on sir, don't mind the disturbance; that fellow disturbs any and every meeting.'

Rann resumed his reading. He had the theatricality of a Seventh Day Adventist. His voice rose and fell as in a sort of declamation. He hissed and snorted, sighed and screamed according to the theme of the drama he was developing. The theme was the collapse of this planet about AD 3000. When he described, holding aloft a specimen, how the tuft of a grass-like vegetation, an obstinate weed, was going to overrun the earth, people watched without response. But then he went on to say: 'This looks insignificant, like the genie within a bottle. Take out the cork and you will see the dimension to which it can grow,' and described its tough, persistent growth, told about how by AD 2500 half the surface of the globe would be covered up.

'It's a cannibal, in certain places along the Amazon it is actually called the Cannibal Herb, which nomenclature was at first mistaken to mean food for the cannibals, but actually means that it fattens itself on other plants. Where it appears no other plant can grow. It swallows every scrap of vegetation near at hand, root, stalk and leaf, it quenches its thirst by sapping up groundwater however deep the water-table may be. I have in my collection a specimen—a wire-like root three hundred feet long when it was pulled out. Under a microscope at the root-terminal were seen sacs to suck up water. Ultimately no water will be left underground, in rivers or in the sea, when billions of such sacs are drawing up water and evaporating them at the surface.

'Scientists, biologists, biochemists are secretly working on formulations that would eliminate this weed. Secretly because they do not want to create a scare. But the weed develops resistance to any chemical or bacteria and in a second generation that particular culture has no effect. Actually any weedicide acts as nutrition for it. Does this not remind us of the demon in our stories whose drop of blood shed on the ground gave rise to a hundred other demons?'

He went on and on thus and then he came to a further menace: 'Are you aware that for one citizen there are eight rats in our country, which means that only one-eighth of the food produced is available for legitimate consumption—'

'What is legitimate consumption?' shouted a voice from the back of the hall. 'Have rats no right to eat? They also are creatures of this earth like any of us.'

The chuckers realized that the interrupter they had thrown out was back in the hall somewhere, though he could not be spotted.

Someone else cried, 'Don't mind him, doctor, go on . . . a crackpot has smuggled himself in.'

'I'm no crackpot but also a scholar. I'm a Ph.D.'

The chuckers stood up to locate the speaker. There was

a slight disturbance. Some of those in the audience who felt bored edged their way towards the door. Rann stood puzzled. I whispered to him, 'Why do you pay attention to these things, go on, go on.'

He continued, 'There are dozens of such problems facing us today,' and then elaborated for the next forty-five minutes all the things that menaced human survival. Ghastly predictions. His voice reached a screaming pitch when he declared, 'The rats will destroy our food stock and the weed will devour everything, including the rats, and grow to gigantic heights although rising in our present observation only at the rate of a tenth of a millimetre per decade, but it will ultimately rise to gigantic heights sticking out of our planet skyward, so that an observer from another planet will notice giant weeds covering the surface of the globe like bristles, having used all the water. If the observer peered closer with his infra-red giant telescope, he would find millions and billions of skeletons of humans and animals strewn about providing bone-meal for this monstrous and dreadful vegetation . . .'

At this point a scream was heard, 'Ah, what is to happen to our grandchildren?'

'The lady has fainted. Get a doctor someone.'

People were crowding round a woman who had fallen down from her chair. They were splashing water on her face and fanning her.

'Give her air, don't crowd.'

Someone was saying soothingly, when she revived, 'After all, madam, it'll only be in AD 3000. Not now.'

'What if?' she retorted.

Another woman was saying, 'We don't want to perish

360

in this manner—our children must be saved.'

At the sound of the word 'children' the fainted lady who had just revived let out a wail and screamed again, 'Oh, the children! Take them away somewhere to safety.' Many other women began to moan in sympathy and tried to rush out of the hall clutching their children, while the children themselves resisted and howled playfully. 'Come away, this place is cursed—not safe. Oh, come away.' Several men tried to calm the women down, saying, 'Be calm, it will happen only one thousand years later, no danger immediately.'

'Who are you to say so? What authority have you to say so? It may happen today.'

People were on their feet and the assembly was in complete disarray. The ex-judge, who had escorted the Deputy Minister, strayed out and ultimately disappeared. So did the police. Various spirited young men lifted and smashed the folding chairs. People rushed to the exit in confusion.

'Cobra! A cobra is crawling under the chair! Take care!' a mischievous urchin shouted.

'Where? Where?' People hoisted themselves on benches and chairs. The smashed chairs were collected, heaped up outside and set on fire. Someone switched off the hall lights in the pandemonium, though somehow the stage lights were still on. A gang of toughs approached the dais, armed with the legs and remnants of the splintered chairs and shouted, 'Down with—'

While Rann continued to sit stupidly watching the show as if gratified with the preview of the cataclysm he forecast, I tugged him up by his collar, crying, 'Come out, you fool, before they kill you.'

'Why? Why?' he asked. I dragged him out to the back of the stage, pushed open a door, propelled him into the darkness at the rear of the Town Hall, and led him out to an open space.

Two men approached saying, 'This way doctor, your car is there.' They hustled him in the dark. Presently I heard the door of a car bang and then move off. That was all, the final glimpse I had of the man called Rann. Never saw him again.

A postcard arrived a few days later from the Commandant: 'This is just a thank-you note. My well-wishers brought Rann to the car in which I was waiting. I am sure he is going to be happy hereafter. I won't let him out of sight again. He asks you please to freight his baggage to our address.'

Gaffur had parked his Ambassador on the drive, a little away from the main entrance to the Town Hall. In half darkness, waiting patiently for his distinguished customer. After the hall emptied, the turbulent crowd had left, and the lights were switched off, I started homeward. As I came down the drive I noticed Gaffur's taxi. 'What are you doing here?'

'You know—he asked me to wait here, I don't know, a long drive ahead to Peak House—I've all his baggage in the boot. Picked it up at your house this evening on his order.'

'You are hoping for your Rolls Royce still?' I asked suppressing a laugh.

'Why not?' he asked. 'At the rate he is giving me

business, I think he'll even want me to drive him to Bombay and Delhi—'

'He's already left for Delhi,' I said, and then I told him the story. 'You can't blame him. After all, he's gone back to his wife, who has a right, holds an authorized certificate for his role as a husband.'

'But what about the girl who is waiting?'

'Where?'

'She has packed up and is waiting at the school veranda. They were supposed to go to Peak House and—'

'Let us go and take her home.'

The girl came out running and crying, 'Ah! The meeting over? How I wished I were there to listen to you and watch your triumph in public—' She blurted out: 'Oh, darling, how happy you must be . . . now we are free—' and checked herself.

Gaffur hurriedly got down from the car and ran to meet her halfway to explain the changed situation. When she saw me, she broke down hysterically. 'I don't believe you people. You are all against him. He was so good, oh, he was kind and generous and loving. You don't understand him, nobody understands him. Take me to him, wherever he may be, let me know the truth from his own lips. Please, please, I beg you.' She went on ranting and lamenting.

I realized that she had a totally different picture of Rann. She worshipped him as a god who could do no wrong. Her face was disfigured with tears and her words, mostly panegyrics of her god, gushed forth in a torrent. I was shocked, never having thought their relationship had grown so deep. I was appalled at the extent to which the affair had grown, and couldn't help picturing it as a spread of the weed Rann was bothered about. No use talking to her about Rann—it would make no impression on her, would not pass through the barrier she had built against the outside world.

We let her go on. Gaffur being my friend, did not mind wasting time with us. He too had known her since childhood and was bewildered by the transformation he saw. It took us time to persuade her to come to the car. Gaffur carried her trunk. She was so dead exhausted that with a little push we got her into the car and with a further push leaned her back against the seat cushions. She was apathetic and did not care where we went. When we took the turn into Palm Grove Street, she just said, 'Don't wake up my grandfather. I'll find my way in.'

I hesitated for a moment—it was midnight—but it would have been futile to argue with her. We put her down noiselessly in front of her door with her trunk and sped away with the least noise. We had nothing to say to each other and remained silent till we came to Kabir Street. Stopping at my house, Gaffur said gruffly (he was choking with emotion and was unusually shaken), 'What shall I do with his baggage?'

'I'll keep it and send it on later.'

'Who pays the meter charge?'

'I'll fix it with the Lotus Club tomorrow.'

He drove off gloomily, remarking, 'She used to be such a sweet creature!'

I found no time to visit the Town Hall library for a week. When I resumed my news-hunting and reporting, I dropped

in at the library quietly one morning, and the old man said,
'Oh, you. I wanted to see you badly. Where have you been?
Do you know Baby has not been well? That outing with her
classmates seems to have upset her somehow, eating all
sorts of things . . . young people . . . she came back sooner
than I expected. I called Dr Krishna and he has given her
some medicine.'

'Oh, she'll be all right,' I said with a forced cheer.

'We must fulfil our vow at our family temple in the
village, and then she will be all right. There has been a lapse
on our part,' he said.

'Quite, surely, go ahead,' I said, suppressing the advice,
'Also propitiate Dr Lazarus, that will also help.'

I rather missed him. Without Rann the front room seemed
barren. I felt lonely and bored. I kept the room vacant,
hoping for another Rann to turn up, or, who could say,
Rann himself might return to complete his masterpiece, or
to resume the mission of minding the librarian's
granddaughter's higher education. Even that question, though
it had upset me at first, didn't seem quite so objectionable
now. I had perhaps misread the situation. Their relationship
might have been purely platonic. I laughed to myself at this
(im)possibility. For platonic purposes one did not have to
take a trip to Peak House in Gaffur's taxi. Platonic love did
not call for secret, long journeys! Let me not gloss over it,
I said to myself. Let me speak the truth unto myself. He was
a callous and indiscriminate lecher, and thank God he did
not try to lodge her in his room in my house! That would
have provoked a riot in Kabir Street, and God knows to

what extremes our people might have gone if anything had happened there.

Luckily, nothing came of it—the girl seemed to come through her escapade unscathed. She resumed her studies and attended college regularly; this I verified from time to time through discreet inquiries at the Town Hall library. The old man was always happy to talk of his granddaughter. 'Oh, she is too studious nowadays. After her school hours, she just comes home, and writes and reads all evening. Her grandmother is rather worried about her, and wants her to go out and relax with her friends. But she seems to have lost interest in her friends and has become very serious-minded.'

In my narrative about Rann at the Boardless, I gave a modified version of the story and generally slurred over all the incidents connected with the girl to save her from gossip. If anyone questioned me concerning the floating rumours about Rann and Girija, I dismissed their curiosity with contempt as being morbid. But no amount of hedging could keep Rann's abrupt exit from being discussed.

Varma was the first to question me. 'So the lady abducted her own husband from the meeting! Wonderful! What happened after that?'

'I may say that they lived happily ever after, from a letter just received yesterday from Commandant Sarasa. She is keeping him in check. I don't think he will try to get away again. After all, husband and wife quarrel, but it can't last: a sound couple will always get over that phase.'

Varma was impressed with the wife's determined pursuit and capture of her husband.

'It reminds one of Savitri and Satyavan of our legends.

How Savitri persistently followed Yama, the God of Death, when he plucked away her husband's life; how she dogged his steps as he tried to move off, pleading and pleading until he yielded, and how Satyavan, whose body had lain inert in the forest, revived and joined his wife. I think this Commandant is a similar one.'

I left him and his cronies to draw whatever conclusion they pleased, without contradicting anyone. I suspected that somewhere in his thirty-year collection of calendars Varma surely had a sheet in colour litho of Savitri pestering Yama; most of his philosophical conclusions were derived from such representations on his walls.

The fiasco at the Town Hall was a passing sensation as far as the Boardless community was concerned; the confusion was a result of some thugs who had got into the hall only to disturb and break chairs. But one of the members explained: 'It seems the lecturer threatened to blow up the earth with an atom bomb. I was not there, of course, but my nephew, who is studying at Albert Mission, told me that the lecturer made a threatening speech.'

His listeners murmured an approval of the manner in which the function ended.

'But the Deputy Minister's speech was wholesome and inspiring, I learn,' added someone else.

I never corrected any statement or defended Rann. Not my business.

But I constantly speculated on Rann's present plight—the tethered domesticity, which he must be facing in far-off Delhi. I was hoping to hear from him, but he never wrote, probably resenting the manner in which he had ended his lecture and fallen into a trap.

Six months later one evening while posting a letter in the mail van of 7 Down, the station master came excitedly to announce, 'The lady is in the waiting room—arrived in a jeep this afternoon!' I looked and there she stood, filling up the threshold of the waiting room in her khaki uniform, an overwhelming presence. She waved to me and turned in, opened the door a few minutes later and came out in civilian dress—a pale yellow saree. She looked enormously powerful as she greeted me with a laugh: 'You never expected to see me, but I am here now.' She had two chairs put out under the tree as before, looked at the station master hovering around to do her bidding. She told him:

'Masterji—I hope the timetable is unchanged, and we won't be disturbed till the goods train arrives at eleven.'

'Yes madam, how well you remember!'

'Tell your good wife, I shall need nothing more than a banana and a glass of milk—advised to avoid all food at all times! I shall call for my milk and fruit by and by—till then please leave us alone, we have to talk over important matters.' Turning to me, she said, 'TM, no excuses today. You will have to sit through and listen to me fully. I'm pressed for time. I've been sent south for a survey of rural areas—last two days I was busy travelling around in a jeep. Painful business, jeep travel. I'm pressed for time, leaving for Trichy airport at five in the morning and then on to Delhi by noon. Have to tell you a lot. Sit down and stay down. If you feel hungry, I'll ask the master to give you something to eat. But don't go. You have to listen to me.'

Without coming to the point she was talking in general

terms, since she suspected that the station master and Muni must still be around, ready to listen to our talks. When she was sure they were gone, she leaned forward and whispered, her voice quivering, 'Your friend has vanished again!'

I had sensed that some such statement was coming and said involuntarily, 'I thought so.'

She begged, 'If he is here, please give him up again—I agreed to this trip in the hope that he might be here again, although I knew it was a hopeless hope.'

'I wish with all my heart I could help you again. But believe me, he is not here. I have no information. I've not heard from him at all.'

I repeated it several times to emphasize that I was speaking the truth. She fished out of her handbag a tiny kerchief, touched her eyes, blew her nose and said, 'These few months have been our happiest ones. It seemed a revival of our far-off days in Madras—he managed to convey the same charm and warmth. But for our physical changes and age, which the outside world might notice. As far as we were concerned, we were back in the days of my father's carpentry, on the bench under the tree, whispering to each other. Such revived moments made one forget the present conditions. The joy in each other's company and the sense of fulfilment were complete and indescribable. At such moments I thought of you with profound gratitude. But alas, I could not give him enough time. I left home for the Parade Ground at six in the morning, returned home off and on, being mostly out on various official duties. Sometimes I had to be away for a couple of days or more touring the countryside. Heavy work, I liked it. He appreciated my work and was full of praise and encouragement, and looked after himself and the home. Such a domesticated creature one could not imagine. He lived a very well regulated life, sought no society-life or diversion, being completely absorbed in his writing and studies. He mentioned that his work was progressing smoothly, at a faster rate than at any time in his life, and regretted that he should have missed this wonderful life with me. We found time to sit and talk only late in the evening after I had shed my official uniform and changed into a saree. We had chairs put out in the garden and sat there till late at night, even carrying our supper out under the stars. At about eleven he would return to his study and shut himself in, worked, I suppose far into the night. He often said that his book, when it came out, would shake all our ideas to the foundation. He jogged in the morning in the park nearby, went for a stroll in the evening through shopping crowds at the market, and demanded nothing more nor sought any other company. I left him absolutely alone, respected his desire for privacy. When I noticed letters coming to him from different countries, I feared he might be in touch with his old friends, but I suppressed that suspicion as unworthy—he was a man to be loved, respected and above all trusted.'

She laughed now bitterly. 'All wrong ideas and misleading notions. I tell you he had unsuspected depths of duplicity. At the initial stages I did not trust him so fully and had his movements watched, but I gave that up in due course, for it seemed unnecessary and mean. Thus we passed our time. It was pleasant but I was also feeling apprehensive without any reason, only because it seemed too good to last. And it actually turned out so.

'Ten days ago I had to be away in Jaipur for three days on special duty. I couldn't take leave of him—he hadn't opened his door yet. It was my usual practice to leave without disturbing him. When I returned home three days later, it was all over, the old story again. The cook told me that he had gone soon after breakfast the day I left, taking a suitcase and a trunk with him. A car came for him with a woman in it. I wondered who she might be and where she came from, and how he could have arranged all this. He had left a letter on the hall table for me.'

She held out the letter for me to read. It just said: 'Good-bye dearest. I have to be off again. It was lovely while it lasted—thanks!'

'What do you make of it?' she asked.

'He must have received a sudden call connected with his research, I think.'

She laughed bitterly. 'But who is the woman?'

'Perhaps a research assistant?'

'No, a nurse from Matilda's. I checked everywhere for missing persons, and one Komal at Matilda's had vanished suddenly, resigning her job. Don't ask me how he could have organized it all, or how he managed to cultivate the nurse or how long it must have gone on. He was an expert in the art of deception. Now I realize that all along he must have lived a parallel secret life while creating the impression of living with me. I visited various airlines and the airport, and got the information that he had taken a flight to Rome on the same day I left for Jaipur. From Rome he could radiate on to any continent with his latest companion! I can only conclude from the description I got at one of the airline counters that the passenger was your Rann of

Malgudi, a special name he seems to have conjured up for your edification. God alone knows under how many names he goes about and how many passports he has manufactured. An expert, really, in his own field. I pray to God that some day he may be caught at least for his passport frauds and made to spend the rest of his life in some hellish prison. I've no hope of seeing him again.'

At this point she broke down, and began to sob uncontrollably. Between her fits of sobbing she managed to say, 'I should have been far happier if I had never met you or noticed your news item about the Timbuctoo man. Or it would have been best if I'd listened to my father's advice to keep away from him.'

It was distressing to see a mighty personality, generally self-possessed, crumbling down. My eyes were wet too. Presently finding it embarrassing to continue in my presence, she abruptly got up, rushed back to the waiting room, and bolted the door.

ಬಿ ಞ

Postscript

I HAD PLANNED *Talkative Man* as a full-length novel. and grandly titled it, 'Novel No. 14'. While it progressed satisfactorily enough, it would not grow beyond 116 typewritten sheets, where it just came to a halt, like a motor car run out of petrol. Talkative Man, the narrator, had nothing more to say, he seemed to feel. What more do you expect? This is only the story of a wife's attempt to reclaim her erratic, elusive husband who is a wanderer, a philanderer on a global scale, abandoning women right and left. I have told you his story as far as I could confine and observe him as a curio in Kabir Street, but I had to manoeuvre to get him out of Malgudi hurriedly, when I found that he was planning to seduce and abduct a young, innocent schoolgirl known to me. So there we are, and 'finis' on page 116 inevitably.

Why *not* only 116 pages, I question. While a poet or dramatist rarely exceeds a hundred pages even in his most ambitious work, and is accepted without anyone commenting on the length of his composition, a writer of fiction is often subject to a quantitative evaluation.

The difficulty lies perhaps in classification. *Talkative Man* is too long to be a short story, but is it too short for a novel? I prefer the shorter form, because it gives me scope for elaboration of details, but within certain limits; I can take up a variety of subjects and get through each in a reasonable time, while a novel ties me down to a single theme for at least two years! When I am at work on a novel, I imagine that I am keeping a crowd of characters waiting outside my door, who are in search of their author.

At the beginning of my career I was advised by my literary agent in London to bear in mind that a novel should run to at least 70,000 words, the minimum standard for fiction in those days. The failure of my first novel, *Swami and Friends*, was attributed to its length: 'Fifty thousand words are an awkward length for a novel,' my agent wrote. A bookbuyer investing 7/6d (in that Golden Age) liked to have his money's worth of reading, I was told. When I mentioned this to Graham Greene in a letter, he wrote back to say, 'I hope you will get a subject next time which will run to a full-length book. But that's on the knees of the gods. Only if you see a choice of subjects and lengths ahead of you, do next time go for the longer.' A welcome advice. Otherwise, I feared that I might be compelled to inflate my stories with laboured detail and description of dress, deportment, facial features, furniture, food and drinks—passages I ruthlessly skip when reading a novel. While writing, I prefer to keep such details to a minimum in order to save my readers the bother of skipping. Also, I have the habit of pruning and trimming, when I look over the first draft, and then in a second draft a further lopping off is certain, until I am satisfied that the narrative progresses smoothly.

The present work has turned out the shortest among my novels, but if I were to blow it up, I could perhaps push it forward from the point where it now ends, with Commandant Sarasa setting out on an odyssey in search of her slippery husband, across several continents and in many societies and hide-and-seek situations, until she tracks him down, corners him, and finally incarcerates him in the prison of domesticity. Thus I might generate 100,000 words or more and give the volume a respectable girth, fit to top a best-seller list. To achieve this end, perhaps I should acquire a word processor, and learn how to handle it without blowing its fuse or allowing it to outwit me by gushing forth phrases faster than I can spell. But alas, I am not inclined to acquire new skills; I cannot handle any mechanical or electronic device. I have given up even typing, finding the typewriter a nuisance and a distraction when its keys stick or the ribbon gets tangled. Apart from this, still bearing in mind Graham Greene's advice of half a century ago, I do not concern myself with quantity while writing.

I speculate, however, what Commandant Sarasa would say if Talkative Man had advised her to set forth in search of her husband. In her present mood, she would probably retort, 'No. Let *him* undertake the pursuit this time when he is finally let out of prison. It will be a long time, though, before that happens. Prison life will have shorn him of his Adolphe Menjou style and his three-piece suit, no woman would even give him a glance, and he will have nowhere to go. At that point he will think of me, but he won't find me. I am going away presently on a UN assignment to a developing country. Your friend won't know where I am gone. Nor am I going to leave my address with you since you are a talkative man and will not keep a secret. The faded Dr Rann, I'm sure, will ultimately seek refuge in your Kabir Street unless he ends up on a footpath in Calcutta or Bombay.'

SHORT STORIES

NARAYAN HAS VERY decided views on the short story, which he began writing early in his career and which he has continued to write throughout. 'The short story affords a writer a welcome diversion from hard work. The novel, whether good or bad, printable or otherwise, involves considerable labour . . . At the end of every novel I have vowed never to write another one—a propitious moment to write a short story or two. I enjoy writing a short story . . . (which) can be brought into existence through a mere suggestion of detail, the focus being kept on a central idea or climax.' Narayan's course through short story writing started with vaguely imitative stories, some purely farcical, some in which he toyed with the supernatural, but soon developed emotional depth and superb characterization. They got longer and more profound (without of course ever losing the light touch). His material he found all around. 'The material available to a story writer in India is limitless . . . It is stimulating to live in a society that is not standardized or mechanized, and is free from monotony. Under such conditions the writer has only to look out of the window to pick up a character (and thereby a story).' He also found material in his family, as in *The Grandmother's Tale*. It is difficult to discuss individual stories, but special mention must be made of *Selvi*, *Annamalai* and *A Horse and Two Goats.* 'Selvi, a taut little story, fired Narayan's imagination when he learnt of a well-known performer being exploited by her agent. *Annamalai*, the story of his illiterate gardener who has been trying to execute a bond without success, and finally decides to go back to his village to die where he will be cremated with the honours due to him, is a truly touching story of master–servant relationship and a brilliant example of Narayan's ability to understand the peasant mind. *A Horse and Two Goats*, inspired by the visit of an American who had a huge clay-horse tucked in the back of his jeep, is a marvellously funny account of the conflict of cultures.

AN ASTROLOGER'S DAY

PUNCTUALLY AT MIDDAY he opened his bag and spread out his professional equipment, which consisted of a dozen cowrie shells, a square piece of cloth with obscure mystic charts on it, a notebook and a bundle of palmyra writing. His forehead was resplendent with sacred ash and vermilion, and his eyes sparkled with a sharp abnormal gleam which was really an outcome of a continual searching look for customers, but which his simple clients took to be a prophetic light and felt comforted. The power of his eyes was considerably enhanced by their position—placed as they were between the painted forehead and the dark whiskers which streamed down his cheeks: even a half-wit's eyes would sparkle in such a setting. To crown the effect he wound a saffron-coloured turban around his head. This colour scheme never failed. People were attracted to him as bees are attracted to cosmos or dahlia stalks. He sat under the boughs of a spreading tamarind tree which flanked a path running through the Town Hall Park. It was a remarkable place in many ways: a surging crowd was always moving up and down this narrow road morning till night. A variety of trades and occupations was represented all along its way: medicine-sellers, sellers of stolen hardware and junk, magicians and, above all, an auctioneer of cheap cloth, who created enough din all day to attract the whole town. Next to him in vociferousness came a vendor of fried groundnuts, who gave his ware a fancy name each day, calling it Bombay Ice-Cream one day, and on the next Delhi Almond, and on the third Raja's Delicacy, and so on and so forth, and people flocked to him. A considerable portion of this crowd dallied before the astrologer too. The astrologer transacted his business by the light of a flare which crackled and smoked up above the groundnut heap nearby. Half the enchantment of the place was due to the fact that it did not have the benefit of municipal lighting. The place was lit up by shop lights. One or two had hissing gaslights, some had naked flares stuck on poles, some were lit up by old cycle lamps and one or two, like the astrologer's, managed without lights of their own. It was a bewildering criss-cross of light rays and moving shadows. This suited the astrologer very well, for the simple reason that he had not in the least intended to be an astrologer when he began life; and he knew no more of what was going to happen to others than he knew what was going to happen to himself next minute. He was as much a stranger to the stars as were his innocent customers. Yet he said things which pleased and astonished everyone: that was more a matter of study, practice and shrewd guesswork. All the same, it was as much an honest man's labour as any other, and he deserved the wages he carried home at the end of a day.

He had left his village without any previous thought or plan. If he had continued there he would have carried on the work of his forefathers—namely, tilling the land, living, marrying and ripening in his cornfield and ancestral home. But that was not to be. He had to leave home without telling anyone, and he could not rest till he left it behind a couple of hundred miles. To a villager it is a great deal, as if an ocean flowed between.

He had a working analysis of mankind's troubles: marriage, money and the tangles of human ties. Long practice had sharpened his perception. Within five minutes he understood what was wrong. He charged three pies per question and never opened his mouth till the other had spoken for at least ten minutes, which provided him enough stuff for a dozen answers and advices. When he told the person before him, gazing at his palm, 'In many ways you are not getting the fullest results for your efforts', nine out of ten were disposed to agree with him. Or he questioned: 'Is there any woman in your family, maybe even a distant relative, who is not well disposed towards you?' Or he gave an analysis of character: 'Most of your troubles are due to your nature. How can you be otherwise with Saturn where he is? You have an impetuous nature and a rough exterior.' This endeared him to their hearts immediately, for even the mildest of us loves to think that he has a forbidding exterior.

The nuts-vendor blew out his flare and rose to go home. This was a signal for the astrologer to bundle up too, since it left him in darkness except for a little shaft of green light which strayed in from somewhere and touched the ground before him. He picked up his cowrie shells and paraphernalia and was putting them back into his bag when the green shaft of light was blotted out; he looked up and saw a man

standing before him. He sensed a possible client and said:
'You look so careworn. It will do you good to sit down for
a while and chat with me.' The other grumbled some vague
reply. The astrologer pressed his invitation; whereupon the
other thrust his palm under his nose, saying: 'You call
yourself an astrologer?' The astrologer felt challenged and
said, tilting the other's palm towards the green shaft of
light: 'Yours is a nature . . .' 'Oh, stop that,' the other said.
'Tell me something worthwhile . . .'

Our friend felt piqued. 'I charge only three pies per
question, and what you get ought to be good enough for
your money . . .' At this the other withdrew his arm, took
out an anna and flung it out to him, saying, 'I have some
questions to ask. If I prove you are bluffing, you must
return that anna to me with interest.'

'If you find my answers satisfactory, will you give me
five rupees?'

'No.'

'Or will you give me eight annas?'

'All right, provided you give me twice as much if you
are wrong,' said the stranger. This pact was accepted after
a little further argument. The astrologer sent up a prayer to
heaven as the other lit a cheroot. The astrologer caught a
glimpse of his face by the matchlight. There was a pause as
cars hooted on the road, *jutka* drivers swore at their horses
and the babble of the crowd agitated the semi-darkness of
the park. The other sat down, sucking his cheroot, puffing
out, sat there ruthlessly. The astrologer felt very
uncomfortable. 'Here, take your anna back. I am not used
to such challenges. It is late for me today . . .' He made
preparations to bundle up. The other held his wrist and

said, 'You can't get out of it now. You dragged me in while I was passing.' The astrologer shivered in his grip; and his voice shook and became faint. 'Leave me today. I will speak to you tomorrow.' The other thrust his palm in his face and said, 'Challenge is challenge. Go on.' The astrologer proceeded with his throat drying up. 'There is a woman . . .'

'Stop,' said the other. 'I don't want all that. Shall I succeed in my present search or not? Answer this and go. Otherwise I will not let you go till you disgorge all your coins.' The astrologer muttered a few incantations and replied, 'All right. I will speak. But will you give me a rupee if what I say is convincing? Otherwise I will not open my mouth, and you may do what you like.' After a good deal of haggling the other agreed. The astrologer said, 'You were left for dead. Am I right?'

'Ah, tell me more.'

'A knife has passed through you once?' said the astrologer.

'Good fellow!' He bared his chest to show the scar. 'What else?'

'And then you were pushed into a well nearby in the field. You were left for dead.'

'I should have been dead if some passer-by had not chanced to peep into the well,' exclaimed the other, overwhelmed by enthusiasm. 'When shall I get at him?' he asked, clenching his fist.

'In the next world,' answered the astrologer. 'He died four months ago in a far-off town. You will never see any more of him.' The other groaned on hearing it. The astrologer proceeded.

'Guru Nayak—'

'You know my name!' the other said, taken aback.

'As I know all other things. Guru Nayak, listen carefully to what I have to say. Your village is two days' journey due north of this town. Take the next train and be gone. I see once again great danger to your life if you go from home.' He took out a pinch of sacred ash and held it out to him. 'Rub it on your forehead and go home. Never travel southward again, and you will live to be a hundred.'

'Why should I leave home again?' the other said reflectively. 'I was only going away now and then to look for him and to choke out his life if I met him.' He shook his head regretfully. 'He has escaped my hands. I hope at least he died as he deserved.' 'Yes,' said the astrologer. 'He was crushed under a lorry.' The other looked gratified to hear it.

The place was deserted by the time the astrologer picked up his articles and put them into his bag. The green shaft was also gone, leaving the place in darkness and silence. The stranger had gone off into the night, after giving the astrologer a handful of coins.

It was nearly midnight when the astrologer reached home. His wife was waiting for him at the door and demanded an explanation. He flung the coins at her and said, 'Count them. One man gave all that.'

'Twelve and a half annas,' she said, counting. She was overjoyed. 'I can buy some jaggery and coconut tomorrow. The child has been asking for sweets for so many days now. I will prepare some nice stuff for her.'

'The swine has cheated me! He promised me a rupee,' said the astrologer. She looked up at him. 'You look worried. What is wrong?'

'Nothing.'

After dinner, sitting on the *pyol*, he told her, 'Do you know a great load is gone from me today? I thought I had the blood of a man on my hands all these years. That was the reason why I ran away from home, settled here and married you. He is alive.'

She gasped. 'You tried to kill!'

'Yes, in our village, when I was a silly youngster. We drank, gambled and quarrelled badly one day—why think of it now? Time to sleep,' he said, yawning, and stretched himself on the *pyol*.

LAWLEY ROAD

THE TALKATIVE MAN said:

For years people were not aware of the existence of a Municipality in Malgudi. The town was none the worse for it. Diseases, if they started, ran their course and disappeared, for even diseases must end someday. Dust and rubbish were blown away by the wind out of sight; drains ebbed and flowed and generally looked after themselves. The Municipality kept itself in the background, and remained so till the country got its independence on the fifteenth of August 1947. History holds few records of such jubilation as was witnessed on that day from the Himalayas to Cape Comorin. Our Municipal Council caught the inspiration. They swept the streets, cleaned the drains and hoisted flags all over the place. Their hearts warmed up when a procession with flags and music passed through their streets.

The Municipal Chairman looked down benignly from his balcony, muttering, 'We have done our bit for this great occasion.' I believe one or two members of the Council who were with him saw tears in his eyes. He was a man who had done well for himself as a supplier of blankets to the army

during the war, later spending a great deal of his gains in
securing the chairmanship. That's an epic by itself and does
not concern us now. My present story is different. The
satisfaction the Chairman now felt was, however, short-
lived. In about a week, when the bunting was torn off, he
became quite dispirited. I used to visit him almost every
day, trying to make a living out of news-reports to an
upcountry paper which paid me two rupees for every inch
of published news. Every month I could measure out about
ten inches of news in that paper, which was mostly a
somewhat idealized account of municipal affairs. This made
me a great favourite there. I walked in and out of the
Municipal Chairman's office constantly. Now he looked so
unhappy that I was forced to ask, 'What is wrong, Mr
Chairman?'

'I feel we have not done enough,' he replied.

'Enough of what?' I asked.

'Nothing to mark off the great event.' He sat brooding
and then announced, 'Come what may, I am going to do
something great!' He called up an Extraordinary Meeting of
the Council, and harangued them, and at once they decided
to nationalize the names of all the streets and parks, in
honour of the birth of independence. They made a start
with the park at the Market Square. It used to be called the
Coronation Park—whose coronation God alone knew; it
might have been the coronation of Victoria or of Asoka. No
one bothered about it. Now the old board was uprooted
and lay on the lawn, and a brand-new sign stood in its
place declaring it henceforth to be Hamara Hindustan Park.

The other transformation, however, could not be so
smoothly worked out. Mahatma Gandhi Road was the

most sought-after name. Eight different ward councillors were after it. There were six others who wanted to call the roads in front of their houses Nehru Road or Netaji Subash Bose Road. Tempers were rising and I feared they might come to blows. There came a point when, I believe, the Council just went mad. It decided to give the same name to four different streets. Well, sir, even in the most democratic or patriotic town it is not feasible to have two roads bearing the same name. The result was seen within a fortnight. The town became unrecognizable with new names. Gone were the Market Road, North Road, Chitra Road, Vinayak Mudali Street and so on. In their place appeared the names, repeated in four different places, of all the ministers, deputy ministers and the members of the Congress Working Committee. Of course, it created a lot of hardship— letters went where they were not wanted, people were not able to say where they lived or direct others there. The town became a wilderness with all its landmarks gone.

The Chairman was gratified with his inspired work— but not for long. He became restless again and looked for fresh fields of action. At the corner of Lawley Extension and Market there used to be a statue. People had got so used to it that they never bothered to ask whose it was or even to look up. It was generally used by the birds as a perch. The Chairman suddenly remembered that it was the statue of Sir Frederick Lawley. The Extension had been named after him. Now it was changed to Gandhi Nagar, and it seemed impossible to keep Lawley's statue there any longer. The Council unanimously resolved to remove it. The Council with the Chairman sallied forth triumphantly next morning and circumambulated the statue. They now realized their mistake. The statue towered twenty feet above them and seemed to arise from a pedestal of molten lead. In their imagination they had thought that a vigorous resolution would be enough to topple down the statue of this satrap, but now they found that it stood with the firmness of a mountain. They realized that Britain, when she was here, had attempted to raise herself on no mean foundation. But it made them only firmer in their resolve. If it was going to mean blasting up that part of the town for the purpose, they would do it. For they unearthed a lot of history about Sir Frederick Lawley. He was a combination of Attila, the Scourge of Europe, and Nadir Shah, with the craftiness of a Machiavelli. He subjugated Indians with the sword and razed to the ground the villages from which he heard the slightest murmur of protest. He never countenanced Indians except when they approached him on their knees.

People dropped their normal occupations and loitered around the statue, wondering how they could have tolerated it for so many years. The gentleman seemed to smile derisively at the nation now, with his arms locked behind and his sword dangling from his belt. There could be no doubt that he must have been the worst tyrant imaginable; the true picture—with breeches and wig and white waistcoat and that hard, determined look—of all that has been hatefully familiar in the British period of Indian history. They shuddered when they thought of the fate of their ancestors who had to bear the tyrannies of this man.

Next the Municipality called for tenders. A dozen contractors sent in their estimates, the lowest standing at fifty thousand rupees, for removing the statue and carting it to the Municipal Office, where they were already worried about the housing of it. The Chairman thought it over and told me, 'Why don't you take it yourself? I will give you the statue free if you do not charge us anything for removing it.' I had thought till then that only my municipal friends were mad, but now I found I could be just as mad as they. I began to calculate the whole affair as a pure investment. Suppose it cost me five thousand rupees to dislodge and move the statue (I knew the contractors were overestimating), and I sold it as metal for six thousand . . . About three tons of metal might fetch anything. Or I could probably sell it to the British Museum or Westminster Abbey. I saw myself throwing up the upcountry paper job.

The Council had no difficulty in passing a resolution permitting me to take the statue away. I made elaborate arrangements for the task . . . I borrowed money from my father-in-law, promising him a fantastic rate of interest. I recruited a team of fifty coolies to hack the pedestal. I stood over them like a slave-driver and kept shouting instructions. They put down their implements at six in the evening and returned to their attack early next day. They were specially recruited from Koppal, where the men's limbs were hardened by generations of teak-cutting in Mempi Forest.

We hacked for ten days. No doubt we succeeded in chipping the pedestal here and there, but that was all; the statue showed no sign of moving. At this rate I feared I might become bankrupt in a fortnight. I received permission from the District Magistrate to acquire a few sticks of dynamite, cordoned off the area and lighted the fuse. I brought down the knight from his pedestal without injuring any limb. Then it took me three days to reach the house with my booty. It was stretched out on a specially designed carriage drawn by several bullocks. The confusion brought about by my passage along Market Road, the crowd that followed uttering jokes, the incessant shouting and instructions I had to be giving, the blinding heat of the day, Sir F's carriage coming to a halt at every inconvenient spot and angle, moving neither forwards nor backwards, holding up the traffic on all sides, and darkness coming on suddenly with the statue nowhere near my home—all this was a nightmare I wish to pass over. I mounted guard over him on the roadside at night. As he lay on his back staring at the stars, I felt sorry for him and said, 'Well, this is what you get for being such a haughty imperialist. It never pays.' In due course, he was safely lodged in my small house. His head and shoulders were in my front hall, and the rest of him stretched out into the street through the doorway. It was an obliging community there at Kabir Lane and nobody minded this obstruction.

The Municipal Council passed a resolution thanking me for my services. I wired this news to my paper, tacking onto it a ten-inch story about the statue. A week later the Chairman came to my house in a state of agitation. I seated him on the chest of the tyrant. He said, 'I have bad news for you. I wish you had not sent up that news item about the statue. See these . . .' He held out a sheaf of telegrams. They were from every kind of historical society in India, all protesting against the removal of the statue. We had all been misled about Sir F. All the present history pertained to a different Lawley of the time of Warren Hastings. This Frederick Lawley (of the statue) was a military governor who had settled down here after the Mutiny. He cleared the jungles and almost built the town of Malgudi. He established here the first cooperative society for the whole of India, and the first canal system by which thousands of acres of land were irrigated from the Sarayu, which had been dissipating itself till then. He established this, he established that, and he died in the great Sarayu floods while attempting to save the lives of villagers living on its banks. He was the first Englishman to advise the British Parliament to involve more and more Indians in all Indian affairs. In one of his despatches he was said to have declared, 'Britain must quit India someday for her own good.'

The Chairman said, 'The government has ordered us to reinstate the statue.' 'Impossible!' I cried. 'This is my statue and I will keep it. I like to collect statues of national heroes.' This heroic sentiment impressed no one. Within a week all the newspapers in the country were full of Sir Frederick Lawley. The public caught the enthusiasm. They paraded in front of my house, shouting slogans. They demanded the statue back. I offered to abandon it if the Municipality at least paid my expenses in bringing it here. The public viewed me as their enemy. 'This man is trying to black-market even a statue,' they remarked. Stung by it, I wrote a placard and hung it on my door: *Statue for sale. Two and a half tons of excellent metal. Ideal gift for a patriotic friend. Offers above ten thousand will be considered.* It infuriated them and made them want to kick me, but they had been brought up in a tradition of non-violence and so they picketed my house; they lay across my door in relays holding a flag and shouting slogans. I had sent away my wife and children to the village in order to make room for the statue in my house, and so this picketing did not bother me—only I had to use the back door a great deal. The Municipality sent me a notice of prosecution under the Ancient Monuments Act which I repudiated in suitable terms. We were getting into bewildering legalities—a battle of wits between me and the municipal lawyer. The only nuisance about it was that an abnormal quantity of correspondence developed and choked up an already congested household.

I clung to my statue, secretly despairing how the matter was ever going to end. I longed to be able to stretch myself fully in my own house.

Six months later relief came. The government demanded a report from the Municipality on the question of the statue, and this together with other lapses on the part of the Municipality made them want to know why the existing Council should not be dissolved and re-elections ordered. I called on the Chairman and said, 'You will have to do something grand now. Why not acquire my house as a National Trust?'

'Why should I?' he asked.

'Because,' I said, 'Sir F is there. You will never be able to cart him to his old place. It'll be a waste of public money. Why not put him up where he is now? He has stayed in the other place too long. I'm prepared to give you my house for a reasonable price.'

'But our funds don't permit it,' he wailed.

'I'm sure you have enough funds of your own. Why should you depend on the municipal funds? It'll indeed be a grand gesture on your part, unique in India . . .' I suggested he ought to relieve himself of some of his old blanket gains. 'After all . . . how much more you will have to spend if you have to fight another election!' It appealed to him. We arrived at a figure. He was very happy when he saw in the papers a few days later: 'The Chairman of Malgudi Municipality has been able to buy back as a present for the nation the statue of Sir Frederick Lawley. He proposed to install it in a newly acquired property which is shortly to be converted into a park. The Municipal Council have resolved that Kabir Lane shall be changed to Lawley Road.'

A NIGHT OF CYCLONE

THE TALKATIVE MAN said:

It was in Vizagapatam that I finally got a job. A *sowcar* was building a mansion on the Beach Road and he gave me twenty-five rupees a month and a small house to live in. He labelled me supervisor of construction. At first the designation seemed to be vague. But I soon learnt what I was expected to do. A supervisor's job is no joke in the beginning: the contractor thinks that you are an upstart; the stone-mason has a feeling that you are an intruder; and the carpenter thinks that he is your equal in status. It is plain sailing when you have discovered your duty which consists in bullying the contractor, frightening the stone-mason, and pretending to be carrying out a general scheme of retrenchment.

Believe me when I tell you that I considered myself the most blessed man in Madras Presidency at that time. Blessing number one: work was easy. I generally conducted my supervision from my bed through a window. Blessing number two: my wife and I were living in a sweet idyll. Her temper was uniformly good in those days. It might have been because she had not brought into the world our first boy; he was due to make his appearance in a couple of months. Blessing number three: our house was situated in the finest locality. The sea was not ten yards from my door.

One November morning I got up at about 9.30 and found it almost dark outside. The workmen were waiting in a body at my door and asked to be let off since it was going to be a rough day. I sternly replied I would not stand any nonsense and ordered them back to work.

A little later I went through the Bazaar street, where everything was oppresively dull and calm. It was half an hour past ten in the morning and yet there was only a faint twilight. Some shops were already closing. Of all things on earth when I see shops closing in daytime I instinctively look forward to something terrible. I could detect something panicky about everybody. Just then a lot of children burst out of a school yelling at the top of their voices. It relieved the monotonous calm a bit. One child however came out bitterly weeping. I asked him what the matter was. He sobbed out, 'Is it true that the world is going to end today? Our teacher said so.'

When I went home my wife told me in a somewhat shaky voice that the world was going to end that day. She took the trouble to assure me at the same time that there was not a word of truth in it, and then gave a hollow laugh. I managed to crack one or two silly jokes about the end of the world, admonishing her to take only her best saris with her when leaving it.

At about midday I found that the workmen had left the work and gone home without my permission.

I do not remember where exactly the game commenced. At about three, I found the elements in a fiendish glee and about to break their accumulated fury on Man. The coconut trees edging the sand were swaying to and fro, almost touching the ground each time. The sea looked sinister in the gloomy light. I wondered if it was the same sea that used to make me poetic and sentimental at times. The water was reddish brown in colour, the colour of dirty blood. Each trembling wave stood half as high as a coconut tree ready to fall on and devour the earth any minute. From that brown simmering expanse terrible gurgling and hissing noises rose in the air.

My wife sat up for a while in dismal silence, and then went to bed saying that she was not feeling well. She was pale and nervous. Lighting a lamp, I say by her side and tried to keep her mind engaged by reading to her interesting bits from a newspaper. By this time the sea was raving and shrieking like a devil, the wind was screaming for blood, and the rain beat down on the roof with the noise of thousand hammers on a zinc sheet. My wife was listening to my most entertaining tit-bits in grim silence. Gradually she began to give low moans. She complained of pain down her sides.

At about eight in the evening she grew worse. I did not know what to do. She blurted out between moans that I was to light the oven and cook the food. I sulked into the kitchen with a groan. Hunger was scalding my stomach. If next to cycling I have failed to learn anything, it is lighting a fire. It has always been a mystery to me how our women do it and all honour to them. I stuffed the oven with firewod till it could hold no more and then looked for the matchbox and found it on the sill of an open window.

Then I struck fifty sticks one by one without producing

so much as a whiff of smoke. With the fifty-first I lighted a newspaper and tried to light the firewood with it. One newspaper after another kept burning. The firewood would not catch fire. Only my fingers did. And by the way, it was then that I genuinely wondered how houses and shops caught fire in this world. The small kitchen was filled with smoke and my nostrils and eyes had their share.

I left the kitchen and went back to the hall, in a very bad temper. My wife asked me if I had eaten anything, to which I gave a biting reply. There was a chance if surviving even the cyclone, but not that hunger. My wife then reminded me that there was a little milk in the store room, which was only a dignified name for a particular corner in my wretched kitchen. I rushed to the store room. I was about to drain off the milk at one pull, when I thought that my wife might need it any time now. I kept the milk back, determined to fill my stomach with any stuff that was available. I ransacked all the things in the store room, plunging my hand into this stuffy pot and that, I then put my hand into the pot containing tamarind and suddenly withdrew it with a howl and looked in. There was a big black scorpion in the pot.

The sting began to take effect. I jumped and howled with pain. I fell down and rolled on the floor.

Now the storm had gathered full strength. Tiles from the roof were flying off. In the best room in my house calendars and pictures were flying like missiles hither and thither. There was no place to stand in. Water was deep everywhere. The house might collapse any moment. I could have borne anything, but not the scorpion sting at that time. I waded through the water in the front room and reached my wife's room. She was wailing and moaning, writhing like a worm on her bed. I had to stand there and look on, not knowing what to do.

She then admitted the fact that it was labour pain. Why were things crowding on me? I was savage enough to curse her for choosing that day.

When her pain gave her respite, she said, 'I do not wish to trouble you, but can you bring some help?' Bringing her help! Where from? Who would come out in that hellish carnival? Whom did I know?

However, I took an umbrella and a lantern, and throwing at her a word of cheer set out. A part of the road in front of my house had collapsed, and there was seawater in its place. I attempted a short cut to my neighbour's' bungalow, which was built on an eminence. Meanwhile, the umbrella was snatched from my hands and went no one knows where. Next, the lantern, the so-called hurricane lantern, went out. I walked in darkness knocking my shins against every stone on the way, stumbling on bushes of cactus, and having the pleasure of cold rain water running down my spine. I felt that I was letting myself into the hands of a demon. It looked as though the wind would fold me up and lift me in the air and dash me down or twist me and tie up my body into a thousand knots. And all this, while trees were crashing down left and right. With bruised and bleeding feet, I panted uphill to the bungalow of my 'neighbour'. Not till I was actually in his porch did I realize how rash I had been. The 'neighbour' was a European: he was a police officer—DSP or something; and he had a ferocious bull dog. A formidable combination of things! I retraced my steps quickly.

Half-way I stood undecided. I was new to the place. I not only did not know anybody, but did not even know where anybody could be found. I suddenly recollected that in the same road a doctor lived in a castle-like house called 'Ocean View'. I started towards it, sucking my scorpion stung finger, in which, it seemed to me, needles, instead of blood, were circulating. Suddenly I found myself weeping loudly like a child.

I ran up the never-ending slopes and steps and stood in the veranda of 'Ocean View'. For about twenty minutes I violently banged on the door. Then I ran round and round the house shouting. A window opened and a lady demanded who I was. What a foolish question! As if she would know all about me the moment I announced my name! All the same I gave her an epitome of my miserable life up to the hour, of which she did not hear a single word. She then asked me my name. I shouted it back. There was so much noise all around that each question and answer had to be repeated a dozen times. It was most exhausting. I must have cut a very homely figure with the rain water dripping from me and my wild wet hair plastered on my face, and my dress swathed in mud. I could clearly see that the lady took me for an apparition or a thug. I asked her in the mildest tone possible if the doctor was in. She summoned her last ounce of courage and replied that he was away at Bombay, and that he wouldn't return for a month. And then she added quite irrelevantly, perhaps to impress the thug, that there were a lot of relatives sleeping in the house and they would be wild if they were disturbed. I assured her that I was not a thug and explained my condition. She was sympathetic enough, no doubt, but what could she do? It was her husband and not she or any of the terrible relatives slumbering in the house that had studied medicine.

I raced back home.

I assured my wife that help would be coming. She brightened up a little at this piece of lie. She then advised me to open the window on the side of the sea since the gale threatened to topple the house down if the closed window resisted it. The house already seemed to be creaking and rocking. But to open the window would be to invite the storm into the room. We were discussing this when all of a sudden there was a crash—the kitchen was down. It was followed by a terrific bang and explosion in our room. The window under discussion was smashed by the wind. The light went out. I sat stunned for a while. Then, groping about in the dark, I tried to fix up the window with my hand (which was still smarting with scorpion venom) against the ferocious gale. And all the time my wife was killing me with her cries pitched in various keys. I became mad with rage, hurt my hand worse, and fell into wild abusing. I dropped the window down and stood agape as the loud, lusty cry of a newborn baby pierced the stormy darkness.

The Talkative Man rose and hallooed, 'Boy! Come here!' A giggling, radiant urchin came in. The Talkative Man patted the urchin on the head and said, 'Well, sir, this is the gentleman who arrived on that fine night.'

SELVI

AT THE END of every concert, she was mobbed by autograph hunters. They would hem her in and not allow her to leave the dais. At that moment Mohan, slowly progressing towards the exit, would turn round and call across the hall, 'Selvi, hurry up. You want to miss the train?' 'Still a lot of time,' she could have said, but she was not in the habit of ever contradicting him; for Mohan this was a golden chance not to be missed, to order her in public and demonstrate his authority. He would then turn to a group of admirers waiting to escort him and Selvi, particularly Selvi, to the car, and remark in apparent jest, 'Left to herself, she'll sit there and fill all the autograph books in the world till doomsday, she has no sense of time.'

The public viewed her as a rare, ethereal entity; but he alone knew her private face. 'Not bad-looking,' he commented within himself when he first saw her, 'but needs touching up.' Her eyebrows, which flourished wildly, were trimmed and arched. For her complexion, by no means fair, but just on the borderline, he discovered the correct skin cream and talcum which imparted to her brow and cheeks a shade confounding classification. Mohan did not want anyone to suspect that he encouraged the use of cosmetics. He had been a follower of Mahatma Gandhi and spent several years in prison, wore only cloth spun by hand and shunned all luxury; there could be no question of his seeking modern, artificial aids to enhance the personality of his wife. But he had discovered at some stage certain subtle cosmetics through a contact in Singapore, an adoring fan of Selvi's, who felt only too honoured to be asked to supply them regularly, and to keep it a secret.

When Selvi came on the stage, she looked radiant, rather than dark, brown or fair, and it left the public guessing and debating, whenever the question came up, as to what colour her skin was. There was a tremendous amount of speculation on all aspects of her life and person wherever her admirers gathered, especially at a place like the Boardless where much town-talk was exchanged over coffee at the tables reserved for the habitués. Varma, the proprietor, loved to overhear such conversation from his pedestal at the cash counter, especially when the subject was Selvi. He was one of her worshippers, but from a distance, often feeling, 'Goddess Lakshmi has favoured me; I have nothing more to pray for in the line of wealth or prosperity, but I crave for the favour of the other goddess, that is Saraswathi, who is in our midst today as Selvi the divine singer; if only she will condescend to accept a cup of coffee or sweets from my hand, how grand it would be! But alas, whenever I bring a gift for her, *he* takes it and turns me back from the porch with a formal word of thanks.' Varma was only one among the thousands who had a longing to meet Selvi. But she was kept in a fortress of invisible walls. It was as if she was fated to spend her life either in solitary confinement or fettered to her gaoler in company. She was never left alone, even for a moment, with anyone. She had been wedded to Mohan for over two decades and had never spoken to anyone except in his presence.

Visitors kept coming all day long for a *darshan* from Selvi, but few ever reached her presence. Some were received on the ground floor, some were received on the lawns, some were encouraged to go up the staircase—but none could get a glimpse of her, only of Mohan's secretary or of the secretary's secretary. Select personalities, however, were received ceremoniously in the main hall upstairs and seated on sofas. Ordinary visitors would not be offered seats, but they could occupy any bench or chair found scattered here and there and wait as long as they pleased—and go back wherever they came from.

Their home was a huge building of East India Company days, displaying arches, columns and gables, once the residence of Sir Frederick Lawley (whose statue stood in the town-square), who had kept a retinue of forty servants to sweep and dust the six oversized halls built on two floors, with tall doors and gothic windows and Venetian shutters, set on several acres of ground five miles away from the city on the road to Mempi Hills. The place was wooded with enormous trees; particularly important was an elm (or oak or beech, no one could say) at the gate, planted by Sir Frederick, who had brought the seedling from England, said to be the only one of its kind in India. No one would tenant the house, since Sir Frederick's spirit was said to hover about the place, and many weird tales were current in

406

Malgudi at that time. The building had been abandoned since 1947, when Britain quit India. Mohan, who at some point made a bid for it, said, 'Let me try. Gandhiji's non-violence rid the country of the British rule. I was a humble disciple of Mahatmaji and I should be able to rid the place of a British ghost by the same technique!' He found money to buy the house when Selvi received a fee for lending her voice to a film star, who just moved her lips, synchronizing with Selvi's singing, and attained much glory for her performance in a film. But thereafter Mohan definitely shut out all film offers. 'I'll establish Selvi as a unique phenomenon on her own, not as a voice for some fat cosmetic-dummy.'

Bit by bit, by assiduous publicity and word-of-mouth recommendation, winning the favour of every journalist and music critic available, he had built up her image to its present stature. Hard work it was over the years. At the end, when it bore fruit, her name acquired a unique charm, her photograph began to appear in one publication or another every week. She was in demand everywhere. Mohan's office was besieged by the organizers of musical events from all over the country. 'Leave your proposal with my secretary, and we will inform you after finalizing our calendar for the quarter,' he would tell one. To another, he would say, 'My schedule is tight till 1982—if there is any cancellation we'll see what can be done. Remind me in October of 1981, I'll give you a final answer.' He rejected several offers for no other reason than to preserve a rarity value for Selvi. When Mohan accepted an engagement, the applicant (more a supplicant) felt grateful, notwithstanding the exorbitant fee, of which half was to be paid immediately in cash without a receipt. He varied his tactics occasionally. He would

specify that all the earnings of a certain concert should go
to some fashionable social service organization carrying
well-known names on its list of patrons. He would accept
no remuneration for the performance itself, but ask for
expenses in cash, which would approximate his normal fee.
He was a financial expert who knew how to conjure up
money and at the same time keep Income Tax at arm's
length. Pacing his lawns and corridors restlessly, his mind
was always busy, planning how to organize and manoeuvre
men and money. Suddenly he would pause, summon his
stenographer and dictate, or pick up the phone and talk at
length into it.

In addition to the actual professional matters, he kept
an eye on public relations, too; he attended select, exclusive
parties, invited eminent men and women to dinner at
Lawley Terrace; among the guests would often be found a
sprinkling of international figures, too; on his walls hung
group photographs of himself and Selvi in the company of
the strangest assortment of personalities—Tito, Bulganin,
Yehudi Menuhin, John Kennedy, the Nehru family, the
Pope, Charlie Chaplin, yogis and sportsmen and political
figures, taken under various circumstances and settings.

At the Boardless there was constant speculation about
Selvi's early life. Varma heard at the gossip table that Selvi
had been brought up by her mother in a back row of
Vinayak Mudali Street, in a small house with tiles falling
off, with not enough cash at home to put the tiles back on
the roof, and had learnt music from her, practising with her
brother and sister accompanying her on their instruments.

At this time Mohan had a photo studio on Market
Road. Once Selvi's mother brought the girl to be

photographed for a school magazine after she had won the first prize in a music competition. Thereafter Mohan visited them casually now and then, as a sort of well-wisher of the family, sat in the single chair their home provided, drank coffee and generally behaved as a benign god to that family by his advice and guidance. Sometimes he would request Selvi to sing, and then dramatically leave the chair and sit down on the floor cross-legged with his eyes shut, in an attitude of total absorption in her melody, to indicate that in the presence of such an inspired artist it would be blasphemous to sit high in a chair.

Day after day, he performed little services for the family, and then gradually took over the management of their affairs. At the Boardless, no one could relate with certainty at what point exactly he began to refer to Selvi as his wife or where, when or how they were married. No one would dare investigate it too closely now.

Mohan had lost no time in investing the money earned from the film in buying Lawley Terrace. After freshening up its walls with lime wash and paints, on an auspicious day he engaged Gaffur's taxi, and took Selvi and the family to the Terrace.

While her mother, brother and sister grew excited at the dimension of the house as they passed through the six halls, looked up at the high ceilings and clicked their tongues, Selvi herself showed no reaction; she went through the house as if through the corridors of a museum. Mohan was a little disappointed and asked, 'How do you like this place?' At that all she could say in answer was, 'It looks big.' At the end of the guided tour, he launched on a description and history (avoiding the hauntings) of the house. She listened, without any show of interest. Her mind seemed to be elsewhere. They were all seated on the gigantic settees of the Company days, which had come with the property, left behind because they could not be moved. She didn't seem to notice even the immensity of the furniture on which she was seated. As a matter of fact, as he came to realize later, in the course of their hundreds of concert tours she was habitually oblivious of her surroundings. In any setting—mansion or five-star hotel with luxurious guest rooms and attendants, or a small-town or village home with no special facilities or privacy—she looked equally indifferent or contented; washed, dressed and was ready for the concert at the appointed time in the evening. Most days she never knew or questioned where she was to sing or what fee they were getting. Whenever he said, 'Pack and get ready,' she filled a trunk with her clothes, toiletry and tonic pills, and was ready, not even questioning where they were going. She sat in a reserved seat in the train when she was asked to do so, and was ready to leave when Mohan warned her they would have to get off at the next stop. She was undemanding, uninquiring, uncomplaining. She seemed to exist without noticing anything or anyone, rapt in some secret melody or thought of her own.

In the course of a quarter-century, she had become a national figure; travelled widely in and out of the country. They named her the Goddess of Melody. When her name was announced, the hall, any hall, filled up to capacity and people fought for seats. When she appeared on the dais, the audience was thrilled as if vouchsafed a vision, and she was accorded a thundering ovation. When she settled down, gently cleared her throat and hummed softly to help the accompanists tune their instruments, a silence fell among the audience. Her voice possessed a versatility and reach which never failed to transport her audience. Her appeal was alike to the common, unsophisticated listener as to pundits, theorists and musicologists, and even those who didn't care for any sort of music liked to be seen at her concerts for prestige's sake.

During a concert, wherever it might be—Madras, Delhi, London, New York or Singapore—Mohan occupied as a rule the centre seat in the first row of the auditorium and rivetted his gaze on the singer, leaving people to wonder whether he was lost in her spell or whether he was inspiring her by thought-transference. Though his eyes were on her, his mind would be busy doing complicated arithmetic with reference to monetary problems, and he would also watch unobtrusively for any tape-recorder that might be smuggled into the hall (he never permitted recording), and note slyly the reactions of the VIPs flanking him.

He planned every concert in detail. He would sit up in the afternoon with Selvi and suggest gently but firmly, 'Wouldn't you like to start with the "Kalyani Varnam"— the minor one?' And she would say, 'Yes,' never having been able to utter any other word in her life. He would continue, 'The second item had better be Thiagaraja's composition in Begada, it'll be good to have a contrasting raga,' and then his list would go on to fill up about four hours. 'Don't bother to elaborate any Pallavi for this audience, but work out briefly a little detail in the Thodi composition. Afterwards you may add any item you like, light Bhajans, Javalis or folk-songs,' offering her a freedom which was worthless since the programme as devised would be tight-fitting for the duration of the concert, which, according to his rule, should never exceed four hours. 'But for my planning and guidance, she'd make a mess, which none realizes,' he often reflected.

Everyone curried Mohan's favour and goodwill in the hope that it would lead him to the proximity of the star. Mohan did encourage a particular class to call on him and received them in the Central Hall of Lawley Terrace; he would call aloud to Selvi when such a person arrived, 'Here is so-and-so come.' It would be no ordinary name, only a minister or an inspector general of police or the managing director of a textile mill, or a newspaper editor, who in his turn would always be eager to do some favour for Mohan, hoping thereby to be recognized eventually by Selvi as a special friend of the family. Selvi would come out of her chamber ten minutes after being summoned and act her part with precision: a wonderful, smile and *namaste* with her palms gently pressed together, which would send a thrill down the spine of the distinguished visitor, who would generally refer to her last concert and confess how deeply moving it had been, and how a particular raga kept ringing in his ears all that evening, long after the performance. Selvi had appropriate lines in reply to such praise: 'Of course, I feel honoured that my little effort has pleased a person of your calibre,' while Mohan would interpose with a joke or a personal remark. He didn't want any visitor, however important, to hold her attention, but would draw it to himself at the right moment. At the end Mohan would feel gratified that his tutored lines, gestures and expressions were perfectly delivered by Selvi. He would congratulate himself on shaping her so successfully into a celebrity. 'But

for my effort, she'd still be another version of her mother
and brother, typical Vinayak Mudali Street products, and
nothing beyond that. I am glad I've been able to train her
so well.'

In order that she might quickly get out of the
contamination of Vinayak Mudali Street, he gently,
unobtrusively, began to isolate her from her mother, brother
and sister. As time went on, she saw less and less of them.
At the beginning a car would be sent to fetch them, once a
week; but as Selvi's public engagements increased, her
mother and others were gradually allowed to fade out of
her life. Selvi tried once or twice to speak to Mohan about
her mother, but he looked annoyed and said, 'They must be
all right. I'll arrange to get them—but where is the time for
it? When we are able to spend at least three days at home,
we will get them here.' Such a break was rare—generally
they came home by train or car and left again within
twenty-four hours. On occasions when they did have the
time, and if she timidly mentioned her mother, he would
almost snap, 'I know, I know, I'll send Mani to Vinayak
Street—but some other time. We have asked the Governor
to lunch tomorrow and they will expect you to sing,
informally of course, for just thirty minutes.' 'The day after
that?' Selvi would put in hesitantly, and he would ignore
her and move off to make a telephone call. Selvi understood,
and resigned herself to it, and never again mentioned her
mother. 'If my own mother can't see me!' she thought again
and again, in secret anguish, having none to whom she
could speak her feelings.

Mohan, noticing that she didn't bother him about her
mother anymore, felt happy that she had got over the

obsession. 'That's the right way. Only a baby would bother about its mother.' He congratulated himself again on the way he was handling her.

Months and years passed thus. Selvi did not keep any reckoning of it, but went through her career like an automaton, switching on and off her music as ordered.

They were in Calcutta for a series of concerts when news of her mother's death reached her. When she heard it, she refused to come out of her room in the hotel, and wanted all her engagements cancelled. Mohan, who went into her room to coax her, swiftly withdrew when he noticed her tear-drenched face and dishevelled hair. All through the train journey back, she kept looking out of the window and never spoke a word, although Mohan did his best to engage her in talk. He was puzzled by her mood. Although she was generally not talkative, she would at least listen to whatever was said to her and intersperse an occasional monosyllabic comment. Now for a stretch of a thirty-six-hour journey she never spoke a word or looked in his direction. When they reached home, he immediately arranged to take her down to Vinayak Mudali Street, and accompanied her himself to honour the dead officially, feeling certain that his gesture would be appreciated by Selvi. Both the big car and Mohan in his whitest handspun clothes seemed ill-fitting in those surroundings. His car blocked half the street in which Selvi's mother had lived. Selvi's sister, who had married and had children in Singapore, could not come, and her brother's whereabouts were unknown. A neighbour dropped in to explain the circumstances of the old lady's death and how they had to take charge of the body and so forth. Mohan tried to cut

short his narration and send him away, since it was unusual
to let a nondescript talk to Selvi directly. But she said to
Mohan, 'You may go back to the Terrace if you like. I'm
staying here.' Mohan had not expected her to talk to him
in that manner. He felt confused and muttered, 'By all
means . . . I'll send back the car . . . When do you want it?'

'Never. I'm staying here as I did before . . .'

'How can you? In this street!' She ignored his objection
and said, 'My mother was my guru; here she taught me
music, lived and died . . . I'll also live and die here; what
was good for her is good for me too . . .'

He had never known her to be so truculent or voluble.
She had been for years so mild and complaisant that he
never thought she could act or speak beyond what she was
taught. He lingered, waited for a while, hoping for a change
of mood. Meanwhile, the neighbour was going on with his
narration, omitting no detail of the old lady's last moments
and the problems that arose in connection with the
performance of the final obsequies. 'I did not know where
to reach you, but finally we carried her across the river and
I lit the pyre with my own hands and dissolved the ashes in
the Sarayu. After all, I'd known her as a boy, and you
remember how I used to call her Auntie and sit up and
listen when you were practising . . . Oh! not these days of
course, I can't afford to buy a ticket, or get anywhere near
the hall where you sing.'

Mohan watched in consternation. He had never known
her to go beyond the script written by him. She had never
spoken to anyone or stayed in a company after receiving his
signal to terminate the interview and withdraw. Today it
didn't work. She ignored his signal, and the man from the

Vinayak neighbourhood went on in a frenzy of reliving the funeral; he felt triumphant to have been of help on a unique occasion.

After waiting impatiently, Mohan rose to go. 'Anything you want to be sent down?'

'Nothing,' she replied. He saw that she had worn an old sari, and had no makeup or jewellery, having left it all behind at the Terrace.

'You mean to say, you'll need nothing?'

'I need nothing . . .'

'How will you manage?' She didn't answer. He asked weakly, 'You have the series at Bhopal, shall I tell them to change the dates?' For the first time he was consulting her on such problems.

She simply said, 'Do what you like.'

'What do you mean by that?' No answer.

He stepped out and drove away; the car had attracted a crowd, which now turned its attention to Selvi. They came forward to stare at her—a rare luxury for most, the citadel having been impregnable all these years; she had been only a hearsay and a myth to most people. Someone said, 'Why did you not come to your mother's help? She was asking for you!' Selvi broke down and was convulsed with sobs.

Three days later Mohan came again to announce, 'On the thirtieth you have to receive an honorary degree at the Delhi University . . .' She just shook her head negatively. 'The Prime Minister will be presiding over the function.'

When pressed, she just said, 'Please leave me out of all this, leave me alone, I want to he alone hereafter. I can't bear the sight of anyone . . .'

416

'Just this one engagement. Do what you like after that. Otherwise it will be most compromising. Only one day at Delhi, we will get back immediately—also you signed the gramophone contract for recording next month . . .' She didn't reply. Her look suggested that it was not her concern. 'You'll be landing me in trouble; at least, the present commitments . . .' It was difficult to carry on negotiations with a crowd watching and following every word of their talk. He wished he could have some privacy with her, but this was a one-room house, where everybody came and stood about or sat down anywhere. If he could get her alone, he would either coax her or wring her neck. He felt helpless and desperate, and suddenly turned round and left.

He came again a week later. But it proved no better. She neither welcomed him nor asked him to leave. He suggested to her to come to the car; this time he had brought his small car. She declined his invitation. 'After all, that woman was old enough to die,' he reflected. 'This fool is ruining her life . . .'

He allowed four more weeks for the mourning period and visited her again, but found a big gathering in her house, overflowing into the street. She sat at the back of the little hall, holding up her *thambura*, and was singing to the audience as if it were an auditorium. A violinist and a drummer had volunteered to play the accompaniments. 'She is frittering away her art,' he thought. She said, 'Come, sit down.' He sat in a corner, listened for a while and slipped away unobtrusively. Again and again, he visited her and found, at all hours of the day, people around her, waiting for her music. News about her free music sessions spread, people thronged there in cars, bicycles and on foot. Varma of the Boardless brought a box of sweets wrapped in gilt paper, and handed it to Selvi silently and went away, having realized his ambition to approach his goddess with an offering. Selvi never spoke unnecessarily. She remained brooding and withdrawn all day, not noticing or minding anyone coming in or going out.

Mohan thought he might be able to find her alone at least at night. At eleven o'clock one night he left his car in Market Road and walked to Vinayak Mudali Street. He called in softly through the door of Selvi's house, 'My dear, it's me, I have to talk to you urgently. Please open the door, please,' appealing desperately through the darkened house. Selvi opened a window shutter just a crack and said firmly, 'Go away, it's not proper to come here at this hour . . .' Mohan turned back with a lump in his throat, swearing half-aloud, 'Ungrateful wretch . . .'

NITYA

'NITYA, AT SIX on Friday morning,' said his father determinedly, 'we leave by bus.' Nitya had noticed preparations at home for this trip, Mother planning a packed lunch for three and filling a basket with coconut, flowers, and incense for worship at the temple. Nitya very well knew how much he was involved in their plans. His mother had talked of nothing else whenever he stepped into the kitchen for coffee. 'After all, a vow has to be fulfilled,' she would keep repeating. Nitya would try to change the subject, banter, joke about it, and run away. They had made a vow to God in a distant hill that Nitya's head would be shaved clean and his hair offered with due rites if his life was spared. That was when he was two years old and stricken with whooping cough and convulsions. Now he was twenty, and although the time limit for fulfilment seemed to be past, yet, they felt, it would not be safe or proper to postpone further. When casually turning the leaves of an old diary, Father discovered the record of their promise to God. Mother, too, recollected having knotted a little coin in a piece of cloth as a reminder, although she could not trace it now. The promise and the diary were lost sight of during Nitya's growing years when the family suddenly found itself drawn into a legal battle over their property. The case was prolonged year after year through the labours of a specially gifted lawyer on the opposite side who could manoeuvre a postponement out of the toughest judge at a crucial point, with the idea of starting it all over again before a new judge in due course. Father was determined to fight it out as the will was unequivocally in his favour and made him sole heir to the property. By the time the final decision came his assets had dwindled, his lawyer himself had changed from a scintillating youth of promise to a toothless character in a frayed gown haunting the corridors of the civil court.

Today, when Father mentioned a firm date for the trip, Nitya protested, 'It doesn't concern me, your twenty-year-old promise. You had no business to pawn my scalp without consulting me.'

'You were only two years old then.'

'You should have done it when you could handle my head as you pleased.'

'But you were very sick and for a long time, too.'

'I have survived, which proves that the disease died rather than me and so where is God's hand in this, if there is a God and if he is interested in my hair?'

His parents were aghast at his manner of talk. Mother pleaded, 'Whatever you do, don't talk like that.'

Father admonished, 'Nitya, you must not be blasphemous. If God hadn't responded to our prayers and saved your life . . .' He could not complete the sentence.

'Was it a bargain?' Nitya asked leeringly.

'Yes,' replied his father. 'It was indeed a bargain and there can be no going back on it.'

'Very well, but the head offered for a shave was not yours. You have been carrying on negotiations with a commodity that did not belong to you.'

'It was for your welfare.'

'Did I ask for it?' Nitya asked puckishly. His mother burst into tears. Father remarked with a scowl, 'You talk like a sinner, cold and godless. Wonder where you inherited it from.'

At this point their neighbour, an alcoholic who had stationed himself in front of the house listening to their debate, suddenly thundered from the street, 'Silence! I am wifeless. Others have two or three—selfish bastards!' He had been a chief engineer in government service, but was dismissed for drunkenness, and later abandoned by his family, too. Nitya loved his antics as he strode up and down the street shouting obscenities after visits to the tavern at the market. Nitya had noted in his private journal: 'The merry engineer mistook the kitchen for the toilet, and that proved too much for his better half.' Now on the pretext of sending him away, Nitya went down the steps and escaped his parents. Later, however, his father kept a close watch on him and clung to him till they reached their seats in the yellow bus at the market gate on Friday.

Father looked triumphant with Nitya secure at his side in the bus, and engaged him in small talk. Mother sat away from them in a back row, enjoying the company of women returning to their villages. The bus passed through Ellaman and crossed Nallappa's Grove and climbed the other bank of the river, splashing up water. The driver displayed immense self-assurance and goaded his bus on with reckless gusto. Passengers were tossed sideways and jolted up and down, but no one minded except Nitya. 'What sort of journey is this?'

'You must learn to be patient, my boy, ours is a poor country. We cannot afford the luxuries they have in Bombay or Madras.' The passengers, mostly villagers, were happy chatting and laughing and also exchanging jokes with the conductor from time to time. Passengers got in and out all along the route whenever the bus stopped, with its wheels screeching and churning up dust. At certain points the bus became almost empty, at others overcrowded, the conductor shouting, 'Move up, move up'. People got in somehow and stayed on somehow, packed to the windscreen. No one protested, but parted with their coins cheerfully. The conductor, hanging on the footboard precariously, pocketed all the cash, which inspired Nitya to note in his diary, 'The bus rocks and sways, and sighs with its burden, but won't burst yet. Perhaps the last straw is yet to arrive. But the real question is, Who owns this? Definitely not this conductor, though he grows heavier every minute with the coins dropping like manna into his pocket.'

'You should get down here and walk up to that hill, the bus can't take you there,' said the conductor at a stop. They struggled their way out of the bus, Mother carrying her bundle of offerings and food delicately through the crush. As the bus started on its way again, Father asked the driver, 'When are you returning?'

'At five, six, or seven; if you miss, tomorrow morning.'

The temple perched on a hillock was visible across the field, but it was impossible to judge the distance. A track formed by the tread of feet meandered through the fields. They had to cross in single file with Nitya in the middle, Father ahead, and Mother bringing up the rear. Nitya reflected, Afraid I might run away, they are sandwiching me. But what chance have I, trapped by slush and vegetation on both sides of this narrow path.

An hour's walk brought them to a hamlet skirting the base of the hillock. Nitya was on the point of asking, Why come so far, if God is everywhere? I could as well have surrendered my head to our Vinayak Street barber, who shaves you at your doorstep. As if reading his mind, Father began to explain, 'This temple was established by our ancestors five hundred years ago—earlier; it's on this hill that Kumara annihilated the demon whose name I can't recollect now.'

'Demon is a demon, whatever the name,' said the young man. Father ignored his quip and continued, 'The temple was built by a Chola king who ruled these parts, and in course of time it was turned over to the care of our ancestors.'

'How are you sure?' Nitya asked.

'You've got into the habit of questioning everything.'

'I just want to know, that's all.'

'Well, it is all recorded in copper plate, stone pillars, and palm leaves, from which deductions are made by scholars. Don't imagine you are the only wise man. There is a document in the temple in palm leaf mentioning my great-grandfather by name and committing our family to the expenses of the annual Chariot Festival. I pay them two hundred rupees a year and twenty measures of rice for a public feast on that day. They come to the town for collections in December, ten days before the festival . . . Luckily, a copy of this document is in my possession with the receipts of annual payments which clinched the issue in our favour at the appellate stage.' Nitya noted later in his diary, 'Even at this distance and on a consecrated spot my father is unable to keep his mind off the civil court, verily like the engineer of his wifelessness.' When they came to the border of the village, Father slowed his steps and, with a slight frown, threw a general question in the air: 'Where is everybody?' as if the reception committee had failed him.

He halted at a corner and shouted, 'Hey, Rama,' and a group of women and boys emerged from some corner and came running on seeing him. They invited him into their homes. Father said impatiently, 'Yes, later. First the temple. Call the headman.'

'They are all away weeding,' said a woman, and turning to a young man jabbed his cheek with her forefinger and said, 'Run up and tell Rama that the Trustee is come.' The boy shot off like an arrow. They dragged out of their homes an assortment of furniture and put it up in the shade of a tree, and then bustled about and conjured up a bunch of bananas and a jug of milk for the visitors and laid the fare on a wooden stool. Nitya cried, 'Oh, just what I need,' and tried to reach out for a fruit, but Father said, 'Not now, after the vow.' (Nitya noted in his diary, 'Not now, but after the vow, says God through my father in a perfect rhyme, while the banana wilts in the tray and the milk curdles irreparably.') The headman arrived. After the initial courtesies, much business talk ensued, with a crowd standing around and listening intently. Father inquired authoritatively, 'Where is the priest? The temple must be opened. We have to leave by the evening bus.'

The headman said out of courtesy, 'Must you? You may spend the night at the rest house, sir. You have come after a long time.'

Immediately, Nitya protested, 'You may both stay back if you choose, but I want to catch the bus,' feeling nostalgic for his evening group at the College Union. Mother said, 'Be patient.' But Nitya replied, 'I've much to do this evening.' Father said, 'What could be more important than your duty to God? Be patient, having come so far.'

The temple priest, his forehead ablaze with sacred ash and vermilion, shoulder wrapped in a red shawl, a lanky person with a booming voice, arrived, dangling a large key in an iron hoop. After greeting the Trustee in the correct manner, he plunged straight into business, cataloguing his demands.

'The well at the temple needs to be deepened. The temple lock must be replaced. It is worn out, sir. These are very bad days. We are finding it difficult to get flowers for the worship. We were getting supplies from the other village. But they raise their rates each time and are very irregular too. They have to come up from the other side of the hill and don't like it, and so have started a rumour that they see a wolf or panther prowling around, and have stopped coming altogether.'

'Nonsense, only an excuse,' cried Father. 'No panther or tiger in these parts, never heard such rubbish in my life.'

'He mentioned wolf, not tiger,' corrected Nitya.

'What if? It is just gossip and nonsense—rumour-mongers!' Father cried with passion, looking outraged at the notion of any wild life in the vicinity of his ancestral temple. He dismissed the subject peremptorily and commanded, 'Get the barber down. My son's tonsure today whatever happens,' and the assembly looked with fresh interest at Nitya's head, at which he simpered, squirmed, and ran his fingers through his crop. The priest turned to a little fellow in the crowd and said, 'Don't bite your nail, you fool! Go to the tank bund and tell Raghavan to come up with his tin box immediately, this very second. Run, run.' The little messenger was off like a shot again.

They started up the hill, led by the priest, a crowd following. It was a short climb, but Nitya's mother panted and rested in three places, while Father hovered around her and fidgeted impatiently. The climb ended at the door of the temple, which was unlocked, and two large doors were pushed open. It was a little shrine with a granite-pillared hall and paved corridor around the sanctum, which housed an image on a pedestal. Father became grim and devout. Mother shut her eyes and recited a prayer. The priest lit the wicks in the sanctum and the image began to glow with the oil anointed on it and gradually took shape. The priest was grumbling, 'Even this oil is adulterated nowadays.' He had managed to secure a handful of marigolds and nerium and stuck them on the image. While they were all in this state of elation, the young messenger returned from his mission and bellowed from the door, 'The barber's house is locked, not a soul there.'

'Did you ask the neighbours?'

'They don't know. They only saw the family go out for the bus with their baggage.'

Nitya cried aloud, 'God is great, really.'

Father commented, 'This is the worst of it, having one

426

barber for the whole place. He thinks he can do what he pleases. One and only Padmavathi for a whole city, as the saying goes,' he said, unable to contain himself. His wife said with a frown, 'Hush! What awful words to utter in this place' (Padmavathi was a reference to a whore). Father glowered at her for checking him, but they were all assembled in the presence of God and could not engage in acrimony. Nitya giggled but suppressed himself when his father glanced in his direction. The headman said in a respectful whisper, 'Raghavan cannot make both ends meet unless he ekes out with the fee for playing the pipe at weddings. It is their family tradition.' Father leaned over to Mother and whispered, 'For thousands of years somehow barbers have also been outstanding pipers and custodians of pure classical music.' While this was going on, the priest sounded a bell and circled a camphor flame around the image and they stopped talking and were lost in meditation.

When the priest came out of the sanctum, bearing a tray with camphor flame, a discussion began as to what course of action the scriptures prescribed when an essential barber was absent.

'We are at the mercy of a single man,' Father kept repeating monotonously, firmly suppressing the name 'Padmavathi', which kept bobbing up again and again on his tongue. The priest put the tray back in the sanctum, came out, and joined the discussion. He finally said, gaping at Nitya's crop, which was the main topic of discussion and purpose of the trip, 'Sometimes, the vow is taken to be fulfilled through a token performance with penalty added. These days young men will not allow barbers to come near them.'

427

'They won't allow their terrifying whiskers to be touched either!' added Father.

'No tonsure is possible unless done in babyhood,' said the priest.

'Too true, well spoken,' said Nitya, pleased with the tenor of talks, and offered, 'Get me a pair of scissors, and I will give you four inches of my front lock, the best available—that's all, and God will be satisfied. After all, with so many offerings, where can he keep his collection?'

The priest said, 'The fruits and coconuts you have brought are adequate, leave them behind, and add whatever cash you can spare.'

Father and Mother looked disappointed and kept throwing covetous glances at Nitya's head. Nitya felt relieved, but the relief threatened to be short-lived. Soon there was a commotion. Someone at the doorway announced excitedly, 'Raghavan is coming up,' followed by the appearance of a fat barber holding in his hand a tiny tin box. He was panting and perspiring; he stared at the gathering from the doorway, and without a word went straight to the well at the backyard, peeled off his vest, drew a pot of water and emptied it over his head, and reappeared, dripping and ready. 'He never opens his razor box without a bath at first when he has to perform a tonsure ceremony,' explained the priest admiringly. The barber explained, 'I had only gone to a nearby farm for a baby's first shave, that was all.'

'Not to play the pipe at a wedding?' someone asked.

'Oh, no. I have jealous neighbours who create false rumours to spoil my business. If I had known the Trustee was coming I would not have accepted even a thousand pieces of gold anywhere outside. When the boy came on a bicycle and told me, I snatched it from his hand and rode down immediately. Now I am ready, my master.' Father and Mother looked pleased at this turn of events. Nitya giggled at the thought of the fat barber on the boy's bicycle. Father took Nitya by hand. 'Let us sit on that stone platform in the corridor, that's where he shaves—'

Nitya shook himself free and said, 'I agreed to give four inches of hair, it was up to you to have taken it. Now you have lost the opportunity, which must be seized by the forelock.'

'Now, with this man here, we must fulfil the vow as originally promised,' said Mother.

'Let Father use the barber if he likes. I'm not interested.'

The barber started pleading and arguing. The priest edged up to Nitya with his pleas and said ingratiatingly, 'You must not hurt your parents' feelings. Please move on to that platform, the barber is ready.'

'But my head is not ready. You promised to accept four inches of my hair. Now you are demanding my head itself. Have you no logic or reason? No contentment or consistency? How can God tolerate fickle-minded people like you! Now I have changed my mind—I won't give even an inch . . .'

Both Father and Mother cried simultaneously, 'Don't talk to the priest like that in his own temple.' Nitya was angry, also hungry. They would not let him touch even one plantain out of the dozens offered by the villagers under the tree. While his parents stood staring at him helplessly, Nitya suddenly turned on his heel, dashed out, and sped downhill saying, 'I will wait for you both at the bus stop, but only till the bus arrives . . .'

THE ROMAN IMAGE

THE TALKATIVE MAN said:

Once I was an archaeologist's assistant. I wandered up and down the country probing, exploring, and digging, in search of antiquities, a most interesting occupation, although cynics sometimes called us 'grave-diggers'. I enjoyed the work immensely. I had a master who was a famous archaeologist called Doctor something or other. He was a superb, timeless being, who lived a thousand years behind the times, and who wanted neither food nor roof nor riches if only he was allowed to gaze on undisturbed at an old coin or chip of a burial urn. He had torn up the earth in almost all parts of India and had brought to light very valuable information concerning the history and outlook of people of remote centuries. His monographs on each of his excavations filled several shelves in all the important libraries. And then, as our good fortune would have it, he received an inspiration that Malgudi district was eminently diggable. I am not competent to explain how he got this idea, but there it was. Word was brought to me that the great man was staying in the dak bungalow and was in need of an assistant. Within an hour of hearing it I stood before the great man. He was sitting on the floor with the most crazy collection of articles in front of him—pots and beads and useless coins and palm leaves, all of them rusty and decaying. He had a lens by his side, through which he looked at these articles and made notes. He asked me: 'What do you know of the archaeological factors of your district?' I blinked. Honestly I didn't know there was any archaeology in our place. He looked at me through his old spectacles, and I realized that my living depended upon my answer. I mustered up all the knowledge of elementary history I had acquired in my boyhood, and replied: 'Well, nothing has so far been done in any methodical manner, although now and then we come across some ignorant villagers ploughing up old unusual bits of pottery and metal.'

'Really,' he asked, pricking up his ears. 'And what do they do with them?'

'They simply throw them away or give them to children to play with,' I replied.

'Oh, too bad,' he muttered. 'Why couldn't you have collected these things in one place?'

'I will take care to do that hereafter, sir,' I said; and that settled it. He engaged me on the spot at fifty rupees a month, and my main business was to follow him about and help him.

I had my wits alive, and within a month I was in a position to lead him by the hand. Not the slightest object escaped my notice. I picked up everything I saw, cleaned and polished it, and held it up for his opinion. Most times, I am sorry to confess, they were useless bits of stuff of known origin—namely, our own times. But I am glad to say that once I scored a hit.

We camped one weekend at Siral—a village sixty miles from the town. It is a lovely ancient place, consisting of a hundred houses. Sarayu river winds its way along the northern boundary of the village. The river here is broader than it is anywhere else in the district. On the other bank of the river we have the beginnings of a magnificent jungle of bamboo and teak. The most modern structure in the place was a small two-roomed inspection lodge. The doctor occupied one room and I the other. We were scouting the surroundings for a mound under which was supposed to be a buried city. This discovery was going to push the earliest known civilization three centuries farther back and rival Mohenjadaro in antiquity. We might be pardoned if we set about our business with some intensity. Our doctor somehow seemed to possess an inexplicable feeling of rivalry with the discoverers of Mohenjadaro and such other places. His greatest desire was to have a monopoly of the earliest known civilization and place it where he chose. This seemed to me a slight weakness in his nature, but pardonable in a great man, who had done so much else in life. This is all beside the point. Let me get on with the story. One day I had gone to the river for a bath. It was an exhilarating evening; I had done a good day's work, assisting the doctor to clean up and study a piece of stained glass picked up in a field outside the village. The doctor kept gazing at this glass all day. He constantly shook his head and said: 'This is easily the most important piece of work which has come under my notice. This bit of glass you see is not ordinary archaeological stuff, but a very important link. This piece of glass is really Florentian, which went out of vogue in AD 5.

How did this come here? It is not found anywhere else in the world. If the identity of this is established properly we may ultimately have a great deal to say about the early Roman Empire and this part of India. This will revolutionize our whole knowledge of history.' He talked of nothing but that the whole day. He trembled with excitement and lost all taste for food. He kept on muttering: 'We must tread warily and not overlook the slightest evidence. Keep your eyes open. We are on the eve of great discoveries . . .' And I caught this excitement and acquired a permanently searching look. I was in this state when I plunged into the waters of Sarayu that evening. I am a good diver. As I went down my hand struck against a hard object in the sandy bed. Feeling with my fingers, I found it to be a stone image. When I came to the surface again I came up bearing that image with me. Dripping with water, I sat on the river step, without even drying myself, and examined the image.

'This takes us on to an entirely new set of possibilities!' exclaimed the doctor in great joy. He keenly examined it by our tin lantern. It was a stone image a foot high, which had acquired a glass-like smoothness, having been under water for years. It had an arm, an eye, the nose, and the mouth missing. There were a few details of ornament and drapery, which the doctor examined with special care. It was 3 a.m. when he went to bed. An hour later the doctor peeped in at my doorway and announced: 'This is a Roman statue. How it came to he found in these parts is a historical fact we have to wrest from evidence. It is going to give an entirely new turn to Indian history.'

Within the next two months all the important papers and periodicals in the world published details of this discovery. Papers were read before historical associations and conferences. I came to be looked upon as a sort of saviour of Indian history, for the doctor insisted upon giving me my due share of fame. University honours came my way. I was offered lucrative positions here and there. It was finally decided that the image was that of a Roman Emperor called Tiberius II. It would be out of place to go into the details that led to this conclusion: but you need have no doubt that the doctor had excellent reasons for it. Besides the study of the image itself he went through some Roman texts which mentioned south India.

For the next few months we toured about a great deal lecturing on this subject and demonstrating. I went with my doctor to Madras and started work on a monograph on the subject. It was to be a monumental work covering over a thousand pages of demy size, full of photographs and sketches. You can understand why it should be so big when I tell you that it was going to be a combined work on early Roman history, Indian history, archaeology, and epigraphy. My name was going to appear as the joint author of the work. I realized that here was my future—fame, position, and perhaps some money, too. The doctor left me in entire charge of this work and went away to upper India to continue a piece of work which he had already been doing. I sat in a large library the whole day, examining, investigating, studying, and writing. I became a fairly important person in learned societies. I worked from seven in the morning to eleven in the evening almost without a break, and throughout the day I had visits from people interested in the discovery. Papers and journals contained paragraphs now and then—'Archaeologist assistant working on monograph . . .'—and its progress was duly reported to the public. And then there came a time when the press could announce: 'Monograph on which —— has been working for months now will be ready for publication in ten days. It is expected that this is going to make the richest contribution to Indian history . . .' My fingers were worn out with writing. My eyes were nearly gone. I looked forward to the end of the work, when, as my doctor wrote: 'You can have a holiday for three months in any hill station you like and forget the whole business . . .' The manuscripts piled a yard high on my table.

It was at this stage that I had to visit Siral once again. I had to obtain measurements of the spot where the image was found. I left my work at that and hurried to the village. I plunged into the river and came up. I sat on the river step, still dripping with water, noting down figures, when a stranger came and sat near me. We fell to talking, and I told him about my work, in the hope of drawing out further facts. He was a rustic, and he listened to me without emotion. At the end of my narration he remained peculiarly moody and asked me to repeat facts about the image. He compressed his lips and asked: 'Where do you say it came from?'

'Rome—'

'Where is that?'

'In Europe,' I said. He stood still, puzzled, and I amplified: 'Where the European people live—'

'I don't know about that—but if it is the image which you found in these parts I can tell you something about it. It is without nose and arm, isn't it?' I assented, not knowing what was coming. He said: 'Follow me, if you want to

know anything more about this image.' He led me up the
bank, along a foot track which wound through the jungle.
We reached a hamlet a mile off. He stopped in front of a
little shrine and said: 'That image belonged to this temple.'
He led me into the shrine. We had to go stooping into it
because of its narrow doorway and low roof. At the inner
sanctum there was an image of Mari with a garland of
yellow chrysanthemums around her neck, lit by a faint wick
lamp. On one side of the sanctum doorway stood a
dwarapalaka—a winged creature a foot high. My friend
pointed at the image and said: 'This formed a pair with the
one you picked up, and it used to adorn that side of the
doorway.' I looked up where he pointed. I noticed a
pedestal without anything on it. A doubt seized me. 'I want
to examine the figure,' I said. He brought down the wick
lamp; I examined by its flickering light the *dwarapalaka*. 'Is
this exactly like the one which was on that side?' It was a
superfluous question. This image was exactly like the image
I had found, but without its injuries.

'Where was this made?'

'I had it done by a stone-image maker, a fellow in
another village. You see that hillock? Its stone is made into
images all over the world, and at its foot is a village where
they make images.'

'Are you sure when it was made?'

'Yes, I gave an advance of twenty rupees for it, and how
that fellow delayed! I went over to the village and sat up
night and day for two months and got the pair done. I
watched them take shape before my eyes. And then we
collected about fifty rupees and gave it to him. We wanted
to improve this temple.' I put back the lamp and walked

out. I sat down on the temple step. 'Why do you look so sad? I thought you'd be pleased to know these things,' he said, watching me.

'I am, I am—only I've been rather unwell,' I assured him. 'Can't you tell me something more about it: how it came to be found in the river?'

'Yes, yes,' said my friend. 'It was carried and thrown into the river; it didn't walk down there.'

'Oh!' I exclaimed.

'That is a story. For this we went to the court and had the priest dismissed and fined. He cannot come near the temple now. We spent one thousand rupees in lawyer fees alone; we were prepared to spend all our fortune if only to see that priest removed. It went up to Malgudi court—we got a vakil from Madras.'

'What was wrong with your priest?'

'No doubt he had a hereditary claim and took up the work when his father died, but the fellow was a devil for drink if ever there was one. Morning till night he was drinking, and he performed all the puja in that condition. We did not know what to do with him. We just tolerated him, hoping that some day the Goddess would teach him a lesson. We did not like to be too harsh, since he was a poor fellow, and he went about his duties quietly. But when we added these two *dwarapalakas* at the doorway he got a queer notion in his head. He used to say that the two doorkeepers constantly harried him by staring at him wherever he went. He said that their look pricked him in the neck. Sometimes he would peep in from within to see if the images were looking away, and he'd scream, 'Ah, still they are watching me,' and shout at them. This went on for months. In course of time he began to shudder whenever he had to pass these doorkeepers. It was an acute moment of suspense for him when he had to cross that pair and get into the sanctum. Gradually he complained that if he ever took his eyes off these figures they butted him from behind, kicked him, and pulled his hair, and so forth. He was afraid to look anywhere else and walked on cautiously with his eyes on the images. But if he had his eyes on one, the other knocked him from behind. He showed us bruises and scratches sometimes. We declared we might treat his complaints seriously if he ever went into the shrine without a drop of drink in him. In course of time he started to seek his own remedy. He carried a small mallet with him, and whenever he got a knock he returned the blow; it fell on a nose today, on an arm tomorrow, and on an ear another day. We didn't notice his handiwork for months. Judging from the mallet blows, the image on the left side seems to have been the greater offender.

'The culmination came when he knocked it off its pedestal and carried it to the river. Next morning he declared he saw it walk off and plunge into the river. He must have felt that this would serve as a lesson to the other image if it should be thinking of any trick. But the other image never got its chance: for we dragged the priest before a law court and had him sent away.'

Thus ended the villager's tale. It took time for me to recover. I asked: 'Didn't you have to pick up the image from the water and show it to the judge?'

'No, because the fellow would not tell us where he had flung it. Did not know till this moment where exactly it could be found.'

When I went back to Madras I was a different man. The doctor had just returned for a short stay. I told him everything. He was furious. 'We have made ourselves mighty fools before the whole world,' he cried.

I didn't know what to say. I mumbled: 'I am so sorry, sir.' He pointed at the pile of manuscripts on the table and cried: 'Throw all that rubbish into the fire, before we are declared mad . . .' I pushed the whole pile off the table and applied a matchstick. We stood frowning at the roaring fire for a moment, and then he asked, pointing at the image: 'And what will you do with it?'

'I don't know,' I said.

'Drown it. After all, you picked it up from the water—that piece of nonsense!' he cried.

I had never seen him in such a rage before. I wrapped the image in a piece of brown paper, carried it to the seashore, and flung it far into the sea. I hope it is still rolling about at the bottom of the Bay of Bengal. I only hope it won't get into some large fish and come back to the study table! Later a brief message appeared in all the important papers: 'The manuscript on which Doctor —— and assistant were engaged has been destroyed, and the work will be suspended.'

The doctor gave me two months' salary and bade me goodbye.

A HORSE AND TWO GOATS

OF THE SEVEN hundred thousand villages dotting the map of India, in which the majority of India's five hundred million live, flourish and die, Kritam was probably the tiniest. It was indicated on the district survey map by a microscopic dot, the map being meant more for the revenue official out to collect tax than for the guidance of the motorist, who in any case could not hope to reach it since it sprawled far from the highway at the end of a rough track furrowed up by the iron-hooped wheels of bullock carts. But its size did not prevent it giving itself the grandiose name Kritam, which meant in Tamil 'coronet' or 'crown' on the brow of this subcontinent. The village consisted of less than thirty houses, only one of them built with brick and cement. Painted a brilliant yellow and blue all over with gorgeous carvings of gods and gargoyles on its balustrade, it was known as the Big House. The other houses, distributed in four streets, were generally of bamboo thatch, straw, mud, and other unspecified material. Muni's was the last house in the fourth street, beyond which stretched the fields. In his prosperous days Muni had owned a flock of forty sheep and goats and sallied forth every morning driving the flock to the highway a couple of miles away. There he would sit on the pedestal of a clay statue of a horse while his cattle grazed around. He carried a crook at the end of a bamboo pole and snapped foliage from the avenue trees to feed his flock; he also gathered faggots and dry sticks, bundled them, and carried them home for fuel at sunset.

His wife lit the domestic fire at dawn, boiled water in a mud pot, threw into it a handful of millet flour, added salt, and gave him his first nourishment for the day. When he started out, she would put in his hand a packed lunch, once again the same millet cooked into a little ball, which he could swallow with a raw onion at midday. She was old, but he was older and needed all the attention she could give him in order to be kept alive.

His fortunes had declined gradually, unnoticed. From a flock of forty which he drove into a pen at night, his stock had now come down to two goats which were not worth the rent of a half rupee a month which the Big House charged for the use of the pen in their backyard. And so the two goats were tethered to the trunk of a drumstick tree which grew in front of his hut and from which occasionally Muni could shake down drumsticks. This morning he got six. He carried them in with a sense of triumph. Although no one could say precisely who owned the tree, it was his because he lived in its shadow.

She said, 'If you were content with the drumstick leaves alone, I could boil and salt some for you.'

'Oh, I am tired of eating those leaves. I have a craving to chew the drumstick out of sauce, I tell you.'

441

'You have only four teeth in your jaw, but your craving is for big things. All right, get the stuff for the sauce, and I will prepare it for you. After all, next year you may not be alive to ask for anything. But first get me all the stuff, including a measure of rice or millet, and I will satisfy your unholy craving. Our store is empty today. Dal, chili, curry leaves, mustard, coriander, gingelley oil, and one large potato. Go out and get all this.' He repeated the list after her in order not to miss any item and walked off to the shop in the third street.

He sat on an upturned packing case below the platform of the shop. The shopman paid no attention to him. Muni kept clearing his throat, coughing and sneezing until the shopman could not stand it any more and demanded, 'What ails you? You will fly off that seat into the gutter if you sneeze so hard, young man.' Muni laughed inordinately, in order to please the shopman, at being called 'young man'. The shopman softened and said, 'You have enough of the imp inside to keep a second wife busy, but for the fact that the old lady is still alive.' Muni laughed appropriately again at this joke. It completely won the shopman over; he liked his sense of humour to be appreciated. Muni engaged his attention in local gossip for a few minutes, which always ended with a reference to the postman's wife, who had eloped to the city some months before.

The shopman felt most pleased to hear the worst of the postman, who had cheated him. Being an itinerant postman, he returned home to Kritam only once in ten days and every time managed to slip away again without passing the shop in the third street. By thus humouring the shopman, Muni could always ask for one or two items of food, promising payment later. Some days the shopman was in a good mood and gave in, and sometimes he would lose his temper suddenly and bark at Muni for daring to ask for credit. This was such a day, and Muni could not progress beyond two items listed as essential components. The shopman was also displaying a remarkable memory for old facts and figures and took out an oblong ledger to support his observations. Muni felt impelled to rise and flee but his self-respect kept him in his seat and made him listen to the worst things about himself. The shopman concluded, 'If you could find five rupees and a quarter, you would pay off an ancient debt and then could apply for admission to swarga. How much have you got now?'

'I will pay you everything on the first of the next month.'

'As always, and whom do you expect to rob by then?'

Muni felt caught and mumbled, 'My daughter has sent word that she will be sending me money.'

'Have you a daughter?' sneered the shopman. 'And she is sending you money! For what purpose, may I know?'

'Birthday, fiftieth birthday,' said Muni quietly.

'Birthday! How old are you?'

Muni repeated weakly, not being sure of it himself, 'Fifty.' He always calculated his age from the time of the great famine when he stood as high as the parapet around the village well, but who could calculate such things accurately nowadays with so many famines occuring? The shopman felt encouraged when other customers stood around to watch and comment. Muni thought helplessly, 'My poverty is exposed to everybody. But what can I do?'

'More likely you are seventy,' said the shopman. 'You

443

also forget that you mentioned a birthday five weeks ago when you wanted castor oil for your holy bath.'

'Bath! Who can dream of a bath when you have to scratch the tank-bed for a bowl of water? We would all be parched and dead but for the Big House, where they let us take a pot of water from their well.' After saying this Muni unobtrusively rose and moved off.

He told his wife, 'That scoundrel would not give me anything. So go out and sell the drumsticks for what they are worth.'

He flung himself down in a corner to recoup from the fatigue of his visit to the shop. His wife said, 'You are getting no sauce today, nor anything else. I can't find anything to give you to eat. Fast till evening, it'll do you good. Take the goats and be gone now,' and added, 'Don't come back before the sun is down.' He knew that if he obeyed her she would somehow conjure up some food for him in the evening. Only he must be careful not to argue and irritate her. Her temper was undependable in the morning but improved by evening time. She was sure to go out and work—grind corn in the Big House, sweep or scrub somewhere, and earn enough to buy some food and keep a dinner ready for him in the evening.

Unleashing the goats from the drumstick tree, Muni started out, driving them ahead and uttering weird cries from time to time in order to urge them on. He passed through the village with his head bowed in thought. He did not want to look at anyone or be accosted. A couple of cronies lounging in the temple corridor hailed him, but he ignored their call. They had known him in the days of affluence when he lorded over a flock of fleecy sheep, and not the miserable gawky goats that he had today. Of course, he also used to have a few goats for those who fancied them, but the real wealth lay in sheep; they bred fast and people came and bought the fleece in the shearing season; and then that famous butcher from the town came over on the weekly market days bringing him betel leaves, tobacco, and often enough some bhang, which they smoked in a hut in the coconut grove, undisturbed by wives and well-wishers. After a smoke one felt light and elated and inclined to forgive everyone including that brother-in-law of his who had once tried to set fire to his home. But all this seemed like the memories of a previous birth. Some pestilence afflicted his cattle (he could of course guess who had laid his animals under a curse) and even the friendly butcher would not touch one at half the price . . . and now here he was left with the two scraggy creatures. He wished someone would rid him of their company too. The shopman had said that he was seventy. At seventy, one only waited to be summoned by God. When he was dead what would his wife do? They had lived in each other's company since they were children. He was told on their day of wedding that he was ten years old and she was eight. During the wedding ceremony they had had to recite their respective ages and names. He had thrashed her only a few times in their career, and later she had had the upper hand. Progeny, none. Perhaps a large progeny would have brought him the blessing of the gods. Fertility brought merit. People with fourteen sons were always so prosperous and at peace with the world and themselves. He recollected the thrill he had felt when he mentioned a daughter to that shopman. Although it was not believed, what if he did not have a daughter?—his cousin in the next village had many daughters, and any one of them was as good as his; he was fond of them all and would buy them sweets if he could afford it. Still, everyone in the village whispered behind their backs that Muni and his wife were a barren couple. He avoided looking at anyone; they all professed to be so high up. And everyone else in the village had more money than he. 'I am the poorest fellow in our caste and no wonder that they spurn me, but I won't look at them either,' and so he passed on along the edge of the street, with his eyes downcast and people also left him alone, commenting only to the extent, 'Ah, there he goes with his two great goats; if he slits their throats, he may have more peace of mind'; 'What has he to worry about anyway? They live on nothing and have nobody to worry about.' Thus people commented when he passed through the village. Only on the outskirts did he lift his head and look up. He urged and bullied the goats until they meandered along to the foot of the horse statue on the edge of the village. He sat on its pedestal for the rest of the day. The advantage of this was that he could watch the highway and see the lorries and buses pass through to the hills, and it gave him a sense of belonging to a larger world. The pedestal of the statue was broad enough for him to move around as the sun travelled up and westward; or he could also crouch under the belly of the horse, for shade.

The horse was nearly life-size, moulded out of clay, baked, burnt and brightly coloured, and reared its head proudly, prancing with its forelegs in the air and flourishing its tail in a loop. Beside the horse stood a warrior with scythe-like mustachios, bulging eyes and aquiline nose. The old image-makers believed in indicating a man of strength by making his eyes bulge and sharpening his moustache tips. They had also decorated the man's chest with beads which looked today like blobs of mud through the ravages of sun and wind and rain (when it came), but Muni would insist that he had known the beads to sparkle like the nine gems at one time in his life. The horse itself was said to have been as white as a *dhobi*-washed sheet, and had had on its back a cover of pure brocade of red-and-black lace, matching the multicoloured sash around the waist of the warrior. But none in the village remembered the splendour as no one noticed its existence. Even Muni, who spent all his waking hours at its foot, never bothered to look up. It was untouched by the young vandals of the village who gashed tree trunks with knives and tried to topple off milestones and inscribed lewd designs on all the walls. This statue had been closer to the population of the village at one time, when this spot bordered the village; but when the highway was laid (or perhaps when the tank and wells dried up completely here) the village moved a couple of miles inland.

Muni sat at the foot of the statue, watching his two goats graze in the arid soil among the cactus and lantana bushes. He looked at the sun; it had tilted westward no doubt, but it was not yet time to go back home; if he went too early his wife would have no food for him. Also, he must give her time to cool off her temper and feel sympathetic, and then she would scrounge and manage to get some food. He watched the mountain road for a time signal. When the green bus appeared around the bend he could leave, and his wife would feel pleased that he had let the goats feed long enough.

He noticed now a new sort of vehicle coming down at full speed. It looked both like a motor car and a bus. He used to be intrigued by the novelty of such spectacles, but of late work was going on at the source of the river on the mountain and an assortment of people and traffic went past him, and he took it all casually and described to his wife, later in the day, not everything as he once did, but only some things, if he noticed anything special. Today, while he observed the yellow vehicle coming down, he was wondering how to describe it later when it sputtered and stopped in front of him. A red-faced foreigner who had been driving it got down and went round it, stooping, looking, and poking under the vehicle; then he straightened himself up, looked at the dashboard, stared in Muni's direction, and approached him. 'Excuse me, is there a gas station nearby, or do I have to wait until another car comes—' He suddenly looked up at the clay horse and cried, 'Marvellous!' without completing his sentence. Muni felt he should get up and run away, and cursed his age. He could not really put his limbs into action; some years ago he could outrun a cheetah, as happened once when he went to the forest to cut fuel and it was then that two of his sheep were mauled—a sign that bad times were coming. Though he tried, he could not extricate himself easily from his seat, besides which there was also the problem of the goats. He could not leave them behind.

The red-faced man wore khaki clothes—evidently a policeman or a soldier. Muni said to himself, 'He will chase or shoot if I start running. Sometimes dogs chase only those who run—O Shiva protect me. I don't know why this man should be after me.' Meanwhile the foreigner cried 'Marvellous!' again, nodding his head. He paced around the

448

statue with his eyes fixed on it. Muni sat frozen for a while, and then fidgeted and tried to edge away. Now the other man suddenly pressed his palms together in a salute, smiled, and said, 'Namaste! How do you do?'

At which Muni spoke the only English expression he had learnt, 'Yes, no.' Having exhausted his English vocabulary, he started in Tamil: 'My name is Muni. These two goats are mine, and no one can gainsay it—though our village is full of slanderers these days who will not hesitate to say that what belongs to a man doesn't belong to him.' He rolled his eyes and shuddered at the thought of the evil-minded men and women peopling his village.

The foreigner faithfully looked in the direction indicated by Muni's fingers, gazed for a while at the two goats and the rocks, and with a puzzled expression took out his silver cigarette-case and lit a cigarette. Suddenly remembering the courtesies of the season, he asked, 'Do you smoke?' Muni answered, 'Yes, no.' Whereupon the red-faced man took a cigarette and gave it to Muni, who received it with surprise, having had no offer of a smoke from anyone for years now. Those days when he smoked bhang were gone with his sheep and the large-hearted butcher. Nowadays he was not able to find even matches, let alone bhang. (His wife went across and borrowed a fire at dawn from a neighbour.) He had always wanted to smoke a cigarette; only once had the shopman given him one on credit, and he remembered how good it had tasted. The other flicked the lighter open and offered a light to Muni. Muni felt so confused about how to act that he blew on it and put it out. The other, puzzled but undaunted, flourished his lighter, presented it again, and lit Muni's cigarette. Muni drew a deep puff and started coughing; it was racking, no doubt, but extremely pleasant. When his cough subsided he wiped his eyes and took stock of the situation, understanding that the other man was not an inquisitor of any kind. Yet, in order to make sure, he remained wary. No need to run away from a man who gave such a potent smoke. His head was reeling from the effect of the strong American cigarette made with roasted tobacco. The man said, 'I come from New York,' took out a wallet from his hip pocket, and presented his card.

Muni shrank away from the card. Perhaps he was trying to present a warrant and arrest him. Beware of khaki, one part of his mind warned. Take all the cigarettes or bhang or whatever is offered, but don't get caught. Beware of khaki. He wished he weren't seventy as the shopman had said. At seventy one didn't run, but surrendered to whatever came. He could only ward off trouble by talk. So he went on, all in the chaste Tamil for which Kritam was famous. (Even the worst detractors could not deny that the famous poetess Avvaiyar was born in this area, although no one could say whether it was in Kritam or Kuppam, the adjoining village.) Out of this heritage the Tamil language gushed through Muni in an unimpeded flow. He said, 'Before God, sir, Bhagavan, who sees everything, I tell you, sir, that we know nothing of the case. If the murder was committed, whoever did it will not escape. Bhagavan is all-seeing. Don't ask me about it. I know nothing.' A body had been found mutilated and thrown under a tamarind tree at the border between Kritam and Kuppam a few weeks before, giving rise to much gossip and speculation. Muni added an explanation, 'Anything is possible there. People over there will stop at nothing.' The foreigner nodded his head and listened courteously though he understood nothing.

'I am sure you know when this horse was made,' said the red man and smiled ingratiatingly.

Muni reacted to the relaxed atmosphere by smiling himself, and pleaded, 'Please go away, sir. I know nothing. I promise we will hold him for you if we see any bad character around, and we will bury him up to his neck in a coconut pit if he tries to escape; but our village has always had a clean record. Must definitely be the other village.'

Now the red man implored, 'Please, please, I will speak slowly, please try to understand me. Can't you understand even a simple word of English? Everyone in this country seems to know English. I have got along with English everywhere in this country, but you don't speak it. Have you any religious or spiritual scruples for avoiding the English speech?'

Muni made some indistinct sounds in his throat and shook his head. Encouraged, the other went on to explain at length, uttering each syllable with care and deliberation. Presently he sidled over and took a seat beside the old man, explaining, 'You see, last August, we probably had the hottest summer in history, and I was working in my shirtsleeves in my office on the fortieth floor of the Empire State Building. You must have heard of the power failure, and there I was stuck for four hours, no elevator, no air-conditioning. All the way in the train I kept thinking, and the minute I reached home in Connecticut, I told my wife Ruth, "We will visit India this winter, it's time to look at other civilizations." Next day she called the travel agent first thing and told him to fix it, and so here I am. Ruth came with me but is staying back at Srinagar, and I am the one doing the rounds and joining her later.'

Muni looked reflective at the end of this long peroration and said, rather feebly, 'Yes, no,' as a concession to the other's language, and went on in Tamil, 'When I was this high,' he indicated a foot high, 'I heard my uncle say . . .'

No one can tell what he was planning to say as the other interrupted him at this stage to ask, 'Boy, what is the secret of your teeth? How old are you?'

The old man forgot what he had started to say and remarked, 'Sometimes we too lose our cattle. Jackals or cheetahs may carry them off, but sometimes it is just theft from over in the next village, and then we will know who has done it. Our priest at the temple can see in the camphor flame the face of the thief, and when he is caught . . .' He gestured with his hands a perfect mincing of meat.

The American watched his hands intently and said, 'I know what you mean. Chop something? Maybe I am holding you up and you want to chop wood? Where is your axe? Hand it to me and show me what to chop. I do enjoy it, you know, just a hobby. We get a lot of driftwood along the backwater near my house, and on Sundays I do nothing but chop wood for the fireplace. I really feel different when I watch the fire in the fireplace, although it may take all the sections of the Sunday *New York Times* to get a fire started,' and he smiled at this reference.

Muni felt totally confused but decided the best thing would be to make an attempt to get away from this place. He tried to edge out, saying, 'Must go home,' and turned to go. The other seized his shoulder and said desperately, 'Is there no one, absolutely no one here, to translate for me?' He looked up and down the road, which was deserted in

452

this hot afternoon. A sudden gust of wind churned up the dust and dead leaves on the roadside into a ghostly column and propelled it towards the mountain road. The stranger almost pinioned Muni's back to the statue and asked, 'Isn't this statue yours? Why don't you sell it to me?'

The old man now understood the reference to the horse, thought for a second, and said in his own language, 'I was an urchin this high when I heard my grandfather explain the story of this horse and warrior, and my grandfather himself was this high when he heard his grandfather, whose grandfather . . .'

The other man interrupted him with, 'I don't want to seem to have stopped here for nothing. I will offer you a good price for this,' he said, indicating the horse. He had concluded without the least doubt that Muni owned this mud horse. Perhaps he guessed by the way he sat at its pedestal, like other souvenir-sellers in this country presiding over their wares.

Muni followed the man's eyes and pointing fingers and dimly understood the subject matter and, feeling relieved that the theme of the mutilated body had been abandoned at least for the time being, said again, enthusiastically, 'I was this high when my grandfather told me about this horse and the warrior, and my grandfather was this high when he himself . . .' and he was getting into a deeper bog of remembering each time he tried to indicate the antiquity of the statue.

The Tamil that Muni spoke was stimulating even as pure sound, and the foreigner listened with fascination. 'I wish I had my tape-recorder here,' he said, assuming the pleasantest expression. 'Your language sounds wonderful. I get a kick out of every word you utter, here'—he indicated his ears—'but you don't have to waste your breath in sales talk. I appreciate the article. You don't have to explain its points.'

'I never went to a school, in those days only brahmins went to schools, but we had to go out and work in the fields morning till night, from sowing to harvest time . . . and when Pongal came and we had cut the harvest, my father allowed me to go out and play with others at the tank, and so I don't know the *Parangi* language you speak, even little fellows in your country probably speak the Parangi language, but here only learned men and officers know it. We had a postman in our village who could speak to you boldly in your language, but his wife ran away with someone and he does not speak to anyone at all nowadays. Who would, if a wife did what she did? Women must be watched; otherwise they will sell themselves and the home,' and he laughed at his own quip.

The foreigner laughed heartily, took out another cigarette, and offered it to Muni, who now smoked with ease, deciding to stay on if the fellow was going to be so good as to keep up his cigarette supply. The American now stood up on the pedestal in the attitude of a demonstrative lecturer and said, running his finger along some of the carved decorations around the horse's neck, speaking slowly and uttering his words syllable by syllable, 'I could give a sales talk for this better than anyone else . . . This is a marvellous combination of yellow and indigo, though faded now . . . How do you people of this country achieve these flaming colours?'

Muni, now assured that the subject was still the horse

and not the dead body, said, 'This is our guardian, it means death to our adversaries. At the end of Kali Yuga, this world and all other worlds will be destroyed, and the Redeemer will come in the shape of a horse called Kalki; then this horse will come to life and gallop and trample down all bad men.' As he spoke of bad men the figures of the shopman and his brother-in-law assumed concrete forms in his mind, and he revelled for a moment in the predicament of the fellow under the horse's hoof: served him right for trying to set fire to his home . . .

While he was brooding on this pleasant vision, the foreigner utilized the pause to say, 'I assure you that this will have the best home in the USA. I'll push away the bookcase, you know I love books and am a member of five book clubs, and the choice and bonus volumes really mount up to a pile in our living-room, as high as this horse itself. But they'll have to go. Ruth may disapprove, but I will convince her. The TV may have to be shifted too. We can't have everything in the living room. Ruth will probably say what about when we have a party? I'm going to keep him right in the middle of the room. I don't see how that can interfere with the party—we'll stand around him and have our drinks.'

Muni continued his description of the end of the world. 'Our pundit discoursed at the temple once how the oceans are going to close over the earth in a huge wave and swallow us—this horse will grow bigger than the biggest wave and carry on its back only the good people and kick into the floods the evil ones—plenty of them about,' he said reflectively. 'Do you know when it is going to happen?' he asked.

The foreigner now understood by the tone of the other that a question was being asked and said, 'How am I transporting it? I can push the seat back and make room in the rear. That van can take in an elephant'—waving precisely at the back of the seat.

Muni was still hovering on visions of avatars and said again, 'I never missed our pundit's discourses at the temple in those days during every bright half of the month, although he'd go on all night, and he told us that Vishnu is the highest god. Whenever evil men trouble us, he comes down to save us. He has come many times. The first time he incarnated as a great fish, and lifted the scriptures on his back when the floods and sea waves . . .'

'I am not a millionaire, but a modest businessman. My trade is coffee.'

Amidst all this wilderness of obscure sounds Muni caught the word 'coffee' and said, 'If you want to drink "kapi", drive further up, in the next town, they have Friday markets, and there they open "kapi-otels"—so I learn from passers-by. Don't think I wander about. I go nowhere and look for nothing.' His thoughts went back to the avatars. 'The first avatar was in the shape of a little fish in a bowl of water, but every hour it grew bigger and bigger and became in the end a huge whale which the seas could not contain, and on the back of the whale the holy books were supported, saved and carried.' Having launched on the first avatar it was inevitable that he should go on to the next, a wild boar on whose tusk the earth was lifted when a vicious conqueror of the earth carried it off and hid it at the bottom of the sea. After describing this avatar Muni concluded, 'God will always save us whenever we are

troubled by evil beings. When we were young we staged at
full moon the story of the avatars. That's how I know the
stories; we played them all night until the sun rose, and
sometimes the European collector would come to watch,
bringing his own chair. I had a good voice and so they
always taught me songs and gave me the women's roles. I
was always Goddess Laxmi, and they dressed me in a
brocade sari, loaned from the Big House . . .'

The foreigner said, 'I repeat I am not a millionaire.
Ours is a modest business; after all, we can't afford to buy
more than sixty minutes' TV time in a month, which works
out to two minutes a day, that's all, although in the course
of time we'll maybe sponsor a one-hour show regularly if
our sales graph continues to go up . . .'

Muni was intoxicated by the memory of his theatrical
days and was about to explain how he had painted his face
and worn a wig and diamond earrings when the visitor,
feeling that he had spent too much time already, said, 'Tell
me, will you accept a hundred rupees or not for the horse?
I'd love to take the whiskered soldier also but I've no space
for him this year. I'll have to cancel my air ticket and take
a boat home, I suppose. Ruth can go by air if she likes, but
I will go with the horse and keep him in my cabin all the
way if necessary,' and he smiled at the picture of himself
voyaging across the seas hugging this horse. He added, 'I
will have to pad it with straw so that it doesn't break . . .'

'When we played Ramayana, they dressed me as Sita,'
added Muni. 'A teacher came and taught us the songs for
the drama and we gave him fifty rupees. He incarnated
himself as Rama, and he alone could destroy Ravana, the
demon with ten heads who shook all the worlds; do you

know the story of Ramayana?'

'I have my station wagon as you see. I can push the seat back and take the horse in if you will just lend me a hand with it.'

'Do you know Mahabharata? Krishna was the eighth avatar of Vishnu, incarnated to help the Five Brothers regain their kingdom. When Krishna was a baby he danced on the thousand-hooded giant serpent and trampled it to death; and then he suckled the breasts of the demoness and left them flat as a disc though when she came to him her bosoms were large, like mounds of earth on the banks of a dug-up canal.' He indicated two mounds with his hands. The stranger was completely mystified by the gesture. For the first time he said, 'I really wonder what you are saying because your answer is crucial. We have come to the point when we should be ready to talk business.'

'When the tenth avatar comes, do you know where you and I will be?' asked the old man.

'Lend me a hand and I can lift off the horse from its pedestal after picking out the cement at the joints. We can do anything if we have a basis of understanding.'

At this stage the mutual mystification was complete, and there was no need even to carry on a guessing game at the meaning of words. The old man chattered away in a spirit of balancing off the credits and debits of conversational exchange, and said in order to be on the credit side, 'O honourable one, I hope God has blessed you with numerous progeny. I say this because you seem to be a good man, willing to stay beside an old man and talk to him, while all day I have none to talk to except when somebody stops by to ask for a piece of tobacco. But I seldom have it, tobacco is not what it used to be at one time, and I have given up chewing. I cannot afford it nowadays.' Noting the other's interest in his speech, Muni felt encouraged to ask, 'How many children have you?' with appropriate gestures with his hands. Realizing that a question was being asked, the red man replied, 'I said a hundred,' which encouraged Muni to go into details, 'How many of your children are boys and how many girls? Where are they? Is your daughter married? Is it difficult to find a son-in-law in your country also?'

In answer to these questions the red man dashed his hand into his pocket and brought forth his wallet in order to take immediate advantage of the bearish trend in the market. He flourished a hundred-rupee currency note and asked, 'Well, this is what I meant.'

The old man now realized that some financial element was entering their talk. He peered closely at the currency note, the like of which he had never seen in his life; he knew the five and ten by their colours although always in other people's hands, while his own earning at any time was in coppers and nickels. What was this man flourishing the note for? Perhaps asking for change. He laughed to himself at the notion of anyone coming to him for changing a thousand—or ten-thousand-rupee note. He said with a grin, 'Ask our village headman, who is also a moneylender; he can change even a lakh of rupees in gold sovereigns if you prefer it that way; he thinks nobody knows, but dig the floor of his puja room and your head will reel at the sight of the hoard. The man disguises himself in rags just to mislead the public. Talk to the headman yourself because he goes mad at the sight of me. Someone took away his pumpkins with the creeper and he, for some reason, thinks it was me and my goats . . . that's why I never let my goats be seen anywhere near the farms.' His eyes travelled to the goats nosing about, attempting to wrest nutrition from the minute greenery peeping out of rock and dry earth.

The foreigner followed his look and decided that it would be a sound policy to show an interest in the old man's pets. He went up casually to them and stroked their backs with every show of courteous attention. Now the truth dawned on the old man. His dream of a lifetime was about to be realized. He understood that the red man was actually making an offer for the goats. He had reared them up in the hope of selling them some day and, with the capital, opening a small shop on this very spot. Sitting here, watching the hills, he had often dreamt how he would put up a thatched roof here, spread a gunny sack out on the ground, and display on it fried nuts, coloured sweets and green coconut for the thirsty and famished wayfarers on the highway, which was sometimes very busy. The animals were not prize ones for a cattle show, but he had spent his occasional savings to provide them some fancy diet now and then, and they did not look too bad. While he was reflecting thus, the red man shook his hand and left on his palm one hundred rupees in tens now. 'It is all for you or you may share it if you have a partner.'

The old man pointed at the station wagon and asked, 'Are you carrying them off in that?'

'Yes, of course,' said the other, understanding the transportation part of it.

The old man said, 'This will be their first ride in a motor car. Carry them off after I get out of sight, otherwise they will never follow you, but only me even if I am travelling on the path to Yama Loka.' He laughed at his own joke, brought his palms together in a salute, turned around and went off, and was soon out of sight beyond a clump of thicket.

The red man looked at the goats grazing peacefully. Perched on the pedestal of the horse, as the westerly sun touched the ancient faded colours of the statue with a fresh splendour, he ruminated, 'He must be gone to fetch some help, I suppose!' and settled down to wait. When a truck came downhill, he stopped it and got the help of a couple of men to detach the horse from its pedestal and place it in his station wagon. He gave them five rupees each, and for a further payment they siphoned off gas from the trucks and helped him to start his engine.

Muni hurried homeward with the cash securely tucked away at his waist in his *dhoti*. He shut the street door and stole up softly to his wife as she squatted before the lit oven wondering if by a miracle food would drop from the sky. Muni displayed his fortune for the day. She snatched the notes from him, counted them by the glow of the fire, and cried, 'One hundred rupees! How did you come by it? Have you been stealing?'

'I have sold our goats to a red-faced man. He was absolutely crazy to have them, gave me all this money and carried them off in his motor car!'

Hardly had these words left his lips when they heard bleating outside. She opened the door and saw the two goats at her door. 'Here they are!' she said. 'What's the meaning of all this?'

He muttered a great curse and seized one of the goats by its ear and shouted, 'Where is that man? Don't you know you are his? Why did you come back?' The goat only wriggled in his grip. He asked the same question of the other too. The goat shook itself off. His wife glared at him and declared, 'If you have thieved, the police will come tonight and break your bones. Don't involve me. I will go away to my parents . . .'

462

A BREATH OF LUCIFER

Prologue

Nature has so designed us that we are compelled to spend at least eight hours out of twenty-four with eyes shut in sleep or in an attempt to sleep. It is a compensatory arrangement, perhaps, for the strain the visual faculty undergoes during our waking hours, owing to the glut of images impinging upon it morning till night. One who seeks serenity should, I suppose, voluntarily restrict one's range of vision. For it is mostly through the eye that the mind is strained or disturbed. Man sees more than what is necessary or good for him. If one does not control one's vision, nature will do it for one sooner or later.

Unnoticed, little by little, my right eye had been growing dimmer in the course of a year or two. I felt annoyed by the presence of a smudge of oil on the lens of my spectacles, which I pulled out and wiped with a handkerchief every other minute. When I tried to read, the smudge appeared on the first line and travelled down line by line, and it also touched up the faces of friends and foes alike whenever I happened to examine a photograph. As I raised my eyes the blot also lifted itself upward. It grew in circumference. I couldn't watch a movie without noticing an unseemly mole on the star's much prized face. No amount of cleaning of my spectacle lens was any use.

My eye doctor, after a dark-room test, pronounced that the spot was not on my spectacle lens but in the God-given lens of the eye itself, which was losing its transparency. He recorded it for my comfort on a piece of paper as 'Lentil Opacity,' to be remedied by means of a simple operation in due course.

Everyone speaks of the simplicity of the operation. It's simple in the sense that it is painless, accomplished without bloodshed. But to the surgeon it is a delicate and responsible task, demanding the utmost concentration of his powers at his fingertips, which will have to hover with the lightness of a butterfly over the patient's eye while detaching a tiny opalescent piece from its surface.

After the operation, total immobility in a state of total blackout for nearly a week, with both eyes sealed up with a bandage; not even the faintest ray of light may pass this barrier. The visual world is shut off. At first I dreaded the prospect. It seemed an inhuman condition of existence. But actually it turned out to be a novel experience. To observe nothing. To be oblivious of the traffic beneath my window, and of the variety of noise-makers passing up and down. I only hear the sound of the traffic but feel no irritation. Perhaps such irritations are caused as much by the sight of the irritant as by its decibel value. When you have no chance of observing the traffic, you cease to bother about it. A soundproof room may not be the only way to attain tranquillity— a bandage over one's eyes may achieve the same result. I never notice the weather, another source of despair, dismay, disappointment, or ecstasy for everyone at all times. I never know whether it is cloudy or sunny outside my window; when it rains I relish the patter of raindrops and the coolness without being aware of the slush and mess of a rain-sodden landscape. I am blissfully free alike from elation as from fury or despair. The joy stimulated by one experience could be as fatiguing as the despair caused by another. I hear words and accept them without any reservation as I am unaware of the accompanying facial expression or gesture which normally modulates the spoken word. In this state, in which one accepts the word absolutely, human relationships become suddenly simplified. For this same reason, I think, the yogis of yore advocated as a first step (and a final step also) in any technique of self-development the unwavering concentration of one's eyes on the tip of one's nose. Mahatma Gandhi himself advised a youth whose heart was constantly agitated by the sight of women to walk with his eyes fixed on his toe, or on the stars above.

When the outside world is screened off thus, one's vision turns immediately inward. In the depths of one's being (according to the terms of philosophers and mystics) or in the folds of one's brain (according to physiologists and psychologists) there is a memory-spot for every faculty. 'Music when soft voices die, vibrates in the memory,' said Shelley. One can recollect the fragrance of a bygone flower or a perfume, the softness of a touch. Similarly there is a visual memory too, which revives in all its sharpness under some extraordinary stimulus. The visual memory brings forth something not only seen and cherished but also wished for. My interests, let me confess, broadly speaking, are archaeological and geological. All my life I have been excessively fond of rocks, monuments, and ancient sculptures. I can never pass by a rock formation indifferently, or an old temple or a monument. So I now watch through my bandaged eyes night and day breathtaking friezes, cornices, pillars, and carvings, countless numbers of them, as on a slow-moving platform, as if one were present at the stone-cluttered yard of a superhuman sculptor. Sometimes I see a goddess enthroned on a lotus seat in a corner, and not far from her is a formless slab smoothed out by time, but faint etchings, possibly edicts of some ancient emperor, are still visible on it. A closer scrutiny reveals that this whole setting is not actually a corner—there is no corner, no direction, east, west, south, or north; it is a spot without our familiar spatial relationships.

Strangely, my visual memory does not present to me any white walls or bright ceilings. Every surface is grey and ancient, as if centuries of the burning of lamps have left congealed layers of holy oil on every surface. Sometimes I am enmeshed in a jumble of chariot wheels, crowns without heads, maces, and fragments of a dilapidated throne; suddenly this jumble sorts itself out and forms into a single regal figure standing on its feet, spanning the ground and the sky. Presently all this melts out of view. The floor is strewn with sawn-off timber, and a lot of grim metallic artefacts, perhaps the leftovers of an ancient torture chamber. A fantastic contrast occurs presently—an endless billowing stretch of tarpaulin or canvas envelops the whole landscape, such enormous billows that I wonder how I can take a step forward without getting enmeshed in them. Now I find myself in a corridor of an ageless cave-temple. Although I am supposed to remain in the dark I find a subdued, serene light illuminating every object and corner softly for me, a light that throws no shadow. Nothing looks fearsome or unpleasant. Everything is in harmony with everything else and has a pleasant quality all its own. Even an occasional specimen of fauna, a tiger in shape but with the face of an angel— it is not clear what creature is represented—smoothly glides past me, throwing a friendly smile at me.

Reality is of the moment and where we are. The immediate present possesses a convincing solid quality; all else is mere recollection or anticipation. This room with the bed on which I lie day and night is very real to me. With all the spectacle that passes before me, other things seem remote and dreamlike. The present rhythm of my life is set by a routine from morning at six (as I guess from the hawkers' voices in the street), when I summon my attendant (whose company and conversation have inspired me to write the accompanying story), till the night, when I am put to bed with the announcement by the same attendant, 'Light is shut off, sir,' punctuated by the arrivals and departures of the doctors' team and visitors who bring me news of the unreal world in which they live. Within the confines of this existence I feel snug and contented. Its routines are of the utmost importance to me. I am so much at home within it that I suspect I shall feel a regret when it ends.

March 1969   *R.K.N.*

SAM WAS ONLY a voice to me, a rich, reverberating baritone. His whispers themselves possessed a solid, rumbling quality. I often speculated, judging from his voice, what he might look like: the possessor of such a voice could be statuesque, with curls falling on his nape, Roman nose, long legs able to cover the distance from my bed to the bathroom in three strides although to me it seemed an endless journey. I asked him on the very first day, 'What do you look like?'

'How can I say? Several years since I looked at a mirror!'

'Why so?'

'The women at home do not give us a chance, that is all. I have even to shave without a mirror.' He added, 'Except once when I came up against a large looking glass at a tailor's and cried out absent-mindedly, "Ah, Errol Flynn in town!" '

'You admired Errol Flynn?'

'Who wouldn't? As Robin Hood, unforgettable; I saw the picture fifty times.'

'What do you look like?'

He paused and answered, 'Next week this time you will see for yourself; be patient till the bandages are taken off . . .'

Sam had taken charge of my bodily self the moment I was wheeled out of the operation theatre at the Malgudi Eye Clinic in New Extension with my eyes padded, bandaged, and sealed. I was to remain blindfolded for nearly a week in bed. During this confinement Sam was engaged for eight rupees a day to act as my eyes.

He was supposed to be a trained 'male nurse,' a term which he abhorred, convinced that nursing was a man's job and that the female in the profession was an impostor. He assumed a defiant and challenging pose whenever the sister at the nursing home came into my room. When she left he always had a remark to make, 'Let this lady take charge of a skull-injury case; I will bet the patient will never see his home again.'

Sam had not started life as a male nurse, if one might judge from his references. He constantly alluded to military matters, commands, campaigns, fatigue duties, and parades. What he actually did in the army was never clear to me. Perhaps if I could have watched his facial expressions and gestures I might have understood or interpreted his words differently, but in my unseeing state I had to accept literally whatever I heard. He often spoke of a colonel who had discovered his talent and encouraged and trained him in nursing. That happened somewhere on the Burma border, Indo-China, or somewhere, when their company was cut off and the medical units completely destroyed. The colonel had to manage with a small band of survivors, the most active among them being Sam, who repaired and rehabilitated the wounded and helped them return home almost intact when the war ended. Which war was it? Where was it fought? Against whom? I could never get an answer to those questions. He always spoke of 'the enemy', but I never understood who it was since Sam's fluency could not be interrupted for a clarification. I had to accept what I heard without question. Before they parted, the colonel composed a certificate which helped Sam in his career. 'I have framed it and hung it in my house beside Jesus,' he said.

At various theatres of war (again, which war I could

never know) his services were in demand, mainly in surgical cases. Sam was not much interested in the physician's job. He had mostly been a surgeon's man. He only spoke of incidents where he had to hold up the guts of someone until the surgeon arrived, of necks half severed, arms amputated, and all aspects of human disjointedness and pain handled without hesitancy or failure. He asserted, 'My two hands and ten fingers are at the disposal of anyone who needs them in war or peace.'

'What do you earn out of such service?' I asked.

He replied, 'Sometimes ten rupees a day, five, two, or nothing. I have eight children, my wife, and two sisters and a niece depending on me, and all of them have to be fed, clothed, sent to schools, and provided with books and medicines. We somehow carry on. God gives me enough. The greater thing for me is the relief that I am able to give anyone in pain . . . Oh, no, do not get up so fast. Not good for you. Don't try to swat that mosquito buzzing at your ear. You may jam your eye. I am here to deal with the mosquito. Hands down, don't put up your hand near your eyes.' He constantly admonished me, ever anxious lest I should by some careless act suffer a setback.

He slept in my room, on a mat a few feet away from my bed. He said that he woke up at five in the morning, but it could be any time since I had no means of verifying his claim by a watch or by observing the light on the walls. Night and day and all days of the week were the same to me. Sam explained that although he woke up early he lay still, without making the slightest noise, until I stirred in bed and called, 'Sam!'

'Good morning, sir,' he answered with alacrity and

added, 'Do not try to get up yet.' Presently he came over
and tucked up the mosquito net with scrupulous care.
'Don't get up yet,' he ordered and moved off. I could hear
him open the bathroom door. Then I noticed his steps move
farther off as he went in to make sure that the window
shutters were secure and would not fly open and hit me in
the face when I got in and fumbled about. After clearing all
possible impediments in my way, he came back and said,
'Righto, sir, now that place is yours, you may go in safely.
Get up slowly. Where is the hurry? Now edge out of your
bed, the floor is only four inches below your feet. Slide
down gently, hold my hand, here it is . . .' Holding both my
hands in his, he walked backward and led me triumphantly
to the bathroom, remarking along the way, 'The ground is
level and plain, walk fearlessly . . .'

With all the assurance that he attempted to give me, the
covering over my eyes subjected me to strange tricks of
vision and made me nervous at every step. I had a feeling
of passing through geological formations, chasms, and
canyons or billowing mounds of cotton wool, tarpaulin, or
heaps of smithy junk or an endless array of baffle walls one
beside another. I had to move with caution. When we
reached the threshold of the bathroom he gave me precise
directions: 'Now move up a little to your left. Raise your
right foot, and there you are. Now you do anything here.
Only don't step back. Turn on your heel, if you must. That
will be fine.' Presently, when I called, he re-entered the
bathroom with a ready compliment on his lips: 'Ah, how
careful and clean! I wish some people supposed to be
endowed with full vision could leave a WC as tidy! Often,
after they have been in, the place will be fit to be burnt

down! However, my business in life is not to complain but to serve.' He then propelled me to the washbasin and handed me the toothbrush. 'Do not brush so fast. May not be good for your eyes. Now stop. I will wash the brush. Here is the water for rinsing. Ready to go back?'

'Yes, Sam!'

He turned me round and led me back towards my bed. 'You want to sit on your bed or in the chair?' he asked at the end of our expedition. While I took time to decide, he suggested, 'Why not the chair? You have been in bed all night. Sometimes I had to mind the casualties until the stretcher-bearers arrived, and I always said to the boys, "Lying in bed makes a man sick, sit up, sit up as long as you can hold yourselves together." While we had no sofas in the jungle, I made them sit and feel comfortable on anything, even on a snake-hole once, after flattening the top.'

'Where did it happen? Did you say Burma?' I asked as he guided me to the cane chair beside the window.

He at once became cautious. 'Burma? Did I say Burma? If I mentioned Burma I must have meant it and not the desert—'

'Which campaign was it?'

'Campaign? Oh, so many, I may not remember. Anyway it was a campaign and we were there. Suppose I fetch you my diary tomorrow? You can look through it when your eyes are all right again, and you will find in it all the answers.'

'Oh! That will be very nice indeed.'

'The colonel gave me such a fat, leather-bound diary, which cost him a hundred rupees in England, before he left, saying, "Sam, put your thoughts into it and all that you see and do, and some day your children will read the pages and feel proud of you." How could I tell the colonel that I could not write or read too well? My father stopped my education when I was that high, and he devoted more time to teach me how to know good toddy from bad.'

'Oh, you drink?' I asked.

'Not now. The colonel whipped me once when he saw me drunk, and I vowed I'd never touch it again,' he added as an afterthought while he poured coffee for me from the thermos flask (which he filled by dashing out to a coffee-house in the neighbourhood; it was amazing with what speed he executed these exits and entrances, although to reach the coffee-house he had to run down a flight of steps, past a veranda on the ground floor, through a gate beyond a drive, and down the street; I didn't understand how he managed it all as he was always present when I called him, and had my coffee ready when I wanted it). He handed me the cup with great care, guiding my fingers around the handle with precision. While I sipped the coffee I could hear him move around the bed, tidying it up. 'When the doctor comes he must find everything neat. Otherwise he will think that a donkey has been in attendance in this ward.' He swept and dusted. He took away the coffee cup, washed it at the sink and put it away, and kept the toilet flush hissing and roaring by repeated pulling of the chain. Thus he set the stage for the doctor's arrival. When the sound of the wheels of the bandage-trolley was heard far off, he helped me back to my bed and stationed himself at the door. When footsteps approached, the baritone greeted: 'Good morning, Doctor sir.'

The doctor asked, 'How is he today?'

'Slept well. Relished his food. No temperature. Conditions normal, Doctor sir.' I felt the doctor's touch on my brow as he untied the bandage, affording me for a tenth of a second a blurred view of assorted faces over me; he examined my eye, applied drops, bandaged again, and left. Sam followed him out as an act of courtesy and came back to say, 'Doctor is satisfied with your progress. I am happy it is so.'

Occasionally I thumbed a little transistor radio, hoping for some music, but turned it off the moment a certain shrill voice came on the air rendering 'film hits'; but I always found the tune continuing in a sort of hum for a minute or two after the radio was put away. Unable to judge the direction of the voice or its source, I used to feel puzzled at first. When I understood, I asked, 'Sam, do you sing?'

The humming ceased. 'I lost practice long ago,' he said, and added, 'When I was at Don Bosco's, the bishop used to encourage me. I sang in the church choir, and also played the harmonium at concerts. We had our dramatic troupe too and I played Lucifer. With my eyebrows painted and turned up, and with a fork at my tail, the bishop often said that never a better Lucifer was seen anywhere; and the public appreciated my performance. In our story the king was a good man, but I had to get inside him and poison his nature. The princess was also pure but I had to spoil her heart and make her commit sins.' He chuckled at the memory of those days.

He disliked the nurse who came on alternate days to give me a sponge bath. Sam never approved of the idea. He said, 'Why can't I do it? I have bathed typhoid patients running one hundred and seven degrees—'

'Oh, yes, of course.' I had to pacify him. 'But this is different, a very special training is necessary for handling an eye patient.'

When the nurse arrived with hot water and towels he would linger on until she said unceremoniously, 'Out you go, I am in a hurry.' He left reluctantly. She bolted the door, seated me in a chair, helped me off with my clothes, and ran a steaming towel over my body, talking all the time of herself, her ambition in life to visit her brother in East Africa, of her three children in school, and so forth.

When she left I asked Sam, 'What does she look like?'

'Looks like herself all right. Why do you want to bother about her? Leave her alone. I know her kind very well.'

'Is she pretty?' I asked persistently, and added, 'At any rate I can swear that her voice is sweet and her touch silken.'

'Oh! Oh!' he cried. 'Take care!'

'Even the faint garlic flavour in her breath is very pleasant, although normally I hate garlic.'

'These are not women you should encourage,' he said. 'Before you know where you are, things will have happened. When I played Lucifer, Marie, who took the part of the king's daughter, made constant attempts to entice me whenever she got a chance. I resisted her stoutly, of course; but once when our troupe was camping out, I found that she had crept into my bed at night. I tried to push her off, but she whispered a threat that she would yell at the top of her voice that I had abducted her. What could I do with such a one!' There was a pause, and he added, 'Even after we returned home from the camp she pursued me, until one day my wife saw what was happening and gashed her face with her fingernails. That taught the slut a lesson.'

'Where is Marie these days?' I asked.

He said, 'Oh! she is married to a fellow who sells raffle tickets, but I ignore her whenever I see her at the market gate helping her husband.'

When the sound of my car was heard outside, he ran to the window to announce, 'Yes sir, they have come.' This would be the evening visit from my family, who brought me my supper. Sam would cry from the window, 'Your brother is there and that good lady his wife also. Your daughter is there and her little son. Oh! What a genius he is going to be! I can see it in him now. Yes, yes, they will be here in a minute now. Let me keep the door open.' He arranged the chairs. Voices outside my door, Sam's voice overwhelming the rest with: 'Good evening, madame. Good evening, sir. Oh! You little man! Come to see your grandfather! Come, come nearer and say hello to him. You must not shy away from him.' Addressing me, he would say, 'He is terrified of your beard, sir,' and, turning back to the boy, 'He will be all right when the bandage is taken off. Then he is going to have a shave and a nice bath, not the sponge bath he is now having, and then you will see how grand your grandfather can be!' He then gave the visitors an up-to-the-minute account of the state of my recovery. He would also throw in a faint complaint. 'He is not very cooperative. Lifts his hands to his eyes constantly, and will not listen to my advice not to exert.' His listeners would comment on this, which would provoke a further comment in the great baritone, the babble maddening to one not able to watch faces and sort out the speakers, until I implored, 'Sam, you can retire for a while and leave us. I can call you later'— thus giving me a chance to have a word with my visitors. I had to assume that he took my advice and departed. At least I did not hear him again until they were ready to leave, when he said, 'Please do not fail to bring the washed clothes tomorrow. Also, the doctor has asked him to eat fruits. If you could find apples—' He carried to the car the vessels brought by them and saw them off.

After their departure he would come and say, 'Your brother, sir, looks a mighty officer. No one can fool him, very strict he must be, and I dare not talk to him. Your daughter is devoted to you, no wonder, if she was motherless and brought up by you. That grandson! Watch my words, some day he is going to be like Nehru. He has that bearing now. Do you know what he said when I took him out for a walk? "If my grandfather does not get well soon I will shoot you."' And he laughed at the memory of that pugnacious remark.

We anticipated with the greatest thrill the day on which the bandages would be taken off my eyes. On the eve of the memorable day Sam said, 'If you don't mind, I will arrange a small celebration. This is very much like the New Year's Eve. You must sanction a small budget for the ceremony, about ten rupees will do. With your permission—' He put his hand in and extracted the purse from under my pillow. He asked for an hour off and left. When he returned I heard him place bottles on the table.

'What have you there?' I asked.

'Soft drinks, orange, Coca-Cola, this also happens to be

my birthday. I have bought cake and candles, my humble contribution for this grand evening.' He was silent and busy for a while and then began a running commentary: 'I'm now cutting the cake, blowing out the candles—'

'How many?'

'I couldn't get more than a dozen, the nearby shop did not have more.'

'Are you only twelve years old?'

He laughed, handed me a glass. 'Coca-Cola, to your health. May you open your eyes on a happy bright world—'

'And also on your face!' I said. He kept filling my glass and toasting to the health of all humanity. I could hear him gulp down his drink again and again. 'What are you drinking?'

'Orange or Coca-Cola, of course.'

'What is the smell?'

'Oh, that smell! Someone broke the spirit lamp in the next ward.'

'I heard them leave this evening!'

'Yes, yes, but just before they left they broke the lamp. I assured them, "Don't worry. I'll clean up." That's the smell on my hands. After all, we must help each other—' Presently he distributed the cake and burst into a song or two: '*He's a jolly good fellow*,' and then, '*The more we are together*—' in a stentorian voice. I could also hear his feet tapping away a dance.

After a while I felt tired and said, 'Sam, give me supper. I feel sleepy.'

After the first spell of sleep I awoke in the middle of the night and called, 'Sam.'

'Yes, sir,' he said with alacrity.

'Will you lead me to the bathroom?'

'Yes, sir.' The next moment he was at my bed, saying, 'Sit up, edge forward, two inches down to your feet; now left, right, left, march, left, right, right turn.' Normally, whenever I described the fantastic things that floated before my bandaged eyes he would reply, 'No, no, no wall, nor a pillar. No junk either, trust me and walk on—' But today when I said, 'You know why I have to walk so slowly?—'

'I know, I know,' he said. 'I won't blame you. The place is cluttered.'

'I see an immense pillar in my way,' I said.

'With carvings,' he added. 'Those lovers again. These two figures! I see them. She is pouting her lips, and he is trying to chew them off, with his arm under her thigh. A sinful spectacle, that's why I gave up looking at sculptures!'

I tried to laugh it off and said, 'The bathroom.'

'The bathroom, the bathroom, that is the problem . . .' He paused and then said all of a sudden, 'The place is on fire.'

'What do you mean on fire?'

'I know my fire when I see one. I was Lucifer once. When I came on stage with fire in my nostrils, children screamed in the auditorium and women fainted. Lucifer has been breathing around. Let us go.' He took me by my hand and hurried me out in some direction.

At the veranda I felt the cold air of the night in my face and asked, 'Are we going out—?'

He would not let me finish my sentence. 'This is no place for us. Hurry up. I have a responsibility. I cannot let you perish in the fire.'

This was the first time I had taken a step outside the bedroom, and I really felt frightened and cried, 'Oh! I feel we are on the edge of a chasm or a cavern, I can't walk.' And he said, 'Softly, softly. Do not make all that noise. I see the tiger's tail sticking out of the cave.'

'Are you joking?'

He didn't answer but gripped my shoulder and led me on. I did not know where we were going. At the stairhead he commanded, 'Halt, we are descending, now your right foot down, there, there, good, now bring the left one, only twenty steps to go.' When I had managed it without stumbling, he complimented me on my smartness.

Now a cold wind blew in my face, and I shivered. I asked, 'Are we inside or outside?' I heard the rustle of tree leaves. I felt the gravel under my bare feet. He did not bother to answer my question. I was taken through a maze of garden paths, and steps. I felt bewildered and exhausted. I suddenly stopped dead in my tracks and demanded, 'Where are you taking me?' Again he did not answer. I said, 'Had we better not go back to my bed?'

He remained silent for a while to consider my proposal and agreed, 'That might be a good idea, but dangerous. They have mined the whole area. Don't touch anything you see, stay here, don't move, I will be back.' He moved off. I was seized with panic when I heard his voice recede. I heard him sing *'He's a jolly good fellow, He's a jolly good fellow,'* followed by *'Has she got lovely cheeks? Yes, she has lovely cheeks,'* which was reassuring as it meant that he was still somewhere around.

I called out, 'Sam.'

He answered from afar, 'Coming, but don't get up yet.'

'Sam, Sam,' I pleaded, 'let me get back to my bed. Is it really on fire?'

He answered, 'Oh, no, who has been putting ideas into your head? I will take you back to your bed, but please give me time to find the way back. There has been foul play and our retreat is cut off, but please stay still and no one will spot you.' His voice still sounded far off.

I pleaded desperately, 'Come nearer.' I had a feeling of being poised over a void. I heard his approaching steps.

'Yes, sir, what is your command?'

'Why have you brought me here?' I asked.

He whispered, 'Marie, she had promised to come, should be here any minute.' He suddenly cried out, 'Marie, where are you?' and mumbled, 'She came into your room last night and the night before, almost every night. Did she disturb you? No. She is such a quiet sort, you would never have known. She came in when I put out the light, and left at sunrise. You are a good officer, have her if you like.'

I could not help remarking, 'Didn't your wife drive her away?'

Promptly came his reply: 'None of her business. How dare she interfere in my affairs? If she tries . . .' He could not complete the sentence, the thought of his wife having infuriated him. He said, 'That woman is no good. All my troubles are due to her.'

I pleaded, 'Sam, take me to my bed.'

'Yes, sir,' he said with alacrity, took my hand, and led me a few steps and said, 'Here is your bed,' and gave me a gentle push down until I sank at my knee and sat on the ground. The stones pricked me, but that seemed better than standing on my feet. He said, 'Well, blanket at your feet.

480

Call out "Sam," I am really not far, not really sleeping .
. Good night, good night, I generally pray and then sleep,
no, I won't really sleep. "Sam," one word will do, one word
will do . . . will do . . .' I heard him snore, he was sound
asleep somewhere in the enormous void. I resigned myself
to my fate. I put out my hand and realized that I was beside
a bush, and I only hoped that some poisonous insect would
not sting me. I was seized with all sorts of fears.

The night was spent thus. I must have fallen into a
drowse, awakened at dawn by the bird-noises around. A
woman took my hand and said, 'Why are you here?'

'Marie?' I asked.

'No, I sweep and clean your room every morning,
before the others come.'

I only said, 'Lead me to my bed.'

She did not waste time on questions. After an endless
journey she said, 'Here is your bed, sir, lie down.'

I suffered a setback, and the unbandaging was postponed.
The doctor struggled and helped me out of a variety of
ailments produced by shock and exposure. A fortnight later
the bandages were taken off, but I never saw Sam again.
Only a postcard addressed to the clinic several days later:

'I wish you a speedy recovery. I do not know what
happened that night. Some foul play, somewhere. The rogue
who brought me the Coca-Cola must have drugged the
drink. I will deal with him yet. I pray that you get well.
After you go home, if you please, send me a money order
for Rs 48/-. I am charging you for only six days and not for
the last day. I wish I could meet you, but my colonel has
summoned me to Madras to attend on a leg amputation.

—Sam.'

UNCLE

I AM THE monarch of all I survey, being the sole occupant of this rambling ancient house in Vinayak Street. I am five-ten, too huge for the easy chair on which I am reclining now. But I remember the time when I could hardly reach the arm of this easy chair. I remember the same chair at the same spot in the hall, with some ancient portrait hanging on a nail over it, with my uncle comfortably lounging and tormenting me by pushing his glittering snuffbox just out of my reach. While trying to reach for it I tumbled down again and again; he emitted a loud guffaw each time I lost my balance and sprawled on the floor. I felt frightened by his loud laughter and whined and cried. At that moment my aunt would scoop down on me and carry me off to the kitchen, set me down in a conrer, and place before me a little basin filled with water, which I splashed about. I needed no further attention except a replenishment of water from time to time. I also watched with wonderment the smoke curling up from the oven when the lady puffed her cheeks and blew on the fire through a hollow bamboo pipe. The spell would suddenly be broken when she picked me up

again, with a bowl of rice in her hand, and carried me off
to the street door. She would carefully seat me on the *pyol*
of the house, my back supported against the slender pillars,
and try to feed me. If I averted my head she gripped my
neck as in a vise and forced the rice between my lips. If I
howled in protest she utilized the chance to thrust more rice
into my open mouth. If I spat it out she would point at a
passer-by and say, 'See that demon, he will carry you off.
He is on the lookout for babies who won't eat.' At that
stage I must have faced the risk of dying of over-rather than
under-feeding. Later in the day she would place a dish of
eatables before me and watch me deal with it. When I
turned the dish over on the floor and messed up the
contents, Uncle and Aunt drew each other's attention to
this marvellous spectacle and nearly danced around me in
joy. In those days my uncle, though portly as ever, possessed
greater agility, I believe.

My uncle stayed at home all day. I was too young to
consider what he did for a living. The question never
occurred to me until I was old enough to sit on a school
bench and discuss life's problems with a class fellow. I was
studying in the first year at Albert Mission School. Our
teacher had written on the blackboard a set of words such
as Man, Dog, Cat, Mat, Taj and Joy, and had asked us to
copy them down on our slates and take them to him for
correction and punishment if necessary. I had copied four
of the six terms and had earned the teacher's approbation.
The boy in the next seat had also done well. Our duties for
the hour were over, and that left us free to talk, in subdued
whispers, though.

'What is your father's name?' he asked.

'I don't know. I call him Uncle.'

'Is he rich?' the boy asked.

'I don't know,' I replied. 'They make plenty of sweets at home.'

'Where does he work?' asked the boy, and the first thing I did when I went home, even before flinging off my books and school bag, was to ask loudly, 'Uncle, where is your office?'

He replied, 'Up above,' pointing heavenward, and I looked up.

'Are you rich?' was my second question.

My aunt emerged from the kitchen and dragged me in, saying, 'Come, I have some very lovely things for you to eat.'

I felt confused and asked my aunt, 'Why won't Uncle . . .?' She merely covered my mouth with her palm and warned, 'Don't talk of all that.'

'Why?' I asked.

'Uncle doesn't like to be asked questions.'

'I will not ask hereafter,' I said and added, 'Only that Suresh, he is a bad boy and he said . . .'

'Hush,' she said.

My world was circumscribed by the boundaries of our house in Vinayak Street, and peopled by Uncle and Aunt mainly. I had no existence separately from my uncle. I clung to him all through the day. Mornings in the garden at the backyard, afternoons inside, and all evening on the front *pyol* of the house squatting beside him. When he prayed or meditated at midday I sat in front of him watching his face and imitating him. When he saw me mutter imaginary prayers with my eyes shut, he became ecstatic and cried aloud to my aunt in the kitchen, 'See this fellow, how well he prays! We must teach him some slokas. No doubt whatever, he is going to be a saint someday. What do you think?' When he prostrated to the gods in the puja room I too threw myself on the floor, encouraged by the compliments showered on me. He would stand staring at me until Aunt reminded him that his lunch was ready. When he sat down to eat I nestled close to him, pressing my elbow on his lap. Aunt would say, 'Move off, little man. Let Uncle eat in peace,' but he always countermanded her and said, 'Stay, stay.' After lunch he chewed betel leaves and areca nut, moved on to his bedroom, and stretched himself on his rosewood bench, with a small pillow under his head. Just when he fell into a doze I demanded, 'Tell me a story,' butting him with my elbow.

He pleaded, 'Let us both sleep. We may have wonderful dreams. After that I will tell you a story.'

'What dreams?' I would persist.

'Shut your eyes and don't talk, and you will get nice dreams.' And while I gave his advice a trial, he closed his eyes.

All too brief a trial. I cried, 'No, I don't see any dream yet. Tell me a story, Uncle.' He patted my head and murmured, 'Once upon a time . . .' with such a hypnotic effect that within a few minutes I fell asleep.

Sometimes I sought a change from the stories and involved him in a game. The bench on which he tried to sleep would be a mountain top, the slight gap between its edge and the wall a gorge with a valley below. I would crawl under the bench, lie on my back, and command, 'Now throw,' having first heaped at his side a variety of articles such as a flashligh without battery, a ping-pong bat, a sandalwood incense holder, a leather wallet, a coat hanger, empty bottles, a tiny stuffed cow, and several other items out of a treasure chest I possessed. And over went the most cherished objects—the more fragile the better for the game, for, in the cool semi-dark world under the bench and by the rules of the game, the possibility of a total annihilation of objects would be perfectly in order.

Ten days after first broaching the subject Suresh cornered me again when we were let off for an hour in the absence of our geography master. We were playing marbles. Suresh suddenly said, 'My father knows your uncle.'

I felt uneasy. But I had not learnt the need for circumspection and asked anxiously, 'What does he say about him?'

'Your uncle came from another country, a far-off place . . .'

'Oh, good, so?' I cried with happiness, feeling relieved that after all some good points about my uncle were emerging.

Suresh said, 'But he impersonated.'

'What is "impersonate"?' I asked.

He said, 'Something not so good. My mother and father were talking, and I heard them use the word.'

The moment I came home from school and flung off my bag my aunt dragged me to the well in the backyard and forced me to wash my hands and feet, although I squirmed and protested vehemently. Next I sat on the arm of my uncle's easy chair with a plate filled with delicacies, ever available under that roof, and ate under the watchful eye of my uncle. Nothing delighted him more than to eat or watch someone eat. 'What is the news in your school today?' he would ask.

'Know what happened, Uncle?' I swallowed a mouthful and took time to suppress the word 'impersonate', which kept welling up from the depths of my being, and invent a story. 'A bad boy from the Third B—big fellow—jabbed me with his elbow . . .'

'Did he? Were you hurt?'

'Oh, no, he came charging but I stepped aside and he banged his head against the wall, and it was covered with blood, and they caried him to the hospital.' My uncle uttered many cries of joy at the fate overtaking my adversary and induced me to develop the details, which always sounded gory.

When they let me go I bounced off to the street, where a gang awaited my arrival. We played marbles or kicked a rubber ball about with war cries and shouts, blissfully unaware of the passers-by and the traffic, until the street end melted into a blaze of luminous dust with the sun gone. We played until my uncle appeared at our doorway and announced, 'Time to turn in,' when we dispersed unceremoniously and noisily. Once again my aunt would want to give my hands and feet a scrubbing. 'How many times!' I protested, 'Won't I catch a cold at this rate?'

She just said, 'You have all the road dust on you now. Come on.' After dousing me she smeared sacred ash on my forehead and made me sit with my uncle in the back veranda of the house and recite holy verse. After which I picked up my school books and, under my uncle's supervision, read my lessons, both the tutor and the taught feeling exhausted at the end of it. By eight-thirty I would be fed and put to sleep in a corner of the hall, at the junction of the two walls where I felt most secure.

On Fridays we visited the little shrine at the end of our street. Rather an exciting outing for me, as we passed along brilliantly lit shops displaying banana bunches, coloured drinks, bottled peppermints, and red and yellow paper kites, every item seming to pulsate with an inner glow.

They both rose at five in the morning and moved about softly so as not to disturb me. The first thing in the day, my uncle drew water from the well for the family, and then watered the plants in the garden. I woke to the sound of the pulley creaking over the well and joined my uncle in the garden. In the morning light he looked like a magician. One asked for nothing more in life than to be up at that hour and watch brilliant eddying columns of water coming through little channels dug along the ground. The hydraulic engineering for the garden was my uncle's own. He had raised the ground beside the well to form a basin, and when he tipped a cauldron of water over it, the column ran down the slope and passed through to the plants according to his dictates. He controlled the supply of water at various stages with a little trowel in hand, with which he scooped up the mud and opened or blocked the water course. I floated little bits of straw or leaves, or picked up ants and helped them have a free swim along the current. Sometimes without my uncle's knowledge I scooped off the mud bank with my hands and diverted the water elsewhere.

I revelled in this world of mud, greens, slush and water, forgetting for the moment such things as homework and teachers. When the sun came over the walls of the house behind our garden, my uncle ended his operations, poured a great quantity of water over himself, and went in dripping, in search of a towel. When I tried to follow him in, my aunt brought out a bucket of hot water and gave me a bath beside the well. Soon I found myself in the puja room murmuring prayers.

A perpetual smell of incense and flowers hung about the puja room, which was actually an alcove in the kitchen where pictures of gods hung on the walls. I loved the pictures: the great god Krishna poised on the hood of a giant serpent; Vishnu, blue-coloured, seated on the back of Garuda, the divine eagle, gliding in space and watching us. As I watched the pictures my mind went off into fantastic speculations while my tongue recited holy verse. 'Was the eagle a sort of aeroplane for Vishnu? Lakshmi stands on lotus! How can anyone stand on a lotus flower without crushing it?' From the fireplace would come my aunt's voice, 'I don't hear you pray.' I would suppress my speculations and recite aloud, addressing the elephant-faced god, '*Gajananam bhutaganadi sevitam* . . .' for three minutes in Sanskrit. I always wanted to ask for its meaning, but if I paused my aunt would shout over the hissing of the frying pan (which, incidentally, was generating an enormously appetizing fragrance). 'Why have you stopped?' Now I would turn to the picture of Saraswati, the goddess of learning, as she sat on a rock with her peacock beside a cool shrubbery, and wonder at her ability to play the veena with one hand while turning the rosary with the other, still leaving two hands free, perhaps to pat the peacock. I would raise my voice and say, '*Saraswati namastubhyam*', which meant 'O goddess of learning, I bow to you,' or some such thing. I secretly added a personal request to this prayer. 'May you help me get through my school hours without being mauled by my teachers or other boys, may I get through this day unscathed.' Although my normal day at school was peaceful, I always approached it at the beginning of each day with dread. My teacher was unshaved and looked villainous. He frequently inhaled a pinch of snuff in the class and spoke in a grating voice, the snuff having ravaged his vocal cords, and he flourished a short, stubby cane menacingly at the whole class every now and then. I had never seen him attack anyone, but his gestures were frightening, and I sat on my bench shuddering lest he should turn in my direction and notice me.

My life was precisely organized by my uncle, and I had little time to waste. When I emerged from the puja I had to go straight to the kitchen and drink off a glass of milk. This would be an occasion for my aunt to comment on my dress or voice. She would suddenly bring her face close to mine and examine my eyes. 'What are you looking for?' I would ask, rearing my head, but she held it firmly between her palms and inspected until she was satisfied that there was no patch of dirt or swelling under my eyes. 'Oh, I was mistaken, nothing,' she would say with relief. 'Anyway, you have grown darker. You must not roast yourself in the sun so much. Why should they make you do all that drill in the sun?'

Next I passed into the jurisdiction of my uncle, who sat leaning against a pillar in the hall with eyes shut in meditation. He said, emerging from his trance, 'Boy, gather all your lessons for the day and put them in your bag. Have you sharpened your pencil? Cleaned your slate? Do you need anything?' In spite of my firm statement that I needed nothing, he came over, seized my school bag, peered into it, and probed its bottom with his fingers. It was surprising how lightly he could abandon his prayers, but he was perhaps an adept who could resume them at will, as his day was mostly divided between munching and meditation. He held up to the light a slate pencil in order to judge whether it could be used for just another day. He would sharpen its point on the stone floor, commenting, 'You must hold it here and write, and don't bite the end; this can be used for a week more.' It was painful to write with such a short stub; my thumb and forefinger became sore, and further, if my teacher noticed it he twisted my ear and snatched away the stub and made me stand on the bench as a punishment. I could not mention these problems explicitly, as I feared that my uncle might don his shirt and offer to visit my school in order to investigate. I had a secret anxiety lest he should ever appear in our school, as I thought that the boys might stand around and make fun of his girth. And so I had to manage with the stub as ordained. When he felt satisfied that I had used the pencil wisely, he would open his wooden cupboard, take out a lacquered casket with a dragon on its lid, and out of it a small cardboard box, and again from it a little package containing long slate pencils. he would take out a brand-new one and hesitate; guessing his intention, I would jump up and snatch it from his hand crying, 'Don't break it, I want it full-length.' Sometimes he gave it whole, sometimes he broke it into two saying, 'Half is long enough.' He then looked through my books page by page, and packed them securely back into the bag. He said from time to time, 'Little man, if you don't read your lessons properly you will never count for anything in life and no one will respect you. Do you understand?' 'Yes, Uncle,' I said, though not very clear in my mind as to what 'respect' meant.

One evening I came home announcing, 'They are going to photograph us in our school.' My uncle, who had been lounging in the easy chair, sprang to his feet and asked, 'Who? Who is going to photograph you?'

'My teacher's brother has a friend who has a camera and he is going to photograph us.'

'Only you or others also?'

'Our class alone, not even the B section will be allowed, although they asked to be photographed too.'

Uncle's face lit up with joy. He called Aunt and said, 'Did you hear, this young man is going to be photographed tomorrow. Dress him properly.'

Next day my uncle spent a lot of time selecting clothes for me, and my aunt gave a double rub to my face and groomed me. My uncle followed me about uttering several pieces of advice before letting me out. 'You must never scowl even if the sun hits you in the eyes. You must try to look pleasant. You know in those days only girls waiting to be married used to have their photos taken. Nowadays everyone is being photographed.'

When I came home from school that evening he asked anxiously, 'How did it go off?'

I flung away the school bag to its corner and said, 'No, nothing happened. He didn't come.'

'Who?'

'Our teacher's brother's friend,' I said. 'It seems his camera has broken down or something like that, and so—no photo.'

My uncle's face fell. Both of them had been waiting at the door to see me return triumphantly from the photographer. He murmured sympathetically, 'Don't worry about it, we will find another photographer; only I thought you should not have taken out the blue shirt until Deepavali—never mind; we will buy you a new one for the festival.'

My aunt said, 'We could fold the shirt neatly and put it away until Deepavali. He has not soiled it.'

'I sat very quietly today lest the clothes should be spoilt,' I said, which was a fact. I had refused to play with my friends for fear that my shirt might get crumpled. This blue shirt was of a special kind; my uncle had bought the cloth from a street hawker, who assured him that the fabric was foreign and could not normally be acquired except through smugglers operating in certain coastal villages. Uncle bought three yards of the blue cloth after a whole afternoon's haggling, and planned to stitch shirts for me and himself. He had sent for an old Muslim tailor who had the original Singer sewing machine set up on the *pyol* of a house in Kabir Lane. He behaved extremely deferentially before my uncle and would not be seated even on the floor. My uncle relaxed in his easy chair and my aunt stood at the kitchen doorway and both discussed with the tailor various matters relating to persons, times, and places which sounded remote and incomprehensible to me. He kept addressing my uncle as his saviour at the end of every sentence, and salaamed him. When the time came to take measurements my uncle stood very erect and muttered numerous instructions as to the length, cut, and number and kind (unbreakable, tin) of buttons that he favoured, and so forth. 'Note the measurements down properly,' he said sternly several times, 'lest you should forget and make a mistake; it is a rare kind of cloth, not obtainable in our country; can't afford to take chances with it, remember.'

The tailor in answer avowed again his indebtedness to my uncle. 'On the road that day if you had not—' he began.

My uncle looked embarrassed and cut him short with, 'Don't go on with all those grandmother's stories now. The past is past, remember.'

'How can I help it, sir? Every morning I and my children think of you and pray for your welfare. When they gave me up for dead with vultures circling above and passed on, you stopped by and revived me, sir, although you had this baby in your arms . . . and you gave me the strength to walk a thousand miles over mountain passes . . .'

My uncle said curtly, 'Why don't you take the measurements?'

'I obey,' said the tailor immediately, and proceeded to measure me. He was not only deferential but also patronizing in his tone. 'Stand up, little master, otherwise you will blame this old man for any mistake that may occur. See how your venerable uncle stands erect at his age!'

He completed the measurements, noted them on a very small roll of paper, probably the torn-off margin of a newspaper, with a stubby pencil which he always carried over his ear, and departed after accepting all the advice given as they kept saying, 'Remember he is a growing boy, make allowance for that; don't want him to feel suffocated in his new shirt after the first wash . . .'

The tailor left after uttering the only word of protest, 'If master had bought just a quarter yard more . . .'

'Not at all necessary,' said my uncle. 'I know how much is needed, seeing that you are going to give me short arms, and no collar is wanted . . .' The shirts came back stitched in due course and were laid away in the big trunk.

Next evening I came home gleefully announcing, 'We were photographed today.'

'Indeed!' cried my uncle. 'How stupid of them when you were not ready for it!'

'Does it mean that you are going to look like this in the photo?' asked my aunt.

'It will not do justice to you,' said my uncle. 'They should have given us at least half an hour's notice, and then you could have . . .'

'Our teacher suddenly said, "Come out, all of you, and stand in a line under the tree." We marched out. A man came with a small camera, lined up all the tall boys first and all the short ones in the second line with our teachers in the centre; and then he cried, 'Stand steady, don't move,' and it was over. Our teacher has promised to give a photo to whoever brings two rupees from home.'

'Two rupees!' repeated my uncle aghast.

Aunt said, 'Never mind, it is the child's first photo.'

'I thought the class would be let off after the photo, but we were marched back for geography lessons.'

My uncle thurst two rupees into my pocket before I left for school next day, cautioning me, 'Take it carefully to your teacher.' He sounded anxious lest I should drop the money or get robbed on the way. He stood on the front step and watched me go. I turned around a couple of times to assure him, 'Don't fear, I will be careful,' dreading lest he should suddenly don his shirt and decide to escort me.

For two weeks there was no sign of the photo. My uncle got quite agitated and asked every day, 'What did your teacher say?' I had to invent an answer each time as I did not have the courage to confront my teacher on the subject. And so I generally said, 'The photographer has been very ill. But tomorrow positively we are getting it.'

Ultimately the photo did arrive and we were given our copies at the end of the day. As I reached home I shouted from the street, 'Photo!' which brought my uncle down the steps of the house. He followed me anxiously about while I took my own time to fish out the photograph from my school bag. 'Such a small one!' my uncle cried on seeing it.

'His camera also was small!' I said.

They carried the print to a corner where a beam of sunlight streamed in through the red pane of a ventilator and observed it closely. Uncle put his spectacles on, but my aunt had to wait for her turn since they managed with a single pair between them. 'Why can't we go out, it is brighter out there, and I won't need glasses?' she suggested.

'No,' he replied firmly. 'Inquisitive fellows all around— fellows ready to peer through the wall if they could, to learn what is happening here,' said my uncle, putting on his spectacles and commenting, 'Our boy has the brightest face in the group, but they have made him look so dark!'

I pointed out my enemies to them: 'This is Suresh—always trying to kill me if I am not careful. This boy also is a bad fellow.' My aunt's eyes met mine significantly at the mention of Suresh, who looked florid by the red light of the ventilator. 'This is our teacher. He will not hesitate to skin alive anyone who is found talking in his class. The man who took the photo is his brother's friend. Own brother, not cousin. Suresh asked if he was a cousin, and it made my teacher so wild!'

My uncle counted the heads and cried, 'Fifty? Two rupees each and they have collected their one hundred rupees! Not even a mount for the photo! They are robbing us in your schools nowadays!'

Next day when I was leaving for school my uncle said, 'Come home early. We will go out to the market. Have you any important lessons?'

'No one,' I said with conviction. 'I will come home for lunch and stay on.'

'Do you wish to come with us?' he asked, aiming his question in the direction of his wife in the kitchen. My aunt, with her years of experience behind her, flung back the responsibility of a decision on him, shouting from the fireplace, 'Do you want me to go with you?' The man was cornered now and answered, 'Not if you have things to mind at home . . .'

'Of course, I have asked that servant woman to come and pound the paddy today. If we miss her today she will not come again.' She trailed off indecisively. This was a diplomatic game which, in spite of my age of innocence, I understood very well, and so I broke in. 'Let Aunt come another day, Uncle. he will want a carriage to be brought and all that trouble,' which was a fact, whenever she wanted to go out she would send me running to the street corner to fetch a *jutka*, and it was not always an easy job. Some days you found six *jutkas* waiting for fares under the margosa shade at the street corner, some days you couldn't find even one at a busy hour; sometimes the *jutka* drivers who knew me would tease and not take me seriously or pass disparaging remarks about my uncle, referring to him as 'that Rangoon man' or mention incidents which I could not comprehend, and generally mumble and smirk among themselves at my expense.

My uncle added, 'Quite right. We can walk to the market.'

'Yes, by all means,' said my aunt, much to everyone's relief.

We sallied out at three o'clock in the afternoon, having finished our tiffin and coffee. The main job for the day was to mount and frame the photograph. Uncle carried it in his hand delicately, enclosed in an old envelope, as if it were fragile and likely to perish at a finger's pressure. As we went down the street a neighbour standing at his door hailed us and demanded, 'Where are you taking the young fellow?' He was an engineer who worked in some distant projects on the hills, coming home once in a while and then again disappearing from our society. He was a particular friend of my uncle as they occasionally gathered for a game of cards in my house. He asked, 'I am here for a few days, can't we have a session sometime?'

'Of course, of course,' said my uncle without much

fervour, 'I will let you know,' and moved on.

'Won't Aunt get angry?' I asked, remembering the arguments they had had after every card session. The card players would have been sitting around in the middle of the hall, demanding coffee and edibles, and playing far into the night. My aunt would complain after the company had dispersed, 'Sitting there with your friends, you lock me up in the kitchen all day! What madness seizes you people when you touch a pack of cards, I wonder!' Worn out by her attacks, my uncle began to avoid his friends, the company gradually dwindled and disappeared. But it did not prevent them from dreaming about cards or luxuriating in visions of a grand session. Somewhere my uncle was supposed to have lost a lot of money through the card games, and my aunt was very definite that he should never go near cards again, although he kept saying, 'We play only Twenty-eight, and not Rummy, after all, Twenty-eight . . .'

'Twenty-eight or forty-eight, it's all the same to me,' said my aunt. 'Fifty thousand rupees just scattered like waste paper, that is all! Sheer madness!' She was rather emphatic. My uncle, not being a quarrelsome sort, just accepted meekly whatever she said, and evidently benefited by her advice.

As we wealked on I asked many questions. This was my opportunity to clear my doubts and learn about new things in life. I asked, 'Why does not Aunt like playing cards? So many nice people gather in our house and it is so interesting!'

He answered, 'It is very expensive, my boy, some people have lost all their fortune and become beggars. Gambling is bad. Don't you know how Nala lost his kingdom?' And he began to narrate the ancient story of Nala. Cyclists passed, a herd of cattle returned from the grazing fields beyond the river, some very young school children emerged from the town primary school, the sun scorching us all. But my uncle noticed nothing while he unfolded to me the fate of Nala, holding me by the wrist lest I should be run over or gored by the cattle. I shrank behind him when we passed my school. I had skipped three classes in the afternoon and did not wish to be seen by my teachers or classmates. We could hear the voices from within the classrooms. Presently the bell for the three-thirty recess would sound and the boys would rush out to drink water at the tap or to make water on the roadside or swarm around the groundnut seller at the school gate. The headmaster was likely to prowl about to prevent the boys from fouling the road. It would be disaster for me to be seen by anyone now. Nor did I wish my uncle to get any ideas while passing the gate—such as stopping to have a word with my teacher. I quickened my steps and tried to dirvert his mind to other matters by suddenly saying, 'Why did Nala lose?'

Before answering he paused for a moment to ask, 'Is that noise all from your school? Why do they make all that row? Glad we don't live next door to your school!' Not wanting him to dwell too much on school matters, I trotted ahead of him, hoping to set the pace for him. But he remarked, 'Do you have to caper like that? No, my boy, I could have given you a beating five years ago, but today I am deliberately slowing my pace.' I paused for him to catch up with me. We had crossed the danger zone, gone past the school.

I asked innocently as we resumed our march, 'What game did Nala play? Did he play cards?'

'Oh no,' uncle said. 'I am sure he would have, if they had invented playing cards in those days. He played dice.' He went on to explain the game to me and continued the story, 'The fellow played with his brother, but malevolent gods had got into the dice and affected his chances, and he lost his kingdom and everything except his wife and had to march out of the capital like a mendicant wearing only a loincloth.'

We turned to our right and took a short cut through Kabir Street and were on Market Road. Not a busy hour, as the high school boys were still not let off. Several donkeys stood about the fountain statuesquely. When the boys emerged from the high school, I imagined, they would shout and frighten the donkeys, provoke them in various ways until they ran helter-skelter, confusing the evening traffic. Street dogs dozing on the edge of the road would join the fray and give them chase, and there would be a hullabaloo. I missed all this imagined spectacle and told my uncle, 'We should have come a little later.'

'Why?' asked my uncle and added, 'You wish that you had attended your classes after all?'

'Oh, no,' I said, and blurted out, 'We could have seen the donkey jump about.' Even without this spectacle Market Road thrilled me every inch, so full of life, movement, and activity. A candy peddler was crying his wares, sounding a bell. This man often established himself at our school gate, drawing out and pinching off portions of a pink, elastic, gluey sweet, stuck in a coil around a bamboo shaft. My mouth watered at the sight of it. I pleaded, 'Uncle, please get me a bit of it!'

He suddenly looked serious and said, 'No, no, it is

dangerous to eat such stuff. You may catch cholera.'

I said with bravado, 'Not likely. He comes to our school every day, and all boys eat it, and also our drawing master. No one has suffered from cholera yet.'

All that he said was, 'I will get you something nicer to eat. Wait.' As we passed a sweetmeat shop he said, 'This is Jagan's shop. No harm in eating here. He makes things out of pure ghee.' He stopped by a resplendently arrayed sweetmeat shop and bought a packet for me.

I swiftly unpacked it and asked out of courtesy, 'Uncle, you want some?' and when he shook his head I ate it, and threw away the wrapper high up and watched it gently floating down on Market Road until Uncle pulled me up, saying, 'Look in front and walk.'

The frame-maker's name was Jayraj. He had hoisted a signboard which was rather pompously worded 'Photographers & Photo-framers', stretching the entire width of the outer wall of the market. Why he chose to display himself in the plural no one could say, since no one ever saw anyone except Mr Jayraj in the proprietor's seat in the inner sanctum. Although there was always a goodly company on the long bench sticking out from his threshold, they were all his friends, well-wishers, customers, and general listeners as Jayraj held forth on his social and personal philosophy all day. Now he gestured to us to be seated on the bench while he went on gently hammering tacks onto the sides of a frame covered with a cardboard. Presently he looked up and greeted my uncle, 'Doctor, where have you been all these days?'

I was surprised at my uncle being addressed as a doctor. Immediately I looked up and asked, 'Uncle, are you a doctor?' He merely rumpled my hair and did not answer.

Jayraj took this occasion to look at me and say, 'Brought this young man along, who is he?'

My uncle simply said, 'He is my boy, our child at home.'

'Oh, I know, yes of course, now grown up so!'

My uncle looked slightly awkward and changed the subject. He held out my photograph and asked with affected cheer, 'Oh, here is this young man's photo which must be framed. Will you do it?'

'Of course, anything for you, sir.' He looked at the photo with disgust. I thought he might fling the picture into the gutter that flowed copiously below the steps of his shop. His brow was furrowed, he pursed his lips, blinked his eyes, placed a straight finger across the picture, shook his head dolefully, and said, 'This is how people cheat schoolboys nowadays. Underexpose and overdevelop or overexpose and underdevelop. This is what they do.'

My uncle added fuel to the fire by saying, 'Not even a mount for the two rupees be charged!'

Jayraj put away the photograph and said, 'Well, mounting and framing is my duty, even if you bring the photo of a donkey's rear.' While he paused for breath my uncle tried to say something, but Jayraj didn't give him the chance. He said, 'Here I am in the heart of the city ready to serve our townfolk. Why can't people make use of me instead of some tenth-rate camera-meddler? I am open twenty-four hours of the day in the service of humanity. I even sleep here when there is work to do, and no factory act applies to me. I can't demand overtime or bonus, but my satisfaction lies in serving humanity.' He pointed at his camera, a hooded apparatus on a tripod in a corner. 'There it is, always ready. If somebody summons me I respond immediately, no matter what the subject is—a wedding, a corpse, prostitute, a minister of state, or a cat on a wall—it's all the same to me. My business is to photograph, and let me tell you straight away that my charges are more than moderate. I don't believe in doing cheap work. I photographed Mahatma Gandhi when he was here. I was summoned to Madras whenever Nehru was on a visit. Dr Radhakrishnan, Tagore, Birla. I could give you a big list of people who were pleased with my work and wrote out testimonials spontaneously. I have locked them in the safe at home. Any day you will be welcome to visit my humble home and peruse them if you like. I don't mind losing all my gold, but not the testimonials from the brilliant sons of our motherland. I want my children and their children to cherish them and say some day, 'We come of a line who served the brilliant sons of Mother India, and here are the tokens.'

While this preamble was going on, his hands were busy giving the finishing touches to a wedding group; he was smoothing off the ripples of glue on the back of the picture. He squatted on his heels on the floor with a little work-bench in front of him. He held the wedding group at arm's length and said, 'Not my business, so many committing the folly every week, the government looking on, while people howl about the population problem, but why can't they ban all marriages for ten years?' He packed the framed picture in an old newspaper, tied a string around it, and put it away. Now my turn. He picked up my photograph, studied it again, and remarked, 'Fifty heads to be compressed on a

postcard. Maybe they are only little men, but still . . .
Unless you look through a magnifying glass you will never
know who is who.' He then asked my uncle, 'Will you leave
the colour of the mount, frame, and style entirely to me or
have you any ideas?'

My uncle was bewildered by this question and said, 'I
want it to look nice, that is all. I want it to look,' he
repeated, 'particularly nice.'

'I don't doubt it,' said Jayraj, who never liked the other
person to end a conversation. 'Well, for the tone of this
print there are certain shades of wooden frames and mounts
suitable, and some not suitable. If you prefer something
unsuitable according to me, it'll still be done. I will wrap it
up, present it to you, and collect my bill; but let me assure
you that my heart will not be in it. Anyway, it is up to you,'
he said challengingly. My uncle seemed bewildered by all
this philosophy and remained silent. He looked apprehensive
and wanted to know the worst quickly. The man had
placed my photograph on his desk, weighting it down with
a steel measuring scale. We awaited his next move.
Meanwhile more people came and took their seats on the
bench, like men at a dentist's parlour. Jayraj did not bother
to notice his visitors, nor did he notice the crowd passing
through the market gateway, shoppers, hawkers, beggars,
dogs and stray cattle and coolies with baskets on their
heads, all kinds of men and women, jostling, shouting,
laughing, cursing, and moving as in a mass trance; they
might have been able to pass in and out more easily but for
Jayraj's bench sticking across the market entrance.

A very bald man came and gingerly sat down on the
bench, announcing, 'The trusteee has sent me.' It made no

impression on Jayraj, who had picked up a length of framing rod and was sawing if off noisily.

My uncle asked suddenly, 'When will you give it?'

Before Jayraj could muster an answer the bald man said for the fourth time, 'The trustee has sent me . . .'

Jayraj chose this moment to tell some other young man leaning on a bicycle, 'Tomorrow at one o'clock.' The young man jumped on his bicycle and rode away.

The bald man began again. 'The trustee . . .'

Jayraj looked at my uncle and said. 'It all depends when you want it.'

The bald man said, 'The trustee . . . is going away to Tirupathi tomorrow . . . and wants . . .'

Jayraj completed his sentence for him, 'Wants me along? Tell him I have no time for a pilgrimage.'

'No, no, he wants the picture.'

'Where is the hurry? Let him come back from Tirupathi.'

The other looked nonplussed.

Meanwhile a woman who sold betel leaves in the market came up with a basket at her hip and asked, 'When should I bring the baby?'

'Whenever the midwife advises,' replied Jayraj. She blushed and threw the end of her sari over her face and laughed. 'Tomorrow evening at three o'clock. Dress him in his best. Put on him all the jewellery you can, and come early. If you come late the sunlight will be gone and there will be no photo. Be sure to bring two rupees with you. No credit, and then you can give me the balance when I give you the photo in a frame.'

'Ah, can't you trust me so much, sir?'

'No argument, that is my system, that is all. If I want

the betel leaves in your basket I pay for it at once, so also for what I do.' She went away laughing, and Jayraj said, addressing no one in particular, 'She has a child every ten months. Mother is constant, but not the father.' His assembly laughed at this quip. 'Not my business to question the parentage. I take the picture and frame it when ordered to do so and that is all.'

My uncle asked all of a sudden, 'Will you be able to frame and give me the photograph now?'

'No,' said Jayraj promptly, 'unless you expect me to stay on and work until midnight.'

'Why not? You said you could.'

'Yes sir,' he replied. 'I said so and I will say so again, if you command me. Will you wait and take it?'

My uncle was flabbergasted. He said, 'No, I cannot. I have to go to the temple,' and he brooded over his inescapable routine of prayer, meditation, dinner, and sleep.

'It's five o'clock now. Your work will take two hours— the paste must dry. We must give the paste its time to dry. But before I can take up your work, you see that man on your side, whose scalp is shining today but once upon a time who had a shock of hair like a coir doormat,' and he nodded in the direction of the bald man who was still waiting for a reply for the trustee. Jayraj continued his theme of bald pate. 'About ten years ago one morning I noticed when he came to frame a calendar portrait of Brahma the Creator that he was growing thin on top; fortunately for us we cannot know the top of our own heads; and I did not tell him so that he might not feel discouraged about his matrimonial future; no one can question the why or wherefore of baldness; it is much like

507

life and death. God gives us the hair and take it away when obviously it is needed elsewhere, that is all.'

Every word that Jayraj uttered pleased the bald man, who remarked at the end of it, 'Don't forget that I save on hair oil!' And he bowed his head to exhibit his shining top, at which I roared with laughter, Jayraj laughed out of courtesy, and my uncle smiled patronizingly, and into this pleasant and well-softened atmosphere the bald man pushed in a word about the business which had brought him there. 'The trustee . . .' he began, and Jayraj repeated, 'Oh, trustee, school trustee, temple trustee, hospital trustee, let him be anything; I have no use for trustees, and so why keep harping on them?'

The bald man sprang to his feet, approached the edge of the inner sanctum, leant forward almost in supplication and prayed, 'Please, please, don't send me back empty-handed; he will be upset, thinking that I have been loafing about.'

Now Jayraj looked properly concerned and said, 'He would think so, would he? All right, he shall have it even if I have to forgo sleep tonight. No more sleep, no more rest, until the trustee is pacified. That settles it.' He said finally, looking at my uncle. 'Yours immediately after the trustee's even if it means an all-night vigil.'

My uncle repeated, 'All night! I may not be able to stay long.'

'You don't have to,' said Jayraj. 'Please be gone, sir, and that is not going to affect my programme or promise. Trust me. You are determined to hang this young person's group picture on your wall tonight, perhaps the most auspicious date in your calendar! Yes, sir. Each unto himself is my philosophy. Tonight it shall be done. I usually charge three rupees for this size, Doctor; does it seem exorbitant to you?'

I felt startled when this man again addressed my uncle as 'Doctor'. My uncle considered the offer and said meekly, 'The print itself costs only two rupees.'

'In that case I will leave it to your sense of justice. Do you assume that frame and mount are in any sense inferior to the photo?'

Everyone on the bench looked concerned and nodded appreciatively at the progress of this dialogue (like the chorus in a Greek play) and my uncle said, 'All right, three.' He peeped out at the municipal clock tower. 'It is past five, you won't take it up before seven?'

Jayraj said, 'Never before eight.'

'I have to be going. How will it reach me?'

Jayraj said, 'I'll knock on your door tonight and deliver it. Maybe you could leave the charges, amounting to three rupees. Don't mistake me for asking for money in advance. You see that room.' He indicated an ante-chamber. 'It is full of pictures of gods, demons, and humans, framed in glass, ordered by people who never turned up again, and in those days I never knew how to ask for payment. If a picture is not claimed immediately I keep it for twenty years in that room. That's the law here. Anyway I don't want to keep your picture for twenty years. I will bring it to you tonight . . . or . . .' A sudden idea struck him. 'Why don't you leave this little fellow behind? He will collect the picture, and I will see that he comes home to you safely tonight.'

An impossible idea it seemed at first. My uncle shook his head and said, 'Oh, not possible. How can he stay here?'

'Trust me, have you no trust in me? Anyway at the end of the day I will deliver him and the photo at your door.'

'If you are coming our way, why do you want this boy to be left here?'

'To be frank, in order to make sure that I keep my promise and don't yield to any sudden impulse to shut my shop and run home.'

'Until midnight?'

'Oh, no, I was joking. Much earlier, much earlier.'

'What will he do for food? He is used to his supper at eight.'

Jayraj pointed to a restaurant across the street and said, 'I will nourish him properly. I love to have children around.'

My uncle looked at me and asked, 'Will you stay?'

I was thrilled. Jayraj was going to give me heavenly things to eat, and I could watch the procession of people and vehicles on Market Road. I pleaded, 'Uncle, don't be afraid.' I recollected all the dare-devilry of young men in the adventure stories I had heard. I wanted to have the pride of some achievement today. I pleaded with my uncle, 'Please leave me and go. I will come home later.'

Jayraj looked up and said, 'Don't worry about him,' and held out his hand. My uncle took out his purse and counted out three rupees on Jayraj's palm saying, 'I have never left him alone before.'

Jayraj said, 'Our boys must learn to get on by themselves. We must become a strong nation.'

After my uncle left, Jayraj pushed away my photo on to the floor and took in its place on the desk a group photo of the trustee's. He kept gazing on it and said, 'Not a very good photo. That Pictograph man again! So proud of his electronic flash! He claims he commands sunlight at his fingertips, but when he throws it on to the faces of a group before the camera, what do they do? They shut their eyes or open them wide as if they saw a ghost. For all the garland on his chest and all his pomposity, the man at the centre and all others in the group look to me like monkeys surprised on a mango tree . . .' The bald head kept swaying in approval. Jayraj constantly looked up from his work to make sure that the fellow was listening. I sat between them. Jayaraj abruptly ordered, 'Child, move over, let that man come nearer.' I obeyed instantly.

This was my first day out, exciting and frightening at the same time. The world looked entirely different—the crowd at the market, which had seemed so entertaining before, was now terrifying. I feared that I might be engulfed and swept off, and never see my home again. As twilight came on and the street lamps were lit, I grew apprehensive. Somehow I felt I could not trust Jayraj. I stole a look at him. He looked forbidding. He wore a pair of glasses with thick lenses through which his eyeballs bulged, lending him a ghoulish look; unshaven chin and grey mottled hair covering his forehead; khaki shirt and a blood-red *dhoti*, a frightening combination. All this smiles and friendly talk before my uncle was a show to entice me. He seemed to have his own sinister plans to deal with me once I was left at his mercy. He had become cold and aloof. Otherwise, why should he have asked me to yield my place to the bald man? The moment my uncle's back was turned this man's manner had changed; he looked grim and ignored me.

Where was the nourishment he had promised? I was afraid
to ask. I kept looking at the restaurant across the road in
the hope that he might follow my gaze and take the hint,
but his hands were sawing, hammering, pasting, and
smoothing while his tongue wagged interruptedly. Having
promised me nourishment, this man was not giving it a
thought. Suppose I reminded him? But I lacked the courage
to speak to him. With unappeased hunger on one side, my
mind was also busy as to how to retrieve my photo from
this horrible man and find my way home. I had not noticed
the landmarks while coming. There were so many lanes
ending on Market Road. I was not sure which one of them
would lead me to Kabir Street, and from Kabir Street
should I go up or down? A well stood right in the middle
of that street, and beside it the striped wall of an abandoned
temple in which the tailor was supposed to live. One went
past it and came through onto Vinayak Street somehow.
Vinayak Street seemed such a distant dream to me now.
Once some gracious god could put me down there, at either
end. I could always find my way home. I was beginning to
feel lost.

Jayraj paused for a moment to look at me and say,
'When I promise a time for delivery, I keep it.' Analysing
his statement, I found no hint of anything to eat. 'When I
promise a time . . . etc.' What of the promise of food? What
did 'delivery' mean? Did it include eating? It was a worrying
situation for me. I could not understand whether he implied
that after delivering his picture to the bald man he would
summon the restaurant-keeper and order a feast, or did he
simply mean that in due course he would nail my photo on
four sides with wood and glass and then say, 'That is all,

512

now get out.' When I tried to declare, 'I am very hungry, are you doing anything about it? A promise is sacred and inescapable,' I found my voice croaking, creaking, and the words in such a jumble and mumble that it only attracted the other's attention and conveyed nothing. He looked up and asked, 'Did you speak?'

He looked fierce under the kerosene 'power-light' hanging from the ceiling, and the huge shadow of its tin reflector left half the shop in darkness. I had no doubt that he enticed people in there, murdered them in cold blood, and stored their bodies in the ante-room. I remembered his mysterious references to the room, and my uncle had understood. The wonder was that Uncle should listen to all that and yet leave me behind. Of course, if it came to it, I could hit him with the little rod on the work bench and run away. This was a testing time, and Uncle perhaps wanted to try me out; hadn't they agreed that little boys should become tough? If he asked me in I should take care not to cross the threshold— but if he ordered food, but kept it as a bait far inside and then said, 'Come in here and eat'—perhaps then I should make a dash for the food, hit him with the steel rod, and run—tactics to be accomplished at lightning speed. Perhaps my uncle expected me to perform such deeds, and would admire my pluck. Hit Jayraj on the head and run and munch while running. While my mind was busy working out the details of my retreat, I noticed that the man had risen to his feet and was rummaging among old paper and cardboard, stacked in the back room. When he stood up he looked lanky and tall, with long legs and long limbs as if he had uncoiled hmself. Rather snakelike, I thought.

For a moment I was seized with panic at the prospect

of combating him. The bald man had edged closer and closer and had now actually stepped into the workshop, anticipating some excitement, the light from the power-lamp imparting a blinding lustre to his bald pate. Jayraj cried from the back room, 'Impossible to get at what one wants in this cursed place, must set apart a day for cleaning up . . . Ah, here it is.' And he brought out a portrait in a grey mount, took it close to the light, and said, 'Come nearer, the print is rather faded.' They examined it with their heads abutting each other. I looked away, I realized that while they were brewing their nefarious plan I should remain alert but without giving them any sign of noticing. 'This is the man; at one time the richest doctor in Burma . . .' I caught these words. Occasionally from time to time I turned my head just to look at them and caught them glancing at me and turning away. I too looked away, sharpening my ears not to miss a single word; somehow I was beginning to feel that their talk had something to do with me. Jayraj's loud and guffawing tone was all gone, he was now talking in a sinister undertone. 'Ten doctors employed under him. But this fellow was only a *chokra*; he sterilized needles and wrapped up powders and medicine bottles and cleansed the syringe; actually he must have started as this man's (tapping the photo) personal bootboy. When the Japanese bombed Rangoon, these people trekked back to our country, leaving behind their palatial home and several cars and everything, but still they managed to carry with them jewellery and much gold, and a bank account in Madras, and above all also a fifteen-day-old baby in arms. The doctor took ill and died on the way. There were rumours that he was pushed off a cliff by so-and-so. The lady reached India half dead, lingered for a year, and died. The baby was all right, so was the *chokra*, all through the expedition. The *chokra*, becoming all in all, took charge of all the cash and gold and bank accounts after reaching this country, impersonating the doctor. That poor woman, the doctor's wife, need not have died, but this fellow kept her a prisoner in the house and gave her some injections and finished her. The cremation was a double-quick affair across the river.'

The bald man now moved back to my side. Jayraj had resumed his seat and was working on a frame. I still kept fixedly looking away, feeling desperate at the prospect before me—a total darkness had now fallen on the city, and there was the hopelessness of getting any refreshment.

They continued their talk in conspiratorial tones all through. The bald man asked some question. Jayraj replied, 'Who could say? I didn't know much about them. I think that the fat woman must also have been there all the time and a party to it. I learnt a lot from a servant maid who brought this picture for framing one day. I told her to call for it next day. She never came. So far no sign of anyone claiming it.'

'The same fellow who sat here a little while ago!' said the bald man in astonishment.

Jayraj lowered his voice and muttered, 'When I called him "Doctor"—you must have seen his face!' and then they carried on their talk for a long while, which was all inaudible to me. I kept glancing at them and feeling their eyes on me all the time. Finally the tap-tap of the hammer ceased and he said, 'All right, this is finished. Let the glue dry a bit. Anyway it must be said to his credit: he tended the child and brought him up—only God knows the full truth.' He suddenly called me, held out to me the photograph salvaged from the dark chamber, and asked, 'Do you wish to take this home? I can give it to you free.' And they both stared at my face and the photo while he held it out. I had a momentary curiosity to look at the face of the man who had been the subject of their talk. The photo was very faded, I could glimpse only a moustache and little else; the man was in European clothes—if what they said was true, this was my father, I looked at their faces and noticed the sneering, leering expressions on them. I flung the photo back, got up without a word, and began to run.

I raced down Market Road, not aware of the direction I was taking. I heard the man shout after me, 'Come, come, I will frame yours and give it to you, and then take you home.' The bald man's squeaky voice added something to support his friend, but I ran. I bumped into people coming to the market and was cursed. 'Have you no eyes, these boys nowadays!' I feared Jayraj might shout, 'Catch him, don't let him get away.' Presently I slowed down my pace. I had no sense of direction but presently noticed Jagan's sweetmart on my right-hand side this time and knew that I was going back the way I had come. My head was drumming with Jayraj's speech. It was agonizing to picture my uncle cheating, murdering, and lying. The references to my father and mother touched me less; they were remote, unconvincing figures.

Blundering and groping along, I reached the end of Market Road. People looked at me curiously. I did not

want to betray that this was my first outing alone, and so
sauntered along, tried to look casual, whistled and hummed
aloud, '*Raghupati Raghava Raja Ram.*' The street lighting
imperceptibly dimmed and grew sparser as I reached the
foot of Lawley Statue. The Lawley Extension homes were
tucked far back into their respective compounds, no way of
knocking on their doors for any help; nor could I approach
the boys leaning on their bicycles and chatting; they were
senior boys who might make fun of me or beat me. A
vagrant lay stretched full length on a side away from others;
he looked wild and dreadful, but he kept looking at me
while others would not even notice my presence. I shrank
away at the foot of this terrible statue, hoping that it would
not suddenly start moving and march over me. The vagrant
held out his hand and said, 'Give me a coin, I will buy
something to eat.'

I turned my shirt pocket inside out to prove my
statement. 'I have no money, not a paisa, and I am also
hungry.'

'Go home then,' he ordered.

'I want to, but where is Vinayak Street?'

It was a grave risk betraying myself in this manner; if
he realized that I was a lost soul he might abduct and sell
me upcountry as a slave. 'I will go with you and show the
way, will you tell your mother to give me a little rice for my
trouble?'

Mother! Mother! My mind fell into a confusion . . . of
that woman who died at Uncle's hand . . . I had all along
felt my aunt was my mother. 'I have only an aunt, no
mother,' I said.

'Aunts don't like me, and so go by yourself. Go back

half the way you came, count three streets and turn on your left, if you know which is your left hand, and then turn right and you will be in Kabir Street . . .'

'Oh, I know Kabir Street, and the well,' I said with relief.

'Get onto it then, and take the turning beyond the well for Vinayak Street, don't wander all over the town like this. Boys like you must stay at home and read your lessons.'

'Yes, sir,' I said respectfully, feeling intimidated. 'Once I am back I promise to read my lessons.'

The directions that he gave helped me. I came through and found myself at the disused well in Kabir Street. When I reached Vinayak Street I felt triumphant. In that feeling of relief, even Jayraj's words ceased to rankle in my mind. The dogs in our street set up a stormy reception for me. At that hour the street was deserted, and the only guardians were the mongrels that roamed up and down in packs. They barked viciously at first but soon recognized me. Escorted by the friendly dogs, wagging their tails and wetting the lampposts in their delight at meeting me, I reached my house. My uncle and aunt were on the front doorstep and flung at me a jumble of inquiries. 'Your uncle wanted to start out again and look for you,' my aunt said.

Uncle lifted me practically half in the air in the sheer joy of our reunion, and asked, 'Where is the framer? He promised to leave you here. It is past ten o'clock now.'

Before I could answer my aunt said, 'I told you not to trust such persons.'

'Where is your photograph?'

I had not thought of an answer for that. What could I say? I only burst into tears and wept at the memory of all

518

the confusion in my mind. Safer to weep than to speak. If I spoke I feared I might blunder into mentioning the other photo out of the darkroom.

My aunt immediately swept me in, remarking sorrowfully, 'Must be very, very hungry, poor child.'

I sobbed, 'He didn't give me anything to eat.'

All night I lay tossing in my bed. I kicked my feet against the wall and groaned and woke up with a start from a medley of nightmares composed of the day's experience. My uncle was snoring peacefully in his room; I could see him through the open door. I sat up and watched him. He had impersonated a doctor, but it didn't seem to be a very serious charge, as I had always thought that all doctors with their rubber tubes and medical smell were play-acting all the time. Imprisoning and poisoning my mother—Mother? My aunt was my mother as far as I could see, and she was quite alive and sound. There wasn't even a faded photo of that mother as there was of my father. The photographer had said something about money and jewellery. I was indifferent to both. My uncle gave me all the money I needed, never refusing me anything at any time. Jewellery—those glittering pieces—one had better not bother about. You could not buy candy with gold, could you? To think that the refugees from Rangoon should have carried such tinsel all the way! In my own way I was analysing and examining the charges against my uncle and found them flimsy, although the picture of him emanating out of dark whispers and furtive glances, in the background of a half-lit back room, was shocking.

I needed some clarifications very urgently. My aunt, sleeping on her mat at the edge of the open courtyard, stirred. I made sure that Uncle's snores were continuing, softly rose from my bed, and went over to her side. I sat on the edge of her mat and looked at her. She had observed my restlessness and asked, 'Why haven't you slept yet?'

I whispered, 'Aunt, are you awake? I want to tell you something.'

She encouraged me to speak. I gave her an account of Jayraj's narrative. She merely said, 'Forget it. Never mention it to your uncle.'

'Why?'

'Don't ask questions. Go back to your bed and sleep.'

I could do nothing more. I took the advice. The next day Jayraj managed to deliver the framed photo through someone who passed this way. My uncle examined it inch by inch by the light from the courtyard, and declared, 'Wonderful, good work, worth three rupees, surely.' He fumbled about with a hammer and nail looking for the right place, and hung it finally over his easy chair, right below the big portrait of his ancestor on the wall.

I acted on my aunt's advice and never asked any question. As I grew up and met more people, I heard oblique references to my uncle here and there, but I ignored whatever I heard. Only once did I try to strangle a classmate at the college hostel in Madras who had gossiped about my uncle. Stirred by such information, sometimes I thought of him as a monster and I felt like pricking and deflating him the next time I met him. But when I saw him on the railway platform, waiting to receive me, the joy in his perspiring face moved me, and I never questioned him in any manner. After seeing me through the Albert Mission High School he had maintained me at a college in Madras; he wrote a postcard at least once a week, and celebrated my arrival during a vacation with continuous feasting at home. He had probably gambled away a lot more money than he had spent on me. It didn't matter. Nothing ever mattered. He never denied me anything. Again and again I was prompted to ask the question, 'What am I worth? What about my parents?' but I rigorously suppressed it. Thus I maintained the delicate fabric of our relationship till the very end of his life. After his death, I examined his records—not a shade of correspondence or account to show any connection with Burma, except the lacquered casket with a dragon on it. He had bequeathed the house and all his possessions and a small annuity in the bank to me and left my aunt in my care.

ANNAMALAI

THE MAIL BROUGHT me only a postcard, with the message in Tamil crammed on the back of it in minute calligraphy. I was curious about it only for a minute—the handwriting, style of address, the black ink, and above all the ceremonial flourish of the language were well known to me. I had deciphered and read out to Annamalai on an average one letter every month for a decade and a half when he was gardener, watchman, and general custodian of me and my property at the New Extension. Now the letter began: 'At the Divine Presence of my old master, do I place with hesitancy this slight epistle for consideration. It's placed at the lotus feet of the great soul who gave me food and shelter and money in my lifetime, and for whose welfare I pray to the Almighty every hour of my waking life. God bless you, sir. By your grace and the grace of gods in the firmament above, I am in excellent health and spirits, and my kith and kin, namely, my younger brother Amavasai and my daughter, son-in-law, and the two grandchildren and my sister who lives four doors from me, and my maternal uncle and his children, who tend the coconut grove, are all well. This year the gods have been kind and have sent us the rains to nourish our lands and gardens and orchards. Our tanks have been full, and we work hard . . .' I was indeed happy to have such a good report of fertility and joy from one who had nothing but problems as far as I could remember. But my happiness was short-lived. The rosy picture lasted about ten closely packed lines, followed by an abrupt transition. I realized all this excellence of reporting was just a formality, following a polite code of epistle-writing and not to be taken literally in part or in whole, for the letter started off in an opposite direction and tone. 'My purpose in addressing your honoured self just today is to inform you that I am in sore need of money. The crops have failed this year and I am without food or money. My health is poor. I am weak, decrepit, and in bed, and need money for food and medicine. My kith and kin are not able to support me; my brother Amavasai is a godly man but he is very poor and is burdened with a family of nine children and two wives, and so I beg you to treat this letter as if it were a telegram and send me money immediately . . .' He did not specify the amount but left it to my good sense, and whatever could be spared seemed welcome. The letter bore his name at the bottom, but I knew he could not sign; he always affixed his signature in the form of a thumb impression whenever he had to deal with any legal document. I should certainly have been glad to send a pension, not once but regularly, in return for all his years of service. But how could I be sure that he had written the letter? I knew that he could neither read nor write, and how could I make sure that the author of the letter was not his brother Amavasai, that father of nine and husband of two, who might have hit upon an excellent scheme to draw a pension in the name of a dead brother? How could I make sure that Annamalai was still alive? His last words to me before he retired were a grand description of his own funeral, which he anticipated with considerable thrill.

I looked at the postmark to make sure that at least the card had originated correctly. But the post-office seal was just a dark smudge as usual. Even if it weren't so, even if the name of his village had been clearly set forth it would not have made any difference. I was never sure at any time of the name of his village, although as I have already said I had written the address for him scores of times in a decade and a half. He would stand behind my chair after placing the postcard to be addressed on the desk. Every time I would say, 'Now recite the address properly.'

'All right, sir,' he would say, while I waited with the pen poised over the postcard. 'My brother's name is Amavasai, and it must be given to his hand.'

'That I know very well, next tell me the address precisely this time.' Because I had never got it right at any time.

He said something that sounded like 'Mara Konam', which always puzzled me. In Tamil it meant either 'wooden angle' or 'cross angle', depending on whether you stressed the first word or the second of that phonetic assemblage. With the pen ready, if I said, 'Repeat it,' he would help me by uttering slowly and deliberately the name—but a new one this time, sounding something like 'Peramanallur'.

'What is it, where is it?' I asked desperately.

'My village, sir,' he replied with a glow of pride—once again leaving me to brood over a likely meaning. Making

524

allowance for wrong utterance you could translate it as 'Peerumai Nallur,' meaning 'town of pride and goodness' or, with a change of the stress of syllables, 'town of fatness and goodness'. Attempting to grope my way through all this verbal wilderness, if I said, 'Repeat it,' he generally came out with a brand-new sound. With a touch of homesickness in his tone and with an air of making a concession to someone lacking understanding, he would say, 'Write clearly NUMTHOD POST,' reviving me again to wrestle with phonetics to derive a meaning. No use, as this seemed to be an example of absolute sound with no sense, with no scope for an interpretation however differently you tried to distribute the syllables and stresses or whether you attempted a translation or speculated on its meaning in Tamil, Telegu, Kannada, or any of the fourteen languages listed in the Indian Constitution. While I sat brooding over all this verbiage flung at me, Annamalai waited silently with an air of supreme tolerance, only suggesting gently, 'Write in English . . .'

'Why in English?'

'If it could be in Tamil I would have asked that chap who writes the card to write the address also; because it must be in English I have to trouble you'—a piece of logic that sounded intricate.

I persisted. 'Why not in Tamil?'

'Letters will not reach in Tamil: what our schoolmaster has often told us. When my uncle died they wrote a letter and addressed it in Tamil to his son in Conjeevaram and the man never turned up for the funeral. We all joined and buried the uncle after waiting for two days, and the son came one year later and asked, 'Where is my father? I want

to ask for money.' And Annamalai laughed at the recollection
of this episode. Realizing that I had better not inquire too
much, I solved the problem by writing briskly one under
another everything as I heard it. And he would conclusively
ask before picking up the card, 'Have you written via
Katpadi?'

All this business would take its own time. While the
space for address on the postcard was getting filled up I
secretly fretted lest any line should be crowded out, but I
always managed it somehow with the edge of my pen-point.
The whole thing took almost an hour each time, but
Annamalai never sent a card home more than once a
month. He often remarked, 'No doubt, sir, that the people
at home would enjoy receiving letters, but if I wrote a card
to everyone who expected it, I would be a bankrupt. When
I become a bankrupt, will there be one soul among all my
relatives who will offer a handful of rice even if I starve to
death?' And so he kept his communications within practical
limits, although they provided a vital link for him with his
village home.

'How does one get to your village?' I asked.

'Buy a railway ticket, that's how,' he answered, feeling
happy that he could talk of home. 'If you get into the
Passenger at night paying two rupees and ten annas, you
will get to Trichy in the morning. Another train leaves
Trichy at eleven, and for seven rupees and four annas, it
used to be only five fourteen before, you can reach
Villipuram. One must be awake all night, otherwise the
train will take you on, and once they demanded two rupees
extra for going further because I had slept over. I begged
and pleaded and they let me go, but I had to buy another

ticket next morning to get back to Katpadi. You can sleep on the station platform until midday. The bus arrives at midday and for twelve annas it will carry you further. After the bus you may hire a *jutka* or a bullock cart for six annas and then on foot you reach home before dark; if it gets late bandits may waylay and beat us. Don't walk too long; if you leave in the afternoon you may reach Marakonam before sunset. But a card reaches there for just nine paise, isn't it wonderful?' he asked.

Once I asked, 'Why do you have the address written before the message?'

'So that I may be sure that the fellow who writes for me does not write to his own relations on my card. Otherwise how can I know?' This seemed to be a good way of ensuring that the postcard was not misused. It indicated a rather strange relationship, as he often spoke warmly of that unseen man who always wrote his messages on postcards, but perhaps a few intelligent reservations in accepting a friendship improve human relations. I often questioned him about his friend.

'He has also the same name as myself,' he said.

I asked, 'What name?'

He bowed his head and mumbled, 'My . . . my own name . . .' Name was a matter of delicacy, something not to be bandied about unnecessarily, a point of view which had not occurred to me at all until one day he spoke to me about a signboard on the gate announcing my name. He told me point blank when I went down to the garden, 'Take away the name-board from that gate, if you will forgive my saying so.'

'Why?'

527

'All sorts of people read your name aloud while passing down the road. It is not good. Often urchins and tots just learning to spell shout your name and run off when I try to catch them. The other day some women also read your name and laughed to themselves. Why should they? I do not like it at all.' What a different world was his where a name was to be concealed rather than blazoned forth in print, ether waves, and celluloid!

'Where should I hang that board now that I have it?'

He just said, 'Why not inside the house, among the pictures in the hall?'

'People who want to find me should know where I live.'

'Everyone ought to know,' he said, 'otherwise why should they come so far?'

Digging the garden he was at his best. We carried on some of our choicest dialogues when his hands were wielding the pickaxe. He dug and kept digging for its own sake all day. While at work he always tied a red bandanna over his head, knotted above his ear in pirate fashion. Wearing a pair of khaki shorts, his bare back roasted to an ebonite shade by the sun, he attained a spontaneous camouflage in a background of mud and greenery; when he stood ankle-deep in slush at the bed of a banana seedling, he was indistinguishable from his surroundings. On stone, slope, and pit, he moved jauntily, with ease, but indoors he shuffled and scratched the cement floor with his feet, his joints creaked and rumbled as he carried himself upstairs. He never felt easy in the presence of walls and books and papers; he looked frightened and self-conscious, tried to mute his steps and his voice when entering my study. He came in only when he had a postcard for me to address.

While I sat at my desk he would stand behind my chair, suppressing even his normal breath lest it should disturb my work, but he could not help the little rumbles and sighs emanating from his throat whenever he attempted to remain still. If I did not notice his presence soon enough, he would look in the direction of the gate and let out a drover's cry, 'Hai, hai!' at a shattering pitch and go on to explain, 'Again those cows, sir. Some day they are going to shatter the gate and swallow our lawn and flowers so laboriously tended by this old fellow. Many strangers passing our gate stop to exclaim, "See those red flowers, how well they have come up! All of it that old fellow's work, at his age!" '

Annamalai might have had other misgivings about himself, but he had no doubt whatever of his stature as a horticulturist. A combination of circumstances helped him to cherish his notions. I did nothing to check him. My compound was a quarter acre in extent and offered him unlimited scope for experimentations. I had been living in Vinayak Street until the owner of a lorry service moved into the neighbourhood. He was a relative of the municipal chairman and so enjoyed the freedom of the city. His lorries rattled up and down all day, and at night they were parked on the roadside and hammered and drilled so as to be made ready for loading in the morning. No one else in my street seemed to notice the nuisance. No use in protesting and complaining, as the relative of a municipal chairman would be beyond reproach. I decided to flee since it was impossible to read or write in that street; it dawned on me that the place was not meant for my kind any more. I began to look about. I liked the lot shown by a broker in the New Extension layout, who also arranged the sale of my ancient house in Vinayak Street to the same lorry-owner. I moved off with my books and writing within six months of making up my mind. A slight upland stretching away to the mountain road; a swell of ground ahead on my left and the railway line passing through a cutting, punctuated with a red gate, was my new setting. Someone had built a small cottage with a room on top and two rooms downstairs, and it was adequate for my purpose, which was to read and write in peace.

On the day I planned to move I requested my neighbour the lorry-owner to lend me a lorry for transporting myself to my new home. He gladly gave me his lorry; the satisfaction was mutual as he could go on with all the repairs and hammerings all night without a word of protest from anyone, and I for my part should look forward to the sound of only birds and breeze in my new home. So I loaded all my books and trunks onto an open truck, with four loaders perched on them. I took my seat beside the driver and bade goodbye to Vinayak Street. No one to sigh over my departure, since gradually, unnoticed, I had become the sole representative of our clan in that street, especially after the death of my uncle.

When we arrived at New Extension the loaders briskly lifted the articles off the lorry and dumped them in the hall. One of them lagged behind while the rest went back to the lorry and shouted, 'Hey, Annamalai, are you coming or not?' He ignored their call, and they made the driver hoot the horn.

I said to the man, 'They seem to want you . . .'

His brief reply was 'Let them.' He was trying to help me put things in order. 'Do you want this to be carried upstairs?' he asked, pointing at my table. The lorry hooted outside belligerently. He was enraged at the display of bad manners, went to the doorway, looked at them, and said, waving his arms, 'Be off if you want, don't stand there and make donkey noise.'

'How will you come back?'

'Is that your business?' he said. 'Go away if you like, don't let that donkey noise trouble this gentleman.'

I was touched by his solicitude, and looked up from the books I was retrieving from the packing cases, and noticed him for the first time. He was a thick-set, heavy-jowled man with a cleanshaven head covered with a turban, a pair of khaki shorts over heavy bow legs, and long arms reaching down to his knees; he had thick fingers, a broad nose, and enormous teeth stained red with betel juice and tobacco permanently pouched in at his cheek. There was something fierce as well as soft about him at the same time.

'They seem to have left,' I remarked as the sound of the lorry receded.

'Let them,' he said, 'I don't care.'

'How will you go back?' I asked.

'Why should I?' he said. 'Your things are all scattered in a jumble here, and they don't have the sense to stop and help. You may have no idea, sir, what they have become nowadays.'

Thus he entered my service and stayed on. He helped me to move my trunks and books and arrange them properly. Later he followed me about faithfully when I went round to inspect the garden. Whoever had owned the house before me had not bothered about the garden. It had a kind of battlement wall to mark off the backyard, and the rest was encircled with hedges of various types. Whenever I paused to examine any plant closely, Annamalai also stood by earnestly. If I asked, 'What is this?' 'This?' he said, stooping close to it, 'this is a *poon chedi* (flowering plant),' and after a second look at it declared what I myself was able to observe, 'Yellow flowers.' I learnt in course of time that his classifications were extremely simple. If he liked a plant he called it '*poon chedi*' and allowed it to flourish. If it appeared suspicious, thorny, or awry in any manner he just declared, 'This is a *poondu* (weed),' and, before I had a chance to observe it, would pull it off and throw it over the wall with a curse.

'Why do you curse that poor thing?'

'It is an evil plant, sir.'

'What kind of evil?'

'Oh, of several kinds. Little children who go near it will have stomach ache.'

'There are no children for miles around.'

'What if? It can send out its poison on the air . . .'

A sort of basement room was available, and I asked Annamalai, 'Can you live in this?'

'I can live even without this,' he said, and explained, 'I am not afraid of devils, spirits, or anything. I can live anywhere. Did I have a room when I lived in those forests?' He flourished his arm in some vague direction. 'That lorry-keeper is a rascal, sir; please forgive my talking like this in the presence of a gentleman. He is a rascal. He carried me one day in his lorry to a forest on the hill and would never let me get away from there. He had signed a contract to collect manure from those forests, and wanted someone to stay there, dig the manure, and heap it in the lorries.'

'What kind of manure?'

'Droppings of birds and dung of tigers and other wild animals, and dead leaves, in deep layers everywhere, and he gave me a rupee and a half a day to stay there and dig up and load the lorry when it came. I lit a fire and boiled rice and ate it, and stayed under the trees, heaped the leaves around and lit them up to scare away the tigers roaring at night.'

'Why did you choose this life just for one rupee and eight annas a day?' I asked.

He stood brooding for a few moments and replied, 'I don't know. I was sitting in a train going somewhere to seek a job. I didn't have a ticket. A fellow got in and demanded, 'Where is your ticket?' I searched for it here and there and said, 'Some son of a bitch has stolen my ticket.' But he understood and said, 'We will find out who that son of a bitch is. Get off the train first.' And they took me out of the train with the bundle of clothes I carried. After the train left we were alone, and he said, 'How much have you?' I had nothing, and he asked, 'Do you want to earn one rupee and eight annas a day?' I begged him to give me work. He led me to a lorry waiting outside the railway station, handed me a spade and pickaxe, and said, 'Go on in that lorry, and the driver will tell you what to do.' The lorry put me down late next day on the mountain. All night I had to keep awake and keep a fire going, otherwise sometimes even elephants came up.'

'Weren't you terrified?'

'They would run away when they saw the fire, and sometimes I chanted aloud wise sayings and philosophies until they withdrew . . . leaving a lot of dung around, just what that man required . . . and he sold it to the coffee estates and made his money . . . When I wanted to come home they would not let me, and so I stayed on. Last week when they came I was down with the shivering fever, but the lorry driver, a good man, allowed me to climb on the lorry and escape from the forest. I will never go back there, sir; that lorry man holds my wages and asserts that he has given it all as rice and potato all these months . . . I don't know, some day you must reckon it all up for me and help me . . .'

He left early on the following morning to fetch his baggage. He asked for an advance of five rupees, but I hesitated. I had not known him for more than twenty-four hours. I told him, 'I don't have change just at this moment.'

He smiled at me, showing his red-tinted teeth. 'You do not trust me, I see. How can you? The world is full of rogues who will do just what you fear. You must be careful with your cash, sir. If you don't protect your cash and wife . . .' I did not hear him fully as he went downstairs muttering his comment. I was busy setting up my desk as I wished to start my work without any more delay. I heard the gate open, producing a single clear note on its hinges (which I later kept purposely on without oiling as that particular sound served as a doorbell). I peeped from my western window and saw him go down the road. I thought he was going away for good, not to return to a man who would not trust him with five rupees! I felt sorry for not giving him money, at least a rupee. I saw him go up the swell of ground and disappear down the slope. He was going by a short cut to the city across the level-crossing gate.

I went back to my desk, cursing my suspiciousness. Here was one who had volunteered to help and I had shown so little grace. That whole day he was away. Next afternoon the gate latch clicked, and the gate hummed its single clear note as it moved on its hinges, and there he was, carrying a big tin trunk on his head, and a gunny sack piled on top of it. I went down to welcome him. By the time I had gone down he had passed round the house and was lowering the trunk at the door of the basement room.

He would stand below my window and announce to the air, 'Sir, I am off for a moment. I have to talk to the man in the other house,' and move off without waiting for my reply. Sometimes if I heard him I said, as a matter of principle, 'Why do you have to go and bother him about our problems now?'

He would look crestfallen and reply, 'If I must not go, I won't go, if you order so.'

How could I or anyone order Annamalai? It was unthinkable, and so to evade such a drastic step I said, 'You know everything, what does he know more than you?'

He would shake his head at this heresy. 'Don't talk so, sir. If you don't want me to go, I won't go, that is all. You think I want to take off the time to gossip and loaf?'

A difficult question to answer, and I said, 'No, no, if it is important, of course . . .'

And he moved off, muttering, 'They pay him a hundred rupees a month not for nothing . . . and I want to make this compound so good that people passing should say "Ah" when they peep through the gate . . . that is all, am I asking to be paid also a hundred rupees like that mali?' He moved off, talking all the way; talking was an activity performed for its own sake and needed no listener for Annamalai. An hour later he returned clutching a drooping sapling (looking more like a shot-down bird) in his hand, held it aloft under my window, and said, 'Only if we go and ask will people give us plants; otherwise why should they be interested?'

'What is it?' I asked dutifully, and his answer I knew even before he uttered it: 'Flower plant.'

Sometimes he displayed a handful of seeds tied to the end of his *dhoti* in a small bundle. Again I asked, 'What is it?'

'Very rare seeds, no one has seen such a thing in this extension. If you think I am lying . . .' He would then ask, 'Where are these to be planted?'

I would point out to a corner of the compound and say, 'Don't you think we need some good covering there? All that portion looks bare . . .' Even as I spoke I would feel the futility of my suggestion, it was just a constitutional procedure and nothing more. He might follow my instructions or his own inclination, no one could guess what he might do. He would dig up the earth earnestly at some corner and create a new bed of his own pattern, poke his forefinger into the soft earth and push the seed or the seedling in. Every morning he would stoop over it to observe minutely how it progressed. If he found a sprouting seed or any sign of life in the seedling, he watered it twice a day, but if it showed no response to his loving touch, he looked outraged. 'This should have come up so well, but it is the Evil Eye that scorches our plants . . . I know what to do now.' He dipped his finger in a solution of white lime and drew grotesque and strange emblems on a broken mud pot and mounted it up prominently on a stick so that those that entered our gate should first see the grotesque painting rather than the plants. He explained, 'When people say, "Ah, how good this garden looks!" they speak with envy and then it burns up the plants, but when they see the picture there, they will be filled with revulsion and our flowers will flourish. That is all.'

He made his own additions to the garden each day, planting wherever he fancied, and soon I found that I could have no say in the matter. I realized that he treated me with tolerant respect rather than trust, and so I let him have his own way. Our plants grew anyhow and anywhere and generally prospered, although the only attention that Annamalai gave them was an ungrudging supply of water out of a hundred-foot hose-pipe, which he turned on every leaf of every plant until it was doused and drowned. He also flung at their roots from time to time every kind of garbage and litter and called it manuring. By such assiduous efforts he created a generous, massive vegetation as a setting for my home. We had many rose plants whose nomenclature we never learnt, which had developed into leafy menacing entanglements, clawing passers-by; canna grew to gigantic heights, jasmine into wild undergrowth with the blooms maliciously out of reach, although they threw their scent into the night. Dahlias pushed themselves above ground after every monsoon, presented their blooms, and wilted and disappeared, but regenerated themselves again at the next season. No one could guess who planted them originally, but nature was responsible for their periodic appearance, although Annamalai took the credit for it unreservedly. Occasionally I protested when Tacoma hedges bordering the compound developed into green ramparts, shutting off the view in every direction. Annamalai, a prince of courtesy at certain moments, would not immediately contradict me but look long and critically at the object of my protest. 'Don't think of them now, I will deal with them.'

'When?' I asked.

'As soon as we have the rains,' he would say.

'Why should it be so late?'

'Because a plant cut in summer will die at the roots.'

'You know how it is with rains these days, we never have them.'

This would make him gaze skyward and remark, 'How can we blame the rains when people are so evil-minded?'

'What evil?'

'Should they sell rice at one rupee a measure? Is it just? How can poor people live?'

When the rains did come eventually it would be no use reminding him of his promise to trim the hedges, for he would definitely declare, 'When the rain stops, of course, for if a plant is trimmed in rain, it rots. If you want the hedges to be removed completely, tell me, I will do it in a few minutes, but you must not blame me later if every passer-by in the street stares and watches the inside of the house all the time . . .'

But suddenly one day, irrespective of his theories, he would arm himself with a scythe and hack blindly whatever came within his reach, not only the hedge I wanted trimmed but also a lot of others I preferred to keep. When I protested against this depredation, he just said, 'The more we cut the better they will grow, sir.' At the end of this activity, all the plants, having lost their outlines, looked battered and stood up like lean ghosts, with the ground littered green all over. At the next stage he swept up the clippings, bundled them neatly, and carried them off to his friend, namesake, and letter-writer, living in the Bamboo Bazaar, who had his cows to feed; in return for Annamalai's generosity, he kept his penmanship ever at Annamalai's service.

His gardening activities ceased late in the evening. He laid away his implements in a corner of his basement room, laboriously coiled up the hose, and locked it away, muttering, 'This is my very life; otherwise how can an old fellow feed his plants and earn a good name? If some devil steals this I am undone, and you will never see me again.' So much lay behind his habit of rolling up the rubber hose, and I fancied that he slept in its coils as an added safety. After putting it away he took off his red bandanna, turned on the tap, and splashed enormous quantities of water over himself, blowing his nose, clearing his throat, and grooming himself noisily; he washed his feet, rubbing his heels on a granite slab until they shone red; now his bandanna would be employed as a towel; wiping himself dry, he disappeared into the basement and came out later wearing a shirt and a white *dhoti*. This was his off hour, when he visited the gate shop at the level crossing in order to replenish his stock of tobacco and gossip with friends seated on a teak log. The railway gatekeeper who owned the shop (although for reasons of policy he gave out that it belonged to his brother-in-law) was a man of information and read out a summary of the day's news to this gathering out of a local news sheet published by the man who owned the Truth Printing Press and who reduced the day's radio broadcasts and the contents of other newspapers into tiny paragraphs on a single sheet of paper, infringing every form of copyright. He brought out his edition in the evening for two paise, perhaps the cheapest newspaper in the world. Annamalai paid close attention to the reading and thus participated in contemporary history. When he returned home I could spot him half a mile away from my window as his red bandanna came into view over the crest of a slope. If he found me near at hand, he passed to me the news of the day. That was how I first heard of John Kennedy's assassination. I had not tuned the radio the whole day, being absorbed in some studies. I was standing at the gate when he returned home, and I asked casually, 'What is your news today?' and he answered without stopping, 'News? I don't go hunting for it, but I overheard that the chief ruler of America was killed today. They said something like *Kannady* (which means glass in Tamil); could any man give himself such a name?'

When I realized the import of his casual reference, I said, 'Look, was it Kennedy?'

'No, they said Kannady, and someone shot him with a gun and killed him, and probably they have already cremated him.' When I tried to get more news, he brushed me off with: 'Don't think I go after gossip, I only tell you what approaches my ears . . . and they were all talking . . .'

'Who?' I asked.

540

'I don't know who they are. Why should I ask for names? They all sit and talk, having nothing else to do.'

He would come into my study bearing a postcard in hand and announcing, 'A letter for you. The postman gave it.' Actually it would be a letter for him, which he'd never know until told, when he would suddenly become tense and take a step nearer in order to absorb all the details.

'What does he say?' he would ask irritably. His only correspondent was his brother Amavasai, and he hated to hear from him. Torn between curiosity and revulsion, he would wait for me to finish reading the postcard to myself first. 'What does that fellow have to say to me?' he would ask in a tone of disgust and add, 'As if I could not survive without such a brother!'

I'd read aloud the postcard, which always began formally with a ceremonial flourish: 'To my Godly brother and protector, this insignificant younger brother Amavasai submits as follows. At this moment we are all flourishing and we also pray for our divine elder brother's welfare in one breath.' This preamble would occupy half the space on the back of the card, to be abruptly followed by mundane matters. 'The boundary stone on the north side of our land was tampered with last night. We know who did it.'

Pushing the tobacco on his tongue out of the way in order to speak without impediment, Annamalai would demand, 'If you really know who, why don't you crack his skull? Are you bereft of all sense? Tell me that first,' and glare angrily at the postcard in my hand.

I'd read the following line by way of an explanation:

541

'But they don't care.'

'They don't? Why not?' The next few lines would agitate him most, but I had to read them out. 'Unless you come and deal with them personally, they will never be afraid. If you keep away, nothing will improve. You are away and do not care for your kith and kin and are indifferent to our welfare or suffering. You did not care to attend even my daughter's naming ceremony. This is not how the head of a family should behave.'

The rest of the letter generally turned out to be a regular charge-sheet, but concluded ceremoniously, mentioning again lotus feet and divinity. If I said, in order to divert his mind, 'Your brother writes well,' he would suddenly grin, very pleased at the compliment, and remark, 'He to write! Oh, oh, he is a lout. That letter is written by our schoolmaster. We generally tell him our thoughts and he will write. A gifted man.' He would prepare to go downstairs, remarking, 'Those fellows in my village are illiterate louts. Do you think my brother could talk to a telephone?' One of his urban triumphs was that he could handle the telephone. In distinguishing the mouthpiece from the earpiece, he displayed the pride of an astronaut strolling in space. He felt an intimacy with the instrument, and whenever it rang he'd run up to announce, 'Telepoon, sami,' even if I happened to be near it. When I came home at night he'd always run forward to declare while opening the gate, 'There was a telepoon—someone asked if you were in . . .'

'Who was it?'

'Who? How could I know? He didn't show his face!'

'Didn't you ask his name?'

'No, what should I do with his name?'

One morning he waited at my bedroom door to tell me, 'At five o'clock there was a telepoon. You were sleeping, and so I asked, 'Who are you?' He said, 'Trunk, trunk,' and I told him, 'Go away, don't trouble us. No trunk or baggage here. Master is sleeping.' To this day I have no idea where the trunk call was from. When I tried to explain to him what a 'trunk call' was (long-distance call) he kept saying, 'When you are sleeping, that fellow asks for a trunk! Why should we care?' I gave up.

The only way to exist in harmony with Annamalai was to take him as he was; to improve or enlighten him would only exhaust the reformer and disrupt nature's design. At first he used to light a fire in the basement itself, his fuel consisting of leaves and all sorts of odds and ends swept up from the garden, which created an enormous pall of smoke and blackened the walls; also there was the danger of his setting fire to himself in that room without a chimney. I admonished him one day and suggested that he use charcoal. He said, 'Impossible! Food cooked over charcoal shortens one's life, sir. Hereafter I will not cook inside the house at all.' Next day he set up three bricks under the pomegranate tree, placed a mud pot over them, and raised a roaring fire. He boiled water and cooked rice, dal, onion, tomato, and a variety of greens picked from the garden, and created a stew whose fragrance rose heavenward and in its passage enticed me to peep over the terrace and imbibe it.

When the monsoon set in I felt anxious as to how he was going to manage, but somehow even when the skies darkened and the rains fell, between two bouts he raised and kept up the fire under the pomegranate shade. When it poured incessantly he held a corrugated iron sheet over the fire and managed, never bothering to shield his own head. He ate at night, and preserved the remnant, and on the following day from time to time quietly dipped his fingers into the pot and ate a mouthful, facing the wall and shielding his aluminum plate from any Evil Eye that might happen to peep in at his door.

There was not a stronger person in the neighbourhood. When he stalked about during his hours of watch, tapping the ground with a metal rod and challenging in a stentorian voice, he created an air of utter intimidation, like a mastiff. God knows we might have needed a mastiff definitely in the early days, but not now. Annamalai did not seem to realize that such an aggressive watch was no longer necessary. He did not seem to have noticed the transition of my surroundings from a lonely outpost (where I had often watched thieves break open a trunk and examine their booty by torchlight in a ditch a hundred yards from my bedroom window) into a populous colony, nor did he take note of the coming of the industrial estate beyond my house. If any person passing my gate dallied a minute, particularly at night after he had had his supper and the stars were out, Annamalai would challenge him to explain his presence. People passing my gate quickened their pace as a general policy. Occasionally he softened when someone asked for flowers for worship. If he saw me noticing the transaction, he would shout in rage, 'Go away. What do you think you are? Do flowers come up by themselves? Here is the old fellow giving his life to tending them, and you think . . .' and charge threateningly towards the would-be worshipper; but if I remained indoors and watched through the window I could see him give a handful of flowers to the person at the gate, muting his steps and tone and glancing over his shoulder to make sure that I was not watching.

Annamalai was believed to earn money by selling my flowers, according to a lady living next door to me, who had constituted herself his implacable enemy. According to Annamalai, whenever I was away on tour she demanded of him the banana leaves grown in my garden, for her guests to dine on, and his steady refusal had angered her. Whenever I passed their compound wall she would whisper, 'You are trusting that fellow too much, he is always talking to the people at the gate and always carrying on some transaction.' A crisis of the first order developed once when she charged him with the theft of her fowls. She reared poultry, which often invaded my compound through a gap in the fence, and every afternoon Annamalai would be chasing them out with stones and war cries. When I was away for weeks on end, according to the lady, every other day she missed a bird when she counted them at night. She explained how Annamalai dazed the fowl by throwing a wet towel over its head, and carried it off to the shop at the level crossing, where his accomplices sold or cooked it.

Once feathers were found scattered around Annamalai's habitat when it was raided by a watchman of the municipal sewage farm, who wore a khaki coat and pretended to he a policeman. Annamalai was duly frightened and upset. Returning home from a tour one afternoon, I found him standing on a foot-high block of stone, in order to be heard better next door, and haranguing, 'You set the police on me, do you, because you have lost a fowl? So what? What have I to do with it? If it strays into my compound I'll twist its neck, no doubt, but don't imagine that I will thieve like a cheap rascal. Why go about fowl-thieving? I care two straws for your police. They come to us for baksheesh in our village; foolish people will not know that. I am a respectable farmer with an acre of land in the village. I grow rice. Amavasai looks after it and writes to me. I receive letters by post. If I am a fowl-thief, what are those that call me so? Anyway, what do you think you are? Whom do you dare to talk to?' In this strain he spoke for about half an hour, addressing the air and the sky, but the direction of his remarks could not he mistaken. Every day at the same hour he delivered his harangue, soon after he had eaten his midday food, chewed tobacco, and tied the red bandanna securely over his ears.

Sometimes he added much autobiographical detail. Although it was beamed in the direction of the lady next door, I gathered a great deal of information in bits and pieces which enabled me to understand his earlier life. Mounted on his block of stone, he said, 'I was this high when I left home. A man who has the stuff to leave home when he is only ten won't be the sort to steal fowl. My father had said, "You are a thief . . ." That night I slipped out of the house and walked . . . I sat in a train going towards Madras . . . They threw me out, but I got into the next train, and although they thrashed me and threw me out again and again, I reached Madras without a ticket. I am that kind, madam, not a fowl-thief, worked as a coolie and lived in the verandas of big buildings. I am an independent man, madam, I don't stand nonsense from others, even if it is my father. One day someone called me and put me on the deck of a steamer and sent me to a tea garden in Ceylon, where I was until the fever got me. Do you think your son will have the courage to face such things?'

At the same hour day after day I listened and could piece together his life. 'When I came back home I was rid of the shivering fever. I gave my father a hundred rupees and told him that a thief would not bring him a hundred rupees. I hated my village, with all those ignorant folk. My father knew I was planning to run away once again. One day all of them held me down, decorated the house, and married me to a girl. I and Amavasai went to the fields and ploughed and weeded. My wife cooked my food. After my daughter appeared I left home and went away to Penang. I worked in the rubber estates, earned money, and sent money home. That is all they care for at home—as long as you send money they don't care where you are or what you do. All that they want is money, money. I was happy in the rubber plantations. When the Japanese came they cut off everybody's head or broke their skulls with their guns, and they made us dig pits to bury the dead and also ourselves in the end. I escaped and was taken to Madras in a boat with a lot of others. At home I found my daughter grown up, but my wife was dead. It seems she had fever every day and was dead and gone. My son-in-law is in a government job in the town. I am not a fowl-thief . . . My granddaughter goes to a school every day carrying a bag of books, with her anklets jingling and flowers in her hair . . . I had brought the jewellery for her from Malaya.' Whatever the contents of his narrative, he always concluded, 'I am not a rascal. If I were a fowl-thief . . . would a government officer be my son-in-law?'

I told him, 'No one is listening. Why do you address the wall?'

'They are crouching behind it, not missing a word anyway,' he said. 'If she is a great person, let her be, what do I care? How dare she say that I stole her fowl? What do I want their fowl for? Let them keep them under their bed. I don't care. But if any creature ever strays here I'll wring its neck, that is certain.'

'And what will you do with it?'

'I don't care what. Why should I watch what happens to a headless fowl?'

The postcard that most upset him was the one which said, after the usual preamble, 'The black sheep has delivered a lamb, which is also black, but the shepherd is claiming it: every day he comes and creates a scene. We have locked up the lamb, but he threatens to break open the door and take away the lamb. He stands in the street and abuses us every day, and curses our family; such curses are not good for us.' Annamalai interrupted the letter to demand, 'Afraid of curses! Haven't you speech enough to outcurse him?' Another postcard three days later said, 'They came yesterday and carried off the black sheep, the mother, when we were away in the fields.'

'Oh, the . . .' He checked the unholy expression that welled up from the bottom of his heart. 'I know how it must have happened. They must have kept the mother tied up in the backyard while locking up the lamb. What use would that be?' He looked at me questioningly.

I felt I must ask at this point, 'Whose sheep was it?'

'The shepherd's, of course, but he borrowed ten rupees and left me the sheep as a pledge. Give me my ten rupees and take away the sheep, that is all. How can you claim the lamb? A lamb that is born under our roof is ours.' This was an intricate legal point, I think the only one of its kind in the world, impossible for anyone to give a verdict on or quote precedents, as it concerned a unique kind of mortgage which multiplied in custody. 'I have a set of senseless dummies managing my affairs; it is people like my brother who made me want to run away from home.'

This proved a lucky break for the lady next door as the following afternoon Annamalai left to seek the company of the level-crossing gateman and other well-wishers in order to evolve a strategy to confound the erring shepherd in their village. As days passed he began to look more and more serene. I sensed that some solution had been found. He explained that someone who had arrived from the village brought the report that one night they had found the black sheep being driven off by the butcher, whereupon they waylaid him and carried it back to the bleating lamb at home. Now both the sheep and the lamb were securely locked up, while his brother and the family slept outside on the *pyol* of the house. I couldn't imagine how long they could continue this arrangement, but Annamalai said, 'Give me back my ten rupees and take away the sheep.'

'What happens to the lamb?'

'It is ours, of course. The sheep was barren until it came to our house; that shepherd boy did not pledge a pregnant sheep.'

It was the tailor incident that ended our association. The postcard from home said, 'The tailor has sold his machine to another tailor and has decamped. Things are bound to happen when you sit so far away from your kith

and kin. You are allowing all your affairs to be spoilt.'
Annamalai held his temples between his hands and shut his
eyes, unable to stand the shock of this revelation. I asked no
questions, he said nothing more and left me, and I saw him
go up the slope towards the level crossing. Later I watched
him from my window as he dug at a banana root; he
paused and stood frozen in a tableau with his pickaxe stuck
in the ground, arms akimbo, staring at the mud at his feet.
I knew at that moment that he was brooding over his
domestic affairs. I went down, gently approached him,
pretended to look at the banana root, but actually was
dying of curiosity to know more about the tailor story. I
asked some casual horticultural questions and when he
started to reply I asked, 'Why are tailors becoming
troublesome, unpunctual, and always stealing bits of cloth?'

My anti-tailor sentiment softened him, and he said,
'Tailor or carpenter or whoever he may be, what do I care,
I am not afraid of them. I don't care for them.'

'Who is the tailor your brother mentions in his letter?'

'Oh, that! A fellow called Ranga in our village, worthless
fellow, got kicked out everywhere,' and there the narrative
for the day ended because of some interruption.

I got him to talk about the tailor a couple of days later.
'People didn't like him, but, he was a good tailor . . . could
stitch kerchief, drawers, banyan, and even women's jackets
. . . but the fellow had no machine and none of his relations
would help him. No one would lend him money. I got a
money order from Ceylon one day for a hundred rupees—
some money I had left behind. When the postman brought
the money order, this tailor also came along with him, at
the same moment. How could he have known? After the

postman left, he asked, 'Can't you give me a hundred rupees? I can buy a machine.' I asked him, 'How did you know that I was receiving a hundred rupees, who told you?' and I slapped his face, spat at him for prying into my affairs. The fellow wept. I was, after all, his elder, and so I felt sorry and said, 'Stop that. If you howl like that l will thrash you.' Then all our village elders assembled and heard both of us, and ordered that I should lend my hundred rupees to him.'

I failed to understand how anyone could order him thus. I asked naïvely, 'Why should they have told you and what have they to do with it?'

He thought for a while and answered, 'That is how we do it, when the elders assemble and order us . . .'

'But you didn't call the assembly?'

'I didn't, but they came and saw us, when the tailor was crying out that I had hurt him. They then wrote a bond on government paper with stamp and made him sign it; the man who sold the paper was also there, and we gave him two rupees for writing the document.'

Later I got a picture of this transaction little by little. The tailor purchased a sewing machine with the loan from Annamalai. Annamalai's brother accommodated the tailor and the machine on the *pyol* of his house; the tailor renewed the bond from time to time, paid the interest regularly and also a daily rent for occupying the *pyol*. This was a sort of gilt-edged security, and Annamalai preserved the bond in the safety of a tin box in my cellar. When the time for its renewal came each year, he undertook a trip to the village and came back after a month with a fresh signature on the bond, attested by the village headman. But now the entire basis of their financial relationship was shaken. The original tailor had decamped, and the new tailor did not recognize his indebtedness, although he sat on the *pyol* of their house and stitched away without speaking to anyone.

'You never asked for your hundred rupees back?' I asked.

'Why should I?' he asked, surprised at my question. 'As long as he was paying the interest, and renewing his signature. He might have been up to some mischief if I didn't go in person; that is why I went there every time.' After all this narration, Annamalai asked, 'What shall I do now? The rascal has decamped.'

'But where is the machine?'

'Still there. The new tailor stitches everybody's clothes in our house but won't speak to us, nor does he go away from the machine. He sleeps under it every night.'

'Why don't you throw him out?'

Annamalai thought for a while and said, 'He will not speak to us and he will not pay us the rent, saying when pressed that he paid all the rent to the first tailor along with the price of the machine . . . Could it be possible? Is it so in the letter you read?'

Very soon another postcard came. It started with the respected preamble, all right, but ended rather abruptly with the words: 'We have nowhere to sleep, the tailor will not move. Inside the house the sheep and the lamb are locked. As the elder of our family, tell us where we should sleep. My wives threaten to go away to their parents' houses. I am sleeping with all the children in the street. Our own house has no place for us. If you keep so far away from your kith and kin, such things are bound to happen. We suffer and you don't care.'

At this point Annamalai indulged in loud thinking. 'Nothing new, these women are always running off to their parents . . . if you sneeze or cough it is enough to make them threaten that they will go away. Unlucky fellow, that brother of mine. He has no guts to say, "All right, begone, you moodhevi," he is afraid of them.'

'Why can't they throw out the tailor and lock up the machine along with the sheep? Then they could all sleep on the *pyol* . . .'

'I think he is the son of our wrestler—that new tailor, and you know my brother is made of straw although he has produced nine children.' He considered the situation in silence for a while and said, 'It is also good in a way. As long as he is not thrown out, the machine is also there . . . God is helping us by keeping him there within our hold. If my brother has no place to sleep in, let him remain awake.'

For the next three days I sensed that much confabulation was going on, as I saw the red bandanna go up the crest more often than usual. His adviser at the Bamboo Bazaar and the well-wishers at the gate shop must have attacked the core of the problem and discovered a solution. When he returned from the gate shop one evening he announced point blank, 'I must go to my village.'

'Yes, why so suddenly?'

'The bond must be changed, renewed in the new tailor's name. You must let me go.'

'When?'

'When? . . . Whenever you think I should go.'

'I don't think you should go at all. I can't let you go
now. I am planning to visit Rameswaram on a pilgrimage.'

'Yes, it is a holy place, good to visit,' he said
patronizingly. 'You will acquire a lot of merit. After you
come back I will go.' So we parted on the best of terms that
day. As if nothing had been spoken on the subject till now,
he came up again next day, stood behind my chair, and said
without any preamble, 'I must go.'

'Yes, after I return from my pilgrimage.'

He turned round and went down half-way, but came up
again to ask, 'When are you going?'

His constant questioning put me on edge; anyway I
suppressed my annoyance and replied calmly, 'I am waiting
for some others to join me, perhaps in ten days.'

He seemed satisfied with the answer and shuffled down.
That night when I returned home he met me at the gate.
Hardly had I stepped in when he said, 'I will be back in ten
days; let me go tomorrow. I will be back in ten days and
I will guard the house when you are away on pilgrimage . . .'

'Should we settle all questions standing in the street?
Can't you wait until I am in?'

He didn't answer but shut the gate and went away to
his room. I felt bad all that night. While I changed my
clothes, ate, and read or wrote, there was an uneasiness at
the back of my mind at the memory of my sharp speech. I
had sounded too severe. I went down to his backyard first
thing in the morning, earlier than usual. He sat under the
tap with the water turned full blast on his head, and then
went dripping to his basement room. He stuck a flower on
a picture of God on his wall, lit an incense stick, stuck a
flower over his ear, put holy ash on his forehead, knotted

the bandanna over his ear, and, dressed in his shorts, emerged ready for the day, but there was no friendliness in his eyes. I spent the time pretending to examine the mango blooms, made some appreciative remarks about the state of the garden, and suddenly said, 'You want to be away for only ten days?'

'Yes, yes,' he replied eagerly, his mood softening. 'I must renew the bond, or gather people to throw out that interloper and seize his machine . . . even if it means bloodshed. Someone has to lose his life in this business. I will come back in ten days.'

It sounded to me too ambitious a programme to be completed in ten days. 'Are you sure that you want only ten days off?' I asked kindly.

'It may be a day more or less, but I promise to be back then. Once I return I won't go for two years, even then I won't go unless . . . I will leave the next renewal in my brother's hands.'

I found myself irritated again and said, 'I cannot let you go now,' in a tone of extreme firmness, at which he came nearer and pleaded with his palms pressed together, 'Please, I must renew the bond now; otherwise, if it is delayed, I will lose everything, and the people in my village will laugh at me.'

'Get me the bond, I will have a look at it,' I said with authority.

I could hear him open his black trunk. He came in bearing a swath of cloth, unwound it with tender care, and took out of its folds a document on parchment paper. I looked through it. The bond was worth a hundred rupees, and whoever had drafted it made no mention of a tailor or his machine. It was just a note promising repayment of a hundred rupees with interest from time to time, stuck with numerous stamps, dates, thumb impressions, and signatures. I really could not see how it was going to help him. I read it out to him and commented, with my fingers drumming effectively on the document, 'Where is any mention of your tailor or his machine?'

'Surely there is the name Ranga on it!'

'But there is no mention of a tailor. For all it says, Ranga could be a scavenger.'

Annamalai looked panic-stricken. He put his eyes close to the document and, jabbing it with his finger, asked, 'What does it say here?'

I read it word by word again. He looked forlorn. I said, 'I will give you a hundred rupees and don't bother about the bond. What does it cost you to reach your village?'

He made loud calculations and said, 'About ten rupees by Passenger from . . .'

'Coming back, ten rupees. You have been going there for years now and you have already spent more than the principal in railway fare alone to get the bond renewed.'

'But he pays interest,' he said.

'Give me the bond. I will pay the amount and you stay on.' I felt desolate at the thought of his going away. At various times I went out on journeys short and long. Each time I just abandoned the house and returned home weeks and months later to find even a scrap of paper in the wastebasket preserved with care. Now I felt desolate.

He brushed aside my economic arguments. 'You don't know these things. I can always go to a court as long as the bond is there . . .'

'And involve yourself in further expenses? It will be cheaper to burn that bond of yours.' He gave me up as a dense, impossible man whose economic notions were too elementary.

Next day and next again and again, I heard his steps on the stairs. 'I will come back in ten days.'

I said, 'All right, all right, you have too many transactions and you have no peace of mind to do your duty here, and you don't care what happens to me. I have to change my plans for your sake, I suppose?'

All this was lost on him, it was gibberish as far as he was concerned. I was obsessed with flimsy, impalpable things while the solid, four-square realities of the earth were really sheep and tailors and bonds. He stared at me pityingly for a moment as at an uncomprehending fool, turned, and went downstairs. The next few days I found him sulking. He answered me sharply whenever I spoke to him. He never watered the plants. He ignored the lady next door. More than all, he did not light the fire, as was his custom, in the shade of the pomegranate shrub. He had taken off the red bandanna and hooded an old blanket over his head as he sat in a corner of the basement room, in a state of mourning. When I went out or came in, he emerged from the basement and opened the gate dutifully. But no word passed between us. Once I tried to draw him into a conversation by asking breezily, 'Did you hear that they are opening a new store over there?'

'I go nowhere and seek no company. Why should you think I go about, gossiping about shops and things? None of my business.'

Another day I asked, 'Did anyone telephone?'

'Wouldn't I mention it if there had been telepoon?' he replied, glaring at me, and withdrew mumbling, 'If you have no trust in me, send me away. Why should I lie that there was no telepoon if there was one? I am not a rascal. I am also a respectable farmer; send me away.' He looked like someone else under his grey hood; his angry eyes peered at me with hostility. It seemed as if he had propped himself up with an effort all these years but now was suddenly falling to pieces.

A week later, one morning I heard a sound at the gate, noticed him standing outside, his tin trunk and a gunny sack stuffed with odds and ends on the ground at his feet. He wore a dark coat which he had preserved for occasions, a white *dhoti*, and a neat turban on his head. He was nearly unrecognizable in this garb. He said, 'I am going by the eight-o'clock train today. Here is the key of the basement room.' He then threw open the lid of his trunk and said, 'See if I have stolen anything of yours, but that lady calls me a fowl-thief. I am not a rascal.'

'Why do you have to go away like this? Is this how you should leave after fifteen years of service?' I asked.

He merely said, 'I am not well. I don't want to die in this house and bring it a bad name. Let me go home and die. There they will put new clothes and a fresh garland on my corpse and carry it in a procession along all the streets of our village with a band. Whereas if I am dead in that basement room while you are away, I will rot there till the municipal scavengers cart me away with the garbage heap. Let me not bring this house an evil reputation. I will go home and die. All the garden tools are in that room. Count them if you like. I am not a thief.' He waited for me to inspect his trunk. I said, 'Shut it, I don't have to search your trunk.' He hoisted it on his head and placed over it the gunny bundle and was starting off.

'Wait,' I said.

'Why?' he asked without stopping, without turning.

'I want to give you—' I began, and dashed in to fetch some money. When I returned with ten rupees, he was gone.

SALT AND SAWDUST

I

BEING A CHILDLESS couple Veena and Swami found their one-and-a-half room tenement adequate. A small window opened on Grove Street, a *pyol* beside the street door served for a sit-out a kitchen to match, and a backyard with access to a common well. The genius who designed this type of dwelling was Coomar of Boeing Silk Centre, who had bought up an entire row of old houses adjoining his Silk Centre, demolished and rebuilt them to house his staff working in the weaving factory beyond the river. It proved a sound investment and also enabled Coomar to keep his men under his thumb.

Swami left (on his bicycle) for his factory at seven-thirty a.m. but got up at five, while his wife was still asleep. He drew water from the common well, lit the stove and prepared coffee and lunch for two, packing up a portion to carry. Veena got up late, gulped down the coffee kept on the stove, swept the floor and cleaned the vessels. After her bath, she lit an oil lamp before the image of a god in a niche. After lunch, she sat on the *pyol*, watched the street, with a magazine in hand, and brooded over a novel she was planning to write, still nebulous.

She felt she could start writing only when she got a proper notebook, which Swami had promised to bring this evening. While returning home Swami stopped by Bari's Stationery Mart on Market Road and announced, 'My wife is going to write a novel. Can you give me a good notebook?'

'How many pages?' Bari asked mechanically. Swami had no idea. He did not want to risk a conjecture.

'Please wait. I'll find out and come back,' he said and tried to leave.

Bari held him back, 'I know what you want. We are supplying notebooks to novelists all the time. Take this home.' He pressed into his hand a brown packet. 'Two hundred pages Hamilton Bond, five rupees. Come back for more—our notebooks are lucky. Many writers have become famous after buying from us.'

Veena was thrilled. She gazed on the green calico binding, flicked the pages, and ran her fingers tenderly over the paper.

'Now I can really start writing. I have been scribbling on slips of paper—old calendar sheets and such things.' She flicked the pages again, and cried, 'Lined too.'

'Lined sheets are a great help. When you want another one, tell me, and I'll get it,' he said.

'I want 400 pages, but this will do for the present,' she was so pleased that she felt she should do him a good turn. She hugged him and asked, 'Shall I cook our dinner tonight?'

'No, no,' he cried desperately.

On earlier occasions when she had cooked he had swallowed each morsel with difficulty, suppressing comment, and silently suffering. He felt that they might have to starve unless he took over the kitchen duties. He realized that she was not made for it. Boiling, baking, spicing, salting, blending were beyond her understanding or conception. He was a good eater with taste and appetite. 'A novelist probably cannot be a good cook,' he concluded, 'just as I cannot write a novel. She has not been taught to distinguish salt from sawdust.' He quietly took over the kitchen leaving her free to write whatever she fancied.

However, he would inquire from time to time, 'What progress?' She answered, 'Can't say anything now, we have to wait.'

Several days later, when he asked for progress, she said, 'The heroine is just emerging.'

'What do you call her?'

'Oh, names come very last in a novel.'

'In that case, how can a reader know who is who?'

'Just wait and see, it is my responsibility.'

'I could write only two pages today,' she said another day.

'Keep it up. Very soon you will fill four, eight, sixteen pages a day.' His vision soared on multiples of four for some obscure reason. 'I think I had better buy another 200-page notebook before Bari's stock is exhausted. He said that the demand from the novelists is rather heavy this season.'

'Did he mention any novelist's name?'

'I will ask next time.' After that he went into his room to change into a garb to suit his kitchen work. When he came out in a knee-length *dhoti* and a towel over his shoulder she said, 'I was asking if he had met any novelist.'

'Bari has met any number. I know only one novelist and she stands before me now.' He then asked, 'What kind of a man is your hero?'

She replied, 'What do you imagine him to be?'

'Tall, and powerful, not a fellow to be trifled with.'

'So be it,' she said, and asked, 'is he a fighting sort?'

'Maybe if he is drawn to it . . .'

She completed his sentence, 'He won't hesitate to knock off the front teeth of anyone—'

Swami found the image of an adversary minus his teeth amusing, and asked, 'What about the rest of his teeth?'

'He will deal with them when he is challenged next.'

'You almost make him a dentist,' he said.

'A Chinese dentist has opened a clinic at New Extension, and a lot of people sit before him open-mouthed.'

'How have you come to know about it?'

'Sometimes I lock the door and wander about till it is time to return home. Otherwise I cannot get ideas.'

'When will you find time to write if you are wandering about?'

'Wandering about is part of a writer's day. I also carry a small book and jot down things that interest me.'

'Excellent plan,' he said, and disappeared into the kitchen as he smelt burning oil from the frying pan.

II

Veena developed the idea further, and said, when they settled down on the hall-bench after supper, 'I think a

Chinese dentist is the hero, it is something original, none has thought of him before. Chinese dentists are famous.'

'But how can a girl of our part of the world marry a Chinese?'

'Why not?' she said and thought it over and said, 'In the novel actually he is not a Chinese. He had only his training in China.'

'Why did he go to China?' asked Swami.

'When he was a boy he ran away from home.'

'Why?'

'His schoolmaster caned him one day and, in sheer disgust, he went and slept on a bench at the railway platform for two days and nights. When a train passed at midnight, he slipped into a carriage and finally joined some monks and sailed for Peking in a boat.'

'Very interesting, very interesting,' Swami cried. 'How do you get these ideas?'

'When one writes, one gets ideas,' she explained, and continued, 'the monks left him at the port and vanished . . .'

'Were they supernatural beings? Could you explain their presence and help?'

'God must have sent them down to help the boy . . .'

'Why should God be interested?' Swami asked.

'God's ways are mysterious.'

'True, God's ways are certainly mysterious,' he endorsed her philosophy. She continued, 'And the young fellow wandered here and there in the streets of Peking, without food or shelter for a couple of days, and fainted in front of a dentist's clinic. In the morning when the dentist came to open the door, he saw the boy and thought he was dead.'

'What do they do in China with the dead?' he asked in genuine concern and added, 'they probably bury . . .'

'No, no, if he was buried that would end my story,' she said. 'The Chinese are probably careful and cautious, unlike in our country, where they immediately carry away a body and dispose of it.'

'Not that way,' Swami said, showing off his better knowledge of the situation. 'Once when I was working in a cloth shop, a body was found in the veranda and they immediately sent for a doctor.'

'Why a doctor when he or she is already dead?'

'That's a routine in such circumstances—' he generalized.

'I want you to find out from someone what the Chinese do when a body is found at the door. I must know before I proceed with the story.'

He said, 'Since he becomes the Chinese dentist of your story later, he was not really dead—so why bother about it?'

'Of course,' she agreed. 'When he came back home, he knew how to work as a dentist, and became prosperous and famous.'

'Readers will question you . . .'

'Oh, leave that to me, it is my business.'

The story was taken one step further at the next conference. They had both got into the habit of talking about it every evening after dinner, and were becoming, unconsciously, collaborators.

'He fell in love with a girl, who had somehow lost all her teeth and come to fit new ones . . . Day by day as he saw her with her jaws open to be fitted up, he began to love her, being physically so close to each other . . .'

Veena gloated over the vision of love blossoming in a dentist's chair . . .

Swami became critical, 'With her jaws open, toothless gums, do you think it is possible for a man to be attracted? Any romance possible in that state?'

'Don't you know that love is blind?'

Not wanting to appear to cross-examine or discourage her, he said, 'Ah, now I understand, it is natural that a man who bends so close over a woman's face cannot help it, and it's his chance to whisper in her ears his passion though if a toothless person comes before me, I would not care for her.' Veena took offence at this point.

'So that means if I lose my teeth, you will desert me?'

'No, no, you will always be my darling wife. But all that I am trying to say is, when the teeth are lost both the cheeks get sucked in and the mouth becomes pouchy, and the whole face loses shape.'

She was upset at this remark, got up and went away to the corner where her books were kept and started reading, ignoring him.

By the time they sat down again next night after dinner, she relented enough to say, 'He need not be a dentist—I agree it's an awkward situation for lovers . . . Shall I say that he is something in a less awkward profession, a silk merchant or a veterinary doctor?'

Swami was pleased that she had conceded his point, and felt that it was now his turn to concede a point and said, 'No, no, let him be what he is, it's very original, don't change—this is probably the first time a dentist comes into a story . . .'

And on that agreeable note, peace was established once

566

again. The dentist had to work on the heroine's gums for a long time taking moulds and preparing her dentures, trying them out, filing, fitting and bridging. All the time Cupid was at work. It took the dentist several weeks to complete his task and beautify her face. When it was accomplished he proposed and they married, overcoming obstacles.

III

As the notebook was getting filled, Veena took an afternoon off to spend time at the Town Hall library, to browse through popular magazines on the hall table and romances in the shelves, desperately seeking ideas. Not a single book in the whole library on the theme of a dentist and a bare-gummed heroine. She returned home and remained silent all through the evening, leaving Swami to concentrate on his duties in the kitchen. She sat in her corner trying to go on with the story until Swami called from the kitchen, 'Dinner ready.'

One evening she confessed: 'I have not been able to write even two lines today. I don't know in which language I should continue.' She was suddenly facing a problem. She was good in English—always remembered her 60 per cent in English Literature in BA. At the same time she felt she could write in Tamil, and felt it her duty to enrich her mother tongue, so that all classes of people could benefit from her writing. It was an inner struggle, which she did not reveal even to her husband, but he sensed something was wrong and inquired tactfully, 'Want anything?'

'What is our language?' she asked.

'Tamil, of course.'

'What was the language of my studies at Albert Mission?'

'English.'

'How did I fare in it?'

'You always got 60 per cent.'

'Why should I not write in English?'

'Nobody said you should not.'

'But my conscience dictates I should write only in my mother tongue.'

'Yes, of course,' he agreed.

'You go on saying "Yes" to everything. You are not helping me.' He uttered some vague mumbling sounds.

'What are you trying to say?' she asked angrily. He remained silent like a schoolboy before an aggressive pedagogue.

'Don't you realize that English will make my novel known all over India if not the whole world?'

'Very true,' he said with a forced smile. 'Why is she grilling me?' he reflected. 'After all, I know nothing about writing novels. I am only a weaving supervisor at Coomar's factory.' He said to himself further, 'Anyway, it's her business. No one compels her to write a novel. Let her throw it away. If she finds time hanging heavily, let her spin yarn on a charka.' He suddenly asked, 'Shall I get you a charka?'

'Why?' she asked, rather alarmed at his irrelevancy.

'Mahatma Gandhi had advised every citizen of India to spin as a patriotic duty. They are distributing charkas almost free at Gandhi Centre . . .' By this time she felt that something was amiss, abruptly got up and went over to her canvas chair in the corner, picking up a book from her cupboard. He sat in his wooden chair without moving or speaking. He began to feel that silence would be the safest course, fearing, as in a law court, any word he uttered might be used against him. He sat looking out of the window though nothing was happening there, except a donkey swishing its tail under the street lamp, 'Flies are bothering it,' he observed to himself, 'otherwise it could be the happiest donkey.' His neighbour was returning home with a green plastic bag filled with vegetables and passed by with a nod. Swami found the silence oppressive, and tried to break it, 'Mahatma Gandhi had advised that every individual should spin morning and evening and did solve a lot of problems.'

'What sort of problems?' she asked gruffly, looking up from her book.

He answered, 'Well, all sorts of problems people face,' he replied from his seat.

'What makes you talk of that subject now?' She was too logical and serious, he commented within himself, 'Has to be. Novelists are probably like that everywhere.' He remained silent, not knowing how to proceed or in which direction. She sued for peace two days later by an abrupt announcement, 'Have decided to write both in Tamil and English, without bothering about the language just as it comes. Sometimes I think in English, sometimes in Tamil, ideas are more important than language. I'll put down the ideas as they occur to me, if in English, it'll be English, if the next paragraph comes in Tamil I'll not hesitate to continue in Tamil, no hard and fast rule.'

'Of course there should be no hard and fast rules in such matters. To be reduced to a single language in the final stage, I suppose?'

'Why should I?' she said, slightly irritated. 'Don't we mix English and Tamil in conversation?'

He wanted to say, 'If you knew Hindi, you could continue a few paragraphs in Hindi too, it being our national language as desired by Mahatma Gandhi,' but he had the wisdom to suppress it. Another mention of Gandhi might destroy the slender fabric of peace, but he asked solicitously, 'Will you need another book for writing?'

'Yes,' she said, 'I am abandoning this notebook, and will make a fresh start on a new notebook . . .' His mind got busy planning what to do with the blank pages of the present notebook. 'I don't want to look at those pages again. I'll start afresh. You may do what you please with this notebook. Get me another one without fail tomorrow . . .'

'Perhaps you may require two books, if you are writing in two languages, it may prove longer.'

'Difficult to say anything about it now, but bring me one book, that will do for the present . . .'

'I will tell Bari to keep one in reserve in any case . . .' he said. It went on like that. It became a routine for her to fill her notebook, adding to the story each day. They used to talk about it, until one day she announced, 'They are married. It is a grand wedding since he was a popular dentist, and a lot of people in the town owed their good looks to him. His clinic was expanded and he engaged several assistants, and he was able to give his wife a car and a big house, and he had a farm outside the city, and they often spent their weekends at the farm.'

'Any children?'

'By and by, inevitably.'

'How many are you going to give him?'

'We will see,' she said, and added, 'at some point I must decide whether to limit their offspring to one or several.'

'But China has the highest population,' he said.

'True, but he is not a real Chinese, he only trained there,' she said, correcting him.

He said, 'Then he must have at least four children. Two sons and two daughters, the first and the third must be daughters.' He noticed that she looked annoyed . . . too much interference, she suddenly felt, and lapsed into silence.

'Suppose they also have twins?' he dared.

'We can't burden them that way, having no knowledge of bringing up a child ourselves.'

'God will give us children at the appointed time . . .'

'But you assume that we could recklessly burden the couple in the story!' she said.

IV

Veena wrote steadily, filled up page after page of a fresh notebook . . . and with a look of triumph told Swami, 'I won't need another notebook . . .' She held up the notebook proudly. He looked through the pages, shook his head in appreciation of her feat in completing the work; not entirely her work, he had a slight share in her accomplishment, of the 200 pages in the book he had contributed ten pages, and was proud of it. In the story, at the dentist's wedding, an elaborate feeding programme was described for a thousand guests. The feast was very well-planned—two days running they served breakfast, coffee and idli and dosai and uppuma and two sweets and fruit preparations, a heavy lunch with six vegetables and rice preparations, concluding with a light elegant supper. Fried almonds and nuts were available in bowls all over the place, all through the day. The bridegroom, the dentist, had expressed a wish that a variety of eatables must be available for those with weak teeth or even no teeth, he had all kinds of patients, capable of different degrees of chewing and mastication.

Food had to be provided for them, in different densities and calibre. Arrangements were made not only to provide for those who could chew hardstuff, masticate a stone with confidence, but also for those who could only swallow a mashed, over-ripe banana. The doctor was saying again and again, 'It is my principle that a marriage feast must be remembered—not only by those endowed with thirty-two teeth, but also by the unfortunate ones who have less or none.' At this stage Swami and Veena lost sight of the fact that it was a piece of fiction that they were engaged in and went on to chart every meal with tremendous zest. Swami would brook no compromise: it had to be the finest cuisine in every aspect. 'Why should you make it so elaborate and gluttonous?' Veena asked.

He answered, 'The guests should have a wide choice, let them take it or leave it. Why should we bother? Anyway, it is to cost us nothing. Why not make it memorable?' So he let himself go. He explained what basic ingredients were required for the special items in the menu, the right stores which supplied only clean grains and pulses imported from Tanjore and Sholapur, honey and saffron from Kashmir, apples from Kulu valley, and rose water from Hyderabad to flavour sherbets to quench the afternoon thirst of guests, spices, cardamom, cinnamon and cloves from Kerala, and chillies and tamarind from Guntur . . . Swami not only knew where to get the best, but also how to process, dry, grind, and pulverize them before cooking. He also knew how to make a variety of sun-dried fritters, wafers and chips. He arranged for sesame from somewhere to extract the best frying oil, butter from somewhere else to melt and obtain fragrant ghee. He wrote down everything including detailed recipes on the blank pages of the notebook that Veena had abandoned. When he presented his composition to Veena, she said, 'Too long, I'll take only what is relevant to my story.' She accepted only ten pages of his writing, rewrote it, and blended it into her narrative—even with that Swami felt proud of his participation in a literary work.

Swami took the completed novel to Bari, who looked through the pages and said, 'The lady, your missus, must be very clever.'

'Yes, she is,' said Swami, 'otherwise how could one write so much? I could only help her with ideas, now and then, but I am no writer.'

Bari said, 'I can't read your language or English very much, but I'll show it to a scholar I know, who buys paper and stationery from me. He is a professor in our college— a master of eighteen languages.'

It took ten days to get an opinion. Ten days of suspense for Veena, who constantly questioned Swami at their night sessions after dinner, 'Suppose the professor says it is no good?' Swami had to reassure again and again, 'Don't worry. He'll like it. If he doesn't, we will show it to another scholar . . .' Every evening he stopped by at Bari's to ask for the verdict, while Veena waited anxiously for Swami's return.

'Wait, wait, don't be nervous. Scholars will take their own time to study any piece of work. We can't rush them . . .'

One evening he brought her the good news. The scholar's verdict was favourable. He approved especially the double language experiment which showed originality. Veena could not sleep peacefully that night, nor let her husband sleep, agitated by dreams of success and fame as a novelist.

She disturbed him through the night in order to discuss the next step. 'Should we not find a publisher in Madras? They know how to reach the readers.'

'Yes, yes,' he muttered sleepily.

'We may have to travel to Madras . . . Can you take leave? If Coomar refuses to let you go, you must resign. If the novel is taken, we may not have to depend upon Coomar. If it becomes a hit, filmmakers will come after us, that'll mean . . .' Her dreams soared higher and higher. Swami was so frequently shaken out of sleep that he wondered why he should not take a pillow and move to the *pyol* outside.

Bari stopped their plan to visit Madras. 'Why should you go so far for this purpose? I have paper and a friend has the best press . . .'

'Where?' asked Swami.

'You know Mango Lane, just at the start of Mempi Hill Road.'

'No, never been there . . .'

'Once it was an orchard, where mangoes were cultivated and exported to Europe and America, till my friend bought the place, cleared the grove, and installed a press there. He prints and publishes many books, also for the government, reports and railway time-tables. I supply all the paper he needs, a good customer—not always for our Hamilton Brand but he buys all sorts. His name is Natesh, a good friend. He will print anything I want. Why should you wait upon publishers in Madras? They may not accept the novel, having their own notions, or if they take it, they may delay for years. I know novelists who have aged while waiting and waiting.'

'Impossible to wait,' said Swami recollecting his wife's anxiety and impatience to see herself in print.

V

Bari had the printer waiting at his shop. He told Swami, 'My friend came to order some thin paper for handbills, and I have held him back.' Natesh was a tall, lean, bearded person who wore a khadi *kurta* and *dhoti*, forehead smeared with vermilion and holy ash. Natesh wished to see the manuscript. Swami produced the notebook for the printer's inspection next day. But when he suggested he take it with him to Mango Lane, for estimating the printing charges, Swami felt embarrassed, not being sure if Veena would like to let it out of sight. He said, 'I'll bring it back later, the author is still revising it.' Natesh went through the pages, counting the lines for about fifteen minutes, noting down the number of lines and pages, and declared, 'I'll give an estimate for printing and binding in two days.'

'I'll give an estimate for the paper required—that's my business,' added Bari. On this hopeful note they parted for the evening.

Coming to brass tacks a couple of days later, Bari made

a proposal: 'I'll supply the paper definitely as your friend, Natesh, has calculated that you will need twenty reams of white printing for the text, extra for covers. We will print 500 copies at first. It would have cost less if the text had been in a single language but now the labour charges are more for two languages, and Natesh wants to print Tamil in black ink and English in red ink on a page, and that'll also cost more. I can supply printing ink also. It would have been cheaper if your missus had written less number of pages and in her mother tongue only.' Swami said, being ignorant of the intricacies of the creative process, 'I will tell her so.'

'No, no,' cried Bari in alarm. 'I'd not like to offend her, sir . . . Novelists must be respected, and must be left to write in as many languages they choose, who are we to question?'

The printer at their next meeting said, 'I can give a rough estimate, not the final one unless I go through the text for two days, and I won't undertake printing without going through the text to assure myself that it contains no blasphemy, treason, obscenity or plagiarism. It's a legal requirement, if there is any of the above I'll be hauled up before a magistrate . . . Swami became panicky, he had not read the manuscript, (but even if he had) he could not say what offences Veena might have committed, but protested aloud, 'Oh, no! Bari knows me and my family, and our reputation . . .' Bari endorsed this sentiment, 'Such offences are unthinkable in their family, they are very well-known, high class, otherwise they can't be my customers: I would not sell Hamilton Bond paper to anyone and everyone unless I am convinced that they are lawful persons belonging to good families. If I gave my best paper to all and sundry, where would I be?' Swami had no answer to this question as he could not follow the logic of Bari's train of thought. They were sitting around on low aluminium stools and Swami's back ached, sitting erect and stiff on a circular seat which had neither an armrest nor a back. He stood up. Bari cried, 'Sit, down, sit down. You must have tea.' He beckoned his servant, an urchin he had brought with him from Aligarh, whom he never let out of sight. 'Jiddu, three cups of tea. Tell that man to give the best tea, otherwise I'll not pay . . .' While the boy dashed out for tea, Natesh said, 'Apart from other things I must guard against plagiarism.' Swami had heard of plague, but not plagiarism. 'Please explain,' he said. When Natesh explained, he grew panicky. He wondered if his wife visited the Town Hall library to lift passages from other books. As soon as he went home, he asked his wife, 'Did you go to the Town Hall library?'

'Not today . . .'

'But when you go there what do you generally do?'

'Why this sudden interest?' she asked. He retreated into his shell again, 'Just wanted to know if you found any story as good as yours in the library . . .' She brushed off his inquiry with a gesture.

He coaxed and persuaded her to give the novel for the printer's inspection next day. With many warnings she let him take the notebook away with him, expressing her own doubt, 'If he copies and sells it?'

'Oh, no, he can't do it. We will hand him over to the police if he does it. Bari will be our witness. We'll take a receipt.'

Next day at Bari's, Swami met Natesh and handed him the notebook.

VI

Natesh took three days to complete his scrutiny of the novel and brought back the manuscript, safely wrapped in brown paper, along with the estimate. They conferred once again behind a stack of paper. There was silence while Jiddu was gone to fetch three cups of tea. After drinking tea Bari said, 'Let us not waste time. Natesh, have you the estimate ready?'

'Here it is,' said Natesh holding out a long envelope, Bari received it and passed it on to Swami with a flourish. Then he asked the printer, 'How do you find the novel?'

'We will talk about it later—'

Bari said, 'If you are not interested, Swami's missus will take it to the Madras printers.'

'Why should she?' asked Natesh, 'While we are here?'

'If so, come to the point. I'll supply the paper at less than cost price, when the book is sold you may pay . . .'

Swami felt rather disturbed. 'But you said the other day, you would supply it . . .'

Bari said, 'I am a business man, sir, I only said I'd supply, I meant I would supply, nothing more and nothing less . . .'

At this point Natesh said, 'You have not seen my estimate yet. Why don't you look through it first . . .' Swami felt he was being crushed between heavyweights. He opened the estimate, took a brief look at the bewildering items, and then at the bottom line giving the total charges, felt dizzy, abruptly got up and rushed out into the street without a word, leaving the two agape.

Veena was standing at the door as usual. Even at a

distance she could sense that something had gone wrong, judging from Swami's gait and downcast eyes. When he arrived and passed in without a word, she felt a lump in her throat. Why was he uncommunicative today? Normally he would greet her while coming up the steps. Today he was silent, could it be that the printer had detected some serious lapse, moral or legal, in her novel and threatened him with action? They ate in silence. When they settled down in their seats in the front room, she ventured to ask, 'What happened?'

'Nothing,' he said. 'I have brought back the book.'

'I see it. Are they not going to print it?'

'No, unless we sell ourselves and all that we have, to pay their bill. Even Bari has proved tricky and backed out though he had almost promised to supply the paper.'

He went over to his cupboard and brought out the estimate. Veena studied it with minute attention, tried to understand the items in the bill, then let out a deep sigh, and showed symptoms of breaking down. Immediately Swami shed his gloom, assumed a tone of reckless cheer and said, 'You should not mind these setbacks, they are incidental in the career of any writer. I do not know very much about these things, but I have heard of authors facing disappointments all through life until a sudden break of good fortune occurred, even Shakespeare, you are a first class literary student and you must have read how downhearted he was till his plays were recognized.'

'Who told you? I have never seen you read Shakespeare.' This piece of conversation, however, diverted her attention, and she said overcoming her grief, 'Let us go away to Madras, where we will find the right persons to appreciate the novel. This is a wretched town. We should leave it.' He felt happy to see her spirit revive, secretly wondering if she was going to force him to lose his job. Without contradicting her, he just murmured, 'Perhaps we should write to the publishers and ask them first.'

'No,' she said, 'it will be no use. Nothing can be done through letters. It will be a waste of time and money . . .' He felt an impulse to ask, 'On reaching Madras are you going to stand outside the railway station and cry out, "I have arrived with my novel, who is buying it?" Will publishers come tumbling over each other to snatch up your notebook?' He suppressed his thoughts as usual.

She watched him for a while and asked, 'What do you think?'

'I'll see Coomar and ask him for a week off . . .'

'If he refuses, you must resign and come out . . .' This was the second time she was toying with the idea of making him jobless, little realizing how they were dependent on Coomar for shelter and food. Somehow she had constituted herself Coomar's foe. This was not the time to argue with her. He merely said, 'Coomar will understand, but this is a busy production season, lot of pressure at the moment.'

She grumbled, 'He wants to make more money, that is all, he is not concerned with other people's interests. That is all . . .' Swami felt distressed at her notion of his boss, whom he respected. He swallowed his words and remained silent.

VII

Some days later, one afternoon they were visited by Bari and Natesh. It was a holiday and Swami was at home. He became fussy and drew the available furniture here and there, dashed next door and borrowed a folding chair, and managed seats for everybody. Veena threw a brief glance at the visitors, and walked past them unceremoniously and was off, while Swami fell into a state of confusion, torn between surprise at the arrival of visitors and an impulse to go after Veena. His eyes constantly wandered to the corner of the street while greeting and welcoming his visitors. 'Your missus going out in a hurry?' asked Bari.

'Yes, yes, she has an engagement in Fourth Lane, busy all day . . .'

'Writing all the time?' asked the bearded man, whose bulging eyes and forehead splashed with holy ash and vermilion gave him a forbidding look. 'Yes, yes, she has to answer so many letters everyday from publishers in Madras . . . before we go there . . .' The two guests looked at each other in consternation.

'No need, no need,' they cried in unison, 'while we are here . . .'

'But she has definite plans to take her novel to Madras . . .' Swami said, When they said,, 'No, sir, please, she will bring fame to Malgudi . . .' Swami felt emboldened by their importunity, and said in a firm tone, 'Your charges for printing will make me bankrupt and a beggar . . .' He looked righteous.

'But, sir, it was only a formality, estimates are only a business formality. You must not take it to heart, estimates are provisional and negotiable . . .'

'Why did you not say so?' asked Swami authoritatively. He felt free to be rude.

'But you went away before we could say anything.'

Swami gave a fitting reply as he imagined. Veena's absence gave him freedom. She would have controlled him with a look or by a thought wave, as he sometimes suspected, whenever a third person was present. He realized suddenly his social obligations, 'May I offer you tea or coffee?'

After coffee and the courtesies, they came down to business. Natesh suddenly said: 'I was in prison during the political struggle for independence, and being a political sufferer our government gave me a pension, and all help to start my printing press—I always remind myself of Mahatmaji's words and conduct myself in all matters according to his commands . . .' He doubtless looked like one in constant traffic with the other world to maintain contact with his Master. 'Why am I saying this to you now?' he suddenly asked. Bari had the answer for it, 'To prove that you will always do your best and that you are a man of truth and non-violence.' The other smiled in satisfaction, and then remarked, 'Your wife has gone out, and yet you have managed to give us coffee, such good coffee!'

'Oh, that's no trouble. She keeps things ready at all times. I leave her as much time as possible for her writing too.' They complimented him on his attitude and domestic philosophy. Bari said, 'We will not allow the novel to go out, we will do it here.'

The other said, 'I am no scholar or professor, but I read the story and found it interesting, and in some places I was in tears when the young couple faced obstacles. I rejoiced when they married . . . Don't you think so?' he asked turning to Bari.

'Alas, I am ignorant of the language. If it had been in

our language I'd have brought it out famously, but you have told me everything, and so I feel I have read it. Yes, it is a very moving story, I'll supply the paper and Natesh will print it . . .'

'Where?' asked Swami.

'In my press of course. At Madras I learnt the ins and outs of the publishing business. Under the British, publishers were persecuted, especially, when we brought out patriotic literature, and then I had to give up my job when Mahatmaji ordered individual Satyagraha . . . I was arrested for burning the Union Jack, and went to prison. After I was released, the Nehru government helped us to start life again. But now I am concentrating on printing . . . but if I find a good author, I am prepared to publish his work. I know how to market any book which seems good.'

'So you think this novel will sell?' asked Swami, buoyed up. 'Yes, by and by, I know when it should be brought out. In this case the novel should be published later as a second book, we will keep it by. Your story portion stands by itself, but without spoiling it we can extract the other portion describing the marriage feast as a separate part, and publish it as the first book, with a little elaboration— perhaps adding more recipes of the items served in the feast—it can then become a best-seller. While reading it, my mouth watered and I felt hungry. It's so successfully presented. With a little elaboration it can be produced as a separate book and will definitely appeal to the reader, sort of an appetizer for the book to follow, that's the novel, readers will race for it when they know that the feast will again be found in the novel. If you accept the idea we may immediately proceed. I know how to sell it all over the country. The author is at her best in describing food and feast. If you can give me a full book on food and feast, I can give you an agreement immediately. On signing it, I'll give you one thousand and one thousand on publication. We will bring it out at our own cost. When it sells, we will give you a royalty of 10 per cent, less the advance.'

Later Swami explained the offer to Veena. Veena immediately said dolefully, 'They want a cookery book, and not a novel.'

'I think so,' Swami said. 'But he will give a thousand rupees if you agree. Imagine one thousand, you may do many things . . .'

'But the novel?'

'He will publish it as a second book, after your name becomes known widely with the first book.'

'But I don't know any cookery . . .'

'It doesn't matter, I will help you . . .'

'You have never allowed me in the kitchen . . .'

'That should make no difference. You will learn about it in no time and become an authority on the subject . . .'

'Are you making fun of me?'

'Oh, no. You are a writer. You can write on any subject under the sun. Wait a minute.' He went up to a little trunk in which he kept his papers, brought out the first green-bound notebook in which he had scribbled notes for the dentist's marriage feast. Veena went through it now carefully, and asked, 'What do you want me to do?'

'You must rewrite each page of my notes in your own words—treat it as a basis for a book on the subject . . .'

'What about the novel?'

'That will follow, when you have a ready-made

public . . .' She sat silently poring over the pages which she had earlier rejected, but now found the contents absorbing. She thought over it, and shook him again that night while he was sound asleep, and said, 'Get me a new notebook tomorrow. I'll try.'

Next evening on his way home, Swami picked up a Hamilton notebook. Veena received it quietly. Swami left it at that till she herself said after three days, 'I'll give it a trial first . . .'

That afternoon after lunch she sat in her easy chair and wrote a few lines, the opening lines being: 'After air and water, man survives by eating, all of us know how to eat, but not how to make what one eats.' She wrote in the same tone for a few pages and explained that the pages following were planned to make even the dull-witted man or woman an expert cook . . . She read it out to Swami that evening. He cried, 'Wonderful, all along I knew you could do it, all that you have to do now is to elaborate the points from my notes in your own style, and that'll make a full book easily . . .'

Swami signed a contract on behalf of Veena, received Rs 1,000 advance in cash. Veena completed her task in three months and received Rs 1,000 due on delivery of the manuscript. Natesh was as good as his word and Bari supplied the best white printing paper at concessional rates. They called the book: *Appetizer—A Guide to Good Eating*. Natesh through his contacts with booksellers sold out the first edition of 2,000 copies within six months. It went through several editions and then was translated into English and several Indian languages, and Veena became famous. She received invitations from various organizations to lecture and demonstrate. Swami drafted her speeches on food subjects, travelled with her, and answered questions at meetings. They were able to move out of Grove Street to a bungalow in New Extension, and Veena realized her long-standing desire to see her husband out of Coomar's service. All his time was needed to look after Veena's business interests and the swelling correspondence, mostly requests for further recipes, and advice on minor problems in the kitchen. Though he offered to continue cooking their meals, Veena prohibited him from stepping into the kitchen, and engaged a master cook. In all this activity the novel was not exactly forgotten, but awaited publication. Natesh always promised to take it up next, as soon as the press was free, but *Appetizer* reprints kept the machines overworked, and there was no sign of the demand slackening. Veena, however, never lost hope of seeing her novel in print and Swami never lost hope that some day he would be allowed to cook; and the master cook could be secretly persuaded or bribed to leave.

THE EDGE

WHEN PRESSED TO state his age, Ranga would generally reply, 'Fifty, sixty or eighty.' You might change your tactics and inquire, 'How long have you been at this job?'

'Which job?'

'Carrying that grinding wheel around and sharpening knives.'

'Not only knives, but also scythes, clippers and every kind of peeler and cutter in your kitchen, also bread knives, even butcher's hatchets in those days when I carried the big grindstone; in those days I could even sharpen a maharaja's sword' (a favourite fantasy of his was that if armies employed swords he could become a millionaire). You might interrupt his loquaciousness and repeat your question: 'How long have you been a sharpener of knives and other things?' 'Ever since a line of moustache began to appear here,' he would say, drawing a finger over his lip. You would not get any further by studying his chin now overlaid with patchy tufts of discoloured hair. Apparently he never looked at a calendar, watch, almanac or even a mirror. In such a blissful state, clad in a *dhoti*, khaki shirt and turban, his was a familiar figure in the streets of Malgudi as he slowly passed in front of homes, offering his service in a high-pitched, sonorous cry, 'Knives and scissors sharpened.'

He stuck his arm through the frame of a portable grinding apparatus; an uncomplicated contraption operated by an old cycle wheel connected to a foot-pedal. At the Market Road he dodged the traffic and paused in front of tailor's and barber's shops, offering his services. But those were an erratic and unreliable lot, encouraging him by word but always suggesting another time for business. If they were not busy cutting hair or clothes (tailors, particularly, never seemed to have a free moment, always stitching away on overdue orders), they locked up and sneaked away, and Ranga had to be watchful and adopt all kinds of strategies in order to catch them. Getting people to see the importance of keeping their edges sharp was indeed a tiresome mission. People's reluctance and lethargy had, initially, to be overcome. At first sight everyone dismissed him with, 'Go away, we have nothing to grind,' but if he persisted and dallied, some member of the family was bound to produce a rusty knife, and others would follow, vying with one another, presently, to ferret out long-forgotten junk and clamour for immediate attention. But it generally involved much canvassing, coaxing and even aggressiveness on Ranga's part; occasionally he would warn, 'If you do not sharpen your articles now, you may not have another chance, since I am going away on a pilgrimage.'

'Makes no difference, we will call in the other fellow,' someone would say, referring to a competitor, a miserable fellow who operated a hand grinder, collected his cash and disappeared, never giving a second look to his handiwork.

He was a fellow without a social standing, and no one knew his name, no spark ever came out of his wheel, while Ranga created a regular pyrotechnic display and passing children stood transfixed by the spectacle. 'All right,' Ranga would retort, 'I do not grudge the poor fellow his luck, but he will impart to your knife the sharpness of an egg; after that I won't be able to do anything for you. You must not think that anyone and everyone could handle steel. Most of these fellows don't know the difference between a knife blade and a hammerhead.'

Ranga's customers loved his banter and appreciated his work, which he always guaranteed for sixty days. 'If it gets dull before then, you may call me son of a . . . Oh, forgive my letting slip such words . . .' If he were to be assailed for defective execution, he could always turn round and retort that so much depended upon the quality of metal, and the action of sun and rain, and above all the care in handling, but he never argued with his customers; he just resharpened the knives free of cost on his next round. Customers always liked to feel that they had won a point, and Ranga would say to himself, 'After all, it costs nothing, only a few more turns of the wheel and a couple of sparks off the stone to please the eye.' On such occasions he invariably asked for compensation in kind: a little rice and buttermilk or some snack—anything that could be found in the pantry (especially if they had children in the house)—not exactly to fill one's belly but just to mitigate the hunger of the moment and keep one on the move. Hunger was, after all, a passing phase which you got over if you ignored it. He saw no need to be preoccupied with food. The utmost that he was prepared to spend on food was perhaps one rupee a day.

For a rupee he could get a heap of rice in an aluminum bowl, with unexpected delicacies thrown in, such as bits of cabbage or potato, pieces of chicken, meat, lime-pickle, or even sweet *rasagulla* if he was lucky. A man of his acquaintance had some arrangement with the nearby restaurants to collect remnants and leftovers in a bucket; he came over at about ten in the night, installed himself on a culvert and imperiously ladled out his hotchpotch—two liberal scoops for a rupee. Unless one looked sharp, one would miss it, for he was mobbed when the evening show ended at Pearl Cinema across the street. Ranga, however, was always ahead of others in the line. He swallowed his share, washed it down at the street tap and retired to his corner at Krishna Hall, an abandoned building (with no tangible owner) which had been tied up in civil litigations for over three generations, with no end in sight. Ranga discovered this hospitable retreat through sheer luck on the very first day he had arrived from his village in search of shelter. He occupied a cozy corner of the hall through the goodwill of the old man, its caretaker from time immemorial, who allotted living space to those whom he favoured.

Ranga physically dwelt in the town no doubt, but his thoughts were always centred round his home in the village where his daughter was growing up under the care of his rather difficult wife. He managed to send home some money every month for their maintenance, particularly to meet the expenses of his daughter's schooling. He was proud that his daughter went to a school, the very first member of his family to take a step in that direction. His wife, however, did not favour the idea, being convinced that a girl was meant to make herself useful at home, marry and bear children. But Ranga rejected this philosophy outright, especially after the village schoolmaster, who gathered and taught the children on the *pyol* of his house, had told him once. 'Your child is very intelligent. You must see that she studies well, and send her later to the Mission School at Paamban' (a nearby town reached by bus).

Originally Ranga had set up his grinding wheel as an adjunct to the village blacksmith under the big tamarind tree, where congregated at all hours of the day peasants from the surrounding country, bringing in their tools and implements for mending. One or the other in the crowd would get an idea to hone his scythe, shears or weeding blade when he noticed Ranga and his grinding wheel. But the blacksmith was avaricious, claimed twenty paise in every rupee Ranga earned, kept watch on the number of customers Ranga got each day, invariably quarrelled when the time came to settle accounts and frequently also demanded a drink at the tavern across the road; which meant that Ranga would have to drink, too, and face his wife's tantrums when he went home. She would shout, rave and refuse to serve him food. Ranga could never understand why she should behave so wildly—after all, a swill of toddy did no one any harm; on the contrary, it mitigated the weariness of the body at the end of a day's labour, but how could one educate a wife and improve her understanding? Once, on an inspiration, he took home a bottle for her and coaxed her to taste the drink, but she retched at the smell of it and knocked the bottle out of his hand, spilling its precious contents on the mud floor. Normally he would have accepted her action without any visible protest, but that day, having had company and drunk more than normal, he felt spirited enough to strike her, whereupon she brought out the broom from its corner and lashed him with it. She then pushed him out and shut the door on him. Even in that inebriated state he felt relieved that their child, fast asleep on her mat, was not watching. He picked himself up at dawn from the lawn and sat ruminating. His wife came over and asked, 'Have you come to your senses?' standing over him menacingly.

After this crisis Ranga decided to avoid the blacksmith and try his luck as a peripatetic sharpener. Carrying his grinding gear, he left home early morning after swallowing a ball of *ragi* with a bite of raw onion and chillies. After he gave up his association with the blacksmith, he noticed an improvement in his wife's temper. She got up at dawn and set the *ragi* on the boil over their mud oven and stirred the gruel tirelessly till it hardened and could be rolled into a ball, and had it ready by the time Ranga had had his wash at the well. He started on his rounds, avoiding the blacksmith under the tamarind tree, crisscrossed the dozen streets of his village, pausing at every door to announce, 'Knives and cutters sharpened.' When he returned home at night and emptied his day's collection on his wife's lap, she would cry greedily, 'Only two rupees! Did you not visit the weekly market at . . .?'

'Yes, I did, but there were ten others before me!'

His income proved inadequate, although eked out with the wages earned by his wife for performing odd jobs at the Big House of the village. Now she began to wear a perpetual look of anxiety. He sounded her once if he should not cultivate the blacksmith's company again, since those who had anything to do with iron gathered there. She snarled back, 'You are longing for that tipsy company again, I suppose!' She accused him of lack of push. 'I suppose you don't cry loud enough, you perhaps just saunter along the streets mumbling to yourself your greatness as a grinder!' At this Ranga felt upset and let out such a deafening yell that she jumped and cried, 'Are you crazy? What has come over you?' He explained, 'Just to demonstrate how I call out to my patrons when I go on my rounds, a fellow told me that he could hear me beyond the slaughteryard . . .'

'Then I suppose people scamper away and hide their knives on hearing your voice!' And they both laughed at the grim joke.

The daughter was now old enough to he sent to the Mission School at Paamban. Ranga had to find the money for her books, uniform, school fee and, above all, the daily bus-fare. His wife insisted that the girl's schooling be stopped, since she was old enough to work; the rich landlords needed hands at their farms, and it was time to train the girl to make herself useful all round. Ranga rejected her philosophy outright. However meek and obedient he might have proved in other matters, over the question of his daughter's education he stood firm. He was convinced that she should have a different life from theirs. What a rebel he was turning out to be, his wife thought, and remained speechless with amazement. To assuage her fears he asked, 'You only want more money, don't you?'

'Yes, let me see what black magic you will perform to produce more money.'

'You leave the girl alone, and I will find a way. . .'

'Between you two . . . well, you are bent upon making her a worthless flirt wearing ribbons in her hair, imitating the rich folk . . . If she develops into a termagant, don't blame me, please. She is already self-willed and talks back.'

Presently he undertook an exploratory trip to Malgudi, only twenty-five miles away. He came back to report: 'Oh, what a place, it is like the world of God Indra that our pundits describe. You find everything there. Thousands and thousands of people live in thousands of homes, and so many buses and motorcars in the streets, and so many barbers and tailors flourishing hundreds of scissors and razors night and day; in addition, countless numbers of peeling and slicing knives and other instruments in every home, enough work there for two hundred grinders like me; and the wages are liberal, they are noble and generous who live there, unlike the petty ones we have around us here.'

'Ah, already you feel so superior and talk as if they have adopted you.'

He ignored her cynicism and continued his dream. 'As soon as our schoolmaster finds me an auspicious date, I will leave for the town to try my luck; if it turns out well, I will find a home for us so that we may all move there; they have many schools and our child will easily find a place.' His wife cut short his plans with, 'You may go where you like, but we don't move out of here. I won't agree to lock up this house, which is our own; also, I won't allow a growing girl to pick up the style and fashions of the city. We are not coming. Do what you like with yourself, but don't try to drag us along.' Ranga was crestfallen and remained brooding for a little while, but realized: 'After all, it is a good thing that's happening to me. God is kind, and wants me to be free and independent in the town . . . If she wants to he left behind, so much the better.'

'What are you muttering to yourself?' she asked pugnaciously. 'Say it aloud.'

'There is wisdom in what you say; you think ahead,' he replied, and she felt pleased at the compliment.

In the course of time a system evolved whereby he came home to visit his family every other month for three or four days. Leaving his grinding apparatus carefully wrapped up in a piece of jute cloth at Krishna Hall, he would take the bus at the Market Gate. He always anticipated his homecoming with joy, although during his stay he would have to bear the barbed comments of his wife or assuage her fears and anxieties—she had a habit of hopping from one anxiety to another; if it was not money, it was health, hers or the daughter's, or some hostile acts of a neighbour, or the late hours his daughter kept at school. After three days, when she came to the point of remarking, 'How are we to face next month if you sit and enjoy life here?' he would leave, happy to go back to his independent life, but heavy at heart at parting from his daughter. For three days he would have derived the utmost enjoyment out of watching his daughter while she bustled about getting ready for school every morning in her uniform—green skirt and yellow jacket—and in the evening when she returned home full of reports of her doings at school. He would follow her about while she went to wash her uniform at the well and put it out to dry; she had two sets of school dress and took good care of them, so that she could leave for school each day spick-and-span, which annoyed her mother, who commented that the girl was self-centred, always fussing about her clothes or books. It saddened Ranga to hear such comments, but he felt reassured that the girl seemed capable of defending herself and putting her mother in her place.

At the end of one of his visits to the family he stood, clutching his little bundle of clothes, on the highway beyond the coconut grove. If he watched and gesticulated, any lorry or bus would stop and carry him towards the city. He waited patiently under a tree. It might be hours but he did not mind, never having known the habit of counting time. A couple of lorries fully laden passed and then a bus driven so rashly that his attempt to stop it passed unnoticed.

'Glad I didn't get into it. God has saved me, that bus will lift off the ground and fly to the moon before long,' he reflected as it churned up a cloud of sunlit dust and vanished beyond it. Some days, if the time was propitious, he would be picked up and deposited right at the door of Krishna Hall; some days he had to wait indefinitely. His daughter, he reflected with admiration, somehow caught a bus every day. 'Very clever for her age.' He prayed that his wife would leave her alone. 'But that girl is too smart,' he said to himself with a chuckle, 'and can put her mother in her place.' He brooded for a moment on this pleasant picture of the girl brushing off her mother, rudely sometimes, gently sometimes, but always with success, so that sometimes her mother herself admired the girl's independent spirit. That was the way to handle that woman. He wished he had learnt the technique, he had let her go on her own way too long. But God was kind and took him away to the retreat of Krishna Hall; but for the daughter he would not be visiting his home even once in three years. The girl must study and become a doctor—a lady doctor was like an empress, as he remembered the occasions when he had to visit a hospital for his wife's sake and wait in the corridor, and noticed how voices were hushed when the 'lady' strode down that way.

He noticed a vehicle coming at the bend of the road. It was painted yellow, a peculiar-looking one, probably belonging to some big persons, and he did not dare to stop it. As it flashed past, he noticed that the car also had some picture painted on its side. But it stopped at a distance and went into reverse. He noticed now that the picture on the car was of a man and a woman and two ugly children with some message. Though he could not read, he knew that the message on it was TWO WILL DO, a propaganda for birth control. His friend the butcher at the Market Road read a newspaper every day and kept him well-informed. The man in the car, who was wearing a blue bush-shirt, put his head out to ask. 'Where are you going?'

'Town,' Ranga said.

The man opened the door and said, 'Get in, we will drop you there.' Seated, Ranga took out one rupee from his pocket, but the man said, 'Keep it.' They drove on. Ranga felt happy to be seated in the front; he always had to stand holding on to the rail or squat on the floor in the back row of a bus. Now he occupied a cushioned seat, and wished that his wife could see and realize how people respected him. He enjoyed the cool breeze blowing on his face as the car sped through an avenue of coconut trees and came to a halt at some kind of a camp consisting of little shacks built of bamboo and coconut thatch. It seemed to be far away from his route, on the outskirts of a cluster of hamlets. He asked his benefactor, 'Where are we?'

The man replied breezily, 'You don't have to worry, you will be taken care of. Let us have coffee.' He got off and hailed someone inside a hut. Some appetizing eatable on a banana leaf and coffee in a little brass cup were brought out and served. Ranga felt revived, having had nothing to eat since his morning *ragi*. He inquired, 'Why all this, sir?'

The man said benignly, 'Go on, you must be hungry, enjoy.'

Ranga had never known such kindness from anyone. This man was conducting himself like a benign god. Ranga expected that after the repast they would resume their journey. But the benign god suddenly got up and said, 'Come with me.' He took him aside and said in a whisper, 'Do not worry about anything. We will take care of you. Do you want to earn thirty rupees?'

'Thirty rupees!' Ranga cried, 'What should I do for it? I have not brought my machine.'

'You know me well enough now, trust me, do as I say. Don't question and you will get thirty rupees if you obey our instruction; we will give you any quantity of food, and I'll take you to the town . . . only you must stay here tonight. You can sleep here comfortably. I'll take you to the town tomorrow morning. Don't talk to others, or tell them anything. They will be jealous and spoil your chance of getting thirty rupees . . . You will also get a transistor radio. Do you like to have one?'

'Oh, I don't know how to operate it. I'm not educated.'

'It is simple, you just push a key and you will hear music.'

He then took Ranga to a secluded part of the camp, spoke to him at length (though much of what he said was obscure) and went away. Ranga stretched himself on the ground under a tree, feeling comfortable, contented and well-fed. The prospect of getting thirty rupees was pleasant enough, though he felt slightly suspicious and confused. But he had to trust that man in the blue shirt. He seemed godlike. Thirty rupees! Wages for ten days' hard work. He could give the money to his daughter to keep or spend as she liked, without any interference from her mother. He could also give her the radio. She was educated and would know how to operate it. He wondered how to get the money through to her without her mother's knowledge. Perhaps send it to her school—the writer of petitions and addresses at the post office in the city would write down the money-order for him and charge only twenty-five paise for the labour. He was a good friend, who also wrote a postcard for him free of charge whenever he had to order a new grinding wheel from Bangalore. Ranga became wary when he saw people passing; he shut his eyes and fell into a drowse.

The blue bush-shirt woke him up and took him along to another part of the camp, where inside a large tent a man was seated at a desk. 'He is our chief,' he whispered. 'Don't speak until he speaks to you. Answer when he questions. Be respectful. He is our officer.' After saying this, he edged away and was not to be seen again.

Ranga felt overawed in the presence of the officer. That man had a sheet of paper in front of him and demanded,

599

'Your name?' He wrote it down. 'Your age?'

Ranga took time to comprehend, and when he did he began to ramble in his usual manner, 'Must be fifty or seventy, because I . . .' He mentioned inevitably how a thin line of moustache began to appear when he first sharpened a knife as a professional. The officer cut him short. 'I don't want all that! Shall I say you are fifty-five?' 'By all means, sir. You are learned and you know best.'

Then the officer asked, 'Are you married?'

Ranga attempted to explain his domestic complications: the temper of his present wife, who was actually his second one; how he had to marry this woman under pressure from his relatives. He explained, 'My uncle and other elders used to say, "Who will be there to bring you a sip of gruel or hot water when you are on your death bed?" It's all God's wish, sir. How can one know what He wills?' The officer was annoyed but tried to cover it up by going on to the next question: 'How many children?'

'My first wife would have borne ten if God had given her long life, but she fell ill and the lady doctor said . . .' He went into details of her sickness and death. He then went on to some more personal tragedies and suddenly asked. 'Why do you want to know about all this sorrowful business, sir?' The officer waved away his query with a frown. Ranga recollected that he had been advised not to be talkative, not to ask, but only to answer questions. Probably all this fortunately was a prelude to their parting with cash and a radio. The officer repeated, 'How many children?'

'Six died before they were a year old. Do you want their names? So long ago, I don't remember, but I can try if you want. Before the seventh I vowed to the Goddess on the hill to shave my head and roll bare-bodied around the temple corridor, and the seventh survived by the Goddess's grace and is the only one left, but my wife does not understand how precious this daughter is, does not like her to study but wants her to become a drudge like herself. But the girl is wonderful. She goes to a school every day and wants to be a lady doctor. She is a match for her mother.'

The officer noted down against the number of children 'Seven' and then said commandingly, 'You must have no more children. Is that understood?' Ranga looked abashed and grinned. The officer began a lecture on population, food production and so forth, and how the government had decreed that no one should have more than two children. He then thrust forward the sheet of paper and ordered, 'Sign here.' Ranga was nonplussed. 'Oh! If I had learnt to read and write . . .!'

The officer said curtly, 'Hold up your left thumb,' and smeared it on an inking pad and pressed it on the sheet of paper. After these exertions, Ranga continued to stand there, hoping that the stage had arrived to collect his reward and depart. He could cross the field, go up to the highway and pay for a bus ride, he would have money for it. But the officer merely handed him a slip of paper and cried, 'Next.' An orderly entered, pushing before him a middle-aged peasant, while another orderly propelled Ranga out of the presence of the officer to another part of the camp, snatched the slip of paper from his hand and went away, ignoring the several questions that Ranga had put to him. Presently Ranga found himself seized by the arm and led into a room where a doctor and his assistants were waiting at a table. On the table Ranga noticed a white tray

with shining knives neatly arrayed. His professional eye
noted how perfectly the instruments had been honed. The
doctor asked, 'How many more?' Someone answered, 'Only
four, sir.' Ranga felt scared when they said, 'Come here and
lie down,' indicating a raised bed. They gently pushed him
onto it. One man held his head down and two others held
his feet. At some stage they had taken off the clothes and
wrapped him in a white sheet. He felt ashamed to be
stripped thus, but bore it as perhaps an inevitable stage in
his progress towards affluence. The blue bush-shirt had
advised him to be submissive. As he was lying on his back
with the hospital staff standing guard over him, his
understanding improved and his earlier suspicions began to
crystallize. He recollected his butcher friend reading from a
newspaper how the government was opening camps all over
the country where men and women were gathered and
operated upon so that they could have no children. So this
was it! He was seized with panic at the prospect of being
sliced up. 'Don't shake, be calm,' someone whispered softly,
and he felt better, hoping that they would let him off at the
last minute after looking him over thoroughly. The blue-
shirt had assured him that they would never hurt or harm
an old man like him. While these thoughts were flitting
across his mind, he noticed a hand reaching for him with a
swab of cotton. When the wrap around him was parted and
fingers probed his genitals, he lost his head and screamed,
'Hands off! Leave me alone!' He shook himself free when
they tried to hold him down, butted with his head the man
nearest to him, rolled over, toppling the white tray with its
knives. Drawing the hospital wrap around, he stormed out,
driven by a desperate energy. He ran across the fields

screaming, 'No, I won't be cut up . . .' which echoed far and wide, issuing from vocal cords cultivated over a lifetime to overwhelm other noises in a city street with the cry, 'Knives sharpened!'

THE MUTE COMPANIONS

OTHER BEGGARS HAD this advantage over him: they could ask for alms, while he could only make a sort of gurgling at the throat. And this gurgling had to serve him for expressing all his ideas, emotions, and appeals. His home was a corner of the Town Hall veranda.

One day, opening his eyes from a stupor, he saw a tiny monkey ransacking his bag, to which were sticking one or two grains of rice he had collected on the previous day.

Sami pretended to be asleep for a moment and then shot out his arm and gripped the monkey's waist, thus securing a companion, his only companion in life. He tied a piece of cord around the monkey's waist and taught him a number of tricks.

The monkey solved for him the problem of food. He performed his tricks in front of houses and earned for his master rice, edibles, and coins. The opening turn, usually, was a walk around, saluting the assembly, which invariably consisted of a boy, a girl carrying a baby, two other small children, and a grandmother; occasionally also the mother, and, very very rarely indeed, the master of the house. Sami was particular that the monkey should salute everyone assembled, including the young one in the girl's arms. If he omitted anyone he received a tug at his waist which made his teeth chatter. The next turn was the Dancer at the Temple. Other monkey-trainers usually introduced the trick with the question, How did the woman at the temple dance? But Sami merely tickled the monkey under the arm and winked. At this the monkey stood up with one hand on his waist and the other on his head and swayed his hips in a manner that would have done credit to any dancer in a temple. Sami noticed that his patrons said when they saw this, 'Ah, really! It is a wonder how he has taught it all this though he is dumb!'

'I don't think he is really dumb. He must be pretending,' the callous boy would say. And then they would all try to find out if he was really deaf and dumb by asking him his name and age or telling him point blank that he was only pretending. At this stage the master of the house would appear on the scene with a scowl on his face. Sami would pick up his bag, staff, and monkey, and hurry away, contented with a handful of rice flung into the bag. There were occasions when he came across amiable patrons, and he held the performance for nearly one hour, exhibiting certain star turns: The Timid Girl Going Back to Her Mother-in-Law. Sami himself played the role of the irate mother-in-law, who, the moment the girl arrived, sent her out to fetch water from a deep well. And then the great Hanuman setting fire to the capital of the Demon King: the monkey would pick up his tail in his hand and prance about. Sami saw, by the laughter in their faces, that his patrons were pleased, and ventured to ask for a little cooked rice for the monkey, a little buttermilk, and sometimes even an old coat or shirt. The stout khaki coat he wore on his bare body had been given him by someone in that bungalow beyond the big shop as a reward for the mother-in-law turn; and the same turn earned him at another place the dark turban on his head.

In the evening he returned to the Town Hall with the monkey serenely riding on his shoulder, and lay down in the corner of the veranda with the monkey snuggling close to him.

There were certain codes of conduct which he expected the monkey to observe. For instance, he never liked his monkey to carry away anything from a house, not even a pebble. Several times the monkey was made to go back and put the stone in its place; and again Sami was very strict in regard to the monkey's behaviour in a front garden: he was never allowed to touch any leaf or flower or even the flower pots. Sami felt that his very existence depended on the behaviour of the monkey.

Thus they spent three years. Three years is a long time when we remember that every second of those three years they were together; they worked, ate, and slept together. Well might this companionship have lasted a lifetime but for a very slight temptation that came the monkey's way.

One day Sami was going up the drive of one of those big bungalows. It was only a sporting mood that made him enter the gate. Usually he avoided those big places where people were haughty, aloof, and inaccessible, and kept formidable dogs and servants. He went up hesitatingly, expecting to be shouted off any moment, when he saw a servant coming towards him. Sami held the monkey tight and turned to flee, but the servant caught up with him and poured out a volley of words. Sami indicated that he could not hear, whereupon the servant explained by signs that the master of the house wanted the monkey to be brought to his presence.

He was invited to come up the front steps and hold the show on the veranda. The show was held for the exclusive pleasure of a little boy who lay on a couch amidst pillows, covered with a green shawl. As he watched the monkey perform, his waxen face lit up with life, and he took his medicine and food without a protest. The master of the house beamed on all those assembled. Sami felt he had discovered a treasure house.

The monkey was performing for the third time the turn of The Sweet-Seller Balancing a Tray on His Head. All eyes were on him. The monkey saw on a side table a dish containing a slice of bread and some fruit. Overpowered by this vision, he suddenly darted forward, grabbed the slice of bread, and knocked down a medicine bottle and a flower vase. Instantly there was confusion. Sami, blind with rage, jumped forward to catch the monkey, and knocked down the furniture and very nearly tumbled over the delicate patient. Strong arms gripped him and dragged him down the veranda steps. He turned and saw his monkey sitting on top of a pillar, enjoying his slice of bread. Everyone scowled at Sami and shook their fists at him. They behaved as though they had just saved the little patient from a serious mishap wilfully designed by Sami. He desperately tried to explain that he had had no designs on the boy but only wanted to get the monkey. 'Send him out,' cried the master of the house. 'He is frightening the child. This excitement won't do for him. It is going to take weeks for him to get over this shock. Take him away, the devil!' The servants pushed Sami out. He resisted. He wanted to ask, Where is my monkey? Where is my monkey? But he could only make wild gestures and gurgle, and they thought he was menacing them. They pushed him down the drive, towards the gate. He turned, and just saw his monkey sitting on the tiled roof. He fell at their feet and cringed and begged them to let him call back his monkey. They relented. He stood below the tile and looked up, and by gesture implored the monkey to come down. The monkey looked at his master patronizingly, munching the slice of bread. He didn't understand what his master was saying. He couldn't make out whether he was going to be forgiven or punished if he returned. In any case, he was not thinking of returning. He liked his freedom. It was exhilarating to be able to run about, having lived at the end of a yard-long cord for three years. He merely turned round, walked up the tiles, and put himself through a ventilator which opened into the house. His waist cord lay outside for a moment and then crawled in like a snake and disappeared.

Day after day Sami waited at his corner in the Town Hall hoping that his monkey would come back to him, just as he had come to him on the very first day. Day after day he stood at the gate of the bungalow intently gazing at the ventilator, the roofs, and the trees. The servants chased him away when they noticed him. One day he fell at their feet and begged them to tell him what had happened to the monkey. They replied that they didn't know. Sami believed that after it had gone through the ventilator it was caught and kept in the house.

After waiting for a few weeks he resigned himself to the loss and returned to his old precarious existence—on alms which he could not demand.

NAGA

THE BOY TOOK off the lid of the circular wicker basket and stood looking at the cobra coiled inside, and then said, 'Naga, I hope you are dead, so that I may sell your skin to the pursemakers; at least that way you may become useful.' He poked it with a finger. Naga raised its head and looked about with a dull wonder. 'You have become too lazy even to open your hood. You are no cobra. You are an earthworm. I am a snake charmer attempting to show you off and make a living. No wonder so often I have to stand at the bus stop pretending to be blind and beg. The trouble is, no one wants to see you, no one has any respect for you and no one is afraid of you, and do you know what that means? I starve, that is all.'

Whenever the boy appeared at the street door, householders shooed him away. He had seen his father operate under similar conditions. His father would climb the steps of the house unmindful of the discouragement, settle down with his basket and go through his act heedless of what anyone said. He would pull out his gourd pipe from the bag and play the snake tune over and over, until its shrill, ear-piercing note induced a torpor and made people listen to his preamble: 'In my dream, God Shiva appeared and said, "Go forth and thrust your hand into that crevice in the floor of my sanctum." As you all know, Shiva is the Lord of Cobras, which he ties his braid with, and its hood canopies his head; the great God Vishnu rests in the coils of Adi-Shesha, the mightiest serpent, who also bears on his thousand heads this Universe. Think of the armlets on goddess Parvathi! Again, elegant little snakes. How can we think that we are wiser than our gods? Snake is a part of a god's ornament, and not an ordinary creature. I obeyed Shiva's command—at midnight walked out and put my arm into the snake hole.'

At this point his audience would shudder and someone would ask, 'Were you bitten?'

'Of course I was bitten, but still you see me here, because the same god commanded, "Find that weed growing on the old fort wall." No, I am not going to mention its name, even if I am offered a handful of sovereigns.'

'What did you do with the weed?'

'I chewed it; thereafter no venom could enter my system. And the terrible fellow inside this basket plunged his fangs into my arms like a baby biting his mother's nipple, but I laughed and pulled him out, and knocked off with a piece of stone the fangs that made him so arrogant; and then he understood that I was only a friend and well-wisher, and no trouble after that. After all, what is a serpent? A great soul in a state of penance waiting to go back to its heavenly world. That is all, sirs.'

After this speech, his father would flick open the basket lid and play the pipe again, whereupon the snake would dart up like spring-work, look about and sway a little; people would be terrified and repelled, but still enthralled. At the end of the performance, they gave him coins and rice, and sometimes an old shirt, too, and occasionally he wangled an egg if he observed a hen around; seizing Naga by the throat, he let the egg slide down its gullet, to the delight of the onlookers. He then packed up and repeated the performance at the next street or at the bazaar, and when he had collected sufficient food and cash he returned to his hut beside the park wall, in the shade of a big tamarind tree. He cooked the rice and fed his son, and they slept outside the hut, under the stars.

The boy had followed his father ever since he could walk, and when he attained the age of ten his father let him handle Naga and harangue his audience in his own style. His father often said, 'We must not fail to give Naga two eggs a week. When he grows old, he will grow shorter each day; someday he will grow wings and fly off, and do you know that at that time he will spit out the poison in his fangs in the form of a brilliant jewel, and if you possessed it you could become a king?'

One day when the boy had stayed beside the hut out of laziness, he noticed a tiny monkey gambolling amidst the branches of the tamarind tree and watched it with open-mouthed wonder, not even noticing his father arrive home.

'Boy, what are you looking at? Here, eat this,' said the father, handing him a packet of sweets. 'They gave it to me at that big house, where some festival is going on. Naga danced to the pipe wonderfully today. He now understands all our speech. At the end of his dance, he stood six feet high on the tip of his tail, spread out his hood, hissed and sent a whole crowd scampering. Those people enjoyed it, though, and gave me money and sweets.' His father looked happy as he opened the lid of the basket. The cobra raised its head. His father held it up by the neck, and forced a bit of a sweet between its jaws, and watched it work its way down. 'He is now one of our family and should learn to eat what we eat,' he said. After struggling through the sweet, Naga coiled itself down, and the man clapped the lid back.

The boy munched the sweet with his eyes still fixed on the monkey. 'Father, I wish I were a monkey: I'd never come down from the tree. See how he is nibbling all that tamarind fruit . . . Hey, monkey, get me a fruit!' he cried.

The man was amused, and said, 'This is no way to befriend him. You should give him something to eat, not ask him to feed you.'

At which the boy spat out his sweet, wiped it clean with his shirt, held it up and cried, 'Come on, monkey! Here!'

His father said, 'If you call him "monkey", he will never like you. You must give him a nice name.'

'What shall we call him?'

'Rama, name of the master of Hanuman, the Divine Monkey. Monkeys adore that name.'

The boy at once called, 'Rama, here, take this.' He flourished his arms, holding up the sweet, and the monkey did pause in its endless antics and notice him. The boy hugged the tree trunk, and heaved himself up, and carefully placed the sweet on the flat surface of a forking branch, and the monkey watched with round-eyed wonder. The boy slid back to the ground and eagerly waited for the monkey to come down and accept the gift. While he watched and the monkey was debating within himself, a crow appeared from somewhere and took away the sweet. The boy shrieked out a curse.

His father cried, 'Hey, what? Where did you learn this foul word? No monkey will respect you if you utter bad words.' Ultimately, when the little monkey was tempted down with another piece of sweet, his father caught him deftly by the wrist, holding him off firmly by the scruff to prevent his biting.

Fifteen days of starvation, bullying, cajoling and dangling of fruit before the monkey's eyes taught him what he was expected to do. First of all, he ceased trying to bite or scratch. And then he realized that his mission in life was to please his master by performing. At a command from his master, he could demonstrate how Hanuman, the Divine Monkey of the Ramayana, strode up and down with tail ablaze and set Ravana's capital on fire; how an oppressed village daughter-in-law would walk home carrying a pitcher of water on her head; how a newly-wed would address his beloved (chatter, blink, raise the brow and grin); and, finally, what was natural to him—tumbling and acrobatics on top of a bamboo pole. When Rama was ready to appear in public, his master took him to a roadside-tailor friend of his and had him measured out for a frilled jacket, leaving the tail out, and a fool's cap held in position with a band under his small chin. Rama constantly tried to push his cap back and rip it off, but whenever he attempted it he was whacked with a switch, and he soon resigned himself to wearing his uniform until the end of the day. When his master stripped off Rama's clothes, the monkey performed spontaneous somersaults in sheer relief.

Rama became popular. Schoolchildren screamed with joy at the sight of him. Householders beckoned to him to step in and divert a crying child. He performed competently, earned money for his master and peanuts for himself. Discarded baby clothes were offered to him as gifts. The father-son team started out each day, the boy with the monkey riding on his shoulder and the cobra basket carried by his father at some distance away—for the monkey chattered and shrank, his face disfigured with fright, whenever the cobra hissed and reared itself up. While the young fellow managed to display the tricks of the monkey to a group, he could hear his father's pipe farther off. At the weekly market fairs in the villages around, they were a familiar pair, and they became prosperous enough to take a bus home at the end of the day. Sometimes as they started to get on, a timid passenger would ask, 'What's to happen if the cobra gets out?'

'No danger. The lid is secured with a rope,' the father replied.

There would always be someone among the passengers to remark, 'A snake minds its business until you step on its tail.'

'But this monkey?' another passenger said. 'God knows what he will be up to!'

'He is gentle and wise,' said the father, and offered a small tip to win the conductor's favour.

They travelled widely, performing at all market fairs, and earned enough money to indulge in an occasional tiffin at a restaurant. The boy's father would part company from him in the evening, saying, 'Stay. I've a stomach ache; I'll get some medicine for it and come back,' and return tottering late at night. The boy felt frightened of his father at such moments, and, lying on his mat, with the monkey tethered to a stake nearby, pretended to be asleep. Father kicked him and said, 'Get up, lazy swine. Sleeping when your father slaving for you all day comes home for speech with you. You are not my son but a bastard.' But the boy would not stir.

One night the boy really fell asleep, and woke up in the morning to find his father gone. The monkey was also missing. 'They must have gone off together!' he cried. He paced up and down and called, 'Father!' several times. He then peered into the hut and found the round basket intact in its corner. He noticed on the lid of the basket some coins, and felt rather pleased when he counted them and found eighty paise in small change. 'It must all be for me,' he said to himself. He felt promoted to adulthood, handling so much cash. He felt rich but also puzzled at his father's tactics. Ever since he could remember, he had never woken up without finding his father at his side. He had a foreboding that he was not going to see his father anymore. Father would never at any time go out without announcing his purpose—for a bath at the street tap, or to seek medicine for a 'stomach ache', or to do a little shopping.

The boy lifted the lid of the basket to make sure that the snake at least was there. It popped up the moment the lid was taken off. He looked at it, and it looked at him for a moment. 'I'm your master now. Take care.' As if understanding the changed circumstances, the snake darted its forked tongue and half-opened its hood. He tapped it

down with his finger, saying, 'Get back. Not yet.' Would it
be any use waiting for his father to turn up? He felt hungry.
Wondered if it'd be proper to buy his breakfast with the
coins left on the basket lid. If his father should suddenly
come back, he would slap him for taking the money. He
put the lid back on the snake, put the coins back on the lid
as he had found them and sat at the mouth of the hut,
vacantly looking at the tamarind tree and sighing for his
monkey, which would have displayed so many fresh and
unexpected pranks early in the morning. He reached for a
little cloth bag in which was stored a variety of nuts and
fried pulses to feed the monkey. He opened the bag,
examined the contents and put a handful into his mouth
and chewed: 'Tastes so good. Too good for a monkey, but
Father will . . .' His father always clouted his head when he
caught him eating nuts meant for the monkey. Today he felt
free to munch the nuts, although worried at the back of his
mind lest his father should suddenly remember and come
back for the monkey food. He found the gourd pipe in its
usual place, stuck in the thatch. He snatched it up and blew
through its reeds, feeling satisfied that he could play as well
as his father and that the public would not know the
difference; only it made him cough a little and gasp for
breath. The shrill notes attracted the attention of people
passing by the hut, mostly day labourers carrying spades
and pickaxes and women carrying baskets, who nodded
their heads approvingly and remarked, 'True son of the
father.' Everyone had a word with him. All knew him in
that colony of huts, which had cropped up around the
water fountain. All the efforts of the municipality to dislodge
these citizens had proved futile; the huts sprang up as often

as they were destroyed, and when the municipal councillors realized the concentration of voting power in this colony, they let the squatters alone, except when some VIP from Delhi passed that way, and then they were asked to stay out of sight, behind the park wall, till the eminent man had flashed past in his car.

'Why are you not out yet?' asked a woman.

'My father is not here,' the boy said pathetically. 'I do not know where he is gone.' He sobbed a little.

The woman put down her basket, sat by his side and asked, 'Are you hungry?'

'I have money,' he said.

She gently patted his head and said, 'Ah, poor child! I knew your mother. She was a good girl. That she should have left you adrift like this and gone heavenward!' Although he had no memory of his mother, at the mention of her, tears rolled down his cheeks, and he licked them off with relish at the corner of his mouth. The woman suddenly said, 'What are you going to do now?'

'I don't know,' he said. 'Wait till my father comes.'

'Foolish and unfortunate child. Your father is gone.'

'Where?' asked the boy.

'Don't ask me,' the woman said. 'I talked to a man who saw him go. He saw him get into the early-morning bus, which goes up the mountains, and that strumpet in the blue sari was with him.'

'What about the monkey?' the boy asked. 'Won't it come back?'

She had no answer to this question. Meanwhile, a man hawking rice cakes on a wooden tray was crying his wares at the end of the lane. The woman hailed him in a shrill voice and ordered, 'Sell this poor child two *idlis*. Give him freshly made ones, not yesterday's.'

'Yesterday's stuff not available even for a gold piece,' said the man.

'Give him the money,' she told the boy. The boy ran in and fetched some money. The woman pleaded with the hawker, 'Give him something extra for the money.'

'What extra?' he snarled.

'This is an unfortunate child.'

'So are others. What can I do? Why don't you sell your earrings and help him? I shall go bankrupt if I listen to people like you and start giving more for less money.' He took the cash and went on. Before he reached the third hut, the boy had polished off the *idlis*—so soft and pungent, with green chutney spread on top.

The boy felt more at peace with the world now, and able to face his problems. After satisfying herself that he had eaten well, the woman rose to go, muttering, 'Awful strumpet, to seduce a man from his child.' The boy sat and brooded over her words. Though he gave no outward sign of it, he knew who the strumpet in the blue sari was. She lived in one of those houses beyond the park wall and was always to be found standing at the door, and seemed to be a fixture there. At the sight of her, his father would slow down his pace and tell the boy, 'You keep going. I'll join you.' The first time it happened, after waiting at the street corner, the boy tied the monkey to a lamppost and went back to the house. He did not find either his father or the woman where he had left them. The door of the house was shut. He raised his hand to pound on it, but restrained himself and sat down on the step, wondering. Presently the door opened and his father emerged, with the basket slung over his shoulder as usual; he appeared displeased at the sight of the boy and raised his hand to strike him, muttering, 'Didn't I say, "Keep going"?' The boy ducked and ran down the street, and heard the blue-sari woman remark, 'Bad, mischievous devil, full of evil curiosity!' Later, his father said, 'When I say go, you must obey.'

'What did you do there?' asked the boy, trying to look and sound innocent, and the man said severely, 'You must not ask questions.'

'Who is she? What is her name?'

'Oh, she is a relative,' the man said. To further probing questions he said, 'I went in to drink tea. You'll be thrashed if you ask more questions, little devil.'

The boy said, as an afterthought, 'I only came back thinking that you might want me to take the basket,' whereupon his father said sternly, 'No more talk. You must know, she is a good and lovely person.' The boy did not accept this description of her. She had called him names. He wanted to shout from the rooftops, 'Bad, bad, and bad woman and not at all lovely!' but kept it to himself. Whenever they passed that way again, the boy quickened his pace, without looking left or right, and waited patiently for his father to join him at the street corner. Occasionally his father followed his example and passed on without glancing at the house if he noticed, in place of the woman, a hairy-chested man standing at the door, massaging his pot-belly.

The boy found that he could play the pipe, handle the snake and feed it also—all in the same manner as his father used to, Also, he could knock off the fangs whenever they started to grow. He earned enough each day, and as the weeks and months passed he grew taller, and the snake became progressively tardy and flabby and hardly stirred its coils. The boy never ceased to sigh for the monkey. The worst blow his father had dealt him was the kidnapping of his monkey.

When a number of days passed without any earnings, he decided to rid himself of the snake, throw away the gourd pipe and do something else for a living. Perhaps catch another monkey and train it. He had watched his father and knew how to go about this. A monkey on his shoulder would gain him admission anywhere, even into a palace. Later on, he would just keep it as a pet and look for some other profession. Start as a porter at the railway station— so many trains to watch every hour—and maybe get into one someday and out into the wide world. But the first step would be to get rid of Naga. He couldn't afford to find eggs and milk for him.

He carried the snake basket along to a lonely spot down the river course, away from human habitation, where a snake could move about in peace without getting killed at sight. In that lonely part of Nallappa's grove, there were many mounds, crevasses and anthills. 'You could make your home anywhere there, and your cousins will be happy to receive you back into their fold,' he said to the snake. 'You should learn to be happy in your own home. You must forget me. You have become useless, and we must part. I don't know where my father is gone. He'd have kept you until you grew wings and all that, but I don't care.' He opened the lid of the basket, lifted the snake and set it free. It lay inert for a while, then raised its head, looked at the outside world without interest, and started to move along tardily, without any aim. After a few yards of slow motion, It turned about, looking for its basket home. At once the boy snatched up the basket and flung it far out of the snake's range. 'You will not go anywhere else as long as I am nearby.' He turned the snake round, to face an anthill, prodded it on and then began to run at full speed in the opposite direction. He stopped at a distance, hid himself behind a tree and watched. The snake was approaching the slope of the anthill. The boy had no doubt now that Naga would find the hole on its top, slip itself in and vanish from his life forever. The snake crawled halfway up the hill, hesitated and then turned round and came along in his direction again. The boy swore, 'Oh, damned snake! Why don't you go back to your world and stay there? You won't find me again.' He ran through Nallappa's grove and stopped to regain his breath. From where he stood, he saw his Naga glide along majestically across the ground, shining like a silver ribbon under the bright sun. The boy paused to say 'Goodbye' before making his exit. But looking up he noticed a white-necked Brahmany kite sailing in the blue sky. 'Garuda,' he said in awe. As was the custom, he made obeisance to it by touching his eyes with his fingertips. Garuda was the vehicle of God Vishnu and was sacred. He shut his eyes in a brief prayer to the bird. 'You are a god, but I know you eat snakes. Please leave Naga alone.' He opened his eyes and saw the kite skimming along a little nearer, its shadow almost trailing the course of the lethargic snake. 'Oh!' he screamed. 'I know your purpose.' Garuda would make a swoop and dive at the right moment and stab his claws into that foolish Naga, who had refused the shelter of the anthill, and carry him off for his dinner. The boy dashed back to the snake, retrieving his basket on the way. When he saw the basket, Naga slithered back into it, as if coming home after a strenuous public performance.

Naga was eventually reinstated in his corner at the hut beside the park wall. The boy said to the snake, 'If you don't grow wings soon enough, I hope you will be hit on the head with a bamboo staff, as it normally happens to any cobra. Know this: I will not be guarding you forever. I'll be away at the railway station, and if you come out of the basket and adventure about, it will be your end. No one can blame me afterward.'

SEVENTH HOUSE

KRISHNA RAN HIS finger over the block of ice in order to wipe away the layer of sawdust, chiselled off a piece, crushed it, and filled the rubber icebag. This activity in the shaded corner of the back veranda gave him an excuse to get away from the sickroom, but he could not dawdle over it, for he had to keep the icebag on his wife's brow continuously, according to the doctor's command. In that battle between ice and mercury column, it was ice that lost its iciness while the mercury column held its ground at a hundred and three degrees Fahrenheit. The doctor had looked triumphant on the day he diagnosed the illness as typhoid, and announced with glee, 'We now know what stick to employ for beating it; they call it Chloromycetin. Don't you worry any more.' He was a good doctor but given to lugubrious humour and monologuing.

The Chloromycetin pills were given to the patient as directed, and at the doctor's next visit Krishna waited for him to pause for breath and then cut in with: 'The fever has not gone down,' holding up the temperature chart.

The doctor threw a brief, detached look at the sheet and

continued, 'The municipality served me a notice to put a slab over the storm drain at my gate, but my lawyer said—'

'Last night she refused food,' Krishna said.

'Good for the country, with its food shortage. Do you know what the fat grain merchant in the market did? When he came to show me his throat, he asked if I was an MD! I don't know where he learned about MDs.'

'She was restless and tugged at her bedclothes,' Krishna said, lowering his voice as he noticed his wife open her eyes.

The doctor touched her pulse with the tip of his finger and said breezily, 'Perhaps she wants a different-coloured sheet, and why not?'

'I have read somewhere the tugging of bedclothes is a bad sign.'

'Oh, you and your reading!'

The patient moved her lips. Krishna bent close to her, and straightened himself to explain, 'She is asking when you will let her get up.'

The doctor said, 'In time for the Olympics . . .' and laughed at his own joke, 'I'd love to be off for the Olympics myself.'

Krishna said, 'The temperature was a hundred and three at one a.m. . . .'

'Didn't you keep the ice going?'

'Till my fingers were numb.'

'We will treat you for cramps by and by, but first let us see the lady of the house back in the kitchen.'

So Krishna found, after all, a point of agreement with the doctor. He wanted his wife back in the kitchen very badly. He miscooked the rice in a different way each day,

and swallowed it with buttermilk at mealtimes and ran
back to his wife's bedside.

The servant maid came in the afternoon to tidy up the
patient and the bed, and relieved Krishna for almost an
hour, which he spent in watching the street from the
doorway; a cyclist passing, schoolchildren running home,
crows perching in a row on the opposite roof, a street
hawker crying his wares—anything seemed interesting
enough to take his mind off the fever.

Another week passed. Sitting there beside her bed,
holding the icebag in position, he brooded over his married
like from its beginning.

When he was studying at Albert Mission he used to see
a great deal of her; they cut their classes, sat on the river's
edge, discussed earnestly their present and future, and
finally decided to marry. The parents on both sides felt that
here was an instance of the evils of modern education:
young people would not wait for their elders to arrange
their marriage but settled things for themselves, aping
Western manners and cinema stories. Except for the lack of
propriety, in all other respects the proposal should have
proved acceptable; financial background of the families, the
caste and group requirements, age, and everything else were
correct. The elders relented eventually, and on a fine day
the horoscopes of the boy and girl were exchanged and
found not suited to each other. The boy's horoscope indicated
Mars in the Seventh House, which spelled disaster for his
bride. The girl's father refused to consider the proposal
further. The boy's parents were outraged at the attitude of
the bride's party—a bride's father was a seeker and the
bridegroom's the giver, and how dare they be finicky? 'Our

son will get a bride a hundred times superior to this girl. After all, what has she to commend her? All college girls make themselves up to look pretty, but that is not everything.' The young couple felt and looked miserable, which induced the parents to reopen negotiations. A wise man suggested that, if other things were all right, they could ask for a sign and go ahead. The parties agreed to a flower test. On an auspicious day they assembled in the temple. The wick lamp in the inner sanctum threw a soft illumination around. The priest lit a piece of camphor and circled it in front of the image in the sanctum. Both sets of parents and their supporters, standing respectfully in the pillared hall, watched the image and prayed for guidance. The priest beckoned to a boy of four who was with another group of worshippers. When he hesitated, the priest dangled a piece of coconut. The child approached the threshold of the santcum greedily. The priest picked off a red and a white flower from the garland on the image, placed them on a tray, and told the boy to choose one.

'Why?' asked the boy, uneasy at being watched by so many people. If the red flower was chosen, it would indicate God's approval. The little boy accepted the piece of coconut and tried to escape, but the priest held him by the shoulder and commanded, 'Take a flower!' at which the child burst into tears and wailed for his mother. The adults despaired. The crying of the child at this point was inauspicious; there should have been laughter and the red flower. The priest said, 'No need to wait for any other sign. The child has shown us the way,' and they all dispersed silently.

Despite the astrologers, Krishna married the girl, and

Mars in the Seventh House was, eventually, forgotten.

The patient seemed to be asleep, Krishna tiptoed out of the room and told the servant maid waiting in the veranda, 'I have to go out and buy medicines. Give her orange juice at six, and look after her until I return.' He stepped out of his house, feeling like a released prisoner. He walked along, enjoying the crowd and bustle of Market Road until the thought of his wife's fever came back to his mind. He desperately needed someone who could tell him the unvarnished truth about his wife's condition. The doctor touched upon all subjects except that. When Chloromycetin failed to bring down the fever, he said cheerfully, 'It only shows that it is not typhoid but something else. We will do other tests tomorrow.' And that morning, before leaving: 'Why don't you pray, instead of all this cross-examination of me?'

'What sort of prayer?' Krishna had asked naïvely.

'Well, you may say, 'O God, if You *are* there, save me if You can!' the doctor replied, and guffawed loudly at his own joke. The doctor's humour was most trying.

Krishna realized that the doctor might sooner or later arrive at the correct diagnosis, but would it be within the patient's lifetime? He was appalled at the prospect of bereavement; his heart pounded wildly at the dreadful thought. Mars, having lain dormant, was astir now. Mars and an unidentified microbe had combined forces. The microbe was the doctor's business, however confused he might look. But the investigation of Mars was not.

Krishna hired a bicycle from a shop and pedalled off in the direction of the coconut grove where the old astrologer lived who had cast the horoscopes. He found the old man sitting in the hall, placidly watching a pack of children climb over walls, windows, furniture, and rice bags stacked in a corner and creating enough din to drown all conversation. He unrolled a mat for Krishna to sit on, and shouted over the noise of the children, 'I told you at the start itself how it was going to turn out, but you people would not listen to my words. Yes, Mars has begun to exercise his most malignant aspect now. Under the circumstances, survival of the person concerned is doubtful.' Krishna groaned. The children in a body had turned their attention to Krishna's bicycle, and were ringing the bell and feverishly attempting to push the machine off its stand. Nothing seemed to matter now. For a man about to lose his wife, the loss of a cycle taken on hire should not matter. Let children demolish all the bicycles in the town and Krishna would not care. Everything could be replaced except a human life.

'What shall I do,' he asked picturing his wife in her bed asleep and never waking. He clung to this old man desperately, for he felt, in his fevered state of mind, that the astrologer could intercede with, influence, or even apologize on his behalf to, a planet in the high heavens. He remembered the reddish Mars he used to be shown in the sky when he was a Boy Scout—reddish on account of his malignity erupting like the lava from its bosom. 'What would you advise me to do? Please help me!' The old man looked over the rim of his spectacles at Krishna menacingly. His eyes were also red. Everything is red, reflected Krishna. He partakes of the tint of Mars. I don't know whether this man is my friend or foe. My doctor also has red eyes. So has the maid servant . . . Red everywhere.

Krishna said, 'I know that the ruling god in Mars is benign. I wish I knew how to propitiate him and gain his compassion.'

The old man said, 'Wait.' He stood before a cupboard, took out a stack of palm-leaf strips with verses etched on them, four lines to a leaf. 'This is one of the four originals of the *Brihad-Jataka*, from which the whole science of astrology is derived. This is what has given me my living; when I speak with the authority of this leaf.' The old man held the palm-leaf to the light as the doorway and read out a Sanskrit aphorism: 'There can be no such thing as evading fate, but you can insulate yourself to some extent from its rigours.' Then he added, 'Listen to this: "Where Angaraka is malevolent, appease him with the following prayer . . . and accompany it with the gift of rice and gram and a piece of red silk. Pour the oblation of pure butter into a fire raised with sandal sticks, for four days continuously, and feed four brahmins" . . . Can you do it?'

Krishna was panic-stricken. How could he organize all this elaborate ritual (which was going to cost a great deal) when every moment and every rupee counted? Who would nurse his wife in his absence? Who would cook the ritual feast for the brahmins? He simply would not be able to manage it unless his wife helped him. He laughed at the irony of it, and the astrologer said, 'Why do you laugh at these things? You think you are completely modern?'

Krishna apologized for his laugh and explained his helpless state. The old man shut the manuscript indignantly, wrapped it in its cover, and put it away, muttering, 'These simple steps you can't take to achieve a profound result. Go, go . . . I can be of no use to you.'

Krishna hesitated, took two rupees from his purse, and held them out to the old man, who waved the money away. 'Let your wife get well first. Then give me the fee. Not now.' And as Krishna turned to go: 'The trouble is, your love is killing your wife. If you were an indifferent husband, she could survive. The malignity of Mars might make her suffer now and then, mentally more than physically, but would not kill her. I have seen horoscopes that were the exact replica of yours and the wife lived to a ripe age. You know why? The husband was disloyal or cruel, and that in some way neutralized the rigour of the planet in the Seventh House. I see your wife's time is getting to be really bad. Before anything happens, save her. If you can bring yourself to be unfaithful to her, try that. Every man with a concubine has a wife who lives long . . .'

A strange philosophy, but it sounded feasible.

Krishna was ignorant of the technique of infidelity, and wished he had the sickness of his old friend Ramu, who in their younger days used to brag of his sexual exploits. It would be impossible to seek Ramu's guidance now, although he lived close by; he had become a senior government officer and a man of family and might not care to lend himself to reminiscences of this kind.

Krishna looked for a pimp representing the prostitutes in Golden Street and could not spot one, although the market gate was reputed to be swarming with them.

He glanced at his watch. Six o'clock. Mars would have to be appeased before midnight. Somehow his mind fixed the line at midnight. He turned homeward, leaned his bicycle on the lamppost, and ran up the steps of his house. At the sight of him the servant maid prepared to leave, but he begged her to stay on. Then he peeped into the sickroom, saw that his wife was asleep, and addressed her mentally, 'You are going to get better soon. But it will cost something. Doesn't matter. Anything to save your life.'

He washed hurriedly and put on a nylon shirt, a lace-edged *dhoti*, and a silk upper cloth; lightly applied some talcum and a strong perfume he had discovered in his wife's cupboard. He was ready for the evening. He had fifty rupees in his purse, and that should be adequate for the wildest evening one could want. For a moment, as he paused to take a final look at himself in the mirror, he was seized with an immense vision of passion and seduction.

He returned the hired cycle to the shop and at seven was walking up Golden Street. In his imagination he had expected glittering females to beckon him from their balconies. The old houses had *pyols*, pillars, and railings, and were painted in garish colours, as the houses of prostitutes were reputed to be in former times, but the signboards on the houses indicated that the occupants were lawyers, tradesmen, and teachers. The only relic of the old days was a little shop in an obscure corner that sold perfumes in coloured bottles and strings of jasmine flowers and roses.

Krishna passed up and down the street, staring hard at a few women here and there, but they were probably ordinary, indifferent housewives. No one returned his stare. No one seemed to notice his silk upper cloth and lace *dhoti*. He paused to consider whether he could rush into a house, seize someone, perform the necessary act, shed his fifty rupees and rush out. Perhaps he might get beaten in the process. How on earth was one to find out which woman among all those he had noticed on the terraces and verandas of the houses, would respond to his appeal?

After walking up and down for two hours he realized that the thing was impossible. He sighed for the freedom between the sexes he read about in the European countries, where you had only to look about and announce your intentions and you could get enough women to confound the most malignant planet in the universe.

He suddenly remembered that the temple dancer lived somewhere here. He knew a lot of stories about Rangi of the temple, who danced before the god's image during the day and took lovers at night. He stopped for a banana and a fruit drink at a shop and asked the little boy serving him, 'Which is the house of the temple dancer Rangi?' The boy was too small to understand the purpose of his inquiry and merely replied, 'I don't know.' Krishna felt abashed and left.

Under a street lamp stood a *jutka*, the horse idly swishing its tail and the old driver waiting for a fare. Krishna asked, 'Are you free?'

The driver sprang to attention. 'Where do you wish to be taken, sir?'

Krishna said timidly, 'I wonder if you know where the temple dancer Rangi lives?'

'Why do you want her?' the driver asked, looking him up and down.

Krishna mumbled some reply about his wanting to see her dance. 'At this hour!' the driver exclaimed. 'With so much silk and so much perfume on! Don't try to deceive me. When you come out of her house, she will have stripped you of all the silk and perfume. But tell me, first, why only Rangi? There are others, both experts and beginners. I will drive you wherever you like. I have carried hundreds like you on such an errand. But shouldn't I first take you to a milk shop where they will give you hot milk with crushed almond to give you stamina? Just as a routine, my boy . . . I will take you wherever you want to go. Not my business anyway. Someone has given you more money than you need? Or is your wife pregnant and away at her mother's house? I have seen all the tricks that husbands play on their wives. I know the world, my master. Now get in. What difference does it make what you will look like when you come out of there? I will take you wherever you like.'

Krishna obediently got into the carriage, filling its interior with perfume and the rustle of his silken robes. Then he said, 'All right. Take me home.'

He gave his address so mournfully that the *jutka* driver, urging his horse, said, 'Don't be depressed, my young master. You are not missing anything. Someday you will think of this old fellow again.'

'I have my reasons,' Krishna began, gloomily.

The horse driver said, 'I have heard it all before. Don't tell me.' And he began a homily on conjugal life.

Krishna gave up all attempts to explain and leaned back, resigning himself to his fate.

UNDER THE BANYAN TREE

THE VILLAGE SOMAL, nestling away in the forest tracts of Mempi, had a population of less than three hundred. It was in every way a village to make the heart of a rural reformer sink. Its tank, a small expanse of water, right in the middle of the village, served for drinking, bathing, and washing the cattle, and it bred malaria, typhoid, and heaven knew what else. The cottages sprawled anyhow and the lanes twisted and wriggled up and down and strangled each other. The population used the highway as the refuse ground and in the backyard of every house drain water stagnated in green puddles.

Such was the village. It is likely that the people of the village were insensitive: but it is more than likely that they never noticed their surroundings because they lived in a kind of perpetual enchantment. The enchanter was Nambi the storyteller. He was a man of about sixty or seventy. Or was he eighty or one hundred and eighty? Who could say? In a place so much cut off as Somal (the nearest bus-stop was ten miles away), reckoning could hardly be in the familiar measures of time. If anyone asked Nambi what his age was he referred to an ancient famine or an invasion or the building of a bridge and indicated how high he had stood from the ground at the time.

He was illiterate, in the sense that the written word was a mystery to him; but he could make up a story, in his head, at the rate of one a month; each story took nearly ten days to narrate.

His home was the little temple which was at the very end of the village. No one could say how he had come to regard himself as the owner of the temple. The temple was a very small structure with red-striped walls, with a stone image of the Goddess Shakti in the sanctum. The front portion of the temple was Nambi's home. For aught it mattered any place might be his home; for he was without possessions. All that he possessed was a broom with which he swept the temple; and he had also a couple of *dhoties* and upper cloth. He spent most of the day in the shade of the banyan which spread out its branches in front of the temple. When he felt hungry he walked into any house that caught his fancy and joined the family at dinner. When he needed new clothes they were brought to him by the villagers. He hardly ever had to go out in search of company; for the banyan shade served as a clubhouse for the village folk. All through the day people came seeking Nambi's company and squatted under the tree. If he was in a mood for it he listened to their talk and entertained them with his own observations and anecdotes. When he was in no mood he looked at the visitors sourly and asked, 'What do you think I am? Don't blame me if you get no story at the next moon. Unless I meditate how can the Goddess give me a story? Do you think stories float in the air?' And he moved out to the edge of the forest and squatted there, contemplating the trees.

On Friday evenings the village turned up at the temple for worship, when Nambi lit a score of mud lamps and arranged them around the threshold of the sanctuary. He decorated the image with flowers, which grew wildly in the backyard of the temple. He acted as the priest and offered to the Goddess fruits and flowers brought in by the villagers.

On the nights he had a story to tell he lit a small lamp and placed it in a niche in the trunk of the banyan tree. Villagers as they returned home in the evening saw this, went home, and said to their wives, 'Now, now, hurry up with the dinner, the storyteller is calling us.' As the moon crept up behind the hillock, men, women, and children gathered under the banyan tree. The storyteller would not appear yet. He would be sitting in the sanctum, before the Goddess, with his eyes shut, in deep meditation. He sat thus as long as he liked and when he came out, with his forehead ablaze with ash and vermilion, he took his seat on a stone platform in front of the temple. He opened the story with a question. Jerking his finger towards a vague, faraway destination, he asked, 'A thousand years ago, a stone's throw in that direction, what do you think there was? It was not the weed-covered waste it is now, for donkeys to roll in. It was not the ash-pit it is now. It was the capital of the king . . .' The king would be Dasaratha, Vikramaditya, Asoka, or anyone that came into the old man's head; the capital was called Kapila, Kridapura, or anything. Opening thus, the old man went on without a pause for three hours. By then brick by brick the palace of the king was raised. The old man described the dazzling durbar hall where sat a hundred vassal kings, ministers, and subjects; in another part of the palace all the musicians in the world assembled and sang; and most of the songs were sung over again by Nambi to his audience; and he described in detail the pictures and trophies that hung on the walls of the palace . . .

It was story-building on an epic scale. The first day barely conveyed the setting of the tale, and Nambi's audience as yet had no idea who were coming into the story. As the moon slipped behind the trees of Mempi Forest Nambi said, 'Now friends, Mother says this will do for the day.' He abruptly rose, went in, lay down, and fell asleep long before the babble of the crowd ceased.

The light in the niche would again be seen two or three days later, and again and again throughout the bright half of the month. Kings and heroes, villains and fairy-like women, gods in human form, saints and assassins, jostled each other in that world which was created under the banyan tree. Nambi's voice rose and fell in an exquisite rhythm, and the moonlight and the hour completed the magic. The villagers laughed with Nambi, they wept with him, they adored the heroes, cursed the villains, groaned when the conspirator had his initial success, and they sent up to the gods a heartfelt prayer for a happy ending . . .

On the day when the story ended, the whole gathering went into the sanctum and prostrated before the Goddess . . .

By the time the next moon peeped over the hillock Nambi was ready with another story. He never repeated the same kind of story or brought in the same set of persons, and the village folk considered Nambi a sort of miracle, quoted his words of wisdom, and lived on the whole in an exalted plane of their own, though their life in all other respects was hard and drab.

And yet it had gone on for years and years. One moon he lit the lamp in the tree. The audience came. The old man took his seat and began the story. '. . . When King Vikramaditya lived, his minister was . . .' He paused. He could not get beyond it. He made a fresh beginning. 'There was the king . . .' he said, repeated it, and then his words trailed off into a vague mumbling. 'What has come over me?' he asked pathetically. 'Oh, Mother, great Mother, why do I stumble and falter? I know the story. I had the whole of it a moment ago. What was it about? I can't understand what has happened.' He faltered and looked so miserable that his audience said, 'Take your own time. You are perhaps tired.'

'Shut up!' he cried. 'Am I tired? Wait a moment; I will tell you the story presently.' Following this there was utter silence. Eager faces looked up at him. 'Don't look at me!' he flared up. Somebody gave him a tumbler of milk. The audience waited patiently. This was a new experience. Some persons expressed their sympathy aloud. Some persons began to talk among themselves. Those who sat in the outer edge of the crowd silently slipped away. Gradually, as it neared midnight, others followed this example. Nambi sat staring at the ground, his head bowed in thought. For the first time he realized that he was old. He felt he would never more be able to control his thoughts or express them cogently. He looked up. Everyone had gone except his friend Mari the blacksmith. 'Mari, why aren't you also gone?'

639

Mari apologized for the rest: 'They didn't want to tire you; so they have gone away.'

Nambi got up. 'You are right. Tomorrow I will make it up. Age, age. What is my age? It has come on suddenly.' He pointed at his head and said, 'This says, "Old fool, don't think I shall be your servant any more. You will be my servant hereafter." It is disobedient and treacherous.'

He lit the lamp in the niche next day. The crowd assembled under the banyan faithfully. Nambi had spent the whole day in meditation. He had been fervently praying to the Goddess not to desert him. He began the story. He went on for an hour without a stop. He felt greatly relieved, so much so that he interrupted his narration to remark, 'Oh, friends. The Mother is always kind. I was seized with a foolish fear . . .' and continued the story. In a few minutes he felt dried up. He struggled hard: 'And then . . . and then . . . what happened?' He stammered. There followed a pause lasting an hour. The audience rose without a word and went home. The old man sat on the stone brooding till the cock crew. 'I can't blame them for it,' he muttered to himself. 'Can they sit down here and mope all night?' Two days later he gave another instalment of the story, and that, too, lasted only a few minutes. The gathering dwindled. Fewer persons began to take notice of the lamp in the niche. Even these came only out of a sense of duty. Nambi realized that there was no use in prolonging the struggle. He brought the story to a speedy and premature end.

He knew what was happening. He was harrowed by the thoughts of his failure. I should have been happier if I had dropped dead years ago, he said to himself Mother, why have you struck me dumb . . .? He shut himself up in the sanctum, hardly ate any food, and spent the greater part of the day sitting motionless in meditation.

The next moon peeped over the hillock, Nambi lit the lamp in the niche. The villagers as they returned home saw the lamp, but only a handful turned up at night. 'Where are the others?' the old man asked. 'Let us wait.' He waited. The moon came up. His handful of audience waited patiently. And then the old man said, 'I won't tell the story today, nor tomorrow unless the whole village comes here. I insist upon it. It is a mighty story. Everyone must hear it.' Next day he went up and down the village street shouting, 'I have a most wonderful tale to tell tonight. Come one and all; don't miss it . . .' This personal appeal had a great effect. At night a large crowd gathered under the banyan. They were happy that the storyteller had regained his powers. Nambi came out of the temple when everyone had settled and said: 'It is the Mother who gives the gifts; and it is she who takes away the gifts. Nambi is a dotard. He speaks when the Mother has anything to say. He is struck dumb when she has nothing to say. But what is the use of the jasmine when it has lost its scent? What is the lamp for when all the oil is gone? Goddess be thanked . . . These are my last words on this earth; and this is my story.' He rose and went into the sanctum. His audience hardly understood what he meant. They sat there till they became weary. And then some of them got up and stepped into the sanctum. There the storyteller sat with eyes shut. 'Aren't you going to tell us a story?' they asked. He opened his eyes, looked at them, and shook his head. He indicated by gesture that he had spoken his last words.

When he felt hungry he walked into any cottage and

PBD
30-3-07

silently sat down for food, and walked away the moment he had eaten. Beyond this he had hardly anything to demand of his fellow beings. The rest of his life (he lived for a few more years) was one great consummate silence.